Edited and with an Introduction by

RALPH G. NEWMAN

Foreword by DAVID C. MEARNS

DOUBLEDAY & COMPANY, INC., GARDEN CITY, NEW YORK

LINCOLN

FOR

THE

AGES

Dedicated to the memory of all Lincoln scholars and
collectors and particularly to five men:

FOREMAN M. LEBOLD

HARRY E. PRATT

JAMES G. RANDALL

ALFRED WHITAL STERN

BENJAMIN P. THOMAS

whose writings and encouragement of others who follow the
Lincoln trail made substantial contributions
to better scholarship and understanding.

CONTENTS

7

CONTENTS

Contents

CONTENTS

Contents

CONTENTS

Contents

CONTENTS

14

Contents

APPENDIX

EDITOR'S NOTE

All direct Lincoln quotations used in the text are reproduced exactly as they appear in the definitive edition of *The Collected Works of Abraham Lincoln,* Rutgers University Press, 1953–55. Errors in spelling and peculiarities in punctuation are as Mr. Lincoln himself wrote them, or as they appeared in the contemporary press. In a few cases where it seemed necessary to make slight corrections in the text, these emandations appear in brackets.

FOREWORD

What has become of Mr. Lincoln? How stands the audit in this, his one hundred and fiftieth year? Does the old gentleman's reputation flourish? Does he prosper everywhere? Is his popularity secure, his primacy assured? Are the investments in him sound and do they still enrich the lives of the shareholders?

Or, conversely, does he suffer a decline, his stature diminishing, the pale vapors that once shadowed him burned away by brighter light? Are there signs of incipient satiety and dreadful dwindling? Do pretenders and usurpers consign him to the commonplace from which he came? Has he been outmoded, a victim fallen to changed vogue and newer fashion? Have divisive cults and sharp schisms quite dissolved him? Has the last mystery been resolved and the final judgment been pronounced? Surely this sesquicentenary calls for an accounting, and, just as surely, this work is not unrelated to it.

But let it be instantly understood that this rendering is not, in any sterile, statistical-columned sense, a balance sheet. As a matter of fact, there are many things that it is not. It is not, for example, a compendium drawn from eager remembrancers such as James Quay Howard, William Henry Herndon, Francis Bicknell Carpenter, and Allen Thorndike Rice produced in the second half of the last century. These *present* writers have been denied contemporaneity with their subject. On the other hand, they enjoy certain advantages not permitted to those former intimates, acquaintances, and garrulous observers. Among these are perspective, sifted evidence, and a confident mastery of material. If it cannot be urged that they have attained complete and deep-frozen detachment, it can, at least, be claimed that these later partisans are absolved of self-magnification, coattail flights, selfishly imposed restraints and prejudices and biases, careless and capricious memories, lymphatic and lugubrious sentimentality.

Neither is this, by usual definition, an anthology, such as has been typified at its finest by Paul Angle's *The Lincoln Reader*. This is no mosaic composed of extracts drawn from longer and previously published studies, brilliantly fitted in chronological sequence, and exquisitely designed to present a familiar, consistent, and strangely attractive character. This is no magnificent tour de force. The conductor has waved no magic baton at his curiously assorted artists and effortlessly, without rehearsal, evoked a symphony. Actually there are no more symmetries in this work than Mr. Lincoln, in his own person, ever possessed.

But it should not be supposed that this is no more than mere collectanea, an omnium-gatherum, held together only by a general thesis, a title, the binder's stitches, and the covers that encase it. On the contrary, this is a report on the Lincoln story and the Lincoln status as they were found to exist at the close of his one hundred and fiftieth year. The statement is, in other words, current and built upon years of patient study and earnest research. For its preparation almost fourscore specialists have been carefully selected and commissioned to discuss that aspect of Mr. Lincoln's life and character with which they have attained widely acknowledged competence. They include poets and priests, collectors and critics and congressmen and chemists, businessmen and bibliographers, governors and widows, lawyers and librarians, editors and sculptors, historians and dramatists, generals and educators, senators and journalists. The candlestickmaker is somehow missing.

by David C. Mearns

In the year that followed his murder, Mr. Lincoln's last partner in practice, William H. Herndon, wrote of him: "The man is not yet understood, his history is not known." Certainly, in the interval, much has been learned and written of that history, and if his personality persists in elusion it cannot be charged to any want of expositors. For, more than any "human clay-pot" (the phrase is Carl Sandburg's), he has been the subject of intensive, widespread, and constant study. He has, as a matter of fact, inspired a literature so vast, so varied, and, in some instances, so evasive as to create a science, a profession, a trade, even, perhaps, an art. On the other hand, much of it—too much of it—has been imitative, minor, guileless, subjective. It had its beginnings, of course, with the campaign lives of the Republican aspirant for the presidency. Following his murder, the hagiographers and the filio-pietists brought forth a spate of mournful, unrestrained, undocumented gospels, written in tears and dedicated to apotheosis. Then came the dangerous Era of Reminiscence and Anecdote. As a consequence, much that was apocryphal, spurious, or at best suspicious and amazingly long-lived, gained wide and thriving distribution. These fables and popular fallacies have not yet been completely exorcised and banished.

Herndon's *Lincoln* did not appear until 1889; the authorized, discursive, and strangely selective *History* of Nicolay and Hay was published in the following year. Thereafter there were a number of sound, earnest, and occasionally distinguished biographies. But the punctilious academicians, formally trained and governed by their science, were slow to take the Lincoln story to themselves. One of them, as late as 1934, when addressing an assemblage of his colleagues, asked the cynical question, "Has the Lincoln Theme Been Exhausted?" and devoted the remainder of his life to demonstrating the fact that, so far from having been worn out and fully exploited, the Lincoln lode is actually boundless and self-replenishing. In the interval, other schoolmen have followed his excellent example and lavished their learning upon an eager and compensatory public.

21

And now Lincolniana has entered that new period, foreseen by Louis A. Warren, who, when touched by prophecy, wrote not so long ago: "It is not the exhaustive biographies of Abraham Lincoln by a single author that students of the future will search for the factual presentation of isolated incidents in the life of the Railsplitter but in that larger accumulative biography whose contributors have specialized in certain important phases of his career." He added: "A greater number of tomorrow's authors are eligible to contribute discussions on different aspects of the Emancipator's life and times."

He had, of course, anticipated just such a study as is here presented, a collective, corporate finding, in which the polygonous prodigy of the prairie is drawn with precision and prepense. But the question will instantly arise: Why is it that today's Lincolnists may write with greater authority than the scribes who preceded them? Someone will make answer that it is because only in recent years have the Lincoln Papers and Herndon's gatherings been made publicly available. These are, to be sure, the primary, the fundamental, the most conspicuous and important sources. Another will reply that only lately has a definitive edition of Mr. Lincoln's *Collected Works* been produced.

But any consideration of the state of the art must with profound gratitude acknowledge the enlightened service of private collectors to the preservation, extension, and enrichment of the record. Their labors have been, and are, devoted. They have sought out, and are seeking, the rare, the scarce, the curious, the stray and, let it not be overlooked, the expensive. Their prizes have been, and are, for them rich rewards. They have been, they are, in the strictest sense, the true Lincoln men. Some of them have been, and are, professionals; most, however, have possessed that heady enthusiasm, unerring appreciation, and rigorous connoisseurship ordinarily reserved to the amateur. They have been, they are, many. To name them all would be tedious and, perhaps, inappropriate.

by David C. Mearns

But it would be a grievous omission not to cite the giants of other years; Andrew Boyd, the directory publisher, who assembled books, eulogies, sermons, portraits, engravings, manuscripts, medals, and a couple of feathers from the pillow Lincoln died on; Major William Harrison Lambert, the insurance executive, "to whom all Lincoln devotees bow as the chief of their tribe," and whose superb library was dispersed by the auctioneer's hammer; Charles W. McClellan, once a Confederate soldier; Daniel Fish, judge and bibliographer; Judd Stewart, auditor of the American Smelting and Refining Company; Joseph B. Oakleaf, lawyer; Ida Tarbell, journalist and editor; H. E. Barker, bookseller; Charles Frederick Gunther, candy manufacturer; Henry Horner, late Governor of Illinois; Oliver R. Barrett, leonine barrister; James W. Bollinger, judge; Albert H. Greenly, loyal Michigander but resident of New York; F. Lauriston Bullard, editor; Foreman M. Lebold, industrialist; Stuart W. Jackson, Yale '98 the munificent Alfred Whital Stern.

They have sired a mighty race in this generation: Frederick Hill Meserve, incomparable iconographer; Squire William H. Townsend, eloquent and learned dweller in Lincoln's wife's home town; Justin G. Turner, generous possessor of priceless relics exhibited here and overseas; Philip D. Sang, happy Americanist; Carl Haverlin, constant and felicitous discoverer; Henry B. Bass, pursuer of the Lincoln muse.

Private collectors have, through publication, counsel, and correspondence, conferred outstanding benefits upon Lincoln scholarship, yet their most important contribution to the good cause has been made by placing their libraries in public repositories, where they have become a community or national resource. From their generosity has come those great research centers in Ann Arbor, Bloomington (Indiana), Chicago, Fort Wayne, Harrogate, Meadville, New Haven, Providence, San Marino, Springfield (Illinois), Urbana, and Washington, D.C. There the preservation of the Lincoln story and its endless continuation are assured.

These are the towering, the enduring monuments to a soaring spirit and to those who have honored it.

And largely because of them the image of Lincoln grows constantly greater and his memory holds renewing meanings for the race.

David C. Mearns

Washington, D.C.
February 1960

INTRODUCTION

On February 12, 1959, twenty-five hundred persons assembled in Springfield, Illinois, to pay tribute to the state's greatest son on the one hundred and fiftieth anniversary of his birth. The host was William G. Stratton, Governor of Illinois. The principal speaker was Willy Brandt, Mayor of West Berlin. Other speakers were Ambassadors Sir Harold Caccia from Great Britain, Herve Alphand from France, and Ernest Bonhomme from Haiti. Seven other ambassadors sat in the audience, with representatives from twenty-one foreign countries as well as distinguished Americans. They had gathered to pay homage to the memory of Abraham Lincoln, whose name has become synonymous around the world with the American philosophy of freedom. It was not ironic but, one hopes, prophetically appropriate that Willy Brandt gave the main address.

Truly ironic and charged with drama was Nikita Khrushchev's visit to the Lincoln Memorial in Washington. Who can guess the thoughts and emotions of the greatest living proponent of all that Lincoln abhorred in social philosophy, as he studied the compassionate face of the statue? No one knows. But in his country, where Americans are viewed with suspicion and the United States is considered the ultimate example of capitalistic evil, Lincoln is regarded as a saint. His speeches, his biographies, are read, and the man himself is almost worshiped. Is this an anomaly?

25

Not long ago a man from far-off Pakistan came to visit me. One of the leading lawyers of his country, and head of one of its principal law schools, he was here as a guest of the State Department. He told me that his primary reason for coming was to visit the Lincoln shrines and the places where Lincoln had lived, worked, and spoken. A devoted Lincoln student since first learning to read, he said that in Pakistan there was a tremendous interest in and love for the sixteenth president of the United States and complained that we do not send enough books about Abraham Lincoln to his country.

Carl Haverlin, speaking recently in Washington before the Lincoln Group of the District of Columbia, advanced a suggestion directly in line with the thinking of my caller from Pakistan. It might be time, he thought, for us to supplement the Marshall Plan with a Lincoln Plan, which would send to the farthest corners of the earth, not material things, but a more precious commodity which we have in unlimited supply and which could do nothing but good wherever it is received: the principles, the philosophy, the concern for humanity, the belief in the people, which were exemplified by Abraham Lincoln. Mr. Haverlin's suggestion and the plea of the lawyer from Pakistan indicate that thoughtful men both here and abroad look to Abraham Lincoln for inspiration, for guidance, and for hope in perilous times.

Though thousands of books have been written about Lincoln, and translated into every language, the flow of biographies—which are bought and read—has sharply increased since the end of World War II. And remember too that particularly in the publishing business the law of demand and supply is inexorable.

Why does Abraham Lincoln endure, one hundred and fifty years after his humble birth in Kentucky, as the man who has affected most profoundly the lives, thoughts, attitudes, and actions of modern Americans? Why does Lincoln continue to grow in our political philosophy, our cultural inheritance, our social and moral consciousness? Why has he remained in death as powerful an influence and reality as he had in life? Why is it that that influence is growing, not fading?

To attempt an objective reappraisal of Abraham Lincoln as a dynamic force in contemporary thought and action, the creative scholarship of the eminent living students of Lincoln and his times has been assembled in this work. It is true that the facts of the Lincoln story have probably all been recorded. But this extraordinary personality so grips the imagination and stirs the faith of living men that it is important that his life be re-examined, but not from the viewpoint of a single scholar or writer. There are so many facets to this complex, dynamic, and mysterious personality that to evaluate properly the many moods, talents, dilemmas, and torments of his life, the knowledge of seventy-seven individuals—historians, statesmen, men and women of letters—has been garnered to present collectively the first one hundred and fifty years of the Lincoln story. Many of the obvious facts in the Lincoln story do not appear in these pages, but they are easily available. It is likely, however, that more appears here on the *meaning* of Lincoln to all mankind than has ever been assembled in a single volume. It is therefore not the biography of a man whose life span was fifty-six years, two months, and four days, or of what he did in that brief time. It is an interpretation of the man, and an explanation of his hold upon the minds of men, and an attempt, we hope, to come closer to a real understanding of why Abraham Lincoln lives for the ages.

"THE BETTER PART OF ONE'S LIFE CONSISTS
OF HIS FRIENDSHIPS"

ACKNOWLEDGMENTS

Credit for the inspiration, imagination, and executive genius for the radio series which ultimately became this book rests solely with Carl Haverlin, President, Broadcast Music, Incorporated. Earl Schenck Miers, one of the most distinguished contemporary experts on Lincoln and the Civil War, helped select the topics and the authors of the studies which are herein assembled. Joyce Peterson was the office manager of the project and helped prepare the radio scripts. She managed to retain both her sanity and good humor while worrying about seventy-seven authors, hundreds of radio stations, and so many details that a mere cataloguing of them would fill many pages. Jane Carroll supervised the correspondence with the contributors, the editor, and others associated with this work and managed to know where everyone associated with this project could be reached at *any* time. The historical background of each paper was checked by Dr. Wayne C. Temple, head of the Department of Lincolniana, Lincoln Memorial University, and by Lloyd A. Dunlap, Administrative Officer for the national Lincoln Sesquicentennial Commission. Valuable editorial assistance was supplied by Samuel S. Vaughan, Marion D. Pratt, Olive Carruthers, and Russell Sanjek. For assistance in the preparation of the manuscript we are indebted to Margaret H. April, Joan Brown, Richard E. Clark, Glenn Dolberg, John A. Janssen,

29

ACKNOWLEDGMENTS

E. B. Long, and Lloyd Ostendorf. Messrs. William I. Nichols and Stewart Beach of *This Week* magazine and Clement Sylvestro and Clifford L. Lord of the American Association for State and Local History supervised and publicized the nationwide competition which resulted in the papers "Reflections While Standing before the Lincoln Memorial."

1

THE MOST ENDURING MEMORIAL TO LINCOLN*

by Carl Sandburg

Among the million words in the Lincoln utterance record he interprets himself with a keener precision than someone else offering to explain him. His simple opening of the House Divided speech in 1858 serves for today: "If we could first know *where* we are, and *whither* we are tending, we could better judge *what* to do, and how do it." To his Kentucky friend Joshua F. Speed he wrote in 1855: "Our progress in degeneracy appears to me to be pretty rapid. As a nation, we began by declaring that *'all men are created equal.'* We now practically read it 'all men are created equal, *except negroes.'* When the Know-Nothings get control, it will read 'all men are created equal, except *negroes, and foreigners and catholics.'* When it comes to this I should prefer emigrating to some country where they make no pretence of loving liberty. . . ." Infinitely tender was his word from a White House balcony to a crowd on the White House lawn, "I have not

* From the Sesquicentennial Tribute before the Joint Session of the Congress of the United States of America, February 12, 1959.

33

willingly planted a thorn in any man's bosom," or to a military governor, "I shall do nothing in malice. What I deal with is too vast for malicious dealing." He wrote for Congress to read on December 1, 1862, "In times like the present, men should utter nothing for which they would not willingly be responsible through time and in eternity." Like an ancient psalmist he warned Congress, "Fellow-citizens, *we* cannot escape history. We . . . will be remembered in spite of ourselves. No personal significance, or insignificance, can spare one or another of us. The fiery trial through which we pass, will light us down, in honor or dishonor, to the latest generation." Wanting Congress to break and forget past traditions, his words came keen and flashing. "The dogmas of the quiet past, are inadequate to the stormy present. . . . As our case is new, so we must think anew, and act anew. We must disenthrall ourselves. . . ." They are the sort of words that actuated the mind and will of the men who created and navigated that marvel of the sea, the *Nautilus,* and her voyage from Pearl Harbor and under the North Pole icecap.

The people of many other countries take Lincoln now for their own. He belongs to them. He stands for decency, honest dealing, plain talk, and funny stories. "Look where he came from—don't he know all us strugglers and wasn't he a kind of tough struggler all his life right up to the finish?" Something like that you can hear in any nearby neighborhood and across the seas. Millions there are who take him as a personal treasure. He had something they would like to see spread everywhere in the world. Democracy? We can't say exactly what it is, but he had it. In his blood and bones he carried it. In the breath of his speeches and writings it is there. Popular government? Republican institutions? Government where the people have the say-so, one way or another telling their elected rulers what they want? He had the idea. It's there in the lights and shadows of his personality, a mystery that can be lived but never fully spoken in words.

How did he say he would like to be remembered? His beloved friend Representative Owen Lovejoy of Illinois died in March of

1864, and friends wrote to Lincoln and he replied that the pressure of duties kept him from joining them in efforts for a marble monument to Lovejoy. "Let him have the marble monument, along with the well-assured and more enduring one in the hearts of those who love liberty, unselfishly, for all men." So perhaps we may say that the well-assured and most enduring memorial to Lincoln is invisible there, today, tomorrow, and for a long time yet to come in the hearts of lovers of liberty, men and women who understand that wherever there is freedom there have been those who fought and sacrificed for it.

Carl Sandburg

2

From THE AUTOBIOGRAPHY OF

ABRAHAM LINCOLN

Abraham Lincoln was born Feb. 12, 1809, then in Hardin, now in the more recently formed county of Larue, Kentucky. His father, Thomas, & grand-father, Abraham, were born in Rockingham county Virginia, whither their ancestors had come from Berks county, Pennsylvania. His lineage has been traced no farther back than this. The family were originally quakers, though in later times they have fallen away from the peculiar habits of that people. The grand-father Abraham, had four brothers—Isaac, Jacob, John & Thomas. So far as known, the descendants of Jacob and John are still in Virginia. Isaac went to a place near where Virginia, North Carolina, and Tennessee, join; and his de[s]cendants are in that region. Thomas came to Kentucky, and after many years, died there, whence his de[s]cendants went to Missouri. Abraham, grandfather of the subject of this sketch, came to Kentucky, and was killed by indians about the year 1784. He left a widow, three sons and two daughters. The eldest son, Mordecai, remained in Kentucky till late in life, when he removed to Hancock county, Illinois, where soon after he died, and where several of his descendants still reside. The second son, Josiah, removed at

36

an early day to a place on Blue River, now within Harrison [Hancock] county, Indiana; but no recent information of him, or his family, has been obtained. The eldest sister, Mary, married Ralph Crume and some of her descendants are now known to be in Breckinridge county Kentucky. The second sister, Nancy, married William Brumfield, and her family are not known to have left Kentucky, but there is no recent information from them. Thomas, the youngest son, and father of the present subject, by the early death of his father, and very narrow circumstances of his mother, even in childhood was a wandering laboring boy, and grew up litterally without education. He never did more in the way of writing than to bunglingly sign his own name. Before he was grown, he passed one year as a hired hand with his uncle Isaac on Wata[u]ga, a branch of the Holsteen [Holston] River. Getting back into Kentucky, and having reached his 28th year, he married Nancy Hanks—mother of the present subject—in the year 1806. She also was born in Virginia; and relatives of hers of the name of Hanks, and of other names, now reside in Coles, in Macon, and in Adams counties, Illinois, and also in Iowa. The present subject has no brother or sister of the whole or half blood. He had a sister, older than himself, who was grown and married, but died many years ago, leaving no child. Also a brother, younger than himself, who died in infancy. Before leaving Kentucky he and his sister were sent for short periods, to A.B.C. schools, the first kept by Zachariah Riney, and the second by Caleb Hazel.

At this time his father resided on Knob-creek, on the road from Bardstown Ky. to Nashville Tenn. at a point three, or three and a half miles South or South-West of Atherton's ferry on the Rolling Fork.

A. Lincoln.

3

THE ANCESTRY OF ABRAHAM LINCOLN

by Louis A. Warren

Abraham Lincoln knew very little about his paternal ancestry. Such information as he had reached back only as far as the grandfather for whom he was named. He knew practically nothing about his mother's people. Such knowledge as he had he summarized with the statement that she came from "a family by the name of Hanks."

When asked about his grandfather he is reported to have said: "I am much more concerned to know what his [grandfather's] grandson would be." Nevertheless Lincoln *was* concerned about who his ancestors were. He wrote to one of his relatives in 1848 asking for information about them. He suggested "tracing them back as far as your knowledge extends." Secretary Welles, a member of Lincoln's Cabinet, said that he had heard the President say more than once that "when he laid down his official life, he would endeavor to trace out his genealogy and family history." Since he was deprived of this opportunity biographers and genealogists have assumed the task and followed the paternal lineage to his first American ancestor bearing the name Lincoln.

by Louis A. Warren

The story of these seven generations of Lincolns begins in Old Salem, Massachusetts, the town where Nathaniel Hawthorne's famous "House of Seven Gables" is located. Samuel Lincoln, a weaver's apprentice, seventeen years of age, arrived there from England on June 20, 1637. In the same town two other paternal ancestors of the President resided: William Bowne, who had come two years earlier than Samuel Lincoln, and Obadiah Holmes, who came two years later.

Samuel soon moved across the bay to Hingham, where two of his brothers, Thomas and Daniel, had already settled. Since there were four adult Lincolns in Hingham bearing the name Thomas, for identification an occupational suffix was added to their given names. They were known as Thomas the Weaver, brother of Samuel, Thomas the Husbandman, Thomas the Cooper, and Thomas the Miller. Samuel married Martha Lewis and they had eleven children, naming the third son Mordecai, apparently after a member of the Lewis family. Mordecai continued to reside in the Hingham community, and his impressive colonial home still stands in a good state of preservation in nearby Scituate.

Mordecai's wife was Sarah, daughter of Abraham and Sarah Jones. They named their first son after the father, Mordecai, and the second son after Sarah's father, Abraham, thus introducing the name Abraham into the Lincoln family. There stands in Hingham a heroic bronze statue of President Lincoln, serving as a memorial to the many Abraham Lincolns who trace their ancestry back to this New England town. Shortly after the President was inaugurated he was presented with a share ticket dated at Boston in 1765, signed by John Hancock, and endorsed by an Abraham Lincoln to whom the donor referred as "one of your ancestors." Although this Abraham was not an ancestor he was a kinsman, as was Amos Lincoln who married a daughter of Paul Revere.

President Lincoln first came in contact with the New England Lincolns in September 1848 when he addressed an assembly of Whigs in Worcester, Massachusetts. Here he was entertained by Levi Lincoln, Jr., mayor of the city. He had served Massachusetts as governor longer than any other incumbent before or since his time. His brother Enoch was a governor of the State of Maine. Their father, Levi Sr., had been Attorney General in the Cabinet of Thomas Jefferson, and his brother Dr. Abraham Lincoln was a prominent citizen and influential officeholder. Both of these brothers, descendants of Samuel Lincoln, were born in Hingham.

Without his knowledge the name of Abraham Lincoln of Illinois was placed in nomination for the Vice Presidency of the United States at the first Republican Convention held in Philadelphia in 1856, and he received 110 votes. Upon hearing about it he remarked: "They can't mean me, they must mean one of those famous Lincolns up in Massachusetts." Before making the trip to Worcester he had received a letter from Solomon Lincoln of Hingham inquiring about his ancestry. Abraham replied: "It is . . . my father's understanding that, Abraham, Mordecai, and Thomas are old family names of ours." Some years later he revised this list of old family names mentioning "Enoch, Levi, Mordecai, Solomon, Abraham and the like." Yet he still insisted that any attempt to connect his family with the New England Lincolns "ended in nothing more than a similarity in Christian names."

The two sons of Mordecai I, Mordecai II and Abraham, migrated from Hingham to Monmouth County, New Jersey, by 1714. Here Mordecai married Hannah, daughter of Richard and Sarah Bowne and granddaughter of both William Bowne and Obadiah Holmes of Old Salem, to whom we have already referred.

President-elect Lincoln on his way to the inaugural ceremonies spoke to both houses of the New Jersey legislature at Trenton. He mentioned that as a boy he had read about the many battles of the Revolutionary War waged in New Jersey and was deeply impressed by visiting Trenton, where the engagement with the Hessians took place. He would have been more impressed had he known that some of the battlefields in Monmouth County embraced the lands of his own ancestors. Two years before his visit one of his own kinsmen, Edwin Saltar, was the speaker of the New Jersey assembly, and one of his ancestors, Captain John Bowne, had presided over the provincial legislature. While at Trenton the President-elect was within a few miles of the early home of Mordecai Lincoln II, the birthplace of his great-grandfather, John Lincoln.

Continuing on its way to Washington the inaugural train en route to Harrisburg stopped at a small station called Leaman Place. Addressing the citizens Lincoln "expressed his pleasure on entering the great county of Lancaster." Loud calls were made for Mrs. Lincoln, and after his wife appeared the President-elect announced "the long and short of it," and this comment on the disparity in their stature produced a burst of laughter. Mordecai II had migrated from New Jersey to the adjacent county of Berks about 1720, and here the third and fourth generation of Lincolns lived for many years. The old stone house which Mordecai II built in Exeter, not far from Reading, still stands as a memorial to the Pennsylvania Lincolns.

Mordecai and Sarah Saltar Lincoln had but one son, John, who married Rebecca Morris Flower. They named their first three sons Abraham, Isaac, and Jacob. When the first child was born the parents were living in Lancaster County, not more than twenty miles from Leaman Place, where the President spoke in 1861. He was under the impression that his grandfather Abraham was born in Virginia, as he had stated in his autobiographical sketch a year before. This sketch also noted that "The family were originally quakers," but the statement lacks confirmation. There were many intermarriages between the Lincolns and their Quaker neighbors in Berks County. Although Mordecai Lincoln lies buried in the cemetery of the Exeter Quaker Meeting House neither his name nor the name of his son appears on any membership list of this religious body. Mordecai's first wife was an ardent Baptist, and apparently she brought up her son John in that faith. The Lynnville Creek Baptist Church to which the President's grandfather belonged was adjacent to the Lincoln acres.

Grandfather Lincoln first came to Kentucky in 1780 and is

41

reported to have been captured by the Indians and made to run the gauntlet. He and his wife Bathsheba returned to Virginia and with their five children migrated to Kentucky in 1782. Four years later the father was massacred by the Indians, in the presence of the President's father, Thomas, then but eight years of age. According to the President his father's oft-repeated recollection of this tragedy became "the legend more strongly than all others imprinted upon my mind and memory."

Beginning with Mordecai II the Lincoln generations present a unique Western migration that traversed seven states and ultimately sent its most noble son to the nation's capital as the Chief Executive. Mordecai was born in Massachusetts, married in New Jersey, and died in Pennsylvania; John was born in New Jersey, married in Pennsylvania, and died in Virginia; Abraham, grandfather of the President, was born in Pennsylvania, married in Virginia, and died in Kentucky; Thomas, father of the President, was born in Virginia, married in Kentucky, and died in Illinois; the President was born in Kentucky, married in Illinois, and died in the District of Columbia.

A period of 228 years elapsed between the arrival of Samuel Lincoln in America and the tragic departure of President Lincoln at the hands of an assassin. These generations of Lincolns, with their eyes toward the setting sun, breathed in the very essence of freedom which was prevalent especially on the frontiers. Their pilgrimage by land was no less significant than the expedition of their forefathers by sea. By the time the Lincolns finally reached the Golden West and its rainbow of promise they had created and nourished one who has best personified the American way of life: Abraham Lincoln, "a man for the ages."

Louis A. Warren

42

4

THE WORLD OF TOM AND NANCY LINCOLN

by R. Gerald McMurtry

Thomas Lincoln married Nancy Hanks in the cabin home of Richard Berry on June 12, 1806, and from this union came the most colossal figure of the age, "The pillar of a people's hope." Nancy found Tom gentle and considerate, even though a little awkward. He was industrious, a man of many handiworks. He was a carpenter and cabinetmaker, militiaman, patroller, juryman, surveyor, road builder, and hunter. His entire life span of some seventy-odd years might be characterized as that of a typical American pioneer.

His Hardin County neighbors knew Tom as a worthy Kentucky citizen and devout Christian. He had a tender heart and a droll sense of humor. His habits were temperate and he was known for his absolute honesty. These were the attributes that a worthy father was destined to bestow upon an immortal son. Tom was born in 1778, according to his son's statement, in Virginia. He did not ever know, and perhaps would not have cared had he known, that one day his lineage would be identified with the famous New England Lincolns.

43

From a maze of reports we believe that Nancy Hanks was born on February 5, 1784, somewhere beyond the dark hills in the then vast wilderness that is now West Virginia. With her mother's people she was brought through Cumberland Gap to Kentucky and was taken into the home of her relative Richard Berry, who had settled in Washington County.

Nancy grew into womanhood in the primeval forest in Kentucky. There are no authentic portraits or photographs of her, but a composite word description of her appearance has been compiled:

> A slender, symmetrical woman of medium stature, a brunette with dark hair, regular features, and soft sparkling eyes. She weighed about 130 pounds. Her skin was dark, her forehead prominent and her face sharp and angular. Her face was marked with an expression of melancholy.

There must have been a deep, inherent culture in Nancy Hanks, not the refinement that comes with book learning or that reflects formal social graces but a type of Old World gentility. Her short life epitomizes the heroic virtues of pioneer women.

When Tom Lincoln stood before the Reverend Jesse Head and promised to take Nancy Hanks as his lawful wedded wife he was a well-dressed bridegroom. A month before the wedding he had purchased one half a calfskin for his wedding boots. Tom's wedding suit was purchased from the Bleakly and Montgomery store in Elizabethtown. Perhaps he wore the hat and suspenders which he had purchased the year earlier. For an added touch he bought a "tipt bridle" to accentuate the beauty of his fine saddle. By horseback, behind the saddle, his bride would ride to their new cabin home in Elizabethtown.

According to a popular belief the wedding stopped the grinding wheels of justice. The Washington County Court in session at Springfield, Kentucky, adjourned on June 12 so that the judges, the lawyers, the plaintiffs, and the defendants could attend the marriage ceremony and wedding festival in rural Beechland. At the reception they feasted on barbecued mutton, bear meat, wild turkey, eggs of wildfowl, bit their sugar off a string for coffee, poured their peach and honey brandy from a gourd, and made a race for the whisky bottle.

Two days after the wedding Tom purchased at the village store "a half-set of knives and forks." Perhaps little thought was given to the pattern or the manufacturer. Anyway, the Lincolns were now at home to their many friends and kinsmen. There is every reason to believe that when they began housekeeping they had almost all of the pioneer necessities and a few of the luxuries.

What kind of life was that of Thomas Lincoln and Nancy Hanks? Their village offered the usual pioneer social customs: churchgoing, dancing, horse racing, patriotic celebrations, and public exhibitions. Elizabethtown had its dancing master, and there was dancing in the courthouse while the Lincolns lived there. A patriotic ball on the Fourth of July was a favorite way to celebrate the anniversary of American independence. On Monday, May 25, 1807, a group of worthy citizens petitioned "the worshipful county court" for permission to use the courthouse. Evidently the hilarious patriotic festival caused some adverse criticism among the more pious citizens, because a later court entry ordered ". . . no more balls be held in the Court House."

Perhaps Tom Lincoln attended the Hardin County Derby that was run annually at Martins Turf on Middle Creek. Horse racing was a chief source of recreation for Kentucky pioneers, and church members could attend if they abstained from gambling. Likely Tom and Nancy also witnessed dramatic presentations; they resided in the county seat. There were theatrical performances, sleight-of-hand magicians, and ropewalkers. School exhibitions were sometimes available to the Lincolns, and the infant Abraham may even have seen an elephant before he was a year old. A "proprietor of an Elephant" contributed nine dollars to the town on June 24, 1809, for the privilege of exhibiting his animal circus. Perhaps Sarah, the Lincolns' first child, enjoyed seeing the strange beast, and no doubt her parents were also thrilled.

The Lincolns moved to a farm on the south fork of Nolin Creek late in 1808, and in 1809, nine years after George Washington's life had ended, Abraham Lincoln's life began. What a wonderful life this child was destined to experience! New nations would be carved out of old empires, fabulous new lands would be explored and opened up for settlement, and new struggles for human freedom would be won. The old slow-moving, horse-drawn, and wind-propelled modes of travel would give way to the steamboat and the railroad train.

Tom Lincoln's boy was born while Jefferson was concluding his eighth year as President of the United States. Early the following month Madison would take over the reins of government. That winter of 1809, while rural neighbors sat by cracking fires and warmed and talked of Jefferson's embargo, Madison's inauguration, and Bonaparte's Spanish invasion, they little realized that Tom Lincoln's boy would one day be President—the first born beyond the confines of the thirteen original states.

In 1811 the Lincolns moved to their third cabin home on Knob Creek. Here was the most fertile land that Tom Lincoln ever owned. At least Tom thought he owned the farm until he was forced off by an ejection suit instituted by a prior claimant.

The Knob Creek farm was located on the Old Cumberland Road leading from Louisville to Nashville, Tennessee. Over this road many slaves were driven in chains to the Southern cotton market. Abraham as a boy must have observed these people, herded much the same as cattle, as they traveled on foot along the public highway.

Then, too, it was difficult for Tom Lincoln, the laborer, to compete with slave labor. When a freeman worked beside a slave the wages were always low. Indiana with its government-surveyed land and its free soil beckoned to the Lincolns. In the fall of 1816, the year that Indiana became a state, the Lincolns were numbered among its citizens. Surely Abe Lincoln's crossing the Ohio was as fateful as Washington's crossing the Delaware.

In Indiana young Lincoln borrowed the basic books which

by R. Gerald McMurtry

were to become the foundation stones of his education. It was Nancy Hanks who first planted in Lincoln's young breast a love of learning. Despite her untutored life and narrow environment she endowed her son with a breadth of vision that saved the Union and made a people free.

Nancy died in the wilderness of Indiana on October 5, 1818, when young Abraham was but nine years old. In days to come Lincoln would tell his friend "Billy" Herndon that she was highly intellectual by nature, had a good memory, and was strangely heroic amid the vicissitudes of life. So the deep impression of his mother left Abe Lincoln with something "that touched his precepts of living and survived all the disquieting years."

R. Gerald McMurtry

5

LINCOLN'S BOYHOOD

by Sterling North

It has been said that American democracy is the product of the American frontier. It has been proclaimed that without the advent of Abraham Lincoln our democracy would never have survived. And there is enough truth in those two statements to make us profoundly grateful that Tom and Nancy Hanks Lincoln, on Sunday, February 12, 1809, became the parents of a male child.

There was little of culture in that one-room log cabin in the brush-covered hills bordering Nolin Creek. Tom Lincoln was a thickset frontiersman who could but "bunglingly sign his own name." Some say that the gentle Nancy could read and write, but this is doubtful. Perhaps there was a copy of the Bible in the cabin, but even the ownership of this one book by the cabin dwellers on that Kentucky farm has been questioned.

Neither the Lincolns of the father's generation nor the Hankses of the mother's amounted to much in Kentucky. Further back in the Lincoln line there had been men of some distinction, yet not even a gypsy reading her tea leaves could have conceived that this homely frontier baby would one day become the best-loved

48

President our nation has ever known. Who was to teach him the wisdom he would one day acquire? The owls of the forest? Who was to lend him the poetry which later gave wings to his words, "With malice toward none; with charity for all . . ."? Would he learn this from the whippoorwills that all night long called to each other across the clearing?

Lincoln's first actual memories were of another farm not many miles away in the fertile valley of Knob Creek. Here Tom built a one-room log cabin beneath the shadow of Muldraugh's Hill. And here, in good soil on the valley bottom, the corn grew high, when it wasn't washed away by floods.

Dennis Hanks, a cousin of Abe's mother, Nancy, was an eye-witness of Abe Lincoln's childhood:

> It didn't seem no time till Abe was runnin' 'round in buckskin moccasins an' breeches, a tow-linen shirt an' coonskin cap. . . . Abe never give Nancy no trouble after he could walk except to keep him in clothes. Most o' the time we went b'ar foot. . . . An' Abe was right out in the woods, about as soon's he was weaned, fishin' in the crick . . . goin' on coon-hunts with Tom an' me an' the dogs; follerin' up bees to find bee-trees, an' drappin' corn fur his pappy. Mighty interestin' life fur a boy, but thar was good many chances he wouldn't live to grow up.

Once when the creek was in flood Abe nearly drowned. He was rescued by a playmate, Austin Gollaher. But this experience did not turn Lincoln against the sound of running water. Twice in his later youth he would take flatboats all the way down the mighty Mississippi to New Orleans. Later, too, he would invent and patent a device for taking boats over shoals and rapids. He loved the streams of the Middle West—the Sangamon, the Ohio, the Mississippi. Very soon now he would be crossing the Ohio with his family to settle in the almost unpopulated state of Indiana on yet another beloved stream, Pigeon Creek.

The trek to Indiana took place in 1816, so cold a year that it

49

was known on the frontier as "Eighteen-Hundred-and-Froze-to-Death." Tom was restless again. He made a pilgrimage to Indiana and staked out 160 forest acres, placing a brush pile at each corner of the quarter section. Then he came home to get his family.

Dennis Hanks was to remember that they moved everything worth taking "on the backs o' two pack hosses. Tom could make new pole beds an' puncheon tables an' stools easier 'n he could carry 'em. Abe toted a gun. . . ."

In Indiana Tom constructed a half-face hunter's camp as their only shelter for part of that first cold winter. It was fourteen feet wide and about as deep, framed with poles and thatched with bark. A fire was kept burning on the open side of this lean-to which gave some protection from the snow and wind and cold but often filled the little hut with the acrid, suffocating fumes of oak and hickory smoke. Leaves were the floor; corn-tick mattresses the bed. Luckily game was plentiful and Abe managed to bring home a wild turkey. He never again pulled the trigger on larger game.

Lincoln was eventually elected as The Rail Splitter, one of the few log-cabin Presidents who was a real artist with the ax. He recalled that almost constantly between his eighth and twenty-third years he had "that most useful instrument" in his hands. Fields had to be cleared from virgin forest, a task almost unimaginable in our softer way of life. Rails were split from the great logs with mall and wedges. Then the rail fences were laid up in a snake pattern. In Indiana, and later in Illinois, patient Abe split many such rails.

But no rail fence could keep the bears from eating the pigs. Lincoln was never a great poet except in his speeches. When he attempted rhymed verse it was likely to go something like this:

> When first my father settled here,
> 'Twas then the frontier line:
> The panther's scream, filled night with fear
> And bears preyed on the swine.

But in this wilderness there were enemies more to be feared than bears or panthers: the plagues and fevers which sometimes carried off whole villages. Most terrifying of all these mysterious diseases was the "milk sickness" which killed cows and human beings alike. Thomas and Betsy Sparrow, Nancy's uncle and aunt, arrived in Indiana in the autumn of 1817. They and Dennis Hanks made their nest in that "darne little half face camp," as Dennis called it, while Tom and Nancy Lincoln and their two children, Abe and Sarah, moved into the new but unchinked cabin he had built. The Sparrows caught the milk sickness and died. Nancy nursed them in their last illness. Then she, too, took to her bed.

The leaves were brilliant against the autumn sky when gentle Nancy called Sarah and Abe to her side. She made them promise to be good children and kind to each other. Then she closed her eyes and the cabin was motherless. She was buried beside the deer run in the woods; deer were the only creatures of the forest which the women did not fear.

Abe and Sarah and Dennis and Tom had a miserable year in the cabin. They grew careless of their cleanliness. Nancy was no longer there to care for them and give them courage, to wash and cook and make candles and cheer them with her presence. In time Tom grew so lonely that he headed back to Kentucky to find himself another wife. In Elizabethtown he went straight to the house of Sarah Bush Johnston, whom he had courted years before when neither had yet been married. Both had since been widowed.

"Well, *Miss* Johnston, I have no wife, and you have no husband. I came a purpose to marry you. I knowed you from a gal, and you knowed me from a boy. I have no time to lose; and, if you are willin', let it be done straight off."

With a few little details attended to, Sarah and her three children, Elizabeth, Matilda, and John, started back for Indiana with a whole load of Sarah's furniture, including an unbelievable bureau which had cost forty-five dollars. Sarah loved Tom Lincoln's two children and they loved her. She soon had the cabin clean and livable. It must have been a particularly comforting Christ-

51

mas on that December 25, 1819, when Sarah stuffed the wild turkey for the Christmas dinner. The cabin had a mother once again. Tom Lincoln must have added a few extra words of thanks to his usually brief blessing as their five children and Dennis Hanks joined Tom and Sarah at the puncheon table.

Sterling North

6

THE INDIANA YEARS OF ABRAHAM LINCOLN

by Philip Van Doren Stern

Abraham Lincoln lived in southern Indiana from the time he was only seven years old until he was twenty-one. When his mother, Nancy Hanks Lincoln, died in 1818 his father married a second time. Sarah Bush Johnston was a widow from Kentucky with three children of her own.

She proved to be a kind stepmother to Thomas Lincoln's two orphans. She brought some of her own furniture, and under her cheerful, energetic guidance the lonely cabin in the woods was improved with a wooden floor and made to look more like a home.

The Lincoln family was only one of the many obscure and forgotten groups moving Westward in the great migration that settled the North American continent. Lincoln himself said that it was folly to try to make anything out of his early life, for it could all be condensed into a single sentence from Gray's *Elegy*: "The short and simple annals of the poor."

Those who knew the adolescent Lincoln say that he spent long hours reading and trying to teach himself arithmetic. He had to work in the fields and the forest with his hands but he was much more interested in words and ideas. There was little formal schooling; he went to school by "littles"; in all it did not amount to more than a year. He was largely self-taught all his life but he never stopped learning. He read everything that was available. There were not many books but he became thoroughly familiar with them: the Bible, Aesop's *Fables, Robinson Crusoe, Pilgrim's Progress*, Ramsey's and Weems's lives of George Washington, and the *Statutes of Indiana*, in which he may have encountered the Constitution of the United States for the first time. He borrowed books from his neighbors. One of the books he borrowed, a life of Washington, became damaged through exposure to rain, and he had to pull fodder for three days to compensate the owner.

Among the few established dates in this part of Lincoln's life is August 2, 1826, when his sister Sarah married Aaron Grigsby. Less than two years later, on January 20, 1828, almost ten years after the death of his mother, young Abe Lincoln again faced personal tragedy. Sarah, the slightly older sister who had been close to him for almost nineteen years, died in childbirth and was buried in the graveyard of the Pigeon Creek Church.

Lincoln once told the members of his Cabinet that he built a boat with his own hands during the Indiana years. With it he earned his wages, two half dollars, by taking passengers out to the river steamers when they stopped in midstream. It was probably Lincoln's experience as a boatman that gave him the first big chance of his life—a chance to break away for a few months from his wilderness environment and go voyaging on a flatboat down the Mississippi River to New Orleans already one of the most important cities in the United States. He was nineteen when he got his first glimpse of a big city.

In 1828 New Orleans was a very picturesque place. Hundreds of flatboats came down the river to sell their cargoes there, and the city throbbed with life. Here Lincoln had his first direct contact with slavery, for he had been only a child when he lived in the slave state of Kentucky, and Indiana was, of course, a free state.

For two years after his return home he continued to do manual labor and tried to improve his education. The same milk sickness which had killed Nancy Hanks again threatened the wilderness community, and Thomas Lincoln, who had heard a great deal about the rich prairie land of Illinois, decided to move there. In the early spring of 1830, when Abraham Lincoln was just twenty-one, they left Indiana, passing through Vincennes, which had long been the gateway to the West. They forded the Wabash River at that point and entered the State of Illinois to seek a new homestead. A symbolic statue of the young Lincoln now stands at the place where they crossed. It shows him trudging on with his family's wagon party toward the unplowed prairies where the soil lay deep and black.

After they crossed the river they headed north across level land where there were no roads and where horse or ox teams wandered on with nothing except mud or an occasional brook to impede their progress. A great deal of effort has been made in modern times to retrace the exact route the Lincolns took, but even those who have studied what little evidence there is have not been able to come to any precise conclusion about the details of the journey. The Lincoln family went through that sparsely settled area making no more of an imprint upon the land than a band of roving Indians does when it casually moves from one hunting ground to another.

In the middle of March they arrived at a tiny new community in central Illinois named Decatur. There they camped in the town square overnight. The next day they traveled about ten miles southwest. Without even bothering to claim a homesite they built a log cabin a few hundred feet from a narrow muddy stream that was to become forever associated with Lincoln's name. This was the Sangamon River, the prairie stream that was to wind in and out of Lincoln's life until he left Illinois forever to go to Washington as President of the United States.

His introduction to the Sangamon River country was an unusually harsh one. No sooner had they got their cabin built and a few acres under cultivation than the dreadful winter of 1830-31 began. It brought the kind of weather that the Illinois pioneers were to talk about for years. Snow fell four feet deep on level ground and piled up in huge drifts that no one could get through.

The Lincoln family lived in their snowbound cabin like hibernating animals. They probably slept most of the time, for there was nothing else for them to do and inactivity helped conserve energy and their meager supply of food. When the spring at last came the melting snow brought great floods.

That spring Lincoln left his father's home to help build another flatboat and take it downriver to New Orleans. He traveled across the water-covered land by canoe to reach the place where the new boat was to be constructed. When it was launched and started on its way it got stuck on a mill dam which had been thrown across the Sangamon just below a newly established village named New Salem. This was Lincoln's introduction to the little town where he spent the next six years of his life. After he returned from his second voyage to New Orleans he left his father's household forever and established himself in the village where he was to study law and be elected to the state legislature. His life for many years to come was difficult, but he had grown up and was on his own.

The early years he had spent in the dark forest land of Indiana and on the wind-swept prairies of Illinois left their mark upon him. In the forest the menace of wild animals and hostile men was always close at hand. Even worse was the threat of unknown danger that might lurk behind every tree. In those woods he had seen death strike down his beloved mother and sister. Two lonely graves in the Indiana wilderness were the landmarks of his adolescent years. And his first years in Illinois had meant hard manual labor, bitter cold, imprisoning deep snow, and devastating floods.

Those who knew Lincoln well said that melancholy lay beneath the surface manifestations of joviality he had trained himself to adopt. Suddenly and without apparent cause his features would often darken and take on an expression of utter gloom.

by Philip Van Doren Stern

The superstitious pioneers believed that a wind blowing across the grave of a beloved one could freeze the heart of someone far away. Perhaps in Lincoln's case that chilling wind came from the depths of his own memory, from the recollections of the hard years he had spent in the raw new land where he had grown up.

Philip Van Doren Stern

7

LINCOLN IN NEW SALEM

by Paul M. Angle

For a time it seemed as if the little town on the bluff along the Sangamon River would really take root. The grist-and-sawmill, the original reason for the town's existence, drew a few settlers, a store owner or two, a "grocery" or tavern keeper, cooper, cobbler, doctor, even a schoolmaster. By 1836, eight years after James Rutledge and John M. Camron, the millwrights, built the first two cabins, New Salem, Sangamon County, Illinois, had attracted a population of twenty-five or thirty families.

But in that same year an event occurred which forecast the town's death. The Postmaster General of the United States closed New Salem's post office and opened one instead at nearby Petersburg, an upstart village four years younger. Beyond question Petersburg would be the seat of the new county soon to be formed from the northern part of overlarge Sangamon. Even settlers of several years' standing began to leave for localities that offered surer promise of growth and prosperity.

No defection hit New Salem harder than that of Abraham Lincoln. The saddlebags that he filled one April day in 1837 were as light as his purse, but in spite of his lack of material possessions he was the town's most prominent citizen—its postmaster until the removal of the office, its one lawyer, its member of the state legislature. With Lincoln gone the decline of New Salem became inevitable.

Lincoln had achieved his status of leading citizen in less than six years. He had first seen the village in the spring of 1831 as a hired hand on a flatboat. Three months later, after completing his second trip to New Orleans, he had settled there in the dual capacity of mill hand and store clerk. His droll humor, his fearlessness and skill in rough-and-tumble sport, his honesty and candor quickly made him popular. Urged by his neighbors, he became a candidate for election to the legislature. His platform, dated March 9, 1832, which advocated improvement of the Sangamon River and the encouragement of education, ended with an unusual confession. "I was born and have ever remained," he said, "in the most humble walks of life. I have no wealthy or popular relations to recommend me. My case is thrown exclusively upon the independent voters of this county, and if elected they will have conferred a favor upon me, for which I shall be unremitting in my labors to compensate. But if the good people in their wisdom shall see fit to keep me in the background, I have been too familiar with disappointments to be very much chagrined."

Before Lincoln could make a real campaign Black Hawk, leader of a renegade band of Sauk and Fox, whose tribe had been removed from Illinois to Iowa the preceding year, crossed the Mississippi near the mouth of the Iowa River and threw the fear of Indian war into the entire state. Before the governor called out the militia Lincoln had volunteered and was elected captain of the local company—a success, he wrote after he had been nominated for the Presidency, that gave him more satisfaction than any other in his life. When his thirty days' enlistment as a captain expired, Lincoln re-enlisted as a private. He served for three months, the last two as a private, saw no action, and returned unscathed to New Salem only a few days before the election.

"The good people in their wisdom" did see fit to keep him in the background, yet the outcome of the voting forecast success in the future. He ran eighth among thirteen candidates in the district. Out of 300 votes cast in the New Salem precinct Lincoln received 277—a remarkable achievement for a young man of twenty-three who had lived in the community for little more than a year.

Yet Lincoln's defeat posed a personal problem: how could he make a living? His employer had failed soon after the Black Hawk War broke out. Lincoln thought for a time of learning the blacksmith's trade, but was saved from that decision when one of the other New Salem storekeepers offered to sell him and another penniless resident a stock of goods on credit. In Lincoln's words, "they did nothing but get deeper and deeper into debt." It was then that a Democratic Administration came to the young Whig's rescue by appointing him postmaster, "the office being too insignificant to make his politics an objection."

There is evidence that Lincoln treated it as insignificant. One Matthew S. Marsh, writing in the fall of 1835, remarked that "the Post Master (Mr. Lincoln) is very careless about leaving his office open and unlocked during the day—half the time I go in and get my papers, etc., without anyone being there as was the case yesterday." Marsh continued: "The letter was only marked twenty-five [cents]"—at that time the recipient rather than the sender paid postage—"and even if he had been there and known it was double, he would not have charged me any more—luckily he is a very clever fellow and a particular friend of mine." Marsh concluded: "If he is there when I carry this to the office—I will get him to 'Frank' it." And Lincoln did, in spite of a law strictly forbidding such a practice.

About the same time Lincoln was made postmaster the county surveyor offered to appoint him a deputy. Lincoln knew nothing of surveying but he could learn. Of that he was sure. In his first months in New Salem he had recognized that his knowledge of grammar was deficient. He had found a book and with the help of the schoolmaster and others had studied until he knew the rules of correct expression in practice as well as precept. Now he followed the same procedure: he obtained a manual and studied ceaselessly until he mastered the art of measuring land. Between the post office, the surveyor's chain, and occasional odd jobs he managed to live in reasonable comfort.

In 1834 Lincoln ran for the legislature again. This time he was not only successful, he ran a mere fourteen votes behind the first of the four candidates who were elected. Late in November, dressed in a new suit bought with borrowed money, he took the stage for Vandalia, the state capital, to mingle there with leading men from all parts of the state.

As soon as the session was over, Lincoln returned to New Salem, the post office, surveying, and, once more, intensive study. John T. Stuart, a Springfield lawyer with whom Lincoln had served in the Black Hawk War, had seen promise in the young legislator and had urged him to study law. Lincoln acquired an old copy of Blackstone's *Commentaries* and borrowed from Stuart the few other texts then considered essential to a lawyer's education. In the fall of 1836 he received a license to practice; formal admission to the bar came on March 1, 1837, when his name was entered on the role of Illinois attorneys.

When Lincoln was formally admitted to the bar he was nearing the end of his second term in the legislature. In that session he had been the Whig leader—testimony to his quick mastery of the art of politics. It had taken all his skill, however, to win the prize on which he and the other members from Sangamon County, now nine in number, had set their hearts—the transfer of the state capital from Vandalia to Springfield. A week before the session ended the necessary votes had been rounded up, and Lincoln came home to his constituents a hero.

But he would remain among his old friends and neighbors only a few weeks. Stuart had asked him to become his partner, and Springfield offered possibilities that New Salem could never hold out even if it would not fade away. A newspaper notice announced Lincoln's decision and his entrance into a new phase of his life. It read: "J. T. Stuart and A. Lincoln, Attorneys and Counsellors at Law, will practice cojointly in the courts of this Judicial Circuit. Office No. 4 Hoffman's Row upstairs. Springfield, April 12, 1837."

Paul M. Angle

8

ABRAHAM LINCOLN'S FIRST LOVES

by Olive Carruthers

Soon after Abraham Lincoln died and increasingly as the years progressed a babble of female voices seemed to rise over the land, speaking through the medium of the biographers and popular writers on the Lincoln theme. These writers claimed that many women, at one time or another in his fabulous career, could have married him. Schoolmates in Indiana, young women from New Salem, Illinois, society belles and farmers' daughters in Springfield—if their stories were to be credited Abe Lincoln was the courtingest swain of his time and one who proposed to practically every woman he met.

Perhaps he did. There is no way to prove it one way or the other. According to Billy Herndon, his law partner and biographer, he was certainly uncommonly interested in women. But there is no way, really, to prove the bittersweet story which has lived persistently in the hearts of the American people until it has become a part of the nation's folklore—Lincoln's romance with Ann Rutledge, reputedly his first real love and some said his only love.

Abe, just past his twenty-second birthday, first came to New Salem in the spring of 1831. He returned to stay in July of that year. One of the early settlers in the little village twenty miles from Springfield was James Rutledge. Rutledge was part owner of the gristmill, and he ran a tavern. The term "tavern" in those days was used indiscriminately for both hotels and boarding-houses. The Rutledge Tavern was a boardinghouse, and Lincoln lived there for a time.

James Rutledge had a daughter, Ann, who seems to have been the rural princess of all the fairy tales. She was five feet two, blonde, with blue eyes, and she excelled in the womanly arts of needlework and cookery. She undoubtedly waited on table at her father's tavern.

Ann was engaged to a man whom New Salem knew as John McNeil, who had lived in New Salem for a short time and had then gone back to New York State for his family, promising to return. Before he left he told Ann that his real name was Mc-Namar and that he had concealed his identity in order to be free of family obligations until he was financially able to take care of them. Now he could do it, he would return, and he and Ann would be wed.

But the days dragged into weeks and the months into years and John McNamar's letters became less and less frequent.

Did Ann tell Abe Lincoln of her vague engagement? Probably. All New Salem knew the story. If he didn't hear it from Ann he could have heard it from any number of others.

So the fact or fiction, whichever it was, ran that Abe and Ann fell in love and that, as time went on with no more word from McNeil-McNamar, young Lincoln considered that he could honorably court the deserted girl.

Ann felt differently, so the tale was told. Torn between two loves, she was so emotionally wracked that she fell ill of a violent fever in the summer of 1835 and in her delirium called for Abe. Her family allowed him to go into the sick room, and left the two alone.

What they talked about nobody knows. Lincoln never told, and within a few days Ann Rutledge was dead.

Lincoln, so Billy Herndon reported more than thirty years later, nearly went out of his mind with grief. His friends feared for his sanity and for his life. And he locked the memory of Ann Rutledge in his heart, the sweetness of his first love enduring as a solace and source of both inspiration and recurring melancholy.

The story, based on a Menard County newspaper account published while Lincoln was President, was given to the public in a lecture by Herndon in 1866, a year after the President's death and while his widow, Mary Todd Lincoln, was still suffering shock from her husband's assassination.

The story of this romance seems to be full of holes. To begin with, even in those days when gently reared women resorted to the "vapors" over distressed love affairs they didn't go into raging fevers and die of indecision. Ann's symptoms, to the modern therapist, would appear to be those of tuberculosis or perhaps sunstroke. More important to the careful historian is the fact that no scrap of paper has ever been discovered on which one of the so-called lovers wrote to the other. Young men and women usually write notes to each other—tender, foolish, or indiscreet, reminders of trysts kept or broken, or silly "double talk" that has meaning only for the two of them. And Lincoln, by later evidence, was a letter-writing man. He had a gift for language and he liked to use it.

Moreover, if he had been so madly in love with Ann, so stricken by her death, how could he have chased his long legs off, within a year and a half of her demise, courting Mary Owens?

For there is ample proof of Lincoln's courtship of Mary Owens, the highly educated daughter of a wealthy Kentucky landowner. He wrote letters to her. And the letters are still extant.

In fact he had seen Miss Owens in 1833, during the time when he was supposedly courting Ann Rutledge. Mary had come to visit her sister, Betsy Abell, wife of one of Lincoln's closest friends, a New Salem farmer. And when he saw her in "the finest trimmings" any man in New Salem had ever seen on a woman, he bragged to friends—who remembered—that if she ever returned to Illinois he would "catch, tie and marry her."

Though Lincoln later, writing to the wife of a state senator, would criticize her appearance Mary was, by some standards, a handsome woman. Tall, a little bit heavy, but with bright blue eyes and dark, curling hair, with the speech and manners of a gentlewoman, to say nothing of a good mind, she was one to excite the ambition of any man who had never known any women except pioneer drudges.

He had his chance when along in 1836 Betsy Abell made him a proposition. "If my sister Mary returns to visit me," she asked him, "will you court and marry her?" Lincoln may have thought it was a joke. But he promised. And when Mary Owens arrived in New Salem he was there, dancing attendance.

The two found that they had much in common: their Kentucky birth; their interest in politics (Mary's father had been a judge); their feeling about temperance, in which Mary was deeply involved; and their convictions about human slavery. Though Mary's father had fourteen slaves she shared Lincoln's attitude toward the evil of the institution. They talked easily together, and each admired the other's mind.

Hardly a basis for romance, but at the start Lincoln was very well pleased with the prospect. Mary was interested. After all Abe Lincoln was an interesting man. Moreover Mary at twenty-six was in danger, it seemed to her sister, of becoming an old maid. Betsy put up a great case for Abe and predicted an unusual future for him, which Mary might share if she chose.

But as this strange courting progressed Abe's lack of social training and the difference in their backgrounds became more and more apparent to Mary. He was thoughtless of women. Once he let a mutual friend, a Mrs. Green, struggle up a long hill lugging her fat baby without offering to carry the child. Another time when Mary and Abe were out riding with a party of young folks they came to a ford which was difficult to cross. The other swains held back to help their ladies across, but Abe plunged ahead with no heed for Mary. She chided him, but he only responded, "I thought you were plenty smart to look out for yourself." She supposed he meant that for a compliment, but to her the remark indicated a basic lack of understanding more than bad manners.

Still, neither gave up. When one blew warm the other blew cold. Abe went off to Vandalia to attend the state legislature, with no understanding between them. He wrote back a curious letter, full of legislative news and complaints of his health. But he pleaded that she write to him, saying that he had not been pleased since he left her.

Sometime during the winter Lincoln definitely proposed to Mary Owens, for he wrote her from Springfield the following May, saying, "I am often thinking about what we said of your coming to live at Springfield. I am afraid you would not be satisfied. . . . You would have to be poor without the means of hiding your poverty." He may have been only cautious, wanting her to understand what his prospects were as he started the practice of law. She must have half promised him, since he continued, "What you have said to me may have been in just, or I may have misunderstood it. . . . What I have said I will most positively abide by, provided you wish it." Nevertheless his opinion was that she had "better not do it."

No one could blame a girl for being hesitant or even confused by such a proposal. A man in love would most certainly throw caution to the wind—or would he, if the man was Abe Lincoln? Mary couldn't make up her mind.

By the following August she had still not said yes or no. And Lincoln, after riding from Springfield to New Salem to have it out, returned without having had a private word with Mary. Late though it was he sat up to write her a final letter. He protested his willingness to keep his word. He wanted to do right at all times, particularly "in all cases with women." But he was willing to release her, if that was what she wanted. He would save her from embarrassment, though, if that would help her any. "If it suits you best to not answer this," he wrote, "farewell—a long life and a merry one attend you. . . ." He signed the letter, "Your friend Lincoln."

Mary Owens never answered the letter, and Lincoln had his no. The next year he made light of the matter in a facetious letter to another woman who was safely married to one of his friends, with no danger of his proposing to her.

The fact remains that Mary Owens could have married the young Lincoln if she had wanted to. She declined because, as she wrote Herndon many years later, she found him "lacking in those little links that make up a woman's chain of happiness." She never regretted her choice but married another man and brought up a family.

Tragedy and farce, or fiction and fact—or a mixture of all, it seems more than coincidence that Mary Todd, the woman Lincoln married, had in her youth as much beauty as Ann Rutledge and as good a mind as Mary Owens. She also had the triumph and the heartbreak that the other two escaped.

Olive Carruthers

"EVERY MAN IS SAID TO HAVE HIS PECULIAR AMBITION"

9

LINCOLN ENTERS POLITICS

by William E. Baringer

On the frontier, the saying went a century and more ago, every man is a politician. In the untamed wilderness there were no classes and hence, fortunately for democracy, no ruling class. Free and equal citizens organized their own governments and ran them. "A freeborn American" was a phrase constantly and proudly in use, to the irritation of aristocratic European visitors.

Young Abraham Lincoln, Kentucky born and Indiana reared, was one of these freeborn Americans whose birthright it was to serve, with their permission, his fellow citizens. His schooling was brief, and by his own admission he did not know much. But he could read, write, and figure, which was more than most of his contemporaries could do. Nature had blessed him with an inquiring mind, and he learned rapidly from the world around him. He experimented with various forms of self-expression, writing, speechmaking, and storytelling, and became proficient in all three, especially in telling stories.

Work on the frontier meant backbreaking toil on the land. That kind of work Abraham disliked; it diverted him from learning. His father, legally the boy's master until he became twenty-one, kept him at work and pocketed his earnings. Young Lincoln decided to leave home at twenty-one and make his own living by his wits and great physical strength.

On February 12, 1830, when Abraham reached his legal maturity, his family was packing to move from the old farm frontier, Indiana, to the new one, Illinois. He moved with them, then worked all summer at starting the new Thomas Lincoln farm in Macon County, on the upper reaches of the Sangamon River. The following spring, having located a job, he bade his family farewell and never lived with them again.

Near Springfield, on the lower Sangamon, he built a flatboat and, as hired riverman, took a load of produce to New Orleans. Returning to Illinois he arrived in the new town of New Salem "like a piece of floating driftwood," to work as grocery clerk for the same employer. Abraham's personality, his strength, honesty, courage, and geniality quickly made him popular, and the next year, 1832, unemployed, he ran for the legislature. He told the voters of Sangamon County that spring, in a long published statement, what he planned to do if elected. Lincoln admitted that he was young and relatively unknown. He had no powerful friends or relatives to recommend him. If elected he would work hard for his constituents; if defeated he would not blame them.

Parties were not yet solidly organized in frontier Illinois, and personal announcement was the regular method of running for office. The legislature in those days held all the power to govern. To our time the candidacy of this unemployed, inexperienced, ungraduated newcomer appears to have been a miracle of presumption. Not at all, however, in 1832. Most of the members of every frontier legislature were no more experienced than Lincoln. Becoming a candidate was thus a perfectly natural move, politics being the most rewarding form of self-expression in his society.

On election day, in August, he lost. Though his campaign was interrupted by the three-month absence during the Black Hawk

War the New Salem area gave him a nearly unanimous vote, but the rest of the huge county of Sangamon did not.

Determined to try again, the young politician contrived a way of making himself better known. He became deputy surveyor of Sangamon County and postmaster in New Salem. Neither appointment paid much. If either had, somebody else, a Democrat, would have filled it. Lincoln joined the minority party, Whig. His two jobs greatly enlarged his circle of friends, and when the next legislature was elected in 1834 he ran again and won a seat in the House of Representatives.

In November Lincoln borrowed two hundred dollars and bought a tailormade suit. Well dressed for the first time in his life, he arrived in Vandalia, the log capital of Illinois, and was sworn into his first elective public office on December 1, 1834. He was completely unknown in the capital. But not for long. His guide, mentor, and future law partner, John T. Stuart of Springfield, introduced him to his colleagues, showed him the ropes, and soon Lincoln was heard from on the floor of the House. On at least one occasion he won the admiration and laughter of the members by a humorous solution to a difficult parliamentary problem.

By session's end in February he had received $225 in per diem pay, and $33 for travel, the most money the towering and impecunious young Solon had ever made. Lincoln had introduced three bills of his own and seen two of them become law. The Honorable Abraham Lincoln returned to New Salem confident that he was going somewhere in politics. He had acquired extensive experience and popularity among the great men of frontier Illinois, and confidence in himself.

One who saw him in Vandalia that winter left this description of the lanky, towering young lawmaker: "rawboned, angular, features deeply furrowed, ungraceful, almost uncouth; having little if any of that polish so important in society life; and yet there was a magnetism and dash about the man that made him a universal favorite. Underneath that rough exterior—it was easy, too,

71

to find out—dwelt a mind and heart of immense powers."

When cold weather returned, Lincoln was back in Vandalia for a short special session to redistrict the state. His county of Sangamon, largest in Illinois in area and population, gained three House members in the new apportionment law, giving it seven representatives and two senators, the largest county delegation in the state. Lincoln announced for re-election in the spring of 1836 and won triumphantly with the largest vote cast for any Sangamon candidate.

Armed with this strong vote of confidence, encouraged by the election of a Sangamon delegation solidly Whig, and ready to take over the duties of Stuart (who ran for Congress and lost) as the House's leading Whig, Lincoln made bold plans to move the capital from Vandalia to Springfield.

The Sangamon delegation rationalized this ambition as a move in the best interests of the state. Vandalia was too far south for the seat of government. The capitol building was about to fall down, and it was too small for the enlarged legislature. Vandalia's constitutional period as the capital, twenty years, was about up anyway. The government was certain to move north, and Lincoln and his eight men, soon to become famous as the Long Nine, for in height they totaled fifty-four feet, thought they could win the prize for Springfield. They had more votes than any other county, and they counted on gaining outside votes by the familiar process of logrolling. In our time, when fewer logs are rolled, this is better known as back-scratching.

To improve its economy Illinois needed internal improvements —railroads, canals, improved roads and waterways. The Long Nine would give some of these good things to every county and in return gain the votes of those counties' lawmakers for Springfield as the next capital. This was the era of internal improvements and a time of the greatest prosperity the country had ever seen. The national debt had been entirely paid off, and an embarrassing surplus accumulated in the Treasury. Congress ordered this distributed to the states, and Illinois expected a million as its share. Since the state itself had very little money and no taxes at all, the Illinois plan for internal improvements was to sell bonds, build railroads and canals, then pay the debt out of earnings.

Vandalia, determined to remain the capital, sought to strike a club from the Long Nine's hands by putting up a new building to impress the lawmakers. This backfired when the new capitol building was not finished in time, December of 1836. For a week the members waited for the plaster to dry. When they moved in the place was still clammy. Several legislators fell sick and some of them died.

The Long Nine efficiently pushed through a ten-million-dollar internal improvement program, all to be built on credit. Then when capital relocation came up they demanded that men from the railroad counties vote for Springfield, and Sangamon County won the prize. Vandalia and southern members resisted to the last, but Lincoln efficiently outmaneuvered them.

At adjournment members of the Long Nine were welcomed home as heroes. Lincoln went on to New Salem, promptly moved to Springfield, and began a new career as practicing lawyer.

Springfield was still celebrating when hard times, the panic of 1837, struck the land. Illinois could not sell its bonds. Public works went unfinished. The state went far into debt in starting these useless monuments to a former prosperity. Vandalia, still fighting against fate, Lincoln, and Sangamon, sadly saw in the summer of 1839 the capital move north.

When his fourth term ended in 1841 Lincoln declined any further re-election. He had proved his skill as a politician, and his sights were now set on a higher office, a seat in the national House of Representatives. After a few terms there he intended to advance to the Senate. That was the extreme limit of his ambition, until May 1860, when lightning struck in the form of a nomination for President of the United States.

William E. Baringer

10

ABRAHAM LINCOLN: ILLINOIS LEGISLATOR

by Clyde C. Walton

Abraham Lincoln cut his political eyeteeth as an Illinois legislator. He was a candidate from Sangamon County for the lower house of the General Assembly six times. In 1834, 1836, 1838, 1840, and 1854 the voters sent him to represent them at the state capital. The last time, he resigned so that he might campaign for United States Senator. Only in 1832, when Lincoln made his first political race, was he defeated, and this was the only defeat he was ever to suffer in a direct election by the people.

When, in the fall of 1834, he took his seat in the legislature at Vandalia, then the capital, the State of Illinois was sixteen years old and Lincoln but twenty-five. He had now entered his life's work, a work which twenty-seven years later would send him to the White House. Even before his election Lincoln had decided to work with his mind as well as with his hands. The next few years were to see him work harder with his lawbooks than with his surveying instruments, more assiduously on the political canvass than with his ax.

In a very real way Lincoln and Illinois grew up together. The state grew from an agrarian, frontier adolescence to the beginnings of a modern industrial commonwealth. Lincoln grew from an eager, rough backwoodsman to a mature, composed lawyer and canny but respected political figure whose words were heard far beyond the city of Springfield, Illinois. As Illinois would prosper so would Lincoln; as the state's political, financial, and social problems became more sophisticated so, too, a greater comprehension of the world around him and the complexities of the people in it smoothed away many of Lincoln's frontier crudities and strengthened his innate humanity. The early years, however, had left their indelible mark upon him.

Lincoln's service in the Ninth General Assembly during the winter of 1834-35 was creditable but not distinguished. As is traditional with freshman legislators he was quiet and unobtrusive; he allowed the senior members to handle affairs. But he was watching and learning about the political process. He saw some men lead and manipulate others, and he resolved to be one of the leaders, not one of the followers. Perhaps most important of all, he saw how legislation was hammered out on the anvil of compromise.

A special session of the legislature was held the winter of 1835-36, and Lincoln was active both on the floor and in the cloakrooms. Encouraged by John T. Stuart, the Whig chieftain, he entered into debate, introduced legislation, offered amendments, and on occasion acted as Whig leader. He had learned his political lessons quickly and well.

After this special session Lincoln returned to New Salem as he had before. He was by now aware that the horizons of this small village were too limiting to his ambitions. A candidate again in 1836, Lincoln led all seventeen Sangamon County hopefuls in the election for members of the Tenth General Assembly. And now, with the complete support of the Sangamon County legislators, Lincoln would apply the legislative lessons he had learned so well.

Briefly, by clever horse-trading and careful bargaining, Lincoln masterminded the political coup that moved the state capital from

Vandalia to Springfield. He here clearly demonstrated native shrewdness, personal persuasiveness and persistence, and thorough knowledge of parliamentary procedure.

And just before the legislature adjourned Lincoln registered a protest against slavery resolutions passed earlier, saying in part that "slavery is founded on both injustice and bad policy" and that the Congress had no Constitutional power "to interfere with the institution of slavery in the different States." He thereby disavowed the evil of slavery publicly in 1837, and in 1860, speaking of the position he took in this 1837 statement, said that "so far as it goes, it was then the same that it is now."

Springfield, obviously a town with a future, attracted Lincoln, and in April 1837 he left New Salem for the greater possibilities of Springfield. He had been admitted to the bar on March 1 and soon thereafter formed his law partnership with John T. Stuart. This would enable him to practice with one of the leading political and legal figures in Illinois. The firm enjoyed a good practice and Lincoln soon was involved in the highly publicized Adams lawsuit, an action which had political as well as legal implications. Lincoln supported the candidacy of his good friend Dr. Anson G. Henry for the office of probate justice of the peace against General James Adams, a veteran of the War of 1812, who had held the office since 1825. Representing a widow, Mrs. Mary Anderson, Lincoln was seeking to recover ten acres of land which he stated Adams had illegally claimed. It was now that Lincoln utilized his close friendship with Simeon Francis of the *Sangamo Journal* and manifested his unusual trait of writing pseudonymous letters to a newspaper. During the Adams case a series of letters signed "Sampson's Ghost" and "Old Settler" appeared. These letters told the story of Adams' supposed fraud against the poor widow. In a reply, published in the *Illinois Republican*, Adams intimated that Stephen T. Logan, later to become Lincoln's law partner, was guilty of forgery. Logan promptly sued for slander. Adams, however, defeated Henry, and many believed it was partly due to the resentment on the part of the people against Lincoln for making his accusations public and attempting to try his case in the newspapers.

In July 1837 he attended a special session of the General Assembly called to consider the tangled finances of Illinois. The panic of 1837 and the debts piled up by the internal-improvement acts of the previous year were responsible for the sad fiscal condition of the state. Lincoln would have to cope with this problem, which he had helped to create, throughout the remainder of his service as a legislator. He took a conservative position—retain the internal-improvements acts and support the state bank. The legislature refused to repeal the improvements and bank acts, and accomplished little.

In the session beginning in December 1838 Lincoln was a candidate for Speaker of the House but was defeated by a vote of forty-three to thirty-eight. For the remainder of his legislative career he was Whig leader and again held to his basic position on the state-bank and improvement bills. He had a bill passed which would have Illinois buy all public lands in the state from the Federal Government for twenty-five cents an acre, resell them to settlers for a dollar and twenty-five cents, and apply the profit to the interest on the debt. The Congress of the United States ignored this novel scheme.

A special session in the winter of 1839–40 addressed itself to the vexatious problem of the debt but reached no solution. This was the first time the legislature met in Springfield, and the House of Representatives met in the Second Presbyterian Church, since the new capitol building was not finished.

Elected again in 1840, Lincoln was also a member of the Whig State Central Committee, a Whig elector in the "Tippecanoe & Tyler Too" presidential campaign, and an active sponsor of a Harrison campaign paper, *The Old Soldier*. He took the stump for Harrison all over Illinois that fall.

Again nominated in 1840 for Speaker and again defeated, forty-six to thirty-six, Lincoln was plunged into his most ludicrous legislative experience. The General Assembly had convened two weeks early, and expected to adjourn before December 7, when the regular session would begin. If it did so the state bank would be compelled by a recent law to resume specie payment, a measure Lincoln opposed. His strategy was to make adjournment impossible by preventing a quorum from being present in the House, and so he had the Whigs absent themselves from the temporary quarters, which had been moved to the Methodist Church. When a quorum was announced by the appearance of several laggard Democrats and a vote taken on adjournment, Lincoln jumped out of a window in a futile attempt to stave off the inevitable.

For a few days in January 1841 Lincoln was absent from the legislature as a result of the physical illness and mental indisposition following the breaking off of his engagement to Mary Todd. Although he had a much better record in February he seems to have lost interest in legislative matters, and when the Assembly adjourned on March 1, 1841, his legislative career came to an end. He was elected again thirteen years later but resigned to be eligible for the United States Senate, although as matters developed that high office went to Lyman Trumbull.

One cannot evaluate Lincoln, the Illinois legislator, without remembering that his legislative service was only one aspect of his busy life during the years 1834-41. It is fair to say, however, that his service as a legislator convinced him that politics was his ruling passion, and that he was well endowed to participate in the political circus. Above all, his horizons were greatly expanded in both practical and speculative matters, he developed an even greater self-confidence, and he had many of his rougher edges smoothed down. His legislative experience saw him grow from the awkward, slightly precocious, eager young man into a mature, competent, precise, and superbly humane individual, ready for further service and infinitely greater responsibilities.

Clyde C. Walton

11

ABRAHAM LINCOLN TAKES A WIFE

by Marion D. Pratt

To relatives and immediate friends of Abraham Lincoln and Mary Todd the following announcement in the November 11, 1842, issue of the *Sangamon Journal* of Springfield, Illinois, was not news. It read: "MARRIED—In this city on the 4th instant, at the residence of N. W. Edwards, Esq., by Rev. C. Dresser, ABRAHAM LINCOLN, Esq. to Miss MARY TODD, daughter of Robert S. Todd, Esq. of Lexington, Ky." But others in Springfield and in county-seat towns where lawyer and former state representative Lincoln was known would be glad that he had finally, as he expressed it, "took a wife."

Located on the site of the Ninian W. Edwards home, where Lincoln courted and later married Mrs. Edwards' sister Mary, is the Centennial Building. On the third floor is the Illinois State Historical Library, in which the marriage license issued to Abraham Lincoln and Mary Todd by the County Clerk of Sangamon County on November 4, 1842, is on permanent exhibition. It bears Reverend Dresser's certification that the marriage was solemnized by him "on the same 4th day of Nov. 1842." This is no proof of a last-minute decision to marry, since the issuance of a license the same day the marriage was performed was not an unusual occurrence in Sangamon County during this period.

There is documentation also in the form of a personal record, the Abraham Lincoln family Bible now in the Library of Congress. On a page headed "Family Record" the first entry under "Marriages" is in Lincoln's handwriting and reads, "Abraham Lincoln and Mary Todd, married, November 4–1842."

Thus the time and the place of the Lincoln-Todd marriage are well documented. But for details of the event we are dependent upon reminiscences related long after. Some are plausible, some are colored by intervening events and are unreliable, and some are contradictory. There is conflicting evidence as to what extent Mr. and Mrs. Edwards may or may not have opposed the marriage. How much can one believe of the purported conversations made during the preparations on the day of the wedding? There is no agreement as to what Mary Todd's wedding dress was like or of what material it was made. Delaine? Embroidered white muslin? Or white satin? Common sense and a study of the existing photographs of Mary should be sufficient evidence that she was appropriately and attractively dressed. Lincoln, too, we can presume, was in proper attire. Had he not received nods of approval from the William Butlers, friends with whom he was living?

It was seven o'clock Friday evening, candlelight time. Outdoors it was drizzling as relatives and friends, variously estimated to forty persons, gathered in the parlor at the Edwards home on "Aristocracy Hill," as it was commonly known. The Reverend Dresser, in vestments of the Episcopal Church, was ready to perform the ceremony. Miss Todd, a Presbyterian in Kentucky, had been attending the Episcopalian Church in Springfield, of which the Edwardses were members. Lincoln was a friend of Reverend Dresser's, who lived on the corner of Eighth and Jackson in a house he was to sell Lincoln in 1844. It was to be the Lincoln family home until 1861.

The members of the bridal party now took their proper places in front of the fireplace. On the mantel two beautiful astral lamps were lighted. There was a hushed silence as the minister commenced reading, "Dearly beloved . . . " It is generally accepted that the couple's friend James Matheny, a deputy in the circuit clerk's office, was best man. As for bridesmaids, recollections vary. It seems plausible that they included Cousin "Lizzie" Todd; Julia Jayne, a close friend during the months Lincoln's courtship of Mary was renewed; and perhaps Anna Rodney, sister of the wife of Congressman May.

The vows were repeated by the groom, who was well in his thirty-third year, and the bride, soon to be twenty-four. The great disparity between their heights—"the long and the short of it," as he expressed it later—was strikingly noticeable. Lincoln, according to his own description, was "six feet, four inches, nearly; lean in flesh, weighing, on an average, one hundred and eighty pounds; dark complexion, with coarse black hair, and grey eyes." Miss Todd was barely five feet, pleasingly plump, with lovely pink wildrose complexion, "light brown hair with a glint of bronze," and "clear blue eyes."

As Abraham's voice repeated the words "With this ring I thee wed" he placed a wide gold band on Mary's finger. At this moment the sentiment expressed in the ring's inscription, "Love is eternal," must have permeated both Abraham and Mary's minds and hearts.

Reminiscences of the best man record that at the point Lincoln said, "And with all my worldly goods I thee endow," Judge Browne blurted out, "Lord A'mighty, Lincoln, the law fixes that!" If true there was a moment of levity before the clergyman pronounced Abraham and Mary man and wife.

One who was present recalled that the wedding ceremony was "pretty, simple, and impressive" and the wedding supper "elegant and bountiful." The wedding cake was displayed "in state" on the mahogany sideboard with its carved claw feet. The sideboard had belonged to Mr. Edwards' father from the time he was territorial governor of Illinois. The serving was done on a long table.

Family tradition records that the table was covered with a beautiful white cloth with two turtledoves as the center design, the gift of a Spanish ambassador to Governor Edwards.

The same day the *Journal* carried the announcement of the Lincoln-Todd marriage of the previous week Lincoln wrote his friend Sam Marshall of Shawneetown in regard to a business matter. He closed with this statement: "Nothing new here, except my marrying, which to me, is matter of profound wonder."

Yes, Abraham Lincoln, for many years one of the "eligibles," had finally decided that his "forebodings" about marriage were "the worst sort of nonsense." He would accept what God had "foreordained." He had not been one to view women with "indifference," but he had been prone to "dream dreams of Elysium far exceeding all that anything earthly can realize."

At a brilliant cotillion at the American House in December 1839 Lincoln had been attracted to Mary Todd, recently come from Kentucky to live with her sister, Mrs. Edwards. By the winter of 1840 Lincoln had found a kindred spirit in lively, intelligent, witty Mary—or "Molly," as he called her. She admired and knew personally Lincoln's beau ideal of a statesman, Henry Clay. She had happily become "quite a *politician*," working zealously for the election of William Henry Harrison. It was natural that Molly and Abraham were contemplating matrimony. But the misgivings which had haunted Lincoln in his relationship with Mary Owens returned full-fold. He wanted Molly to be happy. If he failed he would never forgive himself. There were other suitors who could perhaps make her a better husband: Stephen A. Douglas; James Shields; or particularly widower Webb, who was persistent in his attentions. Abraham was terribly upset, and Mary released him. This was on January 1, 1841. Instead of being relieved he found his emotions more than ever in conflict. "I am now the most miserable man living," he wrote. Friends took for granted that Mary had rejected him, and one wrote sadly, "Poor A—I fear his is a blighted heart."

By June, through confidences expressed in letters Mary wrote

Mercy Levering, we learn that Mary had "some *lingering regrets* over the past," and as for Mr. Webb, her "heart can never be his." She had not seen Lincoln for months and it would afford her "much, much, happiness" if "he would once more resume his station in Society."

Lincoln's intimate friend Joshua Speed had removed to Kentucky. The letters they exchanged are revealing of their innermost thoughts on love and marriage. Speed was not sure he should marry "black eyed Fanny" Henning. Lincoln fortified him with reasons and encouragement. In February 1842 Speed married Fanny and wrote he was far happier than he had ever expected to be. This made Lincoln happier than he had been since "that fatal first of Jan'y. '41," but not "entirely happy," for Molly was "still unhappy." Speed advised Lincoln to put Molly out of his thoughts completely—or marry her. Lincoln agreed, but replied, "I must regain my confidence in my own ability to keep my resolves when they are made." If God had made him an instrument in bringing Speed and Fanny together, then he declared, "Whatever He designs, He will do for *me* yet. . . . Stand *still* and see the salvation of the Lord is my text just now." This was on the Fourth of July, 1842.

During the late summer Lincoln began to see Mary again. There were many meetings at the home of Mr. and Mrs. Simeon Francis. Francis was editor of the Whig *Journal*, in which a series of satires appeared against the Democratic state auditor Shields. Mary and Julia Jayne had written several of the pieces, and Lincoln only one. However, when Shields demanded the name of the pseudonymous author or authors Lincoln took full responsibility. Shields challenged Lincoln to a duel, but it was averted. The whole affair was a dramatic adventure which drew Mary and Abraham closer together.

On October 5, 1842, just barely a month before Mary and Abraham were married, Lincoln wrote to Speed: "Are you now, in *feeling* as well as *judgement*, glad you are married as you are? . . . Please answer it quickly, as I feel impatient to know." Speed's unqualified affirmative reply must have been received by Lincoln within ten days.

A few weeks later the couple took their matrimonial vows. Mary had written, ". . . my hand will never be given where my heart is not." And now Lincoln was certain that he loved Mary and could make her happy.

"For better or for worse . . . " Mary and Abraham Lincoln understood the significance of "Love is eternal."

Marion D. Pratt

12

LINCOLN EMERGES AS A LEADER

by Leo A. Lerner

It was a day when people talked face to face.

It was a day when people who could read and write wrote out what they thought *by* themselves, and read what was written *for* themselves.

The Republic was little more than fifty years old. Abraham Lincoln was little more than half that age.

He had been a natural leader of the neighborhood around New Salem, Illinois.

A young man growing up in a nation growing up.

He talked like and looked like the country—raw, rugged, and earnest.

In 1832 he first ran for the state legislature. It is hard now to say whether he ran because he was personally ambitious or if offering himself as a lawmaker was just a kind of an awakening. Perhaps it was just that he had lost his job and needed something to do. Destiny sometimes has a way of making man's own needs serve larger purposes.

To keep busy, and because he was fascinated by river naviga-
tion, he even worked as a pilot when the first river steamboat
from the Ohio came up the Sangamon past New Salem to Port-
land Landing near Springfield. Then he went with his New Salem
friends to the Black Hawk War as a captain. They never encountered the fierce old Indian, but they sat around the campfires
every night, and Abraham Lincoln was the star of the show.

In the laughter of the men, in the respect he saw in their eyes,
Lincoln felt the power a man feels when he knows he can stir
other men.

These months in 1832 cast the die in Lincoln's life. He had a
crowd of people around him who felt so attached they would
fight for him. He fought for them, too. Mustered out of the militia,
he turned up at a farm auction to campaign and found a bunch
of toughs beating up Rowan Herndon, one of his friends. Lincoln
pitched in, handled the ruffians easily, brushed himself off, and
made his little speech to the voters. But first he remarked that
his friend was capable of whipping the whole lot of them, one
at a time. This was leadership quality, beating up the "ruffings"
and then giving the credit for the prowess to his friend.

You have to be good where you are to be better later some place
else.

The young men rallied around Lincoln with an admiration
nothing short of worship. He could scrap, tell stories, and had
read a lot of books. "My best friend is the man who brings me a
book I haven't read," he is reported to have said.

There is a piece of imitation parchment gotten up nowadays
and sold nearly everywhere, called "Lincoln's Failures." It tells,
with some exaggeration, how he failed at this and he failed at
that. The purpose of it seems to be to make all the downhearted
people in the world get their courage up. They, too, might get to
be Presidents of the United States someday.

But Lincoln seldom failed without a triumph of some sort, and
of course he succeeded often in the way men usually keep score.

As postmaster, every Saturday Lincoln would sit on the stoop and read the newspapers to his friends. He did this because many of the people in New Salem could not read, and also because reading the issues of the day aloud fixed them more firmly in his mind.

Lincoln was lucky enough, around 1832, to know the schoolmaster Mentor Graham, who later helped him learn surveying and who agreed with him that a knowledge of grammar was indispensable to a man who hoped to get ahead in politics. A farmer, John Vance, had a copy of Kirkham's *Grammar*, and Abe walked six miles each way to get it. Graham said Abe Lincoln learned that grammar faster than any man he ever taught.

At the time he walked for the grammar Lincoln was no child but a grown man of twenty-three, perhaps older than the average American college graduate of today. There is general belief that Lincoln performed all these difficult, self-imposed tasks as a boy or an adolescent, but the significant fact is that he did them as a man. He was not too proud or lazy to learn. The prairie and the prairie people stirred the blood in him as they stirred the great rivers that ran toward the sea.

More than anything the prairie-river people needed representation and leadership, both of which they got from Abraham Lincoln.

Lincoln read, talked, thought, worried, and learned. He became the recognized leader of his party and, most important of all for the later years, a serious student of government.

Two big events took place in the life of Lincoln in 1836: he became a lawyer, under the sponsorship of his friends Judge Bowling Green and Major John T. Stuart, who encouraged Lincoln to study the law; and he was re-elected to the state legislature.

Lincoln was emerging as a political leader, engaged in a new profession, and was soon to be called "the foremost Whig in the state."

The terrible seriousness of the period in which Lincoln then lived cannot be exaggerated. The passions of Americans had been raised to fever pitch by the murder at Alton, Illinois, in the fall of 1837, of Elijah Lovejoy, an abolitionist editor. An aroused mob had killed him and destroyed his press. In St. Louis a wild crowd had lynched a mulatto accused of murder. In Mississippi three Northern gamblers were lynched.

That Americans would ignore law and order infuriated Lincoln. He was anxious to tell his opinion of these atrocities. He wanted to rally responsible men to the great principles of constitutional law that had been established in the American Revolution. Less than three months after the killing of Lovejoy Lincoln spoke to the Young Men's Lyceum in Springfield, making a speech that had been given a great deal of thought and care. It was one of his best speeches, at a time when speeches counted because people listened and talked about what was said.

What Lincoln said was fiercely applicable not only to the time but to today.

He saw "the perpetuation of our political institutions" as the only way to avoid mob rule.

He pleaded with the people to remember that they were in peaceful possession of "the fairest portion of the earth" and that they enjoyed "civil and religious liberty." We didn't create all this, he said; it was a legacy from a "*once* hardy, brave, and patriotic . . . race of ancestors."

Gratitude to our fathers and duty to ourselves "imperatively require us faithfully to perform."

The early power of Lincoln as a logical thinker and unifier of the people was in that speech. He was less than twenty-nine years old but his words already contained the basic idea of the Gettysburg Address, delivered twenty-five years later.

Nowadays most people understand why the law and not a mob should deal with punishment. In those days it was not quite so clear.

Lincoln hammered away passionately at his theme: that the "mobocratic spirit" breaks down and destroys government.

When a man makes a speech and means what he says he never

by Leo A. Lerner

forgets what he said. Lincoln made his own policy for the future.

"Let every American, every lover of liberty, every well wisher to his posterity, swear by the blood of the Revolution, never to violate in the least particular, the laws of the country; and never to tolerate their violation by others," he said. "Let reverence for the laws . . . become the *political religion* of the nation. . . ."

In a brilliant paragraph Lincoln anticipated the possibility of an evil genius, thirsting and burning for power, who might rise and "set boldly to the task of pulling down" our freedom.

Only the law and a united people could frustrate the designs of a potential dictator.

He pointed out that the living history behind the people of the Revolution was fading away. These forefathers were the pillars of the temple of liberty, he said. We must supply in their places other pillars, "hewn from the solid quarry of sober reason."

Speaking to his own and to future generations, he concluded that the materials for "our future support and defence," must be molded into *"general intelligence, [sound] morality* and . . . *a reverence for the constitution and laws. . . ."*

Leo A. Lerner

13

LINCOLN THE LAWYER

by Willard L. King

Lincoln was a lawyer's lawyer. The great bulk of his practice in the ten years prior to his election as President came to him from other lawyers. As Judge David Davis, the circuit judge of his circuit, said, "In all the elements that constitute the great lawyer, he had few equals." And as early as 1850, ten years before his election as President, the many communities in which he practiced over the circuit recognized his pre-eminence.

Lincoln was a lawyer of great industry. In his own lexicon "work" came first. "The leading rule for the lawyer," he said in a lecture to law students, "as for the man of every other calling, is diligence. Leave nothing for to-morrow which can be done to-day. . . . Whatever piece of business you have in hand, before stopping, do all the labor pertaining to it which can then be done." Lincoln never relied on the inspiration of the moment. He never tried a case on a catch-as-catch-can basis. He never shot from the hip. He was thorough and exhaustive in his investigation of the facts and of the law. Of course he sometimes lacked full opportunity for preparation. Herndon has told us that Lincoln

90

did not do himself justice in such cases. With all his extraordinary capacities Lincoln had a methodical mind—he moved slowly and carefully. He acted only on his sober second thoughts. "He thought more than any man I have ever known," Herndon said.

Another quality of Lincoln's as a lawyer, was his meticulousness. His early years as a surveyor had made him careful to the nth degree. He prepared his pleadings with scrupulous accuracy as though he were making a survey of an irregular piece of land. His distinctive copperplate handwriting appears on hundreds of these documents. Most of us have one form of penmanship for rough notes taken under hurried or uncomfortable circumstances and another style of handwriting for careful work. Not Lincoln. Every sample of his handwriting is of the same tenor, unhurried, careful, extraordinary in its precision.

Another notable quality of Lincoln's was his scrupulousness. As Mary Lincoln said, "My husband was truth itself." Lincoln's attachment to truth is truly remarkable. One aspect of this quality was his total lack of affectation. Although he was a consummate actor who could mimic a person's accent, his walk, his gestures, his demeanor, he never used this ability to make himself anything else than what he was—the modest, uneducated, uncultured man.

These three qualities of industry, extreme care, and integrity are in themselves sufficient to insure success in the law. Many men of very meager talents, with these three qualities alone, have achieved eminence at the bar. But Lincoln had more extraordinary capacities.

One such quality was his great resourcefulness. The best example is the familiar one of his producing the almanac to refute the witness who testified he had seen a murder by bright moonlight. And there are many other instances of the same thing.

Lincoln was particularly deft at illustration. As Judge Davis said, "His powers of comparison were large and he rarely failed in a legal discussion to use that mode of reasoning." He chose comparisons that people could understand. When, as President, he was urging General McClellan to action and the General was demanding more men before he advanced, Lincoln said: "Sending men to that army is like shoveling fleas across a barnyard; half of them never get there."

Another lawyerlike quality of Lincoln's was his facile speech. He realized that the main task of the lawyer is communication. His ordinary routine letters contain no clichés, no hackneyed phrases; they are clearly but unusually phrased. He had a passion for clarity combined with an accurate sense of rhythm in language.

Of course the outstanding example of Lincoln's skill with words is the Gettysburg Address, which marks as sharp a change in American literature as does the battle of Gettysburg in American history. From that time forward the embellished style was doomed; nearly everyone tried to imitate Lincoln. How wrong he was when he said: "The world will little note, nor long remember what we say here. . . ."

Another eminent quality of Lincoln's was his conscientiousness. He was a poor lawyer in a case in which he did not believe. "In order to bring into full activity his great powers," Davis said, "it was necessary that he should be convinced of the right and justice of the matter which he advocated." The outstanding example is the Patterson homicide case in Champaign, which Lincoln, with Swett and Whitney, was defending. The victim, before his death, had been drunk and had threatened a crowd with a spade. He was a harmless old fellow. The defendant had thrown a two-pound weight with all his force, striking the old man in the head and killing him. As the trial went on, Lincoln became more and more convinced that his client was guilty. Lincoln tried to beg off from making the closing argument, but his colleagues insisted. Afterward they agreed that he made a poor argument. Patterson, convicted of manslaughter, was sentenced to three years in the penitentiary, and after serving a little more than a year he was pardoned upon Lincoln's recommendation.

Lincoln's conscientiousness in fixing his own fees has been commented on by many. Judge Davis said of him: "To his honor be it said that he never took from a client, even when the cause was gained, more than he thought the service was worth and the client could reasonably afford to pay. . . . When he was elected President, I question whether there was a lawyer in the circuit, who had been at the bar as long a time, whose means were not larger."

Another proof of his conscientiousness is the great number of cases in which he induced the parties to compromise. "Persuade your neighbors to compromise whenever you can," he said in his lecture to young lawyers. "Point out to them how the nominal winner is often a loser—in fees, expenses, and waste of time. As a peace-maker the lawyer has a superior opportunity of being a good man."

A quality that we all know was Lincoln's wit and humor. Hardly a case did he try without a scintillating example. His stories were not mere tales told for entertainment; he told them to illustrate a point. An example is Lincoln's dog story. He told it during the Patterson case, in which it was claimed that Patterson had used unnecessary force in repelling an assault. A farmer, Lincalm said, had been attacked by his neighbor's dog and had killed it with a pitchfork. "Why didn't you hit him with the other end of the fork?" the neighbor asked. "Why didn't he come at me with his other end?" the farmer replied.

Another distinctive quality of Lincoln's was his generosity of judgment, his infinite charity. He never thought the worst of any man; he never cherished rancor. Even in the heat of argument he remained courteous to his opponents. "You will find it better," he told the fiery Frank Blair, "not to impute motives to public men that they do not profess." He did not despise his rival, Stephen A. Douglas, who was as unscrupulous in argument as a man could be. Lincoln did not even hate Jefferson Davis, though he believed him guilty of a great wrong. This charity was an acquired characteristic. In the campaign of 1840 Judge Davis was present in Springfield at the "skinning," as it was called, of Jesse B. Thomas by Lincoln. Thomas, a prominent Democrat, in a political speech at the court spoke disparagingly of Lincoln. Someone ran to tell Lincoln, who quickly appeared. When Thomas had finished, Lincoln answered him. He was "terrific in his denunciation," Davis reported; "had no mercy." Lincoln mimicked Thomas, his walk, his gestures, his accent. The crowd loved it and yelled for more. Thomas wept. Lincoln was filled with remorse and the next day hunted up Thomas and apologized. Lincoln always recalled this incident with chagrin, and the several sharp letters marked "not sent" now among his papers are probably a result of this experience.

Another lawyerlike quality of Lincoln's was his power of command. With all his modesty, with all his humility, when the time came to accept command he took it. At his first inauguration, his Illinois friends were worried and tense before he began to speak. But as soon as he started they relaxed. He spoke as though an inaugural address had been his daily duty in Springfield. And when, a few days later, Seward tried to take the command from him Lincoln gently but firmly retained it. His secretary, the young John Hay, educated in the East, was astounded at this capacity of Lincoln's. Hay should not have been surprised. To take command of a courtroom is the effort of every lawyer. Lincoln had done it hundreds of times. When his adversary yelled, "No, No, No," in the middle of a trial Lincoln said firmly, "Yes, yes, yes."

Lincoln had, in an eminent degree, what Justice Holmes called "the instinct for the jugular." He saw the vulnerable spot in an adversary's case and went directly at it. Judge Davis said: "He seized the strong points of a case and presented them with clearness and great compactness. His mind was logical and direct and he did not indulge in extraneous discussion. Generalities and platitudes had no charm for him." Several contemporaries have commented on this characteristic. When he defended a case he made concession after concession. Judge Davis once wrote to his wife during a trial in Springfield that he was always amazed at *by Willard L. King*

Lincoln's fairness. But an adversary who was lulled into complacency by all these concessions would wake up to find himself defeated. Lincoln would narrow the issues to the crucial one and concentrate all attention on that. As a lawyer Lincoln was a master strategist.

Willard L. King

14

CONGRESSMAN ABRAHAM LINCOLN

by Donald W. Riddle

As Lincoln wrote in 1860, he was "always a Whig in politics," and the Whig party had always been in the minority in Illinois except in the Seventh Congressional District, which he represented; this had been a Whig stronghold from the beginning.

After four terms in the state legislature Lincoln had an excellent record which made him a strong candidate for Congress. But he waited until two of his friends served before him. And in 1846, when he was elected by the largest majority yet polled, the Whigs in the nation reduced the Democratic majority in the Senate and won control of the House.

The time was critical. President Polk had settled the Oregon boundary question, and his domestic Administration measures had been adopted before Lincoln took his seat. The war with Mexico was at its culminating stage; victory brought new territory to the United States, and the Wilmot Proviso had already raised the vexed question of slavery in the new lands.

But in a time when greatness was required Lincoln proved to be no more than an exponent of the Whig party view. True, he evinced more than average ability as a Congressman. He was regular in attendance and industrious in assuming his share of work. He deserves high credit for never skulking the vote on dangerous questions. He was a useful member of two committees. He represented his constituents faithfully in the tasks which they asked him to do, he handled patronage applications with a high ethical standard, and he toiled for the election of his party's candidate for the Presidency. Nevertheless his course in Congress caused him to be repudiated at home, led to bitter criticism, lost for his party the district which had always been theirs, and made Lincoln so unpopular that he could not run for office for years to come.

How are these things to be understood? It must be remembered that Lincoln's previous experience had been on the local and state level; now he was in the national arena. Earlier he had been associated with men of his own or of lesser stature; now he was with party leaders of high ability and attainment. Lincoln, as events later proved, was as able as any, but in 1847 he followed party without individual judgment, swayed by Eastern and Southern Whig leaders and reflecting views not accepted by the people of Illinois.

The Mexican War issue was decisive. In Congress Lincoln, following party leaders, took a position which was the reverse of that upon which he had run for election and that held by his constituents, with whom the war was popular and who supported it with warm patriotism. Soon after taking his seat Lincoln presented his "Spot Resolution," questions about the place and the occasion of the start of the war, shrewdly drawn to embarrass the President. Then he supported a resolution that stigmatized the war as "unnecessarily and unconstitutionally begun by the President." Then he made a speech in which he set forth the attitude toward the war held by Eastern Whigs, declaring that the war was deliberately provoked by American aggression, arguing that the United States had no valid claim to that part of Texas where hostilities began.

Home reaction was immediate and devastating. Illinois newspapers sharply criticized these three acts, characterizing them as unpatriotic, unrepresentative, and even treasonable. Towns and counties called mass meetings which adopted resolutions of censure. Many constituents wrote letters in protest. His friends became alarmed, sensing damage to his future career and fearing the loss of the district in the coming election. But Lincoln was so swayed by the viewpoint of national Whig leaders that he defended his course. Events proved that he was wrong and they were right, for in August 1848 the Whig district which had elected Lincoln for the first time elected a Democrat. For the first time in his political career Lincoln had lost touch with politics in his own district and state.

Trying to redeem himself he spoke in defense of the Whig doctrine of internal improvements, making a persuasive case for the building of railroads and canals at Federal expense. In the autumn of 1848 he made an effective appeal for Zachary Taylor—unmindful of their opposition to the war the Whigs nominated a war hero—and with telling humor ridiculed Lewis Cass, the Democratic candidate. Lincoln franked out thousands of campaign documents and electioneered for Taylor near Washington and in Massachusetts. He did little in Illinois, and in that he was roughly handled by opponents who scorned him for his attitude toward the war.

When Lincoln returned to Washington for the short session of Congress he found that the question of slavery in the newly annexed territories was the burning issue. Debate was hot, with all of the arguments of the compromise to come two years later bitterly contested. But Lincoln was quiet, making no speeches and demonstrating conservatism in his votes. He prepared a bill for the abolition of slavery in the District of Columbia but he never introduced it. He favored receiving antislavery petitions but he presented only one. He was opposed to the extension of slavery into the territories but he did not advance any proposal for keeping it out. Although he favored the Wilmot Proviso, which would keep slavery out of the territories, he opposed the extension of the Missouri Compromise line to the Pacific. Congressman Lincolm was far behind the position which he later assumed as a candidate for the Senate.

When the Whig President, Taylor, was inaugurated Lincoln had patronage jobs to dispense. In this taxing and unpleasant task Lincoln's honesty was apparent. He worked hard for his party and for his friends, endeavoring to get worthy men for government service. His experience with the patronage as Congressman was of inestimable value to him when he became President. Toward the end of his term, seeing that he must otherwise return to the practice of law, he sought for himself the job of commissioner of the General Land Office. But he was disappointed. President Taylor favored his appointment, but Lincoln did not have influence with the right people, notably Thomas Ewing, the Secretary of the Interior. It was a humiliating fate to be refused the office which he desired, and to have it go to a man who, however well qualified, had never worked for the advancement of the party. Nor was Lincoln consoled by the offer made at the express direction of the President, of the office of governor of Oregon Territory. He correctly saw that even though his ambition for further office was thwarted by his present unpopularity, his political future was in Illinois.

So Lincoln finished his one term in Congress a failure. A friend declared that he was so low in public esteem that he could not have been elected constable or justice of the peace. Since he was politically unavailable he cultivated his law practice; with more time for his profession he improved his position, increasing the volume of business and qualifying for more difficult cases and larger fees. He traveled the old circuit and took cases elsewhere. He wrote later that during this period he was losing interest in politics. However, the record shows that he was active. He signed calls for conventions and attended them; he gave advice as to candidates, canvassed Illinois as Whig elector in 1852. He was mentioned as candidate for Congress in 1850 but he said that there were others who could be more easily elected than he. He knew that he was not yet available. He had to live down the reputation which his Mexican War stand had given him. Yet he was determined to be elected to the Senate. He had to wait.

Lincoln's re-entry into politics came with the passage in Congress of Douglas' Kansas-Nebraska Act, which left to the people of those territories the status of slavery within them. While in Congress Lincoln had told Governor (now Senator) Seward that hereafter more attention must be given to slavery. For him that time had now arrived. He had never campaigned for office on the slavery issue, but when he ran for the Senate in 1855 and 1858 and for the Presidency in 1860 slavery was his dominating theme. When he first strove for election to the Senate in 1855 he was still conservative on the issue, merely opposing the extension of slavery into the territories. But this sufficed. The repudiated one-term Congressman had lived down his unpopularity. The one Illinois politician who was capable of opposing Douglas was again a candidate, with an issue which would one day carry him to the Presidency. Failure in Congress was balanced with the saving of the Union.

Donald W. Riddle

15

LINCOLN AND HERNDON

by Albert A. Woldman

Early in December of 1844 a shingle bearing the inscription "Lincoln & Herndon" appeared at the foot of a dingy stairway of a building south of the courthouse square in Springfield, Illinois. In 1849 the sign and the office were moved to a location northwest of the square. For almost twenty-two years the names of Lincoln and Herndon were associated in the practice of law, while the first-named was to grow into world prominence, become the leader and deliverer of his nation, the liberator of slaves, and a martyr to be canonized by mankind.

Springfield folks were surprised when Abraham Lincoln chose young William Henry Herndon for a law partner. Billy was still only a law clerk in the office of Logan & Lincoln, the association which Stephen T. Logan, the senior partner, and Lincoln were breaking up by mutual agreement. Not until December 9, 1844, was Herndon admitted to the bar.

But Lincoln had great confidence in the young man. They had known each other for nearly twelve years. They had shared sleeping quarters above Joshua Speed's general store. The future part-

101

ners had seen much of each other, and a degree of intimacy neighboring on brotherly affection had developed between them.

"There was something in his tall and angular frame, his ill-fitting garments, honest face and lively humor that imprinted his individuality on my affection and regard," Herndon said of his friend and idol. Both joined a debating and literary society which met in Speed's establishment or in a lawyer's office. They were also members of the Young Men's Lyceum, where Lincoln delivered an address on "The Perpetuation of Our Political Institutions" and established an early reputation as an orator.

People of Springfield thought it a strange thing for Lincoln to leave his association with Judge Logan, one of the ablest lawyers in the whole Midwest, to form a partnership with a novice. But Lincoln wanted just such an associate as Billy Herndon, a young man whom he could train according to his own methods. He longed for independence from the restraint of a peer or superior. Judge Logan had kept the reins of authority in his hands and Lincoln had chafed under the restraint. He wished to be his own master. With a junior partner like Billy Herndon this could be achieved.

When Herndon was admitted to the bar he was in his twenty-fifth year, ten years Lincoln's junior, a fine-appearing young man, five feet nine inches tall, handsome, energetic, and an all-around good fellow. He was a leader in the ranks of the young Whigs, and Lincoln felt that his political sagacity and aggressiveness would be a great help to him in the political arena as well as in the law office and the courts of justice.

"Billy, I can trust you, if you can trust me," Lincoln drawled earnestly as he shook his young friend's hand. Thus began their historic law partnership. Herndon was to write later, "It had always been a matter of pride with me during our long partnership, continuing on until it was dissolved by the bullet of the assassin Booth, that we never had any personal controversy or disagreement."

How two such conflicting personalities as Lincoln and Herndon managed to get along for so many years in harmonious friendship remains a mystery. It was a curious alliance. They were unlike in temperaments, habits, and natures. Lincoln always called his junior partner "Billy" while the latter addressed him as "Mr. Lincoln." The senior associate was a conservative while Herndon was a radical and militant enthusiast. Lincoln was a total abstainer while Herndon throughout his career was a heavy drinker. Lincoln hated slavery but believed that by confining it to states where it already had a foothold it would gradually disappear in the natural course of events; Herndon, an agitator and abolitionist, was intent upon the immediate destruction of the institution. "Choke down slavery," was his constant cry.

And yet they possessed much in common. They respected each other as comrades, and Billy almost worshiped his friend as a hero. Herndon was his man Friday. Lincoln, by nature so secretive and reticent, poured out his soul to Billy, and though Herndon was far from being a Boswell, the world is indebted to him for the intimate knowledge of his partner's life and character that otherwise would have been irretrievably lost.

Herndon was little more than an office clerk during the first year of his partnership with Lincoln. He developed into a fair lawyer in time, attending to the routine of the office, trying cases in the justices' courts, and preparing for the next term on circuit. At the outset Lincoln personally handled practically all of the important trial work of the firm. But later Herndon began to bear his full share of the labors of the partnership.

The first Lincoln & Herndon office was in a room above the post office and across the hall which led to the headquarters of the clerk of the United States District Court. It was a shabby and unpretentious affair. The dilapidated furnishings consisted of one small desk and a table, a sofa or lounge, and a half-dozen plain wooden chairs.

Lincoln had hoped that Herndon would bring order and system into the office, but soon found the young man had not the slightest conception of either. And if Herndon installed no order or office efficiency Lincoln cared little. Papers and notes he could not carry in his pockets or in his tall stovepipe hat he tossed into a drawer. A large envelope on his desk stuffed full of loose papers bore the significant legend, "When you can't find it anywhere else look in this."

The partners started a firm bank account but they seldom permitted any balance to accumulate. Fees in cash were divided immediately. "There you are, that is your half," Lincoln would tell Herndon as he handed him an equal portion of the fee collected. Their fees, though numerous, were small. In a daybook of the partnership, written mostly in Lincoln's hand, is a record of the fees collected in 182 cases in a period of over three years. They total a trifle more than two thousand dollars. Five and ten dollars appear to be the most common fees charged, as in sixty-four cases the former amount was paid and in sixty-three the latter. But now and then came windfall fees: the fifteen-hundred-dollar fee received by Lincoln & Herndon in the case of Beaver versus Taylor & Gilbert in the United States District Court; the twenty-five-hundred-dollar fee in the McCormick Reaper litigation, exceeded only by the Illinois Central Railroad case fee of five thousand dollars.

Busily occupied by his extensive law practice in Springfield and on the circuit, Lincoln did not neglect his political ambitions. In 1842 and again in 1844 he strove to win the Whig congressional nomination for his district. But first John J. Hardin and then Edward D. Baker became the party choice and then won their respective elections. Lincoln, however, was undaunted. In 1846 there was to be another contest, and this time he was determined to win. At the Whig convention in Petersburg, May 1, 1846, Herndon managed to get himself selected as secretary of the meeting and became instrumental in winning for his senior partner the congressional nomination by acclamation. No one gave Lincoln greater aid in the ensuing election campaign than faithful Billy Herndon. A leader among the young voters of Sangamon County, he brought back into line many who had deserted Lincoln in

1844. And with victory achieved, Billy was jubilant over his comrade's success and proud that he was the only Whig Congressman elected in the State of Illinois.

When Congressman-elect Lincoln came to his law office for a bundle of documents he wanted to take with him to Washington, and to say good-by to his excited young partner, neither Lincoln nor Herndon, in his wildest dreams, could foresee a far more poignant leave-taking some fourteen years in the future.

Fourteen eventful and exhilarating years were to pass until this second leave-taking, years of struggles and of soul-searching—but also of growth! Fourteen years of law practice on the vast judicial circuits of Illinois—but also of politics, caucuses, conventions, speeches, *and* ambitions. Although Lincoln did not seek a second term in Congress, "politics were his life . . . and his great ambition his motive power," Herndon observed. "His ambition was a little engine that knew no rest."

Then the sudden ascent from relative obscurity to national eminence and the senior partner is the President-elect of the United States.

February 10, 1861. On the morrow Lincoln would be leaving Springfield en route to Washington to assume the colossal burden of saving the nation from breaking into pieces. Now the President-elect was back in his unpretentious law office for a final chat with faithful Billy Herndon. Wearily Lincoln threw himself upon the old horsehair sofa. For a few moments he lay silent in deep reflection, gazing up to the ceiling begrimed with smoke from a rusty wood-burning stove. On this very couch he had lain countless times in the past years, thinking over his law cases, arguing with Herndon and with clients the very same issues—slavery, abolition, states' rights, secession—leading to the crisis he was now being called on to avert. On the green-baize-covered pine table where he had prepared his briefs he had also written his epoch-making political addresses. Here in this stuffy office he had struggled on these many years, tasting of bitter failures and soul-crushing defeats—but also of that crowning and surprising ultimate victory.

Presently, with a sigh, Lincoln suddenly inquired, "Billy, how long have we been together?"

The junior partner replied, "Over sixteen years."

"We've never had a cross word during all that time, have we?"

"No, indeed we have not," answered Herndon emphatically.

There was a lump in Lincoln's throat. Billy had been so loyal, so unselfishly self-effacing in his behalf. There was talk about unfinished business and reminiscences about humorous incidents in their practice and about adventures of his circuit-riding days.

The sun was setting and Lincoln hurriedly gathered a bundle of personal papers, when his eye caught the old "Lincoln Herndon" signboard swinging on its rusty hinges at the foot of the stairway.

"Let it hang there undisturbed," he urged in a low voice, poignant with regret and sadness. "Give our clients to understand that the election of a President makes no change in the firm of Lincoln and Herndon. If I live I'm coming back sometime, and we'll go right on practicing law as if nothing had ever happened."

Lincoln took one last lingering look at the old quarters, then slowly walked out. His professional career was over. He would never come back to this office again.

Judge Albert A. Woldman

16

LINCOLN RE-ENTERS POLITICS

by Allan Nevins

On a warm summer day in the late summer of 1854 young James Miner and his father were walking alongside the courthouse square in the hamlet of Winchester, Illinois, about halfway between Springfield and the Mississippi. It was the village where Stephen A. Douglas had begun his Illinois career; his statue now adorns the square. A local dignitary halted Miner's father. "Abe Lincoln is over at the Akin Hotel," he said, "and wants to see you. He is going to speak in the courthouse this afternoon. He has got up a speech on the Kansas-Nebraska Bill which he has never made before, and he has come down here to try it." Young Miner was one of perhaps two hundred people who later that day, August 26, heard the speech. He was deeply impressed. But he did not realize just how historic the occasion was, for it signaled Lincoln's re-entry into politics.

And why had he left it—he to whom politics, says his partner Herndon, sometimes seemed the breath of life? He would spill himself on the sofa in their offices, writes Herndon, and talk politics, politics—never books, history, literature, economics; al-

107

ways politics. He had left it for two reasons. It seemed to hold no future for him, and it failed to grip his deeper emotions.

When his single term in Congress was approaching its end in 1848 he did not run again because it was the turn of another Whig leader; and he failed to obtain from President Zachary Taylor the position he coveted as head of the General Land Office. The road to political opportunity seemed closed. Then in 1850 Henry Clay's Great Compromise put a temporary end to the sectional frictions growing out of the Mexican War. It is probable that Lincoln, always a realist, had no strong faith in the Compromise. But he intensely admired Henry Clay and he hated the extremists on both sides of the slavery question as much as he loved peace and moderation. He was glad to give compromise a trial. Besides, his party accepted it, and this fact committed him. For the time being no issue existed on which he felt strongly.

Thus it was that during five years, 1849 to 1854, he devoted himself primarily to his law practice and his family. He steadily pushed his way toward a position of leadership at the Illinois bar. A friend later recalled how on warm mornings he would often be seen on the sidewalk in front of his house, hauling one of his boys backward and forward in a little cart, dressed so carelessly that the friend wondered how such a rough-looking, abstracted man could own so nice a home.

Then—the thunderclap! In January 1854 Senator Douglas with startling suddenness introduced a bill to abrogate the Compromise of 1850, which had shut slavery out of Western territories above the parallel 36° 30′, and to organize the territories of Kansas and Nebraska with full freedom to choose or reject slavery. The expectation of Southern supporters of this Kansas-Nebraska Bill was that Kansas would enter the Union as the sixteenth slave state. This bill did more than breach what most Northerners regarded as a solemn compact that the region north and west of Missouri should be free soil. It declared that, in principle, the spread of slavery was quite proper. It made an effort to open the free West to a numbing and degrading institution, which could be planted in any future state by a small and transient local majority. The issue of slavery in Kansas was the concern of the whole nation and would affect the interests of every citizen. Yet under Douglas' plan it would be decided not by the national will but by the first small groups to settle on the Kansas plains.

The whole North was fiercely aroused. As Free-Soil Senators rallied to fight the Kansas-Nebraska Bill scores of cities and hundreds of towns held denunciatory mass meetings. The ablest editors of the North—Horace Greeley, William Cullen Bryant, Henry J. Raymond, Samuel Bowles—attacked it angrily. A majority of the clergy fulminated against it from their pulpits. Most significant of all, thousands of merchants, manufacturers, and other businessmen, usually silent, condemned it vigorously. But in the multitude of men aligned against Douglas' rash measure none felt more deeply than Lincoln and none lifted his voice with so much effect. He saw the country on the brink of a moral and material catastrophe. As the bill passed and North and South prepared for a bitter trial of strength in Kansas he resolved to assert his political leadership.

Doubtless the Winchester speech of August 26 contained his subsequent statement of his fundamental objection to Douglas' idea of popular sovereignty. On its face this idea had a specious look of fairness. But the primary question before the Republic was whether slavery should be kept within its existing bounds in the faith that it would soon die or should be allowed to expand in the faith that it would continue indefinitely. How wrong to treat this mighty question casually! "I insist," declared Lincoln, "that if there is *any thing* which it is the duty of the *whole people* to never entrust to any hands but their own, that thing is the preservation and perpetuity, of their own liberties, and institutions. And if they shall think, as I do, that the extension of slavery endangers them, more than any or all other causes, how recreant to themselves, if they submit the question, and with it, the fate of their country, to a mere hand-ful of men, bent only on temporary self-interest."

Lincoln's Winchester speech near the end of August 1854 was the opening gun in an Illinois battle which quickly claimed the attention of the nation. A week later, at the beginning of September, Douglas made his famous effort to speak in self-defense to an angry Chicago crowd of perhaps ten thousand people, who forced him from the platform. He then began speaking to sullen audiences in Rock Island, Geneva, Quincy, and other downstate towns. Lincoln heard him in Bloomington, taking his measure. By the time Douglas came to Springfield to address the crowds brought there by the state fair Lincoln was ready for him. On October 3 the Little Giant delivered his much-rehearsed plea in the hall of the House at the state capitol. Next day, in the same hall and to many of the same people, Lincoln demolished Douglas in a three-hour argument of impressive scope and vigor.

"I heard the whole speech," wrote a Chicago journalist, Horace White. "It was superior to Webster's reply to Hayne, because its theme is loftier. . . . [It was also] superior as an example of English style. . . . The speech made so profound an impression on me that I feel under its spell to this day." The *Illinois Journal* has given us a fuller account. It described Lincoln's feeling as so intense that he quived with emotion. His audience was still as death as he pursued his masterly exhibition of the fraud and sophistry wrapped in Douglas' plan of popular sovereignty. He examined the Kansas-Nebraska Act in all its aspects, analyzed the cheating and violence to which it inevitably gave rise, and held its iniquity up to the crowd with visible scorn.

"At that conclusion of the speech," declared the *Journal*, "every man felt that it was unanswerable—that no human power could overthrow it or trample it underfoot." A few days later he encountered Douglas again at Peoria, and in much the same three-hour speech again completely overthrew him. This time he was fully reported, so that his effort has come down to us as the Peoria speech, one of the most convincing forensic arguments in our history. Accepted everywhere as Douglas' strongest opponent in the West if not in the whole nation, he spoke elsewhere in Illinois.

The immediate political sequel of his return to politics is a minor page in our history. That fall Illinois, as a result of the movement against Kansas-Nebraska, underwent an electoral revolution. All the Democratic fortresses were overthrown, and the opposition, with Lincoln its most powerful leader, gained control of the legislature. That body had the responsibility of electing a Senator. Lincoln at first led the field and but for some devious political plotting would have gone to Washington. When he saw that an unprincipled man might gain the prize he threw his strength to Lyman Trumbull to give the place to a rigid anti-Nebraska man. But these temporary political results are unimportant compared with the large moral consequences of Lincoln's re-emergence.

For in these speeches of the fall of 1854, which were widely reported alongside those of Douglas, he laid down the fundamental principles which were to raise him to the Presidency. The essential iniquity of the Kansas-Nebraska Act, he declared, was its betrayal of the spirit of free institutions. "I particularly object to the *new* position which the avowed principle of this Nebraska law gives to slavery in the body politic. I object to it because it assumes that there *can* be *moral right* in the enslaving of one man by another. I object to it as a dangerous dalliance for a *free* people—a sad evidence that, feeling prosperity, we forget right— that liberty, as a principle, we have ceased to revere. I object to it because the fathers of the republic eschewed, and rejected it. . . . Near eighty years ago we began by declaring that all men are created equal; but now from that beginning we have run down to the other declaration, that for *some* men to enslave *others* is a 'sacred right of self-government.' These principles can not stand together."

The statement that "these principles can not stand together" led straight to the House Divided speech, to the Lincoln-Douglas debates, to the Cooper Union address—and to the White House. It was deep moral conviction and intellectual insight that brought Lincoln back into politics, and these qualities still speak to democracy everywhere.

Allan Nevins

17

LINCOLN IN SPRINGFIELD

by William G. Stratton

"On April 15, 1837 removed to Springfield, and commenced the practice, his old friend, Stuart taking him into partnership." This is how, in his own words, in an autobiographical sketch written for a campaign biographer, Lincoln referred to his taking up permanent residence in the new capital-to-be of the State of Illinois and entering into law partnership with John T. Stuart. "To this place, and the kindness of these people, I owe everything," he would say twenty-four years later.

Sangamon County at this time had a population of over eighteen thousand and an area so large it was, within a short time, to see three additional counties, Menard, Logan, and Dane (now Christian County), carved out of it. Springfield, with fifteen hundred inhabitants, was the largest town in the county. Legislator Abraham Lincoln had led the fight which caused the Illinois legislature to designate Springfield as the next capital, and on February 28, 1837, the action was carried by a majority vote of that body. Less than two weeks after the passage of the bill the commissioners of Sangamon County deeded the public square of

Springfield to Governor Joseph Duncan, and on the Fourth of July of the same year the cornerstone of the new statehouse was laid with great ceremony. Two years later the state offices would be officially removed from Vandalia to Springfield. Within that period the population of the town would more than double.

When the young lawyer and legislator moved to Springfield he was only twenty-eight years old. This self-educated young politician had lived for six years in the little village of New Salem and had attended sessions of the state legislature in Vandalia. With the exception of his occasional visits to Springfield these were the only centers of population he knew. The refinements and demands of life in a larger community, along with the social and cultural opportunities it offered, were all new to the rawboned, awkward, poorly dressed lawmaker.

The center of Springfield, laid out in the classic pattern, was the square where the new statehouse was being built. The courthouse, bank, and other leading business and government enterprises lined the sides of the square. The residential area circled the business district. The town had six churches and there were several private schools. As early as 1831 there were at least nine general stores in the town. Merchandise from New Orleans, Philadelphia, and New York was available to the residents, and the stores offered a wide assortment of such commodities as dry goods, groceries, boots and shoes, liquors, books, stationery, cut glass and china. Tailors, hatters, carpenters, potters and other craftsmen had established themselves, and doctors and lawyers were moving in steadily. By the time Lincoln became a resident there were nineteen dry-goods stores, several groceries and drugstores, and a goodly number of other establishments. You could find a watchmaker, wagonmaker, barber, several hotels, and a bathhouse. There were eighteen doctors and a dozen lawyers, and several brickyards and mills testified to a growing manufacturing activity. The town was enlarging rapidly, and labor, particularly skilled workers and craftsmen, was much in demand.

As the town grew social activity increased. Fourth-of-July celebrations were most elaborate and included parades, the usual orations, public dinners, and fireworks. The young men formed military companies, and their colorful appearance added an exciting social note. Military companies from other communities came to Springfield and in turn the Springfield groups traveled to the other towns. The governor reviewed the troops, and a military ball was always a part of the program.

Three of Lincoln's four law partnerships were in Springfield. He was married in the city, and the only home he ever owned was there. "Here my children have been born, and one is buried," he later said. In June 1839 Lincoln was elected a trustee by the board of trustees of the town to succeed Samuel H. Treat, who had become a judge of the Eighth Judicial Circuit. Lincoln attended the monthly meetings of the board and took an active part in its activities. He served in this capacity until April 1840, when Springfield became chartered as a city. Lincoln had helped pass the bill incorporating the city of Springfield.

His public speaking developed in this community, and it was in January 1838, before the Young Men's Lyceum, that he delivered one of his greatest speeches, "The Perpetuation of Our Political Institutions." Portions of this speech are as great as anything he was to later speak or write. It was in Springfield that Lincoln was to form the most intimate friendship he ever enjoyed. His association with Joshua F. Speed was to influence his personal and, in some ways, his political life. It was to Speed's general store that Lincoln came the day he moved to Springfield. He priced a bed and bedclothes and explained that he would require credit for these articles. Impressed by the sincerity as well as the melancholy of the man, Speed offered to take Lincoln in as a roomer and share the quarters over the store. Supposedly Lincoln brought his saddlebags in and said, "Well, Speed, I'm moved."

Traveling theatrical companies visited the city. Celebrities like Daniel Webster, Martin Van Buren, and Ralph Waldo Emerson lectured here. Musical groups came to Springfield for concerts.

There were parties, picnics, and dances to which a young legislator and lawyer would be invited. When the first session of the legislature was held in Springfield a cotillion party was given by a group of the young ladies of the city. Included among the names of the managers were Abraham Lincoln and Stephen A. Douglas. Springfield was known as a hospitable town. Isaac N. Arnold, the distinguished Chicagoan, many years later spoke of the state capital in these early years and recalled, "We read much of 'Merrie England,' but I doubt if there was anything more 'merrie' than Springfield in those days."

This was Lincoln's home town for twenty-four years. It was from Springfield that he left for his only term in Congress and from the Springfield district that he was elected to that body. It was here, in the statehouse in 1858, that he delivered the House Divided speech. It was in this city that Lincoln brought his bride to live in the Globe Tavern where their first son, Robert Todd, was born in 1843. In January 1844 Lincoln purchased the house on the northeast corner of Eighth and Jackson Streets from the Reverend Charles Dresser. This was to be the home of the Lincoln family until they left for Washington in 1861. It was here in May of 1860 that the official notification committee called on him to advise him that he was the Republican candidate for the Presidency of the United States. When George Ashmun of Massachusetts, the chairman, introduced William D. Kelley of Pennsylvania, Lincoln asked Kelley how tall he was. "Six feet three; what is yours, Mr. Lincoln?" Lincoln replied, "Six feet four." "Pennsylvania bows to Illinois," said Kelley. "My dear man, for years my heart has been aching for a President that I could *look up to*, and I've found him at last in the land where we thought there were none but little *giants*."

The man and the place are inseparable in history. When he left he said, "Here I have lived a quarter of a century, and have passed from a young to an old man." He spent his last months in Springfield preparing for "a task before me greater than that which rested upon Washington." He used an office in the statehouse, an edifice that might not have existed in Springfield had it not been for his efforts. During the summer of 1860 he conducted a "front porch" campaign for the Presidency; he did not make any speeches. He felt that everything he had to say on the great issues of the day was on record. Meetings and grand rallies were held, he greeted many crowds, attended some of the gatherings, and watched the torchlight processions. On November 6, 1860, he casually walked across the street from his statehouse office to the polls in the courthouse and voted a straight Republican ticket. He then returned to his office. As the crowds began gathering the early returns came in and showed a Republican gain over the election results of 1856. Unable to stand the suspense, Lincoln and a few friends walked to the telegraph office. It was there, shortly before midnight, that the dispatches from the East brought word that Lincoln had carried Pennsylvania and New York. The crowds waiting at the statehouse went wild; they ran through the streets, shouted from the housetops, danced, and sang until their voices gave out. Their neighbor and friend, Abraham Lincoln of Springfield, Illinois, was the President-elect of the United States!

In a drizzling rain on the morning of February 11, 1861, Lincoln, his wife and some friends rode to the Great Western station. Despite the weather more than a thousand people were waiting. He spoke slowly and quietly: "No one, not in my situation, can appreciate my feeling of sadness at this parting. . . ."

North of the city he loved, on a small hill, and near many of his beloved Illinois associates, he sleeps in Oak Ridge Cemetery. He has left many monuments and a memory of greater accomplishment for humanity than any other American. Not the least of his memorials is the city of Springfield and the echo of his last words there, "Trusting in Him, who can go with me, and remain with you and be everywhere for good, let us confidently hope that all will yet be well. To His care commending you, as I hope in your prayers you will commend me, I bid you an affectionate farewell."

William G. Stratton

18

THE LINCOLN FAMILY

by Ruth Painter Randall

Abraham Lincoln did not get married until he was thirty-three. His bride was Mary Todd, a bright, attractive belle of Springfield society, who was nearly ten years younger than he was. Few people have had a greater love for children than these two, and it was a cherished fulfillment to them when, in time, four sons were born.

The first baby arrived when they were living, for reasons of economy, at the Globe Tavern in Springfield. They named him Robert Todd, after Mary's father, but called him "Bob" or "Bobbie." Little Edward Baker Lincoln arrived three years later, after they had moved into the home on Eighth Street.

Lincoln as a father had definite opinions about how to bring up a family. People at that time generally believed that children should be seen and not heard and that to spare the rod was to spoil the child. Lincoln did not agree with them.

Here is the way his wife described his views. "Mr. Lincoln," she said, "was the kindest man and most loving husband and father in the world. He gave us all unbounded liberty." He was, she continued, "exceedingly indulgent" to their children. He did not believe in whipping them at all. When they did something wrong he explained why it was wrong, and let the child state his side of the case. He praised them when they were good. Ahead of his time, he had the modern attitude that children should not be frustrated. Mrs. Lincoln quoted what he often said, "Love is the chain whereby to bind a child to its parents."

Their neighbors in Springfield shook their heads and said the Lincolns spoiled their boys outrageously. But never did parents enjoy their children more. One can read today in letters they wrote each other when Bobbie was nearly five and Eddie two. "The dear codgers," as Lincoln called them, were with their mother on a visit to her old home in Kentucky. Reading these letters is like eavesdropping on this couple as they talked about their children.

She wrote him about Eddie's latest baby words, how the boys were, and related a little incident. Bobbie had brought in a stray kitten and as soon as Eddie spied it, she said, "his *tenderness* broke forth" and he wanted to feed it "with his *own dear hands*." She knew the father would like that story especially, because cats, as she wrote, were his "*hobby*."

In one of his letters he told her how he had tried to buy some "little plaid stockings" for Eddie but could not find the right size. What did "dear Bobby" and Eddie "think of the little letters father sent them?" he asked, and added, "Don't let the blessed fellows forget father." Her answering letter brought reassurance about this: "Do not fear the children have forgotten you." Even baby Eddie's eyes, she said, "brighten at the mention of your name."

Eddie died shortly before his fourth birthday. It was a cruel blow to these loving parents, but within eleven months another boy was born, William Wallace. Willie was to prove a bright, lovable, affectionate child, amazingly like his father.

Three years later the Lincolns were ardently hoping for a

daughter. But the baby who arrived was another boy, whom they named Thomas. One day Lincoln, perhaps looking on while the baby was being bathed, called him a little tadpole, and that started the nickname "Tad." Tad, like his mother, was high-strung, excitable, and very affectionate.

The house on Eighth Street in Springfield was a typically happy American home with a husband and wife deeply devoted to each other and to their children. The family had its ups and downs, as all families do. Mrs. Lincoln was subject to migraine headaches and was at times emotionally unstable. Robert as a little fellow had one crossed eye, Tad had a lisp, and there were childhood illnesses.

But when Lincoln walked home from his law office after the day's work Willie and Tad were likely to be watching for him. They would run down the street to meet him and swing on to his long coattails as he approached the house. After supper they would climb all over him as he sat telling them a story, or perhaps they all had a game of blindman's buff.

The days fell into the pleasant pattern of small-town life. The Lincolns were surrounded by helpful friends and were themselves good neighbors. They all, in the fine old-fashioned way, shared one another's joys and trials. At the time Tad was born, a neighbor also had a new baby which she was too ill to nurse, Mrs. Lincoln nursed both babies at her breast. These neighbors saw many comic incidents occur in the Lincoln family. One day when his mother had just undressed him for a bath three-year-old Willie escaped and ran gleefully out of the front door and down the street. Lincoln, in great amusement, gave chase, captured the runaway, kissed the small laughing face, mounted the boy on his shoulders with the little naked legs around his neck, and carried him back in triumph to his mother and the bath.

The natives of Springfield were treated to another diverting street scene one Sunday. Lincoln, in his Sunday best of black cloth swallow-tailed coat and stovepipe hat, was observed leaving church in the middle of the service. Slung over his arm, like a pair of saddlebags, was the wriggling form of little Tad. As the father hurried with long strides down the street toward home he met a group of friends. Seeing them smile, he said to them with twinkling eyes, "Gentlemen, I entered this colt, but he kicked around so I had to withdraw him."

The man next door to the Lincolns remembered how Lincoln would take his boys for walks in the country, explaining to them such things as animal tracks, small stones, or anything else they happened to see. Sometimes he would put his own and the neighbor's children in his carriage and go out to the Sangamon River for a picnic and fishing expedition. It was a glorious day when a circus came to town and he would take the children to see it. Lincoln, who never lost a certain boyishness, enjoyed that circus as much as they did.

Mrs. Lincoln gave little birthday parties for the boys. Both the Lincolns were sociable by nature. After Lincoln became more prominent and the house was enlarged there were big entertainments at which his face beamed with friendliness and pleasure.

When they moved to Washington into the complications of the Presidency and the tragedy of the Civil War the parents tried to keep life normal for their children. Robert was away at Harvard by then, but Willie and Tad, with two new friends, fairly shook the historic timbers of the White House with their noisy romping. When they raced with a clatter through the room Mrs. Lincoln would smile and say, "Let the children have a good time."

Their way of having a good time decidedly scandalized sedate officials who believed in the then current theories of child-rearing. The Lincoln boys, however, like their father, were unimpressed by the officialdom at Washington and remained their natural selves. They seemingly spent their time thinking up new pranks. A prize example of this took place on the day when they saw a group of grave, bearded gentlemen assembling upstairs in the White House. The boys thought it a bright idea to bombard the Cabinet meeting with a toy cannon. The President, as Commander-in-chief of the Army and Navy, had to stop Cabinet proceedings to restore peace.

One cannot avoid the suspicion that the boys would not have worked so hard at inventing pranks if their father had not enjoyed them so much. He seemed to regard the antics of the children as an indication of their brightness.

Thus, in the early months in the White House, family life for the Lincolns went on somewhat as usual. Then, before the end of the first year, the sound of small-boy merriment ceased. Willie, their child of greatest promise, grew ill and died.

It seemed a blow too great to bear. Mrs. Lincoln never got over it; from that time on she had a degree of mental illness. Lincoln, looking down upon his dead child, tried to express acceptance of God's will, but his voice faltered off into that cry of bereaved parents through the ages: "We loved him so."

Like a soldier in the field the President struggled on in the war to save the Union. Tad now became his father's constant companion. Passers-by on Pennsylvania Avenue would often see the tall President and his small, excited son come out of the White House, turn to the right, and walk about four blocks to Stuntz's toy shop on New York Avenue. The father once said, "I want to give him all the toys I did not have and all the toys that I would have given the boy who went away."

When the President worked late at his desk at night Tad would hang around until he fell asleep on the floor. The father, when his work was finished, would gather the child up in his arms, carry him off, and put him to bed. Tad was still harum-scarum and so noisy that it was said of him, "One would suppose there were at least six boys wherever he happened to be." But he made up for this by a very loving and tender heart.

Lincoln's death shattered the family. The broken Mrs. Lincoln knew no peace until she was buried beside her beloved husband. Tad lived only until he was eighteen. Robert, who was a very able man, acquired wealth as a lawyer and in business. He served his country as Secretary of War and as minister to England and lived until 1926.

Lincoln's love for his family seems part of his paternal good will toward mankind. In his mature statesmanship he had come to feel that all peoples belong to the Family of Man and he believed that love was the chain to bind a family together.

Ruth Painter Randall

19

LINCOLN AND DOUGLAS

by Paul H. Douglas

The Republican party of the State of Illinois met in convention in Springfield on June 16, 1858. Just before the assembly recessed that afternoon the following resolution was submitted to the convention and unanimously approved:

> Resolved, that Abraham Lincoln is the first and only choice of the Republicans of Illinois for the United States Senate, as the successor of Stephen A. Douglas.

When the convention reassembled that evening in the state-house their candidate delivered his acceptance address to a crowd that filled every inch of space in the hall of the House of Representatives. Lincoln's opening sentences forever identified the speech in history, and in effect began the Lincoln and Douglas debates. This was the famous House Divided speech, and the exchange of opinion relating to Lincoln's major theme made the formal debates inevitable, though the two men had debated the issues in earlier campaigns.

124

by Paul H. Douglas

In a natural desire to magnify the qualities of our noble politician-saint, Abraham Lincoln, there has been a tendency to disparage and depreciate Stephen A. Douglas, his opponent. As Lincoln has been properly cast in the role of hero, what is more inevitable for those who love sharp contrasts than to assign Douglas the part of villain? So in discussing these memorable debates in which a century ago Illinois' two ablest sons struggled across our hot prairies, and which were in fact the prelude to the Civil War, many writers and orators, swayed by a sense of drama and at times by partisan feeling, have generally drawn a sharp comparison between a Douglas who is pictured as squat, arrogant, morally obtuse, and none too bright and the tall, majestic, all-comprehending Lincoln.

This is a grave distortion of the truth. Without disparaging Lincoln in the slightest, the two debaters should be presented in more accurate perspective.

In the first place Douglas' energy and ability were such as to make him a foeman worthy of Lincoln's steel. No neutral can study the debates (or the Chicago, Bloomington, and Springfield speeches) without concluding that Douglas was very often the superior, and it is well to remember that it was Douglas and not Lincoln who won the election for the Senate.

Born in Vermont in 1813, Douglas came to Illinois at the age of twenty with only a dollar and a quarter in his pocket. After teaching school at Winchester for a few months he was admitted to the bar shortly before he was twenty-one. A few months afterward he was chosen state's attorney of Morgan County. Elected to the legislature at the age of twenty-three, he served with Lincoln and made a distinctly better record than the latter. At twenty-seven he became Secretary of State for Illinois and shortly afterward was the youngest judge ever to serve on the Illinois Supreme Court. Then in 1843, at the age of thirty, he was elected to Congress, and three years afterward to the Senate of the United States. As Clay, Calhoun, Webster, and Benton faded from the

125

scene Douglas became the intellectual leader of the Senate and the voice of young America. He barely missed being nominated for the Presidency in 1856, and by 1858 was one of the foremost statesmen of the nation.

Douglas was the advocate of Western expansion. He had supported the Mexican War and the acquisition of what are now New Mexico, Arizona, California, and Nevada. He worked aggressively for an Oregon treaty which would bring the Pacific Northeast under the American flag, and he looked forward to the day when all of North America would be joined to us in political union, with continental free trade and with democratic institutions prevailing for all. To cement such union he put through the Illinois Central Railroad running from Galena and Chicago in the north to New Orleans in the south, which was designed to tie the Middle West with Mississippi and the Gulf states. In doing so he avoided the later abuses and scandals of the railway grants of the 60's and 70's and gave to the State of Illinois a share of the revenues of the road and a voice in its control. Then he pushed through legislation for a railroad from Chicago to the Pacific Ocean to connect the Middle West with the Far West.

It was here that he helped to set in play the forces which were his ultimate undoing. For the immediate question of the late 40's and of the 50's was whether the new territories which were being acquired were to be slave or free. The ultimate issue was no less than the fate of the nation as a whole. The Southern fire-eaters wanted to extend slavery into the North, and Robert Toombs of Georgia boasted that he was going to call the roll of his slaves from the foot of Bunker Hill Monument. The Northern abolitionists, on the other hand, wanted slavery abolished in the South. If either of these groups was to fail in its objectives each preferred secession and separation to union in a divided country.

Midway between these groups stood Douglas. As a compromise he proposed that the people of the newly established territories should have the right to decide whether or not they wished to legalize slavery, and that the Federal Government should preserve strict neutrality. To obtain Southern support for his Western railway he got Congress in 1854 to pass the Kansas-Nebraska Act, which repealed the Missouri Compromise of 1820. This Compromise had prohibited slavery in new territories north of the extension of the southern boundary of Missouri, but Douglas now opened them up to local option on the question. While disclaiming any moral concern over the question of slavery, and stating that he did not care whether slavery was voted up or down, Douglas nevertheless insisted on the right of the people of the territories to make a free choice and the duty of the Federal Government to be neutral in fact as well as in word. When the Buchanan Administration violated this principle and with the aid of armed bands from Missouri tried to jam a proslavery constitution down the throats of the people of Kansas, Douglas broke with Buchanan and fought with all his strength for fair play and free elections. In the senatorial election of 1858 he was therefore opposed by the Buchanan Democrats as well as by the newly founded Republican party and its candidate, Lincoln. These latter two groups, widely divided as they were in their ultimate aims, were nevertheless united in a common effort to end the political career of Douglas.

Lincoln's opposition was, of course, deeper than any personal rivalry. Like Douglas he occupied a middle ground between the two sets of extremists. But unlike Douglas he maintained that the Federal Government should not merely be neutral—that since slavery was wrong government should instead prevent its extension into the territories. He believed that with the prevention of the spread of slavery into new territory the economic wastes of that institution would ultimately lead to the freeing of the slaves in the South. But he wanted this to be done peacefully, voluntarily, and with full compensation to the owners.

These, then, were the momentous issues which a century ago faced the debaters and were being threshed out on the prairies of Illinois. It was at Freeport that Lincoln asked Douglas the crucial question as to how he could reconcile the Dred Scott decision that slaveowners could take their slaves into free territories, and possibly even into free states, with his doctrine of the supremacy of "popular sovereignty." Douglas' instant reply was that by local police ordinances and by the sentiments of the people the Dred Scott decision could be made inoperative in the territories. This won for him the senatorial election in 1858. But his answer split the Democratic party between its Northern and its Southern wings and led to his own defeat in 1860 as the presidential candidate of the Northern section.

It was in this latter election that Douglas rose to true greatness. Seeing that his defeat was inevitable, he toured the South and begged Southerners not to secede. If they would only let it be freely decided on the frontier, he argued, the divisive issue could be insulated from the main stream of the nation's political life and the Union could thus be preserved.

But neither North nor South would listen. The North went for Lincoln and the South for Breckinridge and Bell, and then the South seceded rather than live under the Presidency of a hated Northerner. When this conclusion was presented to the nation Douglas did not hesitate for a moment. He pledged his support to his rival, Lincoln, and went on an extended speaking trip through southern Ohio, Indiana, and Illinois to rally the Democrats behind the Union cause. In this he was largely successful, and he even brought over such violent Southern sympathizers as John A. Logan and John A. McClernand, who became Union generals. But worn out by heat, overexhaustion, and strain, he succumbed to a fever and died, more or less penniless, on June 3, 1861, at the early age of forty-eight.

Lacking the moral nobility of Lincoln, Douglas nevertheless deserves well of our country, for he was a passionate fighter for American unity. His body lies near the shores of Lake Michigan, and into the coolness of his tomb the stormy waters of the inland sea at times send their clangor. He would have had it thus, and his fiery spirit would take pride in his last words for his children which are engraved upon the base of his monument: "Tell them to obey the laws and support the Constitution of the United States."

Paul H. Douglas

20

ABRAHAM LINCOLN: STORYTELLER

by Mort Reis Lewis

Probably no American President loved to laugh as much as did Abraham Lincoln, or wanted so much to share with others the funny stories he himself enjoyed. It is also probable that no other occupant of the White House was such a master storyteller.

Abraham Lincoln's sense of humor was as important a part of the sum total of his character as was his sensitivity to tragedy. It was the shining obverse side of the coin that would have otherwise been almost completely oxidized by the dank air of gloom. When Lincoln was a lawyer he could weep sincerely over the plight of a deserving client in desperate straits. For reasons which even he didn't know he would sometimes plumb the depths of misery—a victim, as he called it, of "the hypo," or as we would say, hypochondria. Yet this man not only *loved* to laugh, he *needed* laughter for sheer survival.

Laughter was Lincoln's medicine, his safety valve. As he carried his fearful burdens it was, at times, the outlet he needed to preserve his very sanity. Once, at a moment of disaster during the Civil War, Congressman James M. Ashley of Ohio became scandalized at Lincoln's storytelling and told him so. Lincoln, with his characteristic lightning change of mood, replied sadly, "Ashley, were it not for this occasional vent, I should die."

There was nothing either sham or restrained about Lincoln's laughter. George Washington Julian, a Congressman from Indiana who knew him well, said this of Lincoln: "When he told a particularly good story, and the time came to laugh, he would sometimes throw his left foot across his right knee, and clenching his foot with both hands and bending forward, his whole frame seemed to be convulsed with laughter."

Storytelling was to Lincoln, in the words of his good friend lawyer Ward H. Lamon, "a laborsaving contrivance." On occasion Lincoln could use his ready wit to demolish an opponent on the political stump. In 1858, during one of the famous debates with Douglas, at Quincy, Illinois, he described Douglas' idea of popular sovereignty as being "as thin as the homeopathic soup that was made by boiling the shadow of a pigeon that had starved to death!"

But Lincoln's humor could also be as gentle as it was winning. In another debate, this time at Ottawa, Illinois, after thanking Douglas for a series of left-handed compliments, Lincoln said, "I was not very much accustomed to flattery and it came sweeter to me. I was rather like the Hoosier with the gingerbread, when he said he reckoned he loved it better than any other man and got less of it."

His sense of humor was one of the strongest weapons in his legal arsenal. In a court case, angered by what he considered the unfair tactics of an opposing attorney, Lincoln challenged several prospective members of the jury. The judge intervened, saying, "Mr. Lincoln, the mere fact that a juror knows your opponent does not disqualify him." "No, your Honor," Lincoln replied, "But I am afraid some of the gentlemen may *not* know him, which would place me at a disadvantage." (Riling Lincoln could be like tangling with a porcupine. You might wind up looking like a pincushion.)

Lincoln would sometimes use a quip to turn down gently a request he didn't want to or couldn't grant. In refusing a man who wanted a pass to Richmond, President Lincoln replied, "I would gladly give you the pass if it would do any good, but in the last two years I have given passes to Richmond to 250,000 men and not one of them has managed to get there yet."

He would, on occasion, soften a command that was yet more of a command because of a semihumorous approach. For instance, on November 11, 1863, he wrote to his Secretary of War, Stanton, "I personally wish Jacob R. Freese, of New-Jersey to be appointed a Colonel for a colored regiment—and this regardless of whether he can tell the exact shade of Julius Caesar's hair."

He would sometimes use humor to oil the engine of conversation and get it to run more smoothly. In one such conversation Lincoln told about a farmer who bragged about the size of one year's hay crop. The farmer boasted that it was so big that when harvesttime came he stacked all he could outdoors and then put the rest of it in the barn. Another time Lincoln discussed his own impatience with people who talked in circles and made themselves hard to understand. Lincoln said it reminded him of a little Frenchman out West, during the winter of the deep snow, whose legs were so short that as he walked the seat of his trousers rubbed out his footprints.

Yet indicative of Lincoln's basic sense is the fact that in so many of his exaggerations there are tough grains of reality. For instance, there is his description of an attorney who had written an overlong brief. Said Lincoln, "It's like the lazy preacher that used to write long sermons and the explanation was he got to writin' and was too lazy to stop." The fact is, of course, that it does take more effort to write concisely, to compress ideas into few words, than to overwrite. He had a genius for characterization. Speaking about a certain blowhard Lincoln once said, "He can compress the most words in the fewest ideas of any man I ever met."

In 1858 Lincoln talked with his friend David R. Locke, the

comic writer, about an extremely vain politician who had just died and had had a very large funeral. "If General X had known how big a funeral he would have," said Lincoln, "he would have died long ago."

Lincoln could use humor as a device to rid himself of a troublesome visitor without offending him; to clarify important points in discussions; or to dissipate the blues of a melancholy friend. It was indeed for him a laborsaving contrivance.

Many of Lincoln's witticisms and humorous turns of phrase were original with him. (They had to be, under the circumstances which called them forth.) He was a fine ad libber, able to make spontaneous, original quips. The others he remembered from what people had told him or from what he had read.

As distinguished from his humorous remarks or short witticisms, Lincoln probably originated few of the stories he told. As a matter of fact, Lincoln told a New York politician, Chauncey M. Depew, he had originated only two stories. But there is no doubt he was an expert at doing what gag writers call switching a story. That is, could take the nub of a joke he had read or heard and change the externals so as to make what appeared to be a new story out of an old one. Lincoln had a retentive memory for stories he liked. It has been said that sometimes to help his memory he would write them down.

To the majority of us most of the comic writers whose works Lincoln enjoyed, and occasionally borrowed stories from, are as extinct as the dodo. Some of them wrote under such odd pen names as Orpheus C. Kerr, Petroleum V. Nasby, and John Phoenix. Others used pseudonyms like Artemus Ward and Private Miles O'Reilly. Most of these were topical writers. Other Lincoln favorites were Joseph Glover Baldwin, who wrote *The Flush Times of Alabama and Mississippi*, and Thomas Hood, the English humorist and poet. One or another of the many editions of *Joe Miller's Jest Book* was a primary source for the jokes Lincoln told.

Lincoln's stories, as differentiated again from his humorous remarks, were generally pithy, brief, painted a picture, and made a point. They were illustrative anecdotes, capsulized comic short stories, which included background description and character development.

Many of Lincoln's stories are not too funny when you read them. But they were not meant to be read. They were meant to be told by a master storyteller with a mobile face, capable of comic expression . . . a man with a flexible tongue, who could be an expert mimic and had a superb sense of timing . . . a master storyteller like Lincoln.

He had had an excellent schooling in the art of telling funny stories. Both his father, Thomas, and his Uncle Mordecai Lincoln were prime spinners of funny yarns.

Lincoln justified his habit of telling stories to Chauncy M. Depew in these words: "They say I tell a great many stories; I reckon I do, but I have found in the course of a long experience that common people—*common people*—take them as they run, are more easily influenced and informed through the medium of a broad illustration than in any other way, and what the hypercritical few may think, I don't care."

In the human forest the tall tree that was Lincoln would have been stunted had it not been for the strong, nourishing juices of humor that helped give it both sustenance and vitality.

Mort Reis Lewis

21

LINCOLN AT THE COOPER UNION

by Johnson E. Fairchild

The speaker stopped. There was a moment's silence and then thunderous applause and cheers came from the audience in the Great Hall of Cooper Union. Abraham Lincoln had just finished one of his most important speeches. It probably led to his election as President, certainly to his nomination, and as a speech rates with his best.

It would be pleasant and easy to conclude that Lincoln came to Cooper Union as a part of a preconceived and proper plan that fitted the Lincoln pattern and the political pattern of the time and the needs of destiny. We might conclude that it was a carefully planned and well-carried-out move; that it was a "natural." Nothing could be farther from the truth.

The speech was held during a snowstorm, and the opening lines were miserably delivered. The whole affair was the result of an unusual circumstance, a compromise or two, a local political deadlock, and was strongly affected by numerous indirect influences.

Perhaps this speech illustrates the strange patterns of human events and destiny and the close calls or narrow squeaks of civilization and progress, and the importance of indirect effects.

The setting for the speech was the fruition of a dream nurtured by a poor New York City youngster, Peter Cooper, born February 12, 1791. By his enterprise and ability he became a very wealthy businessman and manufacturer. He used his fortune to build the Cooper Union for the Advancement of Science and Art in New York City. The reddish-brown sandstone building with an iron-beam frame was five stories in height and was a direct forerunner of the New York Skyscraper. It even had an elevator shaft.

The school was opened in 1859, and one of its most spectacular features was its auditorium. This was located in the basement, because Peter Cooper reasoned this would prevent fire and limit panic injuries. At the time the Great Hall, as it was named, was the largest and most elegant auditorium in the United States. *The New York Times* stated that "even Exeter Hall in London, in everything but its superb organ, is its inferior."

In 1859 the possibility that Lincoln would become President of the United States seemed remote. He was an ex-Congressman from Illinois and not a wealthy man—hardly a political advantage in the East, where he was known mainly as the lawyer who debated with Stephen A. Douglas and had lost an election. Lincoln hoped to go East to visit his son at Phillips Exeter Academy in New Hampshire. When in October 1859 he received an invitation to speak in a public lecture series being held at Henry Ward Beecher's Plymouth Church in Brooklyn, he was delighted. The fee was two hundred dollars (a fairly high price for a lecture in 1859), and Mr. Lincoln could pick his own topic.

Recalling his failure to achieve any success with his lecture on "Discoveries and Inventions," Lincoln asked his friends for advice as to the choice of subject. They agreed that his best subject would be the national political situation. In a carefully worded letter to James A. Briggs, a member of the committee which had asked him to speak, Lincoln asked if this was acceptable and received an affirmative reply.

Meanwhile the then Young Republicans were in a dispute and deadlock over choosing a candidate. The former New York governor William H. Seward was one of the men frequently mentioned for the nomination, but some—particularly William Cullen Bryant, editor of the New York *Evening Post*—doubted Seward's ability to win the West and unite the East. Further, Bryant, a Jacksonian Democrat, was violently opposed to slavery, and he had followed the Lincoln-Douglas debates with great interest. Apparently he thought that Lincoln could offer some leadership in a fight against slavery.

When it was learned that Abraham Lincoln was going to speak in Brooklyn it seemed like an opportunity for the Republicans to resolve their local problems by compromising on a speaker from the West. Accordingly strings were pulled to get the Lincoln lecture transferred from Brooklyn to Manhattan, where the audience would be larger and the coverage would probably be better. Further, Peter Cooper's new Great Hall would be made available. So it was arranged and, as a result of compromise and circumstance, Abraham Lincoln came to Cooper Union sponsored by the Young Men's Central Republican Union.

Lincoln arrived at the Astor House on Saturday, February 25, 1860, and spent the day revising his speech and inserting some of the better passages from the Douglas debates. He also greeted many visitors who came to pay their respects. Sunday he went to Brooklyn to the Plymouth Church, to hear the great preacher Henry Ward Beecher and to appear in the church where he had originally been scheduled to speak.

On Monday the twenty-seventh the Young Republican committee on arrangements called at the Astor House. Although it was raining they took Lincoln for a ride up Broadway to Mathew B. Brady's studio, where he faced the great photographer's camera for the first time. Apparently they were upset by the unprepossessing appearance of Mr. Lincoln, his bluff, awkward gestures, and his ignorance of the superficial manners and customs of the metropolitan sophisticates. Later on in the day the rain turned to snow, a poor omen for a large crowd. However this was election year and the tall, gaunt, beardless, fifty-one-year-old Illinois lawyer was a potential candidate and he was known to oppose slavery. As a result at least fifteen hundred people, described by the press as "the pick and flower of New York" and "a large and brilliant" group, gathered. On the platform were Horace Greeley, editor of the New York *Tribune*; David Dudley Field, the distinguished New York lawyer; George P. Putnam, the publisher; Theodore Tilton, editor of the *Independent*; and many other notables. The chairman was William Cullen Bryant.

Lincoln's great height and his ill-fitting new suit made him look somewhat peculiar and unusual. His jacket was too small, the sleeves were much too short. His trousers, perhaps wet from the snow or rain, were unpressed, and he seemed to limp or stagger a little. His new shoes hurt his feet.

Lincoln started slowly; in fact he almost lost his audience in the first few sentences. He apparently suffered from stage fright or nervousness at the grandeur and size of the Great Hall and at the importance of the people he was to address. The platform guests alone could help a man a long way toward the Presidency. To top it all, his attack—his first words—failed. His voice cracked into a high falsetto and he referred to William Cullen Bryant as "Mr. Cheerman." Derisive comments were made and people yelled, "Louder!" Many people shook their heads in disappointment, others laughed. The crowd rustle increased. It was a bad opening, but as Lincoln warmed to his speech his voice lowered a little. His Springfield friend Mason Brayman sat at the back of the hall. By arrangement with Lincoln he was to raise his high hat on a cane whenever Lincoln did not speak loudly enough. Joseph R. Choate, the lawyer and diplomat, wrote of Lincoln at Cooper Union that "as he spoke he was transformed; his eyes kindled, his voice rang and his face shone and seemed to light up the whole assembly. For an hour and a half he held the audience in the hollow of his hand."

As Lincoln worked into his theme he appealed for "national

unity against the extension of slavery beyond the Southern States." He argued that slavery could not be called right, secession could not be tolerated, and slavery should not be permitted to extend into the territories. Gradually the audience realized that they were listening to a great man; his awkwardness was of no importance. When Lincoln closed with his now famous words, "Let us have faith that right makes might, and in that faith, let us, to the end, dare to do our duty as we understand it," the audience cheered and applauded. The speech that had started all wrong ended with a great ovation.

Lincoln was treated to a midnight supper and later walked down Broadway toward the Astor House. He apparently did not realize the impact of his speech. He said that "he did not suppose the newspapers would care to print his speech verbatim." By the newspapers and by word of mouth the news of the speech was carried far and wide. It was printed as a pamphlet by newspapers and interested political organizations in many scattered parts of the country. This speech earned for Lincoln the eventual support of some of the New York Republicans and helped him gain the Republican nomination just three months later. Lincoln himself said, "Brady and the Cooper Institute made me President."

Johnson E Fairchild .

22

THE REPUBLICAN PARTY CHOOSES

A CANDIDATE

by Walter Trohan

In the late afternoon of May 18, 1860, burly, pockmarked David K. Cartter, chairman of the Ohio delegation to the Republican National Convention, lumbered to his feet in Chicago's tension-charged "Wigwam." On the fateful third ballot Abraham Lincoln, whose vote had been picking up steadily, had 231½ votes—only 1½ votes short of the 233 necessary to win the nomination—to 180 votes for William H. Seward of New York.

"I arise, Mr. Chairman," stuttered Cartter, who made political capital of his infirmity, "to announce the change of four votes, from Mr. Chase to Mr. Lincoln."

For a moment there was awesome silence as the import of the stuttered words was assessed; then piercing yells loosed what the Chicago *Press and Tribune* reported as the greatest tumult "since the walls of Jericho came tumbling down." Cannons boomed from the convention hall's roof top, bands blared, bells tolled, and whis-

140

tles screamed. Men tossed their hats in ecstacy and embraced in frenzied joy. Horace Greeley, the ebullient and vindictive editor of the New York *Tribune*, beamed as Thurlow Weed, manager for the defeated Seward, wiped tears from his eyes. Huge Judge David Davis, the victorious Lincoln manager, wept openly with joy.

Thus were the doors of immortality opened for the brooding spirit of Abraham Lincoln. Only a few days before, in another Wigwam at Decatur, Illinois, he had become the favorite son of Illinois when old John Hanks carried a pair of rails into the convention hall, proclaiming they had been cut by himself and Lincoln years before. With the Chicago results the railsplitter candidate was measured for history by a destiny that was to bring him to a martyr's grave. When this came to pass men began, as is their wont, to search for the kingmaker, the master mind who won him the nomination over a host of better-known and even revered contestants.

Some saw this Warwick in the portly Davis, who was later to be rewarded by appointment to the United States Supreme Court; or in Ward Hill Lamon, who had supplies of extra tickets printed to pack the hall with Lincoln men; or in Norman Judd, who had managed Lincoln's popularly successful but futile campaign for the Senate against Stephen A. Douglas, which projected him into national contention; or in Jesse W. Fell, who first told Lincoln he would make a formidable candidate. Others saw the hand of the master as that of Joseph Medill, editor of the *Press and Tribune*, who gave Lincoln his first influential backing; or of Charles Ray, Medill's editorial-writing associate; or of Greeley, who sat on the stage during Lincoln's epochal address in New York's Cooper Union.

Various lesser figures have been advanced, but the one man who did the most to nominate the Civil War President has been largely neglected. That man was Abraham Lincoln himself, who had placed his trust in God, saying: "I know that His hand is in it. If He has a place and work for me—and I think He has—I believe I am ready." But Lincoln, for all his confidence in the Almighty, even more devoutly believed God needed a helping hand and gave it to Him in many ways at many times in the months before the Chicago convention on May 16, 1860.

When Lincoln in effect had won the popular election for the Senate but lost the senatorial toga in the voting in the Illinois legislature, he must have been aware that he had propelled himself into presidential contention. A few papers mentioned him as a possibility in Illinois, and the *Press and Tribune* as a possibility before the nation. In December 1858 Jesse Fell journeyed to Springfield from Bloomington, where his brother edited the influential *Pantagraph*, to tell Lincoln he would make a powerful candidate. Lincoln listened attentively and then protested there was "no use of talking to me while we have such men" as Seward and Salmon P. Chase of Ohio. Lincoln acknowledged that there was force in what Fell had to say, and conceded he was ambitious to be President, but concluded there was "no such good luck in store for me."

Just when Lincoln began to take his prospects seriously we do not know, but we do know he began an extensive correspondence. In April 1859 he wrote a Rock Island, Illinois, editor who wanted to organize a "Lincoln for President" movement, "I really think it best for our cause that no concerted effort, such as you suggest, should be made." But he began making himself known by making a speaking tour, cautiously combining one of his most important speeches with a visit to his son, Robert Todd Lincoln, who was at a New England preparatory academy for Harvard University. During 1859, with its ferment over the raid and execution of John Brown, Lincoln traveled more than four thousand miles, speaking to audiences in Ohio, Iowa, Wisconsin, and Kansas. In 1860 he made his trip East, ostensibly to see his son but actually to make the all-important Cooper Union address.

As the convention neared it is evident from Lincoln's correspondence that he felt that there was but one candidate—himself. Seven weeks before the Chicago gathering he wrote a friend in

Ohio: "My name is new in the field; and I suppose I am not the *first* choice of a very great many. Our policy, then, is to give no offence to others—leave them in a mood to come to us, if they shall be compelled to give up their first love."

This was the strategy he had dictated for Judge Davis, Lamon, Medill, and other supporters. They strove to win the votes of dissident groups, to play off rivals one against the other, to play upon Lincoln's humble origins, to confine the boom lest it start prematurely, and to keep him as inconspicuous as possible yet hold him in contention. On his part he maneuvered with greatest adroitness to keep himself from impaling his ambitions on the deadly briar patch of violent issues.

When the convention met in Chicago, Lincoln remained in Springfield, aware that a personal appearance might jeopardize his chances. He authorized his backers, at least by inference, to make political commitments in his behalf, yet he purportedly wired them: "I authorize no bargains and will be bound by none." Wisely his startled managers decided to make believe they never got this message and went ahead making an amazing array of deals, some of which were to plague their man in the White House. Lincoln honored them all, even to taking four of his opponents into his Cabinet: Seward as Secretary of State, Chase as Secretary of the Treasury, Edward Bates of Missouri as Attorney General, and Simon Cameron of Pennsylvania as Secretary of War.

During the hysteria and turbulence of the nominations and the balloting in the Wigwam, Lincoln sat in his Springfield law office with his partner, William Herndon, and a group of friends. On the first ballot Seward had 173½ votes to 102 for Lincoln and the remainder of the 465 votes were divided among favorite sons and other candidates. Lincoln read a telegraphic dispatch on the result of the first roll call without comment. On the second ballot his vote jumped to 181 while Seward's reached only 184½. While he read the second dispatch, also without comment, it was evident that he accepted the results as clinching his nomination, having previously expressed the opinion that if Seward did not succeed on the first or second ballot he was not likely to win.

After receiving news of the second ballot Lincoln left his office for the more crowded editorial rooms of the *Illinois State Journal.* While he sat there a telegraph operator copied a telegraphic dispatch on the third and final ballot. When the sounder died the operator threw down his pencil and took the dispatch to the newspaper office. There the operator capitalized on his moment of glory by calling for three cheers "for the next President of the United States."

These were given with a will. Then the operator read the dispatch. Lincoln rose from his chair, took the telegram, read it again, and said, "When the second ballot came, I knew this must come." Then he jestingly invited those present to congratulate him, saying, "Gentlemen, you had better come up and shake my hands while you can. Honors elevate some men."

His friends crowded around him. When the last hand had been wrung Lincoln said, "Well, gentlemen, there is a little woman at our house who is probably more interested in this dispatch than I am; if you will excuse me, I will take the dispatch up and let her see it."

Then Abraham Lincoln walked up the street into history.

Walter Trahan

23

THE ELECTION OF 1860

by Adlai E. Stevenson

Presidential elections in the United States are always important, touching, as they have in our time, the nerve network of the world and the issues—economic, political, philosophical, even religious—which are vital to peoples of far-distant lands. We are getting used to this. We are coming to accept this as a part of the responsibility which is inherent in the meaning of America in the modern world.

We also take for granted the elaborate campaign—the party organization in every state, the fanfare and oratory from whistle stop to Madison Square Garden, all with benefit of radio and television, to say nothing of armies from the press. We expect the active participation of the candidate in calculated risks decided upon in high-level conferences of the leaders of his party. But in the voting booths the people still speak, as they have done since the beginnings of the American experiment.

It is with surprise, then, that we study the campaign and election of 1860—the election which plunged the nation into a war of brother against brother, the bloodiest in all history; a war which liberated a whole race of human beings from bondage and which proved, we hope, that man is capable of governing himself.

Abraham Lincoln, first Republican President of the United States, was not the popular candidate. He was not the people's choice. Moreover the election was won for him by the campaign work of his personal enemies within his own party, all of whom had aspired to the nomination and whom he later gathered to his bosom as his most valued advisors in the Cabinet.

"Only events can make a President," Lincoln said later, and the events most certainly conspired in an astounding way.

The Democrats brought it on themselves. At their national convention in Charleston, South Carolina, in April a bitter quarrel developed between the Southern and Northern wings of the party. The issue before the nation was slavery in the territories. The majority of the delegates to the Democratic convention favored a platform which would advocate nonintervention by Congress in the institution of slavery in the territories. That was the popular-sovereignty argument of Stephen A. Douglas of Illinois in his debates with Lincoln in 1858. They would support the Compromise of 1850, which ended the Missouri Compromise, and endorse the Supreme Court decision that denied asylum to slaves even in free territory.

But that wasn't enough for the Southern Democrats. Led by William L. Yancey of Alabama, they insisted on a platform that would make it the positive duty of Congress to establish and protect slavery in the territories. This would have meant that even if the people of a territory opposed slavery Congress would impose it upon them against their will. A deadlock ensued. The Douglas supporters had a majority but not the necessary two-thirds vote to carry the convention for their candidate. After many heated sessions the convention adjourned to meet in Baltimore in June.

Meanwhile, in May, at the Chicago convention of the Republican party, in which my great-grandfather, Jesse W. Fell, was an active participant, Lincoln was nominated, and there was much maneuvering and political promising without consultation with the candidate.

When the Democrats met in Baltimore the rift widened. The Northern wing nominated Stephen A. Douglas for President and Herschel V. Johnson of Georgia for Vice President. The Southern wing came up with John C. Breckinridge of Kentucky for President and Joseph Lane of Oregon for Vice President. At a moment when unanimity was imperative the Democrats were hopelessly divided. A common joke of the time, often repeated, was that "Stephen A. Douglas was a greater man than Abraham Lincoln, for while Lincoln split rails Douglas split the Democratic party."

To confuse the issue further the American party, containing remnants of the old Whigs and some Democrats now calling themselves the Constitutional Union party, nominated John Bell of Tennessee for President and Edward Everett of Massachusetts for Vice President.

From May to November the Republican candidate remained in Springfield, Illinois. The work of carrying on his campaign was done by others. He did not make a single speech that could be considered political. While his correspondence was normally heavy he wrote comparatively few letters now. His only notable literary effort was an autobiography which is valued today largely for its glimpses of his early life and its revelation of character. This was an enlargement upon a shorter sketch which Lincoln wrote in December of 1859, at the request of Jesse Fell, a good friend and vigorous supporter, who had wanted it for use in his native state of Pennsylvania and the East.

Now the campaign biographies began to appear. Lincoln was so little known that one of the early biographers misspelled his first name. The work, nevertheless, sold over ten thousand copies in a few weeks.

The "greats" in the new party, those who had dreamed of the White House themselves, put their shoulders to the wheel. William H. Seward, ex-Governor of New York, whom everyone had expected to walk away with the nomination; Salmon P. Chase, the great "runaway slave lawyer" from Ohio; Edward Bates of Missouri, and Simon Cameron of Pennsylvania went to work to elect the one man each envied most. The party exploited Lincoln's humble beginnings, the fact that he had been born in a log cabin and had once split rails. The phrase "The rail candidate for President in 1860" caught on immediately, and two campaign newspapers named *The Rail Splitter* were established, one in Chicago and the other in Cincinnati.

The Republicans used every conceivable vote-getting technique. Most effective was an organization calling itself the "Wide Awakes," a semimilitary group that attracted young men particularly. Wide Awake clubs were established in most population centers, and the boys marched in torchlight parades and made a great deal of noise. It was an era of great exaggeration. Speakers were numerous and distinguished. Each side threatened the electorate with dire consequences if the other candidate should be elected, a technique still too often employed today. There were the customary appeals for solid party support, but new parties had come into existence, and it was necessary to ask for a change in party allegiance. Lincoln's party had gone through only one national election and had lost that one, in 1856.

Even then "socialism" was a political epithet. And Lincoln's opponents charged that the election of the Republican party would bring socialism in its worst form, including women's rights, division of land, and even free love.

With Lincoln not speaking in his own behalf but with many, many prominent Republicans doing the campaigning, the arguments for his party were most diverse. The issue was presented at times as a high moral crusade; in some areas the appeal was on the basis of coming Republican prosperity, in others on the need for a change of Administration following the long period of Democratic ascendency. The new party was represented as embodying both vigor and progressiveness. Support for the Republican party and its candidate was evidence of "the spirit of radical democracy." At the same time other speakers were presenting the party as highly conservative. It was a great balancing act, which in effect promised all things to all men. The issue of slavery, the one real issue, was played down wherever possible.

Douglas campaigned with great energy; he visited nearly every Northern state and many states in the South. He appealed to the spirit of compromise, urging moderation and adjustment. He urged that Lincoln could not conduct a national Administration on the principles he had used in the debates two years before.

Breckinridge was backed by the Administration in power, that of President James Buchanan.

On Tuesday, November 6, 1860, the American people went to the polls. Lincoln was victorious in all but one of the free states—New Jersey, where the vote was divided. Breckinridge carried the Deep South as well as Arkansas, Delaware, Maryland, and North Carolina. The vote in the electoral college was a landslide: for Lincoln, 181; Breckinridge, 72; Bell, 39; and Douglas, 12.

But it was very different as far as the popular vote was concerned. From the people themselves Lincoln received 1,866,452 votes; Douglas, 1,376,957. The combined votes for Douglas, Breckinridge, and Bell outnumbered Lincoln's by nearly a million. He was elected as a minority President.

The people had spoken. But no one was quite sure what they had said. It was for time and events to reveal the meaning of that capricious election—a meaning that is still unfolding in new facets and depths and durability, and will do so, we have the faith to believe, "to the latest generation."

Adlai E. Stevenson

24

THE SELF-EDUCATION OF ABRAHAM LINCOLN

by Robert L. Kincaid

How well educated was Abraham Lincoln? That question is often asked, because it is commonly understood that the great American statesman had less than a year of formal schooling and consequently could not possess the normal culture and mental disciplines which a well-rounded liberal-arts education is supposed to provide. Lincoln himself contributed to his popular conception of his educational deficiency. In a brief statement for the *Dictionary of Congress* made after he had served in that body he used one word, "defective," to describe his education. After he was nominated for the Presidency in 1860 he further elaborated on his educational background in a sketch he wrote for an author who was to prepare his campaign biography.

Writing in the third person about himself, Lincoln said, he went to "A. B. C. schools by littles," that "all his schooling did not amount to one year," that he "was never in a college or Academy as a student; and never inside of a college or accademy building" until after he was licensed to practice law.

"What he has in the way of education, he has picked up," Lincoln continued. "He regrets his want of education, and does what he can to supply the want." He particularized on two points which he thought worthy of mention, saying, "After he was twenty-three . . . he studied English grammar, imperfectly of course, but so as to speak and write as well as he now does." He also said, "He studied and nearly mastered the Six-books of Euclid, since he was a member of Congress."

That was the way Abraham Lincoln, candidate for the Presidency of the United States, described his educational background to the people he was asking to vote for him. Going to school for less than a year! "Nearly mastering" an English grammar and the six books of Euclid after he was a grown man! Yet this man who was thus describing his "want of education," as he put it, had stirred the nation with his debates with Douglas and had profoundly impressed the nation's political leaders with his incomparable Cooper Union speech. Within another five years his First and Second Inaugural Addresses, his Gettysburg speech, and many of his letters and state papers would be applauded by the world as literary masterpieces which would endure for all time.

Why did Lincoln speak in such a deprecatory manner about his educational background? Was it a pose of false modesty? Was it to elicit sympathy because of the handicaps he had to overcome in preparing himself for a public career? We can only speculate on his true motives, but it would seem from what we know about Lincoln that he was so acutely conscious of his lack of formal education that he felt he must speak of it when he was presenting his claims to the people.

Whatever may have been Lincoln's motive in describing his educational background as he did, we know that something set him apart from his boyhood associates. He and his older sister, Sarah, went to school long enough in Kentucky to learn their ABC's and to read a little. When the Lincoln family moved to Indiana the youngsters attended three schools for brief periods and became a little more proficient in reading, spelling, and writing. Then their formal schooling ended forever. Young Abraham was never to enter a schoolhouse again.

Normally that should have been the end of the lad's educational career, if he had been like most of the frontier youth of his time. He could write a fair hand, he could read and spell tolerably well and could "cipher to the Rule of Three." He had reached the level of education which was then accepted as all that was necessary to make a comfortable living. Why should he bother about books any more?

But young Abraham Lincoln had something within him which no fond parent, devoted teacher, or sympathetic friend can implant or inspire. It is something which a person must be born with. It is the little spark within the human heart sometimes called ambition, or the quest to know, or the desire to get ahead or make something of one's self. It is the restlessness of spirit which drives a person onward from one achievement to another. Lincoln had that spark. He was not actuated by an inordinate ambition to attain great fame or to amass tremendous wealth, although he once said he wanted to be "esteemed of my fellow men." Rather, his constant efforts to improve himself came from a restless mind of vast potential capacity, ever probing, ever searching into the insoluble mysteries of the universe. He wanted to know. He wanted to understand.

Young Lincoln had all the elements of intellectual curiosity which portend greatness. His inquiring mind would never be satisfied until it encompassed the knowledge and wisdom of the ages, whether his training was under the supervision of teachers in the classroom or laboratory or whether it was obtained by self-study and application by reading, observing, or listening. He would find knowledge in the fields and forests, in the pulpit and the courtroom, at the country store and the country mill—wherever he might go, whatever he might read, whomever he might talk with. Perhaps his education would have come easier and more readily if he had had the advantages of formal schooling, but it would have been no more important or meaningful to him than what he learned the so-called hard way.

When Lincoln arrived at New Salem, Illinois, at the age of twenty-two he was already, by some standards, well educated. Although his Indiana years had been spent mostly in farmwork either for his father or for neighbors the lad found time to read and study. It was the books which young Lincoln borrowed while living in Indiana which advanced his thinking, expanded his knowledge, and formed the basis for his political philosophy. His stepmother said, "Abe read every book he could get his hands on." The titles of a few are important: Weems's *Life of Washington*, Grimshaw's *History of the United States*, *The Kentucky Preceptor*, the *Statutes of Indiana*, Scott's *Lessons in Elocution*, and Bailey's *Etymological Dictionary*. From the dictionary he built his marvelous vocabulary; from the elocution book he memorized great orations and literary masterpieces. He wrote a little poetry; he declaimed orations he had memorized; he composed some speeches which he tried out on his boyhood friends or alone in the woods. Unconsciously he was developing a literary style and a mental discipline which would someday produce the incomparable speeches now serving as models in the study of English literature.

Young Lincoln continued his self-education after settling in New Salem. It was there he mastered Kirkham's *Grammar* under the tutelage of Mentor Graham and others; it was there he studied enough geometry to become an assistant to the county surveyor. But his greatest intellectual adventure was his study of the great poets. He studied Shakespeare; he reveled in the beauty and universal appeal of the poetry of Burns; he studied Byron, Hood, and other poets. He memorized long passages which he would readily repeat years later. He borrowed books on history, astronomy, philosophy, and chemistry; he kept abreast of current events and political developments by reading the newspapers which came to the New Salem post office. He studied law by reading the books in the law library of John T. Stuart; he mastered Blackstone's *Commentaries.* He was ready to be admitted to the bar by the time he was twenty-eight, and had been licensed to practice law the previous year.

In following the intellectual growth of Abraham Lincoln from his boyhood in Kentucky, his youth in Indiana, his young manhood in New Salem, to his maturity as a lawyer and politician in Springfield, we can think of it only in terms of the miraculous. With little help from tutors, with few books of his own, with no standards to follow in developing his intellectual potentialities, he became one of the best-educated men of his time. Nothing in his speeches and writings betrays his humble origin and the deficiencies in the educational processes he followed. What he attained by his own efforts can only be explained by the magnitude of his mind and his never-ending quest for knowledge. It was his superior qualities of mind and heart which lifted him from the ranks of oblivion into the small circle of the immortals of history.

25

LINCOLN'S LAST DAYS IN ILLINOIS

by Earl Schenck Miers

With February the prairie winds turned cold and damp. Lincoln could feel the weather in his joints; hot summer was the time he liked best, for he always brimmed over with vigor then. And he was tired from the long journey to Coles County, where he had visited his beloved stepmother.

"Abe, I'll never see you alive again," some claimed Sarah Bush Lincoln said. "They will kill you."

The President-elect laughed. "Don't worry," he said consolingly. "Everything will come out all right."

Now he was back in Springfield, seeing the familiar streets and houses with perhaps a sudden wrench of heart. Here he had lived for a quarter of a century and in his own phrase had passed "from a young to an old man." Here he had married and had paced the floor, waiting for his children to be born. Here one child was buried. For Lincoln as husband, father, and neighbor Springfield had become the sum of life.

But he was also the President-elect. In less than two weeks the long journey to Washington must begin. Everywhere people

155

would be asking questions, poking into his mind, trying to seize on any slip of the tongue for a clue to where he stood on secession and the possibility of war. For weeks newspaper correspondents, overrunning Springfield, had been playing this game of Paul Pry. In a way trying to read Lincoln's mind had become a national pastime.

Sometimes the journalists grasped at pretty thin straws. "Disunion, by armed force, is TREASON," editorialized the *Illinois State Journal*, and reporters, discovering that the *Journal's* editor, E. L. Baker, was a cousin by marriage to Mrs. Lincoln, wondered if he might not speak for the President-elect. Baker did not, and no one knew that fact better than Baker. Next the gentlemen of the fourth estate had expected to gain a hint to Lincoln's attitude at the inaugural of Governor Yates. That affair had turned into a Springfield scandal, owing to what friends called the governor's "indisposition." After the first few sentences the clerk of the House had wisely read the remainder of the governor's remarks, which were so antislavery and anticompromise that everyone knew they were without a trace of Lincoln's tact and wisdom.

So the guessing game continued. To only a few had Lincoln given any glimpse of whither his thoughts were tending, and they weren't talking. On the first of February, for example, the President-elect wrote a *"Private & confidential"* letter to William H. Seward, his future Secretary of State and a compromiser at heart. On the question of extending slavery "under the national auspices," Lincoln said: "I am inflexible." He left Seward no grounds for mistaking his position: "I am for no compromise which *assists or permits* the extension of the institution on soil owned by the nation. And any trick by which the nation is to acquire territory, and then allow some local authority to spread slavery over it, is as obnoxious as any other."

As yet Seward did not really know "the prairie politician" who had beaten him out of the Presidency; Seward still hoped to bend Lincoln. But the Crittenden Compromise that Seward had favored was already dead. Lincoln had killed it in Springfield, smelling out the "old Douglas sham" of popular sovereignty and lecturing John D. Defrees of Indiana: "It acknowledges that slavery has equal rights with liberty, and surrenders all we have contended for." In time Seward would come to know his man and then he would understand why Billy Herndon, Lincoln's law partner, had advised Senator Henry Wilson of Massachusetts: ". . . when on justice, right, liberty, the government and constitution, union, humanity, *then you may all stand aside*; he will rule then and no man can move him, no set of men can. There is no fail *here*. This is Lincoln, and you mark what I say. You and I must keep the people right; God will keep Lincoln right."

On frosty afternoons, very much in need of God's counsel, the President-elect escaped to the privacy of a vacant room over a store belonging to C. M. Smith, his brother-in-law. Here were the copies Herndon had collected for him of the Federal Constitution, Andrew Jackson's Proclamation of 1832 against Nullification, Webster's reply to Hayne during that crisis, and Henry Clay's speech on the Compromise of 1850. Many of the documents were in the two volumes of the *Statesman's Manual* which he borrowed from the Illinois State Library. These he read and re-read, groping for ideas and facts to go into his inaugural address. The task was proving hard and troublesome; and on February 2 he wrote to George D. Prentice of the *Louisville Journal*, who had requested an advance copy: "I have the document already blocked out; but in the now rapidly shifting scenes, I shall have to hold it subject to revision up to near the time of delivery."

Meanwhile the pressure of the approaching trip to Washington mounted. In the span of a few days he accepted invitations to speak in Cincinnati, Albany, Trenton, Columbus, Dayton, and Cleveland but declined an invitation to visit Massachusetts for "want of time." From Titsworth & Brother of Chicago came a gift of a suit of clothes to be worn on March 4, which he accepted; and he also received a whistle made from a pig's tail, for what purpose remained unexplained.

Politics refused to give him any respite, though he shortened his office hours. Horace Greeley came to Springfield, and Lincoln and the editor were closeted for several hours in a hotel room, discussing governmental policies. At the same time a letter going to Thurlow Weed said emphatically: ". . . my name *must* not be used in the Senatorial election, in favor of, or against any one." On February 4 he told Henry Villard of the New York *Herald* that he was suspending all considerations for his Cabinet until he reached Washington, but next day he was confronted by an "unwelcome" Indiana delegation pushing the appointment of Caleb B. Smith.

Still, Lincoln remained cheerful, surrounded by a procession of old friends wanting to wish him well. One was Hannah Armstrong, who had mended his trousers and buckskins in the old New Salem days and whose boy Lincoln had saved from a charge of murder. Like Sarah Bush Lincoln the old woman doubted if she ever would see the President-elect again. Good-humoredly Lincoln said: "Hannah, if they do kill me I shall never die again." According to Herndon another New Salem friend who called was Isaac Cogadall, and they talked about the Rutledges, Ann in particular; but most historians doubt that story.

On February 6 the Lincolns held a farewell reception for their Springfield friends. The Baltimore *Sun* described the occasion as "a brilliant affair [of] 700 ladies and gentlemen, composing the political elite of Illinois and the beauty and fashion of the area." Some sources say that a thousand attended, and all agree that within twenty minutes the jam was so great it required a major military maneuver to move from door to parlor.

About Lincoln's last act in Springfield was to call on Herndon in the offices they had so long shared. By one version Lincoln "recalled some incidents of his early practice and took great pleasure in delineating the ludicrous features of many a lawsuit on the circuit"; and by another version Lincoln asked: "Billy, how many times have you been drunk?" Lincoln, a lifelong teetotaler and at times a vociferous cold-water crusader, had pricked Billy's most vulnerable spot. But no lecture followed.

The old partners walked down the stairs. Lincoln felt the sadness of the moment. Suddenly Billy heard him say: "I am sick of office-holding already, and I shudder when I think of the tasks that are still ahead.

"If I live . . . "

This thought he waved aside when Sarah Bush Lincoln mentioned it, joked over with Hannah Armstrong, admitted bluntly to Herndon. The same thought was on his mind as he rode through the drizzling rain to the Great Western station on the morning of February 11. More than a thousand of his fellow citizens were there, and for twenty minutes he stood in the waiting room, shaking hands. No one could doubt his deep emotion. His face looked pale. He could hardly speak. Then he mounted the rear platform of the train, looking down into the faces of his neighbors. "I now leave," he said, "not knowing when, or whether ever, I may return, with a task before me greater than that which rested upon Washington." Yet with God's help he could not fail. And he said: "To His care commending you, as I hope in your prayers you will commend me, I bid you an affectionate farewell."

They watched, in the rain, as the train bore him away. They knew he was a great man. When another train brought him back they knew that he was also an immortal one.

Earl Schenck Miers

26

THE FACE OF ABRAHAM LINCOLN

by Avard Fairbanks

The face of Abraham Lincoln stirs people in all walks of life to a better understanding of mankind. In that face depth of thought, of feeling, and of understanding have outward expression which become significant of American ideals. Presentations, through works of art, of Lincoln's features give to all who behold them greater awareness of the inner character of that unique individual.

Lincoln's face shows his true character to be full of compassion for the sufferer, with a deep sense of love for those who have devotion to duty, and a determination that right shall prevail—that mankind will have a better world because of that right. He is the son for whom every mother can hope. Misunderstood and opposed by those primarily interested in self-gain, he was the devoted servant of the deprived, the hungry, the oppressed. In the world-wide sense he is the ideal of those who struggle.

In the monuments and paintings dedicated to this humble man the features of his face are symbolic to liberty-loving people throughout the world. For in a face can be found the secret of

160

the power of communication with others, in times past as well as our own. Here are the hopes, understandings, feelings, attitudes, and aspirations toward which one strives in life's pursuits. As we come to know those of Abraham Lincoln, we draw even closer to a great friend.

John G. Nicolay, his private secretary, observed Lincoln on many occasions and in many moods. He described him as follows: "Large head, with high crown of skull; thick, bushy hair; large and deep eye caverns; heavy eyebrows; a large nose; large ears; large mouth, thin upper and somewhat thick under lip; very high and prominent cheekbones; cheeks thin and sunken; strongly developed jawbones; chin slightly upturned; a thin but sinewy neck, rather long . . ."

The distinguished correspondent for the London *Times* William Howard Russell met Lincoln for the first time in the spring of 1861 when Frederick Seward, the son of the Secretary of State, took the reporter to the White House. In the diary Russell recalls his first glimpse of the Lincoln features. "The impression produced by the size of his extremities, and by his flapping and wide projecting ears, may be removed by the appearance of kindliness, sagacity, and the awkward bonhommie of his face; the mouth is absolutely prodigious; the lips, straggling and extending almost from one line of black beard to the other, are only kept in order by two deep furrows from the nostril to the chin; the nose itself —prominent organ—stands out from the face, with an inquiring, anxious air, as though it were sniffing for some good thing in the wind; the eyes dark, full, and deeply set, are penetrating, but full of an expression which almost amounts to tenderness; and above them projects the shaggy brow, running into the small hard frontal space, the development of which can scarcely be estimated accurately, owing to the irregular flocks of thick hair carelessly brushed across it. One would say that, although the mouth was made to enjoy a joke, it could also utter the severest sentence which the head could dictate, but that Mr. Lincoln would be ever more willing to temper justice with mercy, and to enjoy what he considers the amenities of life, than to take a harsh view of men's nature and of the world. . . ."

As we come to sense the significance of life we gain a greater understanding of Lincoln as a world character and of his part in the great drama of civilization. For the face of Lincoln is as great as the world itself. He is the symbol of those universal principles which are the aspiration of all mankind. To gaze upon his face is like beholding the grandeur of a rugged mountain.

There are no photographs or other representations from life which show Lincoln as a child. But we know something of the type of life he lived and the surroundings in which he had his development and training. From this knowledge a sculptor or painter can assemble data to help him mold the forms of Lincoln's face and body in that period. In his youth he lived on a frontier and moved with its expansions. He had close associations with nature and with people who led rugged lives. In addition to his meager formal education he was taught by the woods and life itself. The brooksides were the school benches he sat upon as the streams whispered their stories and laughed at his delight in fishing in them. He knew the solitude of the glades. He listened to the music of the birds.

Lincoln grew to meet the responsibilities of manhood. He experienced the toils of life. He suffered the loss of his natural mother and, later, of his sister. Each experience had a part in molding the expressions of his face. His bony frame and his muscles developed. His world demanded tremendous energy to till the land and build the fences. He learned to live with people. In the little Illinois village of New Salem he associated with varied personalities and learned that one must prove himself by his wits as well as by physical strength. Stories and humor became part of his ability to gain recognition. And the quiet laughter is apparent in the Lincoln face. He was confronted with a new approach to freedom and liberty, different from what he had learned in his youth. In this atmosphere Lincoln found a place for himself as a man among men. Unusual experiences gave him a better understanding of his fellow beings, and this, too, is seen in the Lincoln face.

Lincoln was a man of many faces, and the great portraits and works of sculpture reveal this variety. His partner, William H. Herndon, who had watched Lincoln's face for more than twenty years, in many moods, under happy and difficult circumstances, said, ". . . he was not a pretty man . . . nor was he an ugly one: he was a homely man, careless of his looks, plain looking and plain acting: he had . . . that inner quality which distinguishes one person from another, as much as to say 'I am myself and not you.' . . . Mr. Lincoln was sad and . . . humorous by turns. . . . You will find the plains, mountains & outlines of Lincoln's head & face hard to catch: they are so subtle." The distinguished Lincoln scholar James G. Randall summed it all up by saying, "This aspect of singular attractiveness in Lincoln's countenance in moments of animation, something of the inner man shining through the weather-beaten countenance, was so clearly noted by various observers that it comes down to us with as much authenticity as the photographs themselves."

Fortunately the Lincoln face has been preserved for us through the work of a Chicago sculptor, Leonard Wells Volk, who in the spring of 1860 made a life mask of the future President. This event has been hailed by a great art critic as one of the two most important accomplishments in American portraiture; the other is the life mask of George Washington made by the French sculptor Houdon in 1785. Virtually every sculptor and artist uses the Volk mask for Lincoln. I have committed its lines to memory; it is the most reliable document of the Lincoln face, and far more valuable than photographs, for it is actual form. All the world is indebted to Leonard Volk for his contribution.

An eminent sculptor once described the Lincoln face as viewed from an examination of the life mask by Volk in these words: ". . . a projecting face with unusual vigor and contrasts of planes; long, large, protruding ears, strong, angular lower jaw, and high chin; all lines of face muscular or bony, strongly, firmly, and delicately marked; the forehead wrinkled to the roots of the hair; the fullness above and immediately back of the temples very rich and firm, giving not only an important contrast to the line of the face below, but finishing that part of the head with a commanding form and outline. The profile is also unusual, in the character of the lines and in their construction: first, the full line of the forehead, carried from the top of the nose upward; second, the projecting nose, practically straight, and the distance from its end back to the upper lip, which is rather more than an eighth of an inch greater than with ordinary noses. The nose is thick in its body and wide on the top when looked at in front, and thus helps to make a harmonious face, because it catches so much light. The distance from the top of the nose, when seen in profile, to the inner core of the eye, is again unusual. The end of the nose appears almost blunt, but its outline, when carefully examined, is very delicate. The skin accords with Herndon's statement that it had a smooth and leathery surface. It is this kind of skin that gives such incisive directness and decision to all the lines of the face. The mask is especially living, in that it strongly suggests Lincoln's undemonstrative self-consciousness, as well as a knightly readiness. It bears the marks of both youth and age. Lincoln was in his fifty-second year. The mask is in short a perfect reproduction of Lincoln's face, and greatly beautiful in its human style and graity."

Only America could have produced an Abraham Lincoln. He portrays the American ideal for all people to behold and respect. He represents this great nation as no other could because he is so much a part of it aand so close to the people—in his time, in our time, and forever. To behold the Lincoln features in sculpture, portrait, or photograph creates emotions to which all mankind responds. When the artist or sculptor portrays the character of Lincoln we come close to him, face to face, as did the artist, sculptor, and photographer of his own time. As we respond with our inner consciousness we know that he is our friend. His implied approval of our efforts gives us strength and courage. Though separated from Abraham Lincoln in time and physical being, the living can feel close to him, his dreams, his ideas, and the life which he gave to a noble cause.

Avard Fairbanks

27

LINCOLN GOES TO WASHINGTON

by Shelby Foote

The tall man and his party of fifteen, together with those who had come to say good-by, assembled in the waiting room of the Great Western depot. After the feverish elation of the election three months back they felt unaccountably depressed. There was a gloom about the gathering, no laughter and few smiles, as people came forward for handshakes and farewells. When the stub, funnel-stack locomotive blew the all-aboard they filed out of the station and onto the quay. The President-elect and those who were going with him boarded the single passenger car, while those who were staying collected about the back platform, the rain making a steady murmur against the taut cotton or silk of their umbrellas. Lincoln stood at the rail, chin down, and his look of sadness deepened. Tomorrow he would be fifty-two, one of the youngest men ever to fill the office he had won. Then he raised his head and spoke briefly and the people were hushed as he looked into their faces.

The train pulled out and the people stood and watched it go, some with tears on their faces. Four years and two months later, down in Coles County, Illinois, his stepmother, Sally Bush Lincoln, was to say: "I knowed when he went away he wasn't ever coming back alive."

Throughout the twelve days of his roundabout trip to Washington, traversing five states along an itinerary that called for many speeches and an endless series of conferences with prominent men who boarded the train at every station, Lincoln found his resolution to keep silent on the vital issues increasingly more difficult, if not impossible, to keep. Determined to withhold his plans until the inauguration had given him the authority to *act* as well as to declare, he attempted to say nothing even as he spoke. And in this he was surprisingly successful. He met the crowds with generalities and the dignitaries with jokes, to the confusion and outrage of both. He told the Ohio legislature, "There is nothing going wrong. It is a consoling circumstance that when we look out there is nothing that really hurts anybody. We entertain different views upon political questions, but nobody is suffering anything."

With seven states out of the Union, arsenals and mints seized along with vessels and forts, the Mississippi obstructed, the flag itself fired upon, this man could say there was nothing going wrong. His listeners shrugged and muttered at his ostrich policy. They had come prepared for cheers, and they did cheer him loudly each time he seemed ready to face the issue, as when he warned in New Jersey that if it became necessary "to put the foot down firmly," as he said, they must support him. Even so his appearance was not reassuring to the Easterners. Taken in conjunction with the frontier accent and the shambling Western gait it made them wonder what manner of man they had entrusted with their destinies. Hostile newspapers called him "gorilla" and "baboon," and as caricature the words seemed unpleasantly fitting.

At Independence Hall in Philadelphia he touched a theme he would return to: "I have often inquired of myself, what great principle or idea it was that kept this Confederacy so long together. It was not the mere matter of the separation of the colonies from the mother land; but something in that Declaration giving liberty, not alone to the people of this country, but hope to the world for all future time. It was that which gave promise that in due time the weights should be lifted from the shoulders of all men, and that *all* should have an equal chance."

Men stood and listened with upturned faces, wanting fire for the tinder of their wrath, not ointment for their fears, and the music crept by them. It was not this they had come to hear.

So far Lincoln had seemed merely inadequate, inept—at worst a bumpkin; but now the trip was given a comic-opera finish in which he was called upon to play the part not only of a fool but of a coward. Baltimore, the last scheduled stop before Washington, would mark his first entry into a slavery region as President-elect. The city had *not* sent him a welcome message, as all the others had done, and apparently had made no official plans for receiving him or even acknowledging his presence as he passed through. Unofficially, however—according to reports—there awaited him a reception quite different from any he had been tendered along the way. Bands of toughs, called Blood Tubs, roamed the streets, plotting his abduction or assassination. He would be stabbed or shot, or both; or he would be hustled aboard a boat and taken south, the ransom being Southern independence.

All this was no more than gossip until the night before the flag-raising ceremony in Philadelphia, when news came from reliable sources that much of it was fact. General Winfield Scott, head of the armed forces, wrote warnings; Senator William Seward, slated for Secretary of State, sent his son with documentary evidence; and now came the railroad president with his chief detective, Allan Pinkerton, whose operatives had joined such Maryland bands, he said, and as members had taken deep and bloody oaths. Such threats and warnings had become familiar over the past three months, but hearing all this Lincoln was disturbed. The last thing he wanted just now was an "incident," least of all one with himself as a corpse to be squabbled over. His friends urged him to cancel the schedule and leave for Washington immediately. Lincoln refused, but agreed that if after he had spoken at Philadelphia next morning and at Harrisburg in the afternoon no Baltimore delegation had come to welcome him to that city, he would by-pass it or go through unobserved.

Next afternoon, when no such group had come to meet him, he returned to his hotel, put on an overcoat, stuffed a wool hat into his pocket, and went to the railroad station. There he boarded a special car, accompanied by his friend Ward Hill Lamon, who was known to be a good man in a fight. As the train pulled out, all telegraph wires out of Harrisburg were cut. When the travelers reached Philadelphia about ten o'clock that night Pinkerton was waiting. He put them aboard the Baltimore train; they had berths reserved by a female operative for her "invalid brother" and his companion. At three thirty in the morning the sleeping car was drawn through the quiet Baltimore streets to Camden Station. While they waited Lincoln heard a drunk bawling "Dixie" on the ramp. Lamon, with his bulging eyes and sad frontier mustache, sat clutching four pistols and two large knives. At last the car was picked up by a train from the West, and Lincoln stepped onto the Washington platform at six o'clock in the morning.

"You can't play that on me," a man said, coming forward. Lamon drew back his fist.

"Don't strike him!" Lincoln cried, and caught Lamon's arm, recognizing Elihu Washburne, an Illinois Congressman.

They went to Willard's Hotel for breakfast.

Such was the manner in which the new leader entered his capital to take the oath of office. Though the friendly press was embarrassed to explain it the hostile papers had a field day, using the basic facts of the incident as notes of a theme particularly suited for variations. The overcoat became "a long military cloak," draping the lanky form from eyes to heels, and the wool hat became a Scotch-plaid cap, a sort of tam-o'-shanter. Cartoonists drew what they called "fugitive sketches," showing Lincoln with his hair on end, the elongated figure surrounded by squiggles to show how he quaked as he ran from the threats of the Blood Tubs. "Only an attack of *ager*," they had his friends explaining. Before long the Scotch-plaid pattern was transferred from the cap to the cloak, which at last became a garment he had borrowed from his wife, whom he had left to the mercy of the assassins.

In the North, where there was a need for unity and national pride as never before in the nation's history, there was shame behind the laughter and the sighs. Conversely, elation was high in the South, where people found themselves confirmed in their decision to leave a Union which soon would have such a coward for its leader.

Shelby Foote

28

LINCOLN ORGANIZES THE GOVERNMENT

by Richard N. Current

Day after day crowds had made their way up the dark stairs of the state capitol in Springfield, Illinois. Among the crowds were reporters seeking news, politicians hoping for jobs, and curious citizens—farmers in muddy boots, ladies in their Sunday best—wanting merely to see what the newly elected President looked like.

At first Lincoln welcomed all the visitors. He shook hands with everyone and joked and told stories as if he were still plain Old Abe and had no responsibility for the future of the nation. But after several weeks a change came over him. New lines of worry began to show on his face, and he seemed to be growing more and more troubled. Finally he put an end to his daily receptions. Much of the time he hid out, alone, in a dingy room above a store across the street from the capitol.

During those months from his election to his inauguration, from November 1860 to March 1861, Lincoln was preoccupied with a twofold task. He had to organize a new government and

171

at the same time hold a dividing nation together. One by one the states of the lower South were leaving the Union. Lincoln had to bring them back and do it without war, if he could. His success would depend in part on how he went about organizing his Administration.

This was a matter of personnel. It was a question of what men to appoint to government positions, especially to the highest ones —those of the Cabinet.

Naturally Lincoln wished to put at the head of each department a man well qualified for the work of that particular department. He needed a Secretary of State who knew something about diplomacy, a Secretary of the Treasury experienced in public finance, and so on. To find the right person for each place would have been hard enough, even if Lincoln had had to take nothing into account except the fitness of the man for the post.

But Lincoln also had to take other things into account. He needed a Cabinet that would strengthen his party and his Administration. He needed a Cabinet that by its very membership would help to reunite the country. The Republican party, as well as the American people, was badly divided. So Lincoln hoped to appoint someone to represent every faction of the party and every section of the country—even the South, if possible.

There were further complications. In choosing the members of his Cabinet Lincoln did not have a completely free hand. At the Chicago convention, where he was nominated in May of 1860, his friends and managers had promised positions to certain prominent Republicans in exchange for their support. Lincoln himself had not taken part in any of these deals yet afterward he felt obligated to do what he could to honor them. He could not very well honor them all. He was reported as saying of his Chicago managers: "They have gambled me all around, bought and sold me a hundred times. I cannot begin to fill all the pledges made in my name."

There was no lack of candidates for any of the seven places in the Cabinet. That was part of the trouble. There were too many applicants, and it was hard for Lincoln to choose any of them without antagonizing others.

For the number-one position, that of Secretary of State, Lincoln did not hesitate in making a choice. The obvious man for the place was William H. Seward, the beak-nosed, cigar-chewing, cheerful, and ingratiating Senator from New York. Not that Seward possessed any special knowledge of foreign affairs. But he was the outstanding Republican in the country, next to the President-elect himself. When the Chicago convention met, Seward had been the leading contender for the nomination, and his friends still were convinced that he, not Lincoln, really ought to be President. Seward was a member of the Republican machine that dominated New York State. Though he had made remarks that sounded radical—for instance, he had spoken of an "irrepressible conflict" between the North and the South—he actually was a conservative at heart. He advocated compromise to bring the seceding states back into the Union.

For the next most important Cabinet position, that of Secretary of the Treasury, Lincoln decided upon Governor Salmon P. Chase of Ohio. Chase was a large, statesmanlike-appearing man, conscientious, ambitious, and a bit self-righteous. The extreme opposite of Seward in both personality and political views, Chase represented the radical, uncompromising, antislavery wing of the Republican party.

Some position in the Cabinet had to be set aside for a New Englander. New England demanded representation, even though the Vice President, Hannibal Hamlin, came from Maine. Lincoln left to Hamlin the choice of the New England member, and Hamlin selected Gideon Welles, whom Lincoln put down for Secretary of the Navy. Welles, a newspaperman of Hartford, Connecticut, was not especially experienced in naval matters. Still, with his copious brown wig and his long gray beard he looked something like Father Neptune, the god of the sea. Besides, he was thought to have the administrative abilities that the Navy Department required.

For one of the remaining places Lincoln for a while hoped to find some loyal Unionist from the South. He considered several men from states like Virginia and North Carolina, which as late as his inauguration were still in the Union. Finally he gave up. He could come to no satisfactory understanding with any of the Southerners whose names were suggested to him.

But he appointed two men from the border slave states. From Missouri he chose Edward Bates for the office of Attorney General. Bates, a constitutional lawyer with a manner of an old-fashioned Southern gentleman, disliked slavery but was not extreme on the subject. From Maryland, another border slave state, Lincoln selected Montgomery Blair as Postmaster General. Blair, whose father had been a member of Andrew Jackson's "kitchen Cabinet," belonged to a family that wielded much influence in Missouri as well as Maryland.

There remained a couple of positions which Lincoln used for paying political debts. At the Chicago convention his managers had made promises to Caleb B. Smith, the favorite son of Indiana, and Simon Cameron, the favorite son of Pennsylvania. Smith was honest enough but not particularly distinguished—a run-of-the-mill politician. Cameron, a canny Scot, had a reputation as political wizard, but some who knew him had doubts about his honesty. Still, as Lincoln saw it a debt was a debt. He offered the Interior Department to Smith and the War Department to Cameron.

The Cameron appointment brought Lincoln nothing but trouble. He was plagued by letters and callers protesting that Cameron was unfit for office. In desperation Lincoln asked him to let him withdraw the offer, but Cameron did not even reply. Eventually he took office as Secretary of War.

Before the inauguration Lincoln faced another Cabinet crisis. Seward, having learned that Chase was to be in the Cabinet, refused to serve. While Lincoln would have been glad to get rid of Cameron he could not afford to lose such an important party leader as Seward. He persuaded him to remain.

When the official family at last was publicly known the list did not entirely please anyone, even Lincoln himself. A number of former hopefuls were disappointed, and he had to take care of them with appointments to diplomatic posts and other government jobs. Some newspapers ridiculed the Cabinet as a kind of political menagerie. It contained four former Democrats and only three former Whigs. It represented practically all shades of Republican opinion. It included no less than four of Lincoln's rivals for the presidential nomination in 1860.

Yet on the whole this was a strong Cabinet. It was strong in administrative ability. With one exception the secretaries were to run their departments fairly well. The exception was Cameron, whom Lincoln after about a year removed and replaced with the stern and incorruptible Edwin M. Stanton. Seward proved to be exceptionally able. Serving throughout Lincoln's Presidency and then Andrew Johnson's, Seward made a record that entitles him to rank as one of the greatest Secretaries of State of all time.

The Cabinet also was strong as a political body. Most of its members were themselves powerful in politics. Lincoln had not surrounded himself with yes men. Indeed some observers thought he had gone too far in appointing such a variety of strong-minded advisors. Perhaps they would wrangle so much with him and with one another that the Administration could never get anything done.

But Lincoln succeeded in making himself master in his own house. Calmly but firmly he took Seward down a peg when Seward brashly offered to run the government for him. On the other hand he cleverly thwarted the effort of Chase's friends to oust Seward from the Cabinet.

Lincoln, by organizing the government as he did, failed to prevent the Civil War. But he succeeded in holding the border states, uniting the North, and preparing the way for eventual reunion of the entire country.

Rich'd N. Current

29

THE SIX MOST FATEFUL WEEKS
IN AMERICAN HISTORY

by David M. Potter

When Lincoln took the presidential oath on March 4, 1861, seven states, extending from South Carolina to Texas, had formally voted in state conventions to withdraw or, as the term went, secede from the Union. They had then hastened to form a new Southern republic, the Confederate States of America, elected Jefferson Davis of Mississippi to be their President, and inaugurated Davis at Montgomery, Alabama, just ten days before Lincoln took the oath at Washington. In complete defiance of the Federal Government the secessionists had taken over all of the Federal functions and had seized forts and arsenals. In all the states of the lower South only two forts remained in Federal hands. Fort Pickens at Pensacola, Florida, and Fort Sumter in the harbor at Charleston, South Carolina, alone continued to symbolize the authority of the United States in the region from North Carolina to the Rio Grande.

What could Lincoln do in this situation? What should he do?

The Confederates, of course, thought he should let them go, and there were a good many Northerners who also felt that the easiest way to rid themselves of the problem of slavery was to tell the seceding slave states good-by. But Lincoln believed that this alternative was impossible. In his inaugural address on March 4 he expressed his conviction that under the Constitution "the Union of these States is perpetual" and that "no State . . . can lawfully get out of the Union. . . ." Moreover he felt deep conviction that if the cause of union should fail in the United States it would be a blow to the cause of democracy throughout the world. The world must be shown that democracy did not mean weakness and that a nation conceived in liberty and dedicated to equality could endure. This must be done to protect liberty as "the heritage of all men in all lands, every where." Therefore Lincoln announced, quietly but firmly, "I . . . consider that . . . the Union is unbroken; and . . . I trust this will not be regarded as a menace, but only as the declared purpose of the Union that it *will* constitutionally defend, and maintain itself."

Did this mean, then, that Lincoln had decided to resort to force, to wage war, and to bring bloodshed upon the land? The answer is not easy, and some writers have argued that he had. But certainly we know that Lincoln was profoundly peaceful by temperament, a man who abhorred violence and force. A man so gentle in his ways that after shooting a turkey when he was eight years old he never subsequently "pulled a trigger on any larger game," as he himself said. If he did ultimately come to accept armed conflict as a necessity he certainly did not do so until it seemed inescapable, and on March 4 it still appeared to him that if violence could be avoided the tide of secession might turn and the Southerners' loyalty to the Union might reassert itself. Moreover there were circumstances which made this hope seem reasonable. For one thing the South was by no means united. If seven slave states had seceded there were eight other slave states —Delaware and Maryland, Missouri and Arkansas, Kentucky and Tennessee, and even Virginia and North Carolina—which had shown that they did not want to secede. For another the seceding states had acted amid great excitement and in the almost hysterical belief that Lincoln would revolutionize the South by forcing the emancipation of the region's four million slaves. True, Lincoln was deeply opposed to slavery. "If slavery is not wrong," he said, "nothing is wrong." But he believed that this wrong within the Union could not be dealt with recklessly. To do so would mean to destroy the Union. Therefore Lincoln was prepared to recognize the rights of slaveholders under the Constitution and to tolerate the institution where it already existed, though he would resist its extension. When the South realized that he was not a flaming abolitionist, perhaps the fever of secession would die down.

With this hope in his mind Lincoln pleaded with the people of the South to come back to the Union. At his inaugural he assured them, "I have no purpose, directly or indirectly, to interfere with the institution of slavery in the States where it exists." He reminded them that physically North and South could not separate and move apart in the manner of a divorced husband and wife. And he invoked the "mystic chords of memory, stre[t]ching from every battle-field, and patriot grave," in an appeal to them to renew their devotion to the Union.

When he made this plea Lincoln was planning to avoid decisive action and to allow time to do its healing work. He said quite openly that he would not force the issue by sending in new Federal marshals and judges where the old ones had resigned, as they had done throughout most of the South. He would not try to maintain delivery of the mail if it was repelled. He would not try to reoccupy the forts and arsenals that had fallen. He would simply wait for the Union forces in the South to rally, and while he was waiting Major Robert Anderson and his garrison at Fort Sumter would keep the flag of the Union flying over Charleston Harbor to show that the authority of the Union remained.

On March 4 Lincoln was under the impression that Major Anderson could make a stand at Fort Sumter for as long as need be. But on March 5 he received the crucial news that Anderson's supplies were running low and that the fort would have to surrender unless it received new supplies within a few weeks. This changed the entire picture, for it meant that Lincoln could not play a waiting game. He would be forced either to abandon the fort, which meant to surrender to the secessionists, or to send aid to the fort, which would be likely to precipitate armed conflict. Accordingly Lincoln spent the next six weeks in a desperate effort to find some way of upholding the principle of union without precipitating a war. He sent a message to Sam Houston asking him, as governor of Texas, to lead a Unionist movement in the South, but Houston replied that he was too old. He tried to get reinforcements into Fort Pickens at Pensacola, thinking that if the Union could hold Pickens securely enough it could perhaps afford to surrender Sumter. He sought the advice of his Cabinet and of General Scott, who counseled him to let Sumter go. He listened to the pleadings of Virginia Unionists who counseled the same thing. But he could find no way to shift the question of the authority of the Union away from Sumter, and he grew increasingly reluctant to give up the Charleston fort. Perhaps, also, he was forced increasingly to recognize that he might have to choose between disunion and war, and that if it had to be war he must see that the hostilities did not begin in a way that would be harmful to the Union cause.

By the end of March the force of circumstances was closing in. The appeal to Sam Houston had failed. The attempt to reinforce Fort Pickens had failed because of a miscarriage of orders. The Southern Unionists had not responded to the pleas in the inaugural address. And Major Anderson faced starvation at the end of two more weeks. In the face of these developments Lincoln decided to act. On March 29 he ordered a naval expedition to be prepared for the relief of Fort Sumter, "to be used or not, according to circumstances." Six days later, on April 4 he sent Major Anderson a message that "the expedition will go forward." Then, on April 6 in an hour of decision, he took a crucial step which would have the double effect of saving peace, if it could be saved without surrender, or of shifting blame to the Confederates for starting the war, if war should come. He sent a message to the governor of South Carolina, telling him that an expedition would attempt to bring "provisions only" to Fort Sumter and that no effort would be made to send in reinforcements except "in case of an attack upon the Fort."

Historians still argue whether this was a threat to force the issue if the Confederates prevented food from being sent in or a promise not to force the issue if the food was allowed. They also argue whether this meant that Lincoln was still hanging onto a forlorn hope of peace or whether he had decided that there had to be war and this was the best way, from the standpoint of the Union, for it to begin. All we can say with certainty is that if there was any lingering chance of keeping peace without surrendering the fort this was it.

Between April 6 and April 9 seven vessels sailed from Northern navy yards with orders to assemble off Charleston. On April 12 some of these vessels arrived at the rendezvous outside of Charleston Harbor. But on the previous day Pierre G. T. Beauregard, the Confederate general commanding at Charleston, had demanded that Major Anderson surrender. When this demand was refused he opened fire on the fort in the gray hours before dawn on the twelfth. The bombardment continued until the fort was in flames and no longer defensible, and Major Anderson was forced to surrender.

The fall of Fort Sumter ended a fateful period of agonizing uncertainty and indecision. It broke a tension that had become almost unbearable, and men who could not know that four years of grim war awaited them hailed the result almost with a sense of relief. Decisions that had seemed impossible to make now seemed clear. To the people of Arkansas and Tennessee, North Carolina and Virginia, it seemed plain that if they had to fight either for the South or against it they must fight for it, and so they followed the Gulf states into secession. To the people of the

North it seemed that if the choice was clearly between war and disunion they must accept war. To the lonely man in the White House the events at Sumter meant both a defeat and a challenge. His policy of peace had failed. His policy of union must not fail. But when the cause of union should prevail it must be a victory not for the god of war, nor for the North alone, but for the nation.

David M. Potter

30

FORT SUMTER AND WAR

by W. A. Swanberg

On March 4, 1861, probably the most famous soldier in the nation, North and South, was a fifty-five-year-old artillerist, Major Robert Anderson. Anderson won fame without firing a shot. He won it by being in possession of Fort Sumter, in Charleston Harbor, with a force of seventy-odd men. He unwittingly presented both the North and South with a crisis and a challenge that had to be solved or there would be war.

At Lincoln's inauguration the nation was already dismembered. Senator Louis Wigfall of Texas had said in the Capitol, "This Federal Government is dead. The only question is, whether we will give it a decent . . . burial. . . ."

Lincoln never doubted that it was his clear duty to bring the Union back together—peaceably, if possible. From the start these two aims, based on opposing ideas of right, were irreconcilable by peaceful means. Yet each side, misjudging the determination of the other, still thought to win its point without war—a hope whose hopelessness few in either section understood until later.

Lincoln was immediately confronted by the Sumter problem.

182

by W. A. Swanberg

The eyes of the whole nation, the *two* nations, were focused on Major Anderson because his presence in the fort was a symbol and a test of the North-South quarrel. The South Carolinians, having seceded ten weeks earlier, were outraged over what they considered a "foreign" garrison manning a fort commanding their biggest harbor. They had parleyed vainly with President Buchanan for the fort. Buchanan had refused to recognize the Confederacy; refused to abandon Sumter, which he said was a Federal fort and must be occupied by Federal soldiers. Now the question was in the hands of the new President, Lincoln, and the patience of the Confederacy was growing short.

To Unionists, Anderson had to stay in Sumter to show that the government was not surrendering to what they called rebels and outlaws. To Confederates, Anderson had to get out or their claims to independent statehood would become a laughingstock.

Never has the nation changed horses in such a perilous stream. The new Administration was led by men unfamiliar with their tasks and with one another. Not surprisingly there was a period of fumbling and floundering as Major Anderson waited anxiously at Sumter for news of his fate.

The Carolinians had long since surrounded Sumter with a ring of batteries manned by some six thousand soldiers under General Pierre Beauregard, an old West Point colleague of Anderson's. The fort was cut off from aid. Any help reaching it would have to pass Confederate guns, and the Confederates made it plain that they would fire. The position of Anderson, an idealist devoted to his flag, was rendered all the more painful because he was himself a Kentuckian with Southern sympathies. For him the worst possible result of the quarrel was fratricidal war. Earlier he had pleaded for reinforcements. Now that the government had failed to help him when there was yet time he felt that the wisest course was to abandon Sumter peaceably. He informed Lincoln that he believed it would take a fleet of ships and a force of twenty thousand men to fight their way to the fort and reinforce him.

Lincoln was dumfounded. He had not known the position

was so grave, and in fact he even entertained doubts of Anderson's loyalty. The whole Federal Army, scattered over the country, numbered only sixteen thousand men. But aged General-in-chief Winfield Scott backed up Anderson saying, "Evacuation seems almost inevitable. . . ." As Lincoln himself put it his duty seemed reduced "to the mere matter of getting the garrison safely out of the fort."

Such a move would be a supreme humiliation. It would bring despair to Northern Unionists and would strengthen the young Confederacy, which Lincoln did not recognize as a nation. Fort Sumter, of small importance in itself, loomed before every Unionist as a crucial trial of the new Administration's courage and ability to resist rebellion. At Lincoln's inaugural he had pronounced secession illegal, had promised to the extent of his ability to maintain Federal authority in the seceded states, and to "hold, occupy and possess" Federal forts. That meant Sumter above all. Abandoning it was a step so distasteful that he probed every other possibility as days passed and Anderson's food supply dwindled.

Unhappily Lincoln did not yet have firm control over his Cabinet. Secretary of State Seward, who had expected to become President himself, was regarded by many—including Seward—as the real leader of the Administration. Seward had an odd theory that if the Confederacy was allowed to break away in peace it would soon discover its error and rejoin the Union voluntarily. He felt so sure he could bring Lincoln around to this belief that on his own he conducted secret and unofficial negotiations with Confederate agents, assuring them that Sumter would be evacuated.

This was glad news to the Confederates. The rumor even reached Major Anderson at Sumter. In fact the Major got nothing but rumors, for the Secretary of War failed to communicate with him for weeks. At Sumter the men packed their belongings in the belief that they would soon abandon the fort and sail home.

Seward was horrified when Lincoln decided he could not

shrink from his duty and must make an effort to hold Sumter, even though the effort fail. In New York a relief expedition was prepared under Captain Gustavus Fox. Fox had orders to sail south and offer only to supply Sumter with food. If he was attacked Fox was to make an all-out effort to steam past the Confederate batteries and not only supply the fort but reinforce it.

South Carolina's governor was given official notice that the attempt would be made. At Sumter Anderson received his first word of any kind from the Administration that had been in office a month—a note from Secretary Cameron telling him of the expedition, asking him to hold out, and adding that the President "has entire confidence that you will act as becomes a patriot and soldier. . . ."

Anderson, with only salt pork left in his larder, was appalled. The expedition, he knew, meant war. Although in entire disagreement with the Administration's policy, he was indeed a patriot and soldier to whom duty took precedence over his own feelings. He readied his guns.

The Confederates, with some justice, felt they had been trifled with. General Beauregard was ordered to deliver an ultimatum to Major Anderson. Hoping to win the fort intact Beauregard sent aides who courteously offered Anderson and his men safe conduct if they would clear out. Anderson as courteously refused. He was handed a note:

"Sir: By authority of Brigadier-General Beauregard . . . we have the honor to notify you that he will open the fire of his batteries on Fort Sumter in one hour from this time."

Never was carnage ushered in more politely. But there was nothing polite about the cannonballs that began battering Sumter at four thirty on the morning of April 12, 1861. The Civil War, which both sides had hoped to avoid, was suddenly a roaring reality that would not end for four long years. It was typical of the tragedy and drama of this conflict that the opposing commanders, Anderson and Beauregard, were friends.

Anderson, with only enough soldiers to man three guns at a

time, fired back methodically. Although his men were weakened by confinement and poor food they fought with zest, looking for the relief expedition to smash its way in with provisions and reinforcements that would enable them to give as well as they got. Unluckily, mistaken orders and violent storms deprived Captain Fox of his most vital warships and the expedition was a failure. Red-hot shot set fire to Sumter's barracks, a blaze that finally got out of control. The men in the casemates almost suffocated from heat and smoke. There was danger that the powder magazine would explode and blow the fort sky-high. Yet the men of Sumter continued to fire—an exhibition of gallantry that made the watching Confederates, seeing that black cloud of smoke, cheer their enemy.

With the interior of the fort an inferno, cartridge bags running low, food almost gone, the men exhausted, Anderson bowed to the inevitable. After thirty-three hours of fighting he surrendered. There were a few minor wounds, but the only fatality on either side was a Confederate horse, killed by a Union solid shot.

It was the almost bloodless beginning of the bloodiest war this land ever knew. The Confederates took over the fort, allowing Anderson and his men to return to New York, where they were greeted as heroes. An era had ended. No longer was it safe to talk of peace. Now it was war to the hilt, and patriots on each side were predicting victory within three months—an estimate that every American would come to realize was sheer folly.

W A Swanberg

31

WASHINGTON IN LINCOLN'S TIME

by Herbert Mitgang

The Washington to which Lincoln came in 1861 was not only a capital, it was an armed camp. At the beginning of Lincoln's first term, Washington was a small city where some hundred thousand people lived and worked. But soon the shacks of war began to rise and the capital assumed a temporary, transient look that it never totally lost. Lincoln's Washington was the so-called "city of magnificent distances" but without a magnificence in appearance. The Army and Navy Departments were housed inconspicuously in old buildings near the Executive Mansion; Lincoln walked across a wooded lawn to them from the White House. There were unsightly sewage marshes at the foot of the President's park south of the old mansion. But the Capitol building was impressive. It seemed to be identified with the growth and the war spirit of Washington. The Capitol dominated the city, its dome half finished like the Union itself.

No sooner had the President been sworn in than he was exercising his constitutional role of Commander-in-chief. Never once in uniform (his brief, informal experience in the Black Hawk War could not really be counted), he symbolized the American instinct for civilian control over the military. The capital began to look like an armed camp when five hundred Pennsylvania troops, the first to answer the President's call for volunteers, entered the city on April 18, 1861. Soon lines of blue riflemen infused optimism into every department and corner of the city. Squads of cavalry took possession of the Virginia end of the Long Bridge at Washington and the Aqueduct Bridge at Georgetown, as well as the Chain Bridge four miles above Georgetown. By October 1862 there were a quarter of a million Union soldiers encamped on both sides of the Potomac River.

An intimate picture of the President and the city at war has been handed down in history by Lincoln's closest friend among newspaper correspondents in the capital, Noah Brooks of the Sacramento *Union*. Brooks visited Lincoln in the White House several times each week and was an intimate of the President and Mrs. Lincoln. He had met Lincoln during the Illinois campaign days in 1856, and when they met again at the White House the President greeted Brooks in these words: "Do you suppose I ever forget an old acquaintance? I reckon not."

Whenever he could the President went to the front to see the troops. Leaving Washington he would proceed to the Navy Yard and board his little steamer, the *Carrie Martin*, anchored in a cove on the Potomac near the encamped army. At headquarters Lincoln would take the review, wearing a high hat and riding like a veteran. With him sometimes would be his son Tad, in the care of a mounted orderly. On one such visit the President was driven by an ambulance driver over a rough road. The driver let fly a volley of curses at his team of mules. Lincoln tapped the driver on the shoulder and said, "Excuse me, my friend, are you an Episcopalian?" The startled driver said, "No, Mr. President; I am a Methodist." "Well," said Lincoln, "I thought you must be an Episcopalian, because you swear just like Governor Seward, who is a churchwarden." The driver swore no more.

Often the news was bad. Lincoln went over to the telegraph

office every day, impatient to check the latest from the front.
When one of the Army of the Potomac's "strategic withdrawals"
was made Lincoln walked around the White House sadly remark-
ing, "My God! My God! What will the country say!" Lincoln had
to keep prodding his generals, who had "the slows." His manner
toward enlisted men, Brooks recalls, was always delightful in its
bonhommie and absolute freedom from anything like condescen-
sion.

There was much routine Washington politicking in the midst of
war, and Lincoln, trying to watch the progress of the conflict,
also had to protect his flank in Congress and the government
departments. Secretary Chase seemed more concerned with running for President in 1864 than with helping Lincoln run the war,
yet the latter allowed that Chase had full right to indulge in his
ambition. In spite of Chase's maneuvering, when the office of
Chief Justice of the Supreme Court became vacant Lincoln declared, "But I shall nominate him for Chief Justice, nevertheless."
It was considered a sign of the President's willingness to put the
country ahead of political battles. In the disputes between the
War Democrats and the Peace Democrats, the Radical and the
conservative Republicans, in his messages to Congress, Lincoln
continually kept his eye on the target. His aim was to expedite
the war to a just conclusion for the benefit of the Union and the
country as a whole.

During the election in 1864 the President spent time in the
War Office with friends, following the returns over the telegraph
wires. He amused the little company with anecdotes. He remained optimistic despite some of the political pundits of the
press, who existed in those days, too.

After midnight on the day of the election he was warmly con-
gratulated. About two in the morning a messenger came over from
the White House with the news that a crowd of Pennsylvanians
was serenading his empty chamber, whereupon the President
went home, stopping to make a speech to those in the streets: "If
I know my heart, my gratitude is free from any taint of personal

triumph. I do not impugn the motives of anyone opposed to me. It is no pleasure to me to triumph over anyone; but I give thanks to the Almighty for this evidence of the people's resolution to stand by free government and the rights of humanity."

One final story by Noah Brooks is worth retelling. The President and Brooks were walking back to the White House through the grounds of the War Department building when Brooks fancied he saw in the misty moonlight a man dodging behind one of the trees. Brooks told the President, as they parted at the door of the White House, that he thought this going to and fro in the dark of night, as was usually his custom, was dangerously reckless. Lincoln laughed and then said with some seriousness: "I long ago made up my mind that if anybody wants to kill me, he will do it. If I wore a shirt of mail, and kept myself surrounded by a bodyguard, it would be all the same. There are a thousand ways of getting at a man if it is desired that he should be killed. Besides, in this case, it seems to me the man who would come after me would be just as objectionable to my enemies—if I have any."

And so he went among the people of Washington and, eventually, of the whole country, until he returned to Springfield.

Herbert Mitgang

32

LINCOLN AND THE COMMITTEE
ON THE CONDUCT OF THE WAR

by T. Harry Williams

"Mr. President," cried the angry Senator, "this country is headed straight for hell." Abraham Lincoln looked at "Bluff Ben" Wade and then down the stretch of Pennsylvania Avenue from the White House to the Capitol. "Yes, sir, Senator," he said, "and it's not more than a mile from there right now." Wade's reply is not recorded, but the exchange epitomizes the relations between Lincoln and the chairman of the most powerful congressional committee that functioned during the Civil War. This was the Committee on the Conduct of the War, a joint agency of both houses, dominated by Wade and other Radical Republicans, the faction of Lincoln's party most ardently opposed to slavery. The Committee kept political Washington in almost constant turmoil. It fought Lincoln on many issues and sometimes criticized him bitterly. And yet, as Lincoln himself admitted, it played a vital part in winning the war. Its role was a necessary one in the struggle that preserved the American nation. To save the Union a number of different and not completely harmonious groups had to unite in a common effort. The coalition of opinion that supported the war had to include some men who wanted to go too fast, to balance those who wanted to go too slow.

The Committee came into being in the first year of the war, in December 1861. Behind its creation were two motives. The Radicals wanted to find out why the generals were losing so many battles. And Congress, through the medium of an agency of its own, wanted to secure a voice in the conduct of the war. Thus the Committee was intended to be two things. It was to be an investigative mechanism and also a policy-making body. Congressional committees to inquire into the causes of past defeats had been known before. They were as old as our military history. But a committee that would participate with the President, the Commander-in-chief, in framing present and future decisions, was something new. Nothing quite like the Committee on the Conduct of the War had been seen before or would be seen after. It was a unique experiment in civil-military relations, a peculiar product of the special situation prevailing in our Civil War.

The men who brought about the establishment of the Committee made no secret of their grim purpose. With complete frankness they announced that the agency would be expected to dig into the reasons for recent military reverses, or, as one Radical put it, "to probe the sore spots to the bottom." But the Committee had a more important function than to expose past mistakes. Its big job was to see that the same thing did not occur again. Cried one Senator: "We should teach men in civil and military authority that the people expect they will not make mistakes, and we shall not be easy with their errors." The Committee accepted this most spacious definition of its authority. Chairman Wade, in describing its work, said that it had "gone forth" in the "spirit" of the resolution creating it to ferret out any and all delinquencies in the conduct of the war. When the Committee found a failure, he said, it went to the Lincoln Administration and "demanded" a remedy, "any remedy that may be necessary."

Wade used the term "demand" deliberately and accurately. Frequently during the war the Committee would ask for an interview with the President, sometimes requesting that the Cabinet be present. At these often stormy meetings Wade would inform Lincoln of the Committee's latest finding. Then he would demand that Lincoln remove some general the Committee thought was incompetent or order some movement the Committee believed was militarily feasible. If Lincoln demurred the Committee would threaten to stir up Congress to adopt a resolution supporting its position. Or Wade would warn that the Committee would make its evidence public, with, he said once, "such comments as the circumstances of the case seemed to require." The Committee made plenty of comments during the war. They were in the form of reports interpreting the testimony and information it secured. Backed up by the great prestige of the Committee, these reports had an immense circulation in the North. Not infrequently they bristled with criticisms of the way Lincoln was conducting the war.

Fundamentally the Committee was an expression of a new force in war—the emergence of the civilian as a directing factor in the making of military policy. As modern war became more technological and political it became infinitely more complex. It required the services and talents of people in many areas, men who knew how to run railroads or operate munitions factories or invent new weapons. The civilian came into war and he came to stay. Modern wars are "popular" wars. They have political objectives. Governments, and especially democratic governments, have to have a basis of popular support in war. Hence the function of the civilian political leader has expanded enormously. Lincoln, who both formed and reflected public opinion, demonstrated perfectly the new role of the politician in war. Lincoln the war leader represented one aspect of the civilian force in war. The Committee on the Conduct of the War represented another.

The key to the Committee's concept of its function lies in the previously quoted words of one of its sponsors: The people expected that military men would not make mistakes. And if soldiers did make mistakes the people, through their representatives in Congress, would correct the errors. The process of correction might mean that the offending generals had to be eliminated from military life. If this had to be done it should be done, quickly and ruthlessly. No individual, whatever his reputation, should be permitted to stand in the way of the general good—the winning of the war. This spirit, of course, is the same impulse that controlled the men who directed the French Revolution. The French generals had to succeed or go. Like the French Revolution the Civil War was a popular and political war. The Northern people were called on to make great sacrifices for the war, and they were determined to have something to say about how it was carried on. They meant to see that their generals fought it right.

The Committee was convinced from the first that most of the generals were not fighting it right. Not a single member possessed either a military education or any military experience. But none of them considered that this made the Committee incompetent to evaluate the abilities of soldiers. Like the mass of Americans of the time the members were not awed by any claims that the military was a specialized, mysterious profession. Wade asserted that the average intelligent American could easily become a master of military science in a short time. Consequently the Committee never hesitated to impose its judgment of what was correct strategy on the generals or on Lincoln. The members had a simple recipe for victory. Wars were won by fighting. The thing to do was to attack and then attack again. The Committee put its strategic ideas in a maxim: "In military movements delay is generally bad—indecision is almost always fatal." One general told the Committee that he could not get the enemy to give battle on disadvantageous ground. Wade snapped: "Push on the expedition until he will fight."

What bothered the Committee was that the generals did not seem to want to fight. And the Committee was right in this judgment of many of the generals in the first years of the war. George B. McClellan and other officers like him were in many ways competent commanders. But they shrank from seeking the ultimate and awful decision of battle. The Committee sensed this fatal hesitation but ascribed it to the wrong reason. The Radical members thought that the generals had a secret sympathy for the South and slavery. They believed that the generals had been indoctrinated with pro-Southern propaganda when they were students at West Point.

Thus Wade and his colleagues explained the failure of Northern commanders to smash the Southern armies. The suspicion had no basis in fact. The supercaution of the generals was the result not of any sympathy for the enemy but of their military education. They had been educated in eighteenth-century ways of warfare. They thought of war as bloodless strategy. They believed that wars were won by maneuvering, as on a gigantic chessboard, and that hardly ever did armies come to combat. They viewed war as a kind of game. It was played by professionals and it had no relation to the society that supported the war. Generals fought battles when the conditions were exactly right. They did not fight because the civil authorities wanted a battle to sustain popular morale. In short, many of the generals were unfit to command in a modern political war like the Civil War.

The Committee labored mightily to purge the Army of generals of the McClellan type. Most of the men it would have put in command, the Fremonts and the Butlers, would have been as bad as the officers it wanted to supplant. And in its slanted investigations and biased reports the Committee did some grave injustices to some honorable soldiers. But the ultimate effect of its activities was to spur the war effort to greater intensity. The Committee helped Lincoln get rid of the timid generals. It infused into the conduct of the war a needed driving spirit that would accept nothing but success. The final victory of the Union owed much to Lincoln. It also owed something to the Radicals of the Committee, who fought Lincoln and yet worked with him to attain the same great objective.

T. Harry Williams

33

PRESIDENT LINCOLN AND GENERAL McCLELLAN

by Bruce Catton

The military experience which Abraham Lincoln brought to the Presidency was very sketchy. He had been captain of volunteers in the Black Hawk War, and years later he made a little speech in Congress poking fun at his brief and inglorious career as a soldier. He had had no combat service. It is said that he once was ordered to carry a wooden sword for two days as penalty for his inability to maintain discipline over his rowdy frontiersmen. Once when an old Potawatomi Indian wandered into camp Lincoln kept his men from lynching the poor creature only by taking off his coat and offering to thrash each man personally, one at a time.

That was the extent of Lincoln's military background. Then, for four years beginning in the spring of 1861, Lincoln found himself Commander-in-chief of the nation's armed forces in the nation's most searching war.

During the all-important formative period of this war, from July 1861 to November 1862, Lincoln's principal lieutenant was

Major General George B. McClellan. A brilliant young West Point graduate, McClellan had fought with distinction in the Mexican War. He had gone to the Crimea as official War Department observer to report on the way European armies were handled in the field. He was, in short, a soldier with solid professional training and experience, possessed of vast administrative ability and a high degree of personal magnetism.

The contrast between President and General could not have been more striking. McClellan knew all the things about war that Lincoln did not know, with one significant exception. He never quite understood what the American Civil War was all about or how it had to be won. Lincoln did. So, in the end, it was Lincoln who saved the Union and McClellan who went down in history as a gifted and devoted soldier who somehow did not quite measure up.

For a time the two made a good team. An expert organizer, McClellan took the formless mass of raw recruits who were pouring into Washington after the Bull Run disaster and created the superb Army of the Potomac. He trained that army, organized and equipped it, and infused it with magnificent morale—a belief in itself that endured through four years of terrible fighting. Long after he himself had left the service the veterans spoke of themselves as McClellan's men. For no other soldier did they have the intense personal loyalty they had for McClellan.

But McClellan was also gravely handicapped. He was excessively cautious, and his caution kept him from realizing that the great function of a Federal troop commander was to take the North's immense advantage in muscle and apply it inexorably against the weaker Confederates. He was always convinced that he was outnumbered, and this strange delusion kept him from waging war in the remorseless, unceasing way of a Grant or a Sherman.

Nor was McClellan ever able to see that this war was not going according to the traditional European pattern. Traditionally two nations which went to war followed certain rules. They did not

198

make war on civilians; war was strictly a matter for soldiers. They campaigned, fought, maneuvered, seized strategic points—and sooner or later one side would find itself at a ruinous disadvantage and would sue for peace. Then some sort of treaty would be worked out and the war would end.

But there could be no treaty to end this war. It had to go to a finish. The South wanted absolute independence and it would agree to nothing less, and until it was made literally incapable of fighting any longer the war would go on. This meant that the war would be very grim and merciless. It was not enough for the Federals to defeat opposing armies; they had to destroy them, had to destroy also the economic and political foundation which supported them. They had, for instance, to dismantle the institution of human slavery, not because they necessarily had anything against slavery but simply because slavery made it possible for the Confederate armies to go on fighting. On the surface the whole thing looked like a regular war, but in fact it was a civil war, which meant that the traditional military rules were of very little use.

Of all the men in the North, Abraham Lincoln was the one who understood this the most clearly. From the beginning he treated the conflict as a revolutionary situation and used revolutionary means to fight it. Like Clausewitz he saw war as an extension of politics, and he played politics vigorously. He made generals out of political leaders, not because he supposed that they knew anything about military affairs but because he wanted to bring to the Northern war effort the political support which these leaders could command. He let his attitude toward slavery be governed by the political necessities of the moment; until the Northern attitude hardened he refused to let emancipation be made government policy, but once the political atmosphere changed he had no hesitation in issuing the Emancipation Proclamation, even though he had to stretch his legal authority to or beyond the breaking point in order to do it. Quite simply he was out to destroy the Southern Confederacy in any way possible, using any implement that came to his hand.

All of this meant that the President and the General were forever cut off from a complete meeting of minds. McClellan, always moving slowly and cautiously, insisting on treating this as another war in the established military pattern, was bound to seem—to ardent patriots in the Administration, at least—as a man of lukewarm loyalties. When he took his army down to the Virginia peninsula in the spring of 1862 and lost first the initiative and then the campaign to the hard-hitting Robert E. Lee, leaders in Congress and in the Cabinet muttered that he did not really want to win. McClellan's army was pulled back to Washington and most of his troops were entrusted to the inexpert General John Pope, who led them to a crushing defeat at the second battle of Bull Run. Over the violent objection of most of his advisors Lincoln restored McClellan to the command, knowing that only he could pull the dejected army together again. McClellan performed this task expertly, and when Lee crossed the Potomac to invade the North McClellan followed, brought him to battle at Antietam Creek, beat him, and sent him back into Virginia. Then, with all of the advantage on his side, McClellan refused to conduct a vigorous pursuit. As a matter of fact he made no pursuit at all for some weeks, and Lee was granted the breathing space he needed so desperately to reorganize and re-equip his shattered army. In the end Lincoln finally lost patience and removed McClellan from command. As a soldier McClellan's career ended in November 1862.

Ironically enough the one victory McClellan won—the tremendous battle of Antietam—accomplished precisely what McClellan himself did not want accomplished. It changed the pattern of the whole war, turning it unmistakably into the kind of war which McClellan did not approve. For it was the victory at Antietam which persuaded Lincoln to issue the Emancipation Proclamation. From that moment on the North was fighting not merely for reunion but also for the abolition of slavery. If before this there had ever been a chance that the war might someday end in a compromise, with a restored Union and ample guarantee for Southern rights, that chance was gone after Antietam. Now the last chance for compromise was ruled out. The war could end only in Southern independence or in total destruction of the Confederacy *and* of the social, political, and economic framework which characterized Southern society as a whole.

McClellan's removal, in short, was inevitable after Antietam. Whether he himself realized the fact or not McClellan by this time had become the representative of the substantial number of people in the North who wanted the Union restored but did not want the South wrecked in the process; the Northerners who saw no reason why they should interfere with slavery and who detested the abolitionists nearly as heartily as did the Southerners themselves. McClellan embodied that point of view, and his great victory left him with no place to stand.

Up to this point the relationship between Lincoln and McClellan had been basically that of two men who in spite of friction are working together for the same end. McClellan would have been driven out of the Army much earlier if he had not had Lincoln's support; without Lincoln he assuredly would not have been restored to command for the Antietam campaign. In turn he had not served Lincoln too badly. He had created a magnificent army and he had done some good things with it. If Antietam was in many ways the decisive battle of the entire war McClellan has to be recorded as the general who won it.

But before the war ended the two appeared as open antagonists. In the late summer of 1864 the Democratic party nominated McClellan as its candidate for the Presidency. McClellan himself had no notion of stopping the war before reunion had been won, but many of his supporters had other ideas, and Lincoln himself believed that if McClellan won the election he would do so on terms which would make it impossible for him to overthrow the Confederacy. Justly or otherwise the election came to be regarded as the decisive test of the Northern electorate's willingness to carry the war to a victorious conclusion. Lincoln won, and Mc-Clellan went off to join the shadows.

Of the two men—co-workers, first, and then opponents—it was obviously Lincoln who had the broader concept of things. He understood McClellan and he understood the war; McClellan understood Lincoln very imperfectly and understood the war little better, nor did he like what he understood of either. But although he goes down in history simply as one of the men whom Lincoln used and then discarded he had his own place in the story of the struggle. He created the Army of the Potomac and gave it the character that carried it through the war, and he left in the hearts of his soldiers an image which the passing years never dimmed. To the end of their lives the veterans of that army had a special place in their affections for George B. McClellan. They were not impressionable men; the man who won and kept that place in their emotions had a quality whose distinctive essence should not be dimmed by the fact that the President he served was incomparably the greater man of the two.

Bruce Catton

34

LINCOLN AND THE SOUTH

by Richard B. Harwell

Familiar to boys and girls of the Southern states for two generations after the Civil War was a play song:

> Jeff Davis rides a snow-white horse;
> Abe Lincoln rides a mule.
> Jeff Davis is a gentleman;
> Abe Lincoln is a fool.

Childhood songs were never meant to be taken too seriously.
Yet they undoubtedly reflect a popular spirit more deeply rooted
than that reflected in the newspaper comment of a day or the
political bombast of an hour.

Southern antipathy for Abraham Lincoln has died slowly, but
now, nearly a century after his death, it is gone. Lincoln has taken
his place in the hearts of Southerners, as in those of all Americans,
as a national hero along with Washington and, in the South at
least, along with Lee. What has changed? Is it that the Southerner now is different from the Southerner of the 1860's? Or is it
that the Lincoln the South opposed, even hated, in the 1860's

has suffered a change in the minds of men, and that the South has come to accept and admire the Lincoln of legend as opposed to the Lincoln of life? Neither. The South has learned the real Lincoln.

The Lincoln of 1860 was all the South feared in politics. His party espoused the end of domestic slavery, an institution which many Southerners believed morally sound and in the interests of the colored race, and which Southerners recognized as the basis of much of their prosperity. For years the South had produced the leaders of the national government. It was difficult to realize that a changing America was rendering the region's role in American life less influential. It was easier to attach blame to the upstart political party organized as Republicans and to its spokesman.

Lincoln, in the months before the civil war, became as much a symbol of division as he would, after the war, become a symbol of unity. All through the South the election of 1860 was regarded as a time of decision. Lincoln's victory was a signal to set in motion the machinery which would catapult the South into secession and the nation into war..

As a presidential candidate Lincoln was a figure of scorn and hate as well as a figure of admiration. He was elected President by a minority vote in a bitter campaign. Opposition newspapers in the North denounced him as violently as did the press of the South. Vilification of him continued after his election. It was magnified after each military reverse of the Federals and reached its peak in the presidential canvass of 1864. In the Confederacy Lincoln was quickly seized upon as a focus of hate. Denunciation of him became a shibboleth of loyalty to the South.

Lincoln was represented as the tool of vicious politicians. A Confederate historian asserted: "War, not peace, filled the hearts of Lincoln and his Cabinet." "Mr. Lincoln," he argued, "was president of a faction, and not of his country, and the unhallowed designs of that faction called for war, and forbade all acts tending to maintain the peace. . . . The quiet of the continent was sacrificed to the ambitious views of the Republican party, and to their rankling hatred of the Southern people."

The President was the butt of Southern jokes, the subject of grotesque caricature, the personification of evil in wartime sermons. Every reference the Confederates heard made to Lincoln was unfavorable. In a bit of doggerel he was described by a Southern minister-poet:

> His cheekbones were high and his visage was rough,
> Like a middling of bacon, all wrinkled and tough;
> His nose was as long, and as ugly and big
> As the snout of a half-starved Illinois pig.

Such interpretations were the daily fare of the Confederates. Even *The Southern Literary Messenger*, once the most dignified of periodicals, lost its dignity in writing of the Northern President. His name was made into "Ape," and he was repeatedly referred to as "gorilla." A Southern play about him was called *The Royal Ape.*

A leading Southern novelist, John Esten Cooke, took time from his Confederate military duties to write articles for a Richmond paper. In one written at the height of Confederate optimism he lampooned Lincoln and his failure to find an effective general. "Bankrupt of generals," Cooke wrote, "and fired by the genius of battle, King Abraham himself will don the nodding plume and buckle on the panoply of war. . . . From the awful picture thus evoked from the realms of the imagination, the mind recoils with horror. King Abraham charging at the head of his victorious legions, and joking even in the heat of battle, is a thought too terrific to dwell upon. Let us hope that this is only imagination . . . that if the great Abraham is to join the headless procession, his ugly visage will be removed by his own betrayed countrymen —by the men whose rights he has denied, whose persons he has immured in his loathsome bastiles, whose sons and brothers he has murdered upon Southern battlefields—by that nation which the whole world despises now, because they regard this Buffoon as its type."

The minds of Confederates were trained to abhor Lincoln. Yet the essential humanity of the man crossed the battle lines and filtered past the barriers of the South's propaganda. Confederates could remember how Lincoln had pledged himself to uphold the Union, and knew that his pledge meant a place for each state in a reconstructed nation. They could view favorably his efforts at reconstruction in areas which had come back under Federal control as Union armies advanced deeper into the South.

The political leaders and the press of the South held out to the last. A Petersburg, Virginia, editor described Lincoln as taking the oath for his second term "with hands red with the slaughter of his fellow beings—with a soul loaded down with the guilt of wholesale murder, robbery and arson." But the words of Lincoln himself would soon be known to the South, and Southerners would, in their hearts, believe him. His words were chiseled with truth. They bore a promise of renewed national life to a people weary of war. Lincoln, once a frontier politician, enunciated a new promise for his country in the full maturity achieved through four years in the Presidency.

Lincoln's plan to unite the nation was embodied in the simple and eloquent words of his Second Inaugural Address. If it was, in detail, no plan at all—that is the way Lincoln thought and worked. That is the way he led the Union safely through the war. Determination in Congress to enforce a radical reconstruction was strong. Even with Lincoln alive Congress and its radical leadership might have forced vindictive postwar government on the South—the kind it eventually got; but Lincoln's Second Inaugural Address and his other statements on reconstruction argued well for a reunited country. They paved the way for the South to see him in a new light. As the years have passed, Southerners have recognized Lincoln for the leader he was. As the scars of war have faded, the South has become more and more a part of the nation and more and more able to recognize Lincoln as a truly national hero.

An assassin's bullet killed President Lincoln, but that same bullet described forever a halo about his head. The years since have created an unreal myth instead of a personality for him. This is unfortunate; the man was fine enough to stand every test of history. It is equally unfortunate to imply that the South has discovered in the Lincoln myth a hero who did not exist in reality. The reality of Lincoln as the hope of the South was expressed by a Richmond pastor on April 23, 1865, less than ten days after the President's death: "In the present aspect of political affairs, the bitterest enemy of the South could not have devised a deeper injury, a direr mischief to the people than the murder of President Lincoln. The malignity of a demon could not have concocted a more effective scheme for damaging the South than this. Just at the point of time . . . when a policy of conciliation looking to a general amnesty and a resumption of peaceful relations was announced as the purpose of the President of the United States, as if deliberately intended to thwart this benevolent policy; to overthrow these plans of peace; to kindle into a fiercer flame the embers of suspicion and jealousy, and rancor, this assassin hurls his bloody dagger. . . . If the deed was a calamity to the North, it was a more harmful calamity to the South. . . . *It was a stupendous crime against the South.* We have even more reason to mourn over this murder than the people of the North. Its tendencies are to inflict a deeper injury upon us than even upon them. May God in His providences overrule these reactionary tendencies, and . . . carry forward His own gracious purposes of mercy and peace."

Richard B Harwell

207

35

THE LINCOLNS IN THE EXECUTIVE MANSION

by Margaret A. Flint

It was March 4, 1861. Washington was thronged with visitors and the streets were lined not only with spectators but with armed soldiers. Mounted guards were at the intersections and sharpshooters on the roofs overlooking Pennsylvania Avenue. President Lincoln had finished his inaugural address with its moving appeal to the "better angels of our nature" to preserve the bond of Union. Now the procession moved over the cobbled stones to the White House and a new Administration had begun.

That evening the inaugural ball was held in the Muslin Palace, a temporary structure, hung with white and blue muslin, located in nearby Judiciary Square. Guests began to assemble before nine o'clock and numbered several thousand by the time the official party arrived at eleven. The grand march was led by President Lincoln and Mayor James E. Berret of Washington, followed by Mrs. Lincoln on the arm of Senator Stephen A. Douglas of Illinois. Her costume of blue silk trimmed in Alençon lace, a blue ostrich feather in her hair, and gold and pearl jewelry was duly recorded in the press. Music for dancing, which continued long after midnight, was furnished by the Marine Band.

The White House, "built to be looked at by visitors and strangers," was a two-story stone building painted white with Ionic columns in front and the malarial Potomac flats in the rear. The usual outbuildings and gardens were fenced front and rear, but the wooded lawns extended without barriers to the Departments of War and Navy on the west and State and Treasury on the east. The first floor, with the exception of the family dining room, was "devoted to occasions of ceremony." The stately East Room occupied one end of the first floor, flanked on either side of the long hall by the smaller Green, Blue, and Red Rooms and the dining rooms. The second floor was about equally divided between living quarters and affairs of state. The family occupied the west end. The President and his young secretaries, Nicolay and Hay, had offices in the east end. An arrangement less conducive to privacy can hardly be imagined.

White House entertaining followed established custom. Public receptions were held weekly during the winter. At these inevitably overcrowded functions the President shook countless hands "as if he were mauling rails," according to an Illinois friend. There were state dinners, diplomats to receive, delegations to hear, troops to review, hospitals to visit, and the countless lesser duties that nibble away the hours of the presidential day.

When no official function was scheduled the Lincolns often gave small private receptions. One such occasion was in honor of "General" Tom Thumb and his bride. The General wore his wedding suit and his wife appeared in white satin with a train, orange blossoms, and pearls. The guest list included Cabinet members, Senators, Congressmen, and the military. Tad was delighted with the tiny guests of honor and most solicitous of their comfort.

In the summer of 1861 Mrs. Lincoln gave a formal dinner for Prince Napoleon of France. This has been the subject of some slight controversy, as Secretary Seward, still in some doubt as to who was President, suggested that he do the honors. It was all settled amicably, and the Secretary and his son were among the twenty-seven guests in attendance. Fortunately the Prince arrived early enough to make a balcony appearance for the crowd that had been enjoying the regular Saturday concert of the Marine Band on the south lawn of the White House.

New Years' receptions were a regular and popular event. The diplomatic corps, the Army and Navy and public officials usually paid their respects early. At noon the doors were opened to the general public. The 1865 reception was particularly well attended and the guests in a jubilant mood, for General Sherman had completed his successful march to the sea. When the rush was finally over, a group of Negroes who had waited on the White House grounds came forward and received a hearty welcome from the weary President and his wife.

In December 1863 there was a White House reception for the officers of the Russian Atlantic fleet which had been in American waters since September. Some thought it should have been a grand ball, considering the fact that the visit of the fleet was a palpable "show of force" (a political gambit still in use) to demonstrate Russian and American solidarity in the face of the Confederate leanings of the British and the French. Actually the main purpose of the visit was to get Russian ships out of ice in case England sided with the Poles in their uprising.

Mrs. Lincoln had looked forward to being mistress of the White House and entered on her role with enthusiasm. It was a bitter blow to find this predominantly Southern city hostile and suspicious and her position so difficult that she would finally cry: "I seem to be the scapegoat for both North and South."

Death that follows in the train of war did not spare the White House family. In May 1861 word came that Colonel Elmer E. Ellsworth, who had accompanied the Lincolns from Springfield, had been shot taking down a Confederate flag at Alexandria. His body lay in state in the East Room of the White House and the President wrote the sorrowing parents: ". . . our affliction here, is scarcely less than your own." The same year saw the passing of Senator Douglas. The Little Giant was no less a casualty of war than Colonel Edward D. Baker, who fell leading his troops at the battle of Ball's Bluff. To Fanny McCullough, daughter of a long-time friend who died at Vicksburg, Lincoln wrote: "In this sad world of ours, sorrow comes to all; and, to the young, it comes with bitterest agony. . . ." Mrs. Lincoln's "fiery furnace of affliction" was even more severe since it could have no public expression. Three brothers were to die in the Confederate Army, as was General Ben Hardin Helm, husband of her favorite sister.

The presidential family in 1861 consisted of Robert, nearly nineteen, who has been characterized as "all Todd"; Willie, going on eleven and most like his father; and lisping, mischievous, seven-year old Tad. The Lincolns were no less fond and indulgent parents in Washington than they had been in Springfield. One of Herndon's kinder observations, that the children were "an annoyance to the visitor," was to find some agreement in the White House.

Robert soon returned to his studies at Harvard, but Willie and Tad made themselves thoroughly at home in their new surroundings. Their boon companions the first exciting year were Bud and Holly Taft, whose sister Julia has left stories of many childish pranks. The White House attic proved to be a fascinating place. Once it was the scene of a simulated snowstorm with calling cards from previous Administrations providing the snow, and later it was the setting for a children's circus with Mrs. Lincoln's clothes and the President's spectacles among the principal props. Other activities reflected a capital "bristling with bayonets." Willie wrote a Springfield playmate that after several failures he had finally succeeded in raising a military company "which is in a high state of efficiency and discipline." Tad's Zouave doll Jack was subject to numerous courts-martial and burials until the White House gardener suggested a presidential pardon, which was duly written and signed by Lincoln.

Robert graduated from Harvard in 1864 and entered law school the following fall. He early accepted his responsibilities. It was he who wrote his Aunt Elizabeth Edwards to come to Washington when his parents were overwhelmed by Willie's death in 1862. On vacations and holidays he was at the White House or escorting his mother on one of her many trips. Just when he met Mary Harlan, the eighteen-year-old daughter of the Senator from Iowa, is not known, but by early 1865 his interest was apparent. It was a popular choice with his parents, and the courtship progressed steadily, although the couple weren't married until three years later. Robert's position as the President's son was not an easy one, and the fact that he was of military age and not in uniform made it more difficult. By February 1865 Mrs. Lincoln's objections were finally overcome and he entered the service as a member of General Grant's staff with the rank of captain.

Meanwhile Lincoln had been re-elected and the presidential family looked to the future brightened by the certainty that the long and devastating war was drawing to a close. But who can know the future? Life in the White House is dictated by the past and the present. On all who dwell within its walls it leaves a mark. On this close-knit family from Illinois it was an indelible mark.

Margaret G. Flint

36

LINCOLN AND THE PRESS

by Louis M. Starr

Visitors from abroad often marvel at that strange and uniquely American institution the President's press conference. The very idea that the head of a great nation should lay himself open to public questioning by mere reporters astonishes the Britisher, the Frenchman, the German. Though their press is as free as ours such a proceeding in their own countries is quite beyond their imagining.

To twentieth-century Americans, of course, there is nothing strange about it. If we are to govern ourselves we must look to the press, television, and radio for news of public affairs and thereby make them our own affairs. Since we cannot readily question the President ourselves the press does it for us. The President uses the occasion to tell the people what's on his mind as well as to answer the questions of the press as best he can. Men as different in temperament as Franklin Roosevelt, Harry S. Truman, and Dwight Eisenhower have all spent a good many of their precious hours in the White House in such conferences. That fact alone suggests the usefulness and importance they have come to have in our version of democracy.

It was not always so. Historians credit Theodore Roosevelt with originating the White House press conference in the early years of this century. The press conference is the culmination of a long series of steps which brought the nation's Chief Executive into a working relationship with the newsmen. It is a relationship which would have astonished George Washington quite as much as it astonishes the foreign visitor today.

But it would not have astonished Abraham Lincoln. Imagine the tall, angular form of Honest Abe on the dais where the President faces several hundred newsmen today. How he would have relished the ready give-and-take, bringing his quick wit into play and larding his answers with anecdotes! And how the newsmen would have loved it!

It is appropriate that we consider Lincoln's relations with the press of his own day. We will find that he did more to advance the kind of working relationship we have been talking about than any President before him.

From Jefferson's time on custom had dictated that the Administration release its news and views through pet newspapers— "organs," as they were called. These organs were run by the political supporters of the party in power, usually men who were close to the President. In addition to a great deal of exclusive news they received lucrative government printing and advertising patronage. The editorials of such papers of course faithfully reflected official policy.

But Lincoln did not strictly follow this precedent. By having no "official" news outlet Lincoln helped make the collection of news in Washington the free-for-all it has remained ever since.

We have nothing in Lincoln's words to explain why he took this step. But it fitted his constant purpose of marshaling the broadest possible support from both Republicans and Democrats. An organ, useful as it may be as an official mouthpiece, makes for partisanship in journalism as in politics.

There was plenty of partisanship in journalism as it was. Lincoln drew criticism as bitter and vitriolic as that directed at any

President in history. "The bone, sinew, and intelligence of America utterly repudiate Mr. Lincoln and all his works." That was one of the milder editorial comments of the day. The New York *World* was particularly rancorous. Unlike many other Presidents, before and since, Lincoln took it all in good humor. John Hay, one of his secretaries, set down in his diary once that the President came "loafing into my room, picked up a paper and read the Richmond *Examiner's* recent attack of Jeff Davis. It amused him. 'Why,' said he, 'the *Examiner* seems ab[ou]t as fond of Jeff as the *World* is of me.'" Then there was the time Lincoln was shown a new repeating gun that was equipped with a device to prevent the escape of gas. "Well," he told his callers, "I believe this really does what it is represented to do. Now have any of you heard of any machine, or invention, for preventing the escape of gas from newspaper establishments?" No one who heard such comments could doubt that he was aware of his newspaper critics—nor that he was unruffled by them.

After Lincoln came to the White House his chief contact with the press was not as a reader. Like most of his successors he had little time for newspaper reading. His chief association, and the one of most interest to us today, was with the reporters themselves. Bear in mind that reporters did not enjoy anything like the prestige they enjoy in Washington a century later. Newspapers, until the Civil War, were largely concerned with views rather than news—with opinion rather than pure information. Editors like Horace Greeley loomed very large indeed; reporters, on the other hand, were accounted mere penny-a-liners, newsmongers, busybodies of no standing. Then the war came along and editors discovered that readers were no longer half so interested in what to think as they were in what was doing—what was going on in Washington and on the battlefronts. From the moment Fort Sumter was fired upon, interest was at fever pitch.

Of course this turnabout in journalism did not change the status of the lowly reporter overnight. Far from it. Most of the members of Lincoln's Cabinet, for example, held the working press in contempt. Salmon P. Chase, Lincoln's Secretary of the Treasury, was pompous and distant save to a few of his political friends among the reporters. The mere name of Edwin M. Stanton, the terrible-tempered Secretary of War, was a scourge among the newsmen. Edward Bates, Lincoln's Attorney General, was put down by a reporter as "Of the order of fossils who endure newspapers as necessary evils." Many another official was of like mind.

This prevailing attitude toward newsmen makes Lincoln's seem all the more remarkable. A half dozen or more came to the White House daily, and he welcomed them at all hours. Once they were in his office Lincoln put them at ease, usually lounging in his chair and asking *them* more questions than he answered. Gideon Welles, his Secretary of the Navy, thought it deplorable. "It is an infirmity of the President," Welles noted in his diary, "that he permits the little newsmongers to come around him and be intimate. He has great inquisitiveness. Likes to hear all the political gossip. . . ." William O. Stoddard, one of the President's young secretaries, understood Lincoln's purpose a good deal better than Gideon Welles. Referring to these informal sessions Stoddard wrote of the reporters: "Probably they have no idea how much they tell him. As if through so many human magnetic wires, he receives message after message from the current thought and purpose of the popular masses whom he understands so much better than they do."

In other words Lincoln found in these private sessions with newsmen one of the values that modern Presidents have seen in the press conference. They helped him keep an ear to the ground. By the convention of the time reporters did not quote him directly. But they in turn found him remarkably co-operative in furnishing information they could use either indirectly or for background. It is interesting that the next step in the development of a working relationship between press and President, the formal interview designed for publication, came in the very next Administration. Andrew Johnson was the first President to grant such an interview.

by Louis M. Starr

Lincoln went out of his way in many little ways to accommodate his friends the newsmen. This is not to say that he got along with them perfectly at all times. On one occasion, when a New York *Evening Post* reporter sent his paper secret information on a major troop movement, Lincoln was said to be "mad enough to cry." On another a reporter who had used his access to the White House to secure official documents for the New York *Herald* roused Mr. Lincoln's ire to the extent that the culprit was told to get out and stay out.

But for every incident of this kind a dozen could be cited showing Lincoln's kindly understanding in dealing with reporters, particularly those who followed the armies. "You gentlemen of the press seem to be pretty much like soldiers, who have to go wherever sent," he said to one of them. On half a dozen occasions he circumvented Stanton, his Secretary of War, to get passes for them so they could go to the battle fronts. When he visited himself the Virginia front on occasion he recognized some of them. He would pause to chat with them. If he heard one of them was in Washington he would invite him to the White House to talk of army news. Usually he would ask the young man to come back next time he was in town.

Partly, of course, this interest can be explained in terms of Lincoln's favorite question whenever he saw one of them. It was, "What news have you?" His quest for news of the armies, as anyone could testify who saw him striding to the War Department's telegraph office in the lonely hours of the night, was ceaseless. In this connection it is interesting to note that he first learned of most of the major battles—of Shiloh, Antietam, Gettysburg, and the Wilderness, for example—from news dispatches, not from the official messages.

Then, too, of course, his interest in these lowly reporters can be explained in political terms. Lincoln desperately needed all the support he could muster. A liberal policy toward a press that was hot in pursuit of news served this end. Considering the great care he took in dealing with Greeley, Bennett, and other editors, there is no doubt this thought influenced him. Many reporters were appointed to government jobs. Among those were Whitelaw Reid, Noah Brooks, William Dean Howells, and Edward McPherson.

But Lincoln's thoroughly unconventional ways with the reporters can be best explained in his own words, words that a New York *Tribune* reporter remembered years later. The reporter had obtained Lincoln's consent to be present at a conference with the state governors, but some of the governors objected. The President said, "We shall not do anything today that is secret, in any sense," and then he added: *"Our only chance is to take the American people frankly into our confidence."*

Lincoln called the Civil War "a people's war." These young men with their flying pencils were, in a sense, the people's representatives, no less than the formally elected ones. Only through them could the people be informed of the course of their war. And so Lincoln, very likely without any such conscious rationalizing as this but simply because his instinct was right, adopted a liberal policy toward the working press. It was a policy that advanced the press a long ways toward the responsible role we have assigned it today.

37

LINCOLN AND AMERICAN FOREIGN AFFAIRS

by Wayne C. Temple

Diplomatic relations with foreign powers have always presented problems for our Presidents, but certainly few Chief Executives ever faced such a difficult task as did Abraham Lincoln. Soon after his inauguration in 1861 the United States was torn asunder by a civil war. One false move and Lincoln might find himself also engaged in open warfare with a foreign state. In addition to this grave threat one member of Lincoln's Cabinet was determined to be the power behind the throne. This man considered himself the leader of the Republican party and looked upon Lincoln as a backwoods lawyer who knew little about political affairs. Seward was his name, of course, and he was Secretary of State. Lincoln could not dismiss Seward for fear Charles Francis Adams and Thurlow Weed might withdraw their support from the Administration. Tactfully Lincoln indicated to Seward that the President himself would lead but would call upon him for counsel. Having united his Cabinet as well as he could Lincoln was in a better position to cope with foreign relations.

In an attempt to win recognition from Great Britain and France the Confederate government chose James M. Mason and John Slidell as its envoys to London and Paris. On November 7, 1861, these diplomats began their voyage to Europe on the British mail packet *Trent*, which sailed from Havana. But one day later the *Trent* was stopped by the U.S.S. *San Jacinto*, under the command of Captain Charles Wilkes. Both of the Confederate envoys were removed and later incarcerated in Fort Warren at Boston. This maneuver immediately posed a threat to Lincoln's policy of moderation in international affairs. To further complicate this diplomatic tangle Wilkes was given a hero's welcome in the North, and his bold act was praised not only by the Secretary of the Navy but also by the House of Representatives. Yet Wilkes had never been officially authorized to capture Mason and Slidell. Several British authorities screamed immediately that an insult had been shown to their flag; British prestige had received a slap in the face on the open seas. Outwardly Great Britain appeared to be preparing for war. She dispatched eight thousand troops to Canada and alerted her powerful fleet.

Lincoln remarked that it would be sheer folly for his government to engage in two wars at the same time, but across the Atlantic Ocean Prime Minister Palmerston played recklessly with threats of war. However Queen Victoria and her consort appealed to their ministers for peaceful negotiations. Lincoln shared the Queen's feelings and declared that if Great Britain demanded the release of the Confederate envoys he would allow them to depart from the United States. Secretaries Seward and Welles finally agreed that Lincoln's conciliatory attitude was the wisest choice, and Senator Charles Sumner offered his good services by writing diplomatic letters to both John Bright and Richard Cobden, very influential politicians in Great Britain. Charles Francis Adams, the United States Ambassador in England, and Secretary Seward officially announced to the British that Captain Wilkes had acted without authority. When Lincoln sent his annual message to Congress on December 3, 1861, he tactfully omitted any reference to the *Trent* affair. Sumner, at a Cabinet meeting held

December 25, reported to Lincoln that Bright and Cobden had answered his correspondence with gracious and friendly letters. An apology was tendered to Great Britain, and the controversial Confederate agents were released.

Gradually the pendulum of public opinion in Great Britain swung back in favor of the North, but Lincoln still faced the problem of keeping the Confederate States of America from being officially recognized by the British government. With Lincoln's issuance of the Emancipation Proclamation many British subjects saw the Civil War in a new perspective; now it seemed a crusade for human freedom instead of a struggle for the establishment of a Southern nation. The first Union victories on the battlefields also deterred the British from recognizing the Confederacy.

After having solved one problem in British-American relations Lincoln was quickly faced with another. The Confederate raider *Alabama* had been built in England, and still others were being constructed there. By 1863 Lincoln had decided to act. He suggested that it would be very difficult to preserve friendship with Britain if the Laird shipyard was permitted to sell ships to the Confederacy. Quickly the sales ceased.

Lincoln and John Bright never corresponded directly with each other. Both men probably thought that it would be improper to exchange letters instead of using diplomatic channels. Charles Sumner was the man who served as an intermediary between Lincoln and Bright. And diplomatic relations with Great Britain were more firmly cemented in 1863, when, at the urging of Bright, Lincoln pardoned a British subject, Alfred Rubery, who had been convicted in a Federal court of privateering.

France favored Lincoln's Administration. The French disliked the theory of secession and they could see no justice in human slavery. There was also a tradition of friendship between the two countries because Lafayette had helped Washington win independence from England. But in the fall of 1862 the French Emperor, Napoleon III, announced that he was willing to serve as a mediator in the American Civil War. He implored Great Britain and Russia to join France in a petition for an armistice of six months. Fortunately for Lincoln, Russia and Britain refused. Again, in January of 1863, Napoleon III attempted to halt the bloody conflict. This time Seward and Congress informed the Emperor that the United States would brook no foreign intervention, and very little aid was received by the Confederacy from France after this date. Mrs. Lincoln also did her bit in the field of diplomacy by paying a social call to the French frigate *La Guerrière* at its dock in New York City on August 20, 1863.

Mexico inadvertently gave birth to a crisis in foreign affairs. Benito Pablo Juárez had previously won a Mexican revolution, and the United States had recognized his administration. Juárez, whose government had borrowed money abroad, suspended the interest payments to foreign creditor nations, and in October of 1861 France, Spain, and Great Britain signed an agreement whereby they would support one another in collecting their debts from Mexico. These European powers invited Lincoln to join their pact, but he declined. Ignoring Lincoln's wishes these three allies had landed ten thousand soldiers in Mexico by January of 1862. Juárez quickly capitulated, and Britain as well as Spain withdrew her forces. Napoleon III of France, however, decided to seize control of Mexico. Maximilian and Carlotta of the Austrian Hapsburg dynasty were sent to rule the Mexicans in 1864. But Juárez continued to fight against France. Here was a serious threat to the Monroe Doctrine, but a civil war made it impossible for Lincoln to intervene. Lincoln and Seward relied upon diplomatic negotiations with France for a peaceful solution. They constantly hinted about the Monroe Doctrine, and finally France gave her promise that she would not remain permanently in Mexico.

Lincoln's administration continued to recognize the Juárez government while the Confederacy recognized the French puppet. In an attempt to remove the French from Mexico the House of Representatives passed a resolution which denounced kingships in the Western Hemisphere, but it was not until the end of the Civil War, when the United States sent troops to the Mexican border, that the last of the French soldiers were finally withdrawn. Lincoln's diplomacy had been successful in that he avoided a foreign war. A strict neutrality had been observed by the United States, and in the end Napoleon's Mexican empire collapsed without the use of Federal forces.

Lincoln's cordial relations with Russia provided a lever which he could use to advantage when dealing with Great Britain and France. Tsar Alexander II experienced many of the same problems which Lincoln encountered. The Tsar freed the Russian serfs in 1861, and later the Poles rebelled against Russian rule. Lincoln refused to intervene in the Polish question even though France and Britain invited him to do so.

Since Russia feared a war with Great Britain might develop over the Polish uprising the Russian fleets were sent to the United States, where they would be safe from the Royal Navy and at the same time be in a position to harass British shipping in case of open hostilities. Russia's Atlantic fleet sailed for New York, and on the morning of September 11, 1863, the frigate *Osliaba* dropped anchor. Five days later Mrs. Lincoln, who happened to be in New York on a shopping trip, paid a visit to the *Osliaba*. This was the first time that an American President's wife had ever been aboard a Russian warship. Other units of Russia's Atlantic fleet soon arrived in New York Harbor, and then the squadron sailed down the coast to the Potomac River, anchoring near Alexandria on December 2. Seward gave a banquet for the Russian naval officers on December 7, and twelve days later Lincoln tendered them a special reception at the White House.

Russia's Pacific fleet was ordered to San Francisco and remained there during the winter of 1863-64. The Tsar's naval officers gave every indication of being in sympathy with the North's cause. By exhibiting the utmost kindness toward the Russians Lincoln was able to keep them on his side. His diplomatic maneuvers were also greatly aided by the fact that Russia was still licking her wounds as a result of her defeat at the hands of the British in the Crimean War.

Any nation which attempted to secure diplomatic relations with Japan during the mid-nineteenth century faced a difficult assignment. The local barons disliked foreigners, and there was no central power to control them. At Tokyo lived the Tycoon (or Shogun) who was somewhat analogous to a prime minister, and at Kyoto lived the Mikado, the spiritual emperor of the Japanese. While it appeared that Japan was about to close her ports to foreign trade again, Lincoln was fortunate in having able envoys in this country. And friendship was established and secured. Nevertheless a local baron did fire upon an American merchantman, the *Pembroke*, during the summer of 1863. All foreigners were targets for this local potentate. In retaliation the U.S.S. *Wyoming* bombarded his stronghold on the shore. For a while it seemed that the United States might become embroiled in a war with Japan, but fortuitously the Tycoon gained strength and refused to follow the dictates of the Mikado. American vessels did, however, join with British, Dutch, and French warships in subduing the shore battery of a hostile baron. After this show of force, trade with Japan was re-established. Lincoln's policy here was largely a demonstration of patience wrapped securely around a mailed fist. Oriental suspicions had to be allayed, but gradually Japan did abandon her policy of isolation.

By dealing tactfully with foreign nations during the Civil War Lincoln was able to avoid an additional conflict which probably would have destroyed his government. Our traditional ties with Great Britain and France were not broken, and these same two powers still stand beside us in our European defenses today. Lincoln's acts of friendship toward the Russians enabled us to purchase Alaska in 1867, and even though Russian and the United States face each other today from hostile armed camps open hostilities have been avoided. The Latin American countries certainly appreciated Lincoln's attitude of support for Mexico, and today the Pan-American Union is a strong factor on the side of world peace and understanding. Japan made an attempt to copy the industrial might of the United States and as a result found herself our rival in the world markets. This factor certainly figured in her attack upon Pearl Harbor in 1941. Despite World War II friendly relations have been re-established with the Japanese people, and many of the Japanese certainly remember the tradition of friendship which had existed previously.

Lincoln did not establish personal contact with foreign states but rather left the international affairs to his Secretary of State. Woodrow Wilson, in contrast to Lincoln, many times served as his own Secretary of State. Lincoln's forte was a spirit of fairness coupled with a reverence for legality, and few Presidents have had an equal amount of success with their foreign policies. None save Lincoln has ever been called upon to steer a course through foreign relations while at the same time being engaged in a fratricidal conflict where the booming of cannon was sometimes heard in the streets of Washington, D. C.

Wayne C. Temple

38

LINCOLN AND THE POLITICS OF WAR

by John Hope Franklin

It would be a fatal miscalculation of the role of Lincoln to regard him as an amateur politician groping for some pattern by which to conduct the highest political office in the land. He was a professional politician with much experience in his state of Illinois and on the national scene. As a veteran Whig he had performed yeoman service for his party. As an early if somewhat reluctant Republican he had done much to strengthen the new party. He had traveled from Kansas to Massachusetts in the party's interest. He had cheerfully taken on the impossible assignment of opposing Douglas in the senatorial campaign of 1858. By 1860 he was a seasoned politician, fully aware of the requirements necessary to gain and hold office. His election to the Presidency was not alone the result of a divided Democratic party or even of superior Republican strategy. It was to a great degree the result of his astute political sense and his determination to move to the top regardless of obstacles.

From the beginning of his tenure in the White House Lincoln was keenly aware of the fact that there were many other Republicans who greatly coveted the Presidency. Seward of New York, Chase of Ohio, Cameron of Pennsylvania, and Bates of Missouri are cases in point. He brought them into the Cabinet not only to profit from their talent and experience but also to keep a weather eye on their political activities. Other powerful Republican Congressmen such as Sumner and Stevens he sought to cultivate in a number of ways and with varying degrees of success. Still others, the nameless hundreds of the party faithful, Lincoln sought to satisfy and retain the support of through the use of patronage. In those early months in office, even as the nation was falling apart, Lincoln fully appreciated the importance of building an organization that would help perpetuate the party in power.

Lincoln's political position was of course vitally affected by the outbreak of the war. The need for truly loyal support increased. Violent criticism of the Administration seemed to mount as the war progressed. The first critics, largely but not wholly in the Democratic party, were frequently suspected of disloyalty. If they were Democrats they were often branded as traitors. If they were Republicans they were punished by withholding the patronage, by political ostracism, or the like.

As the war progressed the President kept his eyes on many things, the theaters of war and the increasing complexities of life on the home front. But he never neglected the political scene. He was greatly apprehensive over the fact that a good deal of the criticism of the war was not partisan. Late in 1861 the Committee on the Conduct of the War, composed largely of members of the President's party, was severe in its strictures of the Administration for the disasters at Bull Run, Ball's Bluff, and other places. This was ammunition for the Democrats, and they did not fail to use it.

Thus Lincoln was early thrown on the political defensive, and his acts during the second year of the war reflect, in part, this defensive posture. In September 1862 his proclamation of emancipation and his suspension of the writ of habeas corpus had distinct political overtones. While these measures offended the conservatives of both parties they appealed to those who felt that the President had been equivocal on the crucial questions of slavery and loyalty. There was little the President could do, however, to stem the tide of disaffection as the congressional elections approached. War Democrats joined with Republicans to form the Union party to promote a vigorous prosecution of the war. Even they were mildly critical of the President. The regular Democrats supported the government of the United States but sought the defeat of Lincoln in order to achieve efficiency in the prosecution of the war. These developments depressed Lincoln but he held to his policies, convinced that in the end they would triumph.

The disaffection against Lincoln and his party was so great at the time of the election of 1862 that he lost valuable ground that he had won in 1860. Five states that had gone for Lincoln in 1860 now sent Democratic delegations to the House of Representatives. They were New York, Pennsylvania, Ohio, Indiana, and his own Illinois. A sixth, Wisconsin, sent three members from each party. In Illinois Lincoln's former law partner, John T. Stuart, had gone over to the Democrats and defeated the Administration candidate. Lincoln's working majority in the House of Representatives had dwindled from more than sixty to a mere eighteen. In analyzing the election *The New York Times* said: "The very qualities which have made Abraham Lincoln so well liked in private life . . . his kindheartedness, his concern for fair play, his placidity of temper—in a manner unfit him for the stern requirements of deadly war. . . . There is something . . . we miss—the high sacred vehemence, inspired by the consciousness of infinite interests at stake. . . ."

While Lincoln must have been distressed by the outcome of the elections of 1862 he was unwilling to concede irretrievable defeat. Almost immediately he plunged into the task of recouping his political losses in the same way that he had sought to recover from the early military disasters. In the succeeding months he weathered a Cabinet crisis as well as an increase in the temper of congressional criticism of his policies. Among the general public were severe if friendly critics like Horace Greeley whose arraignments were distracting and, at times, damaging. Add to this the public resentment against measures such as conscription and the military reverses such as Chancellorsville and one can see the manner in which, by the summer of 1863, Lincoln's difficulties were compounded. Happily the gloom was somewhat relieved by the news from Gettysburg and Vicksburg, but it was not sufficient to quiet the critics, particularly with the approach of the presidential election.

In and out of the administration ambitious men preened themselves for the Presidency. The Chase boom was launched by many friends of the Secretary of the Treasury, but Lincoln's refusal to accept his resignation from the Cabinet until Lincoln's nomination was secure had the effect of thwarting the movement. The disaffection of General Fremont was used by the General himself to launch a movement on his own behalf. But it did not get off the ground. The carefully constructed political organization that was Lincoln's handiwork now went into action. When the Republican party, temporarily renamed the Union party, met in Baltimore in June 1864 the anti-Lincoln forces were easily crushed, and every vote was recorded for Lincoln's renomination. There were some later efforts to reverse the decision of the nomination convention but they were, of course, unsuccessful.

It is said that Lincoln was pessimistic about his re-election. He was certainly disheartened by the move within his own party to ditch him after his renomination. The ill-counseled peace overtures of men like Greeley must have discouraged him. The denunciation of Lincoln's conduct of the war by the Democratic nominee, General McClellan, had a ring of authenticity that gave Lincoln some anxiety. Through it all he held firm, defensive where possible, and he illustrated the impracticability of his critics' suggestions by giving them the opportunity to attempt to carry them out and fail.

Events played into Lincoln's hands. In early September 1864 the fall of Atlanta gave him the military victory he needed. Then came the Republican victories in the elections in Maine and Vermont. Fremont withdrew from the race in late September. Gradually Republican ranks closed behind the President. Meanwhile Lincoln was not idle. He successfully urged the admission of Republican-dominated Nevada in time for its electoral votes to be counted. He ordered the furlough of many soldiers who wanted to go to their homes to vote, confident that the majority of them would vote for their Commander-in-chief. He had been responsible for the disintegration of the opposition within the party and for undermining the arguments and proposals advanced by the Democrats. The political victory of 1864 was therefore in a real sense a Lincoln victory.

Thus the entire career of Lincoln points up his sensitivity to political currents. He appreciated, as few Americans have, the political nature of the office of the Presidency. He never forgot this hard fact, and he always acted in a manner that demonstrated his full appreciation of the fact. Far from obscuring the importance of politics to the Presidency the war illustrated to Lincoln a new significance of the political role of the President. He therefore could see clearly the relationship between military and political victories and could function effectively in this context. Whether it was in dealing with a Cameron or a Seward or a Chase, President Lincoln knew full well the political implications of any contact he had with them. Likewise he fully appreciated the importance of the use of political spoils to strengthen the Administration and thus enhance the possibilities of military success. In his presidential career we can see and learn what it means to function in a context in which politics and war are major ingredients. Lincoln's lesson in this regard is valuable and timeless.

John Hope Franklin

39

THE EMANCIPATION PROCLAMATION

by Jay Monaghan

We all remember the Emancipation Proclamation as the document which initiated the freeing of the slaves and, with subsequent legislation, ended human bondage in the United States—important, surely, to all lovers of freedom. The problem which confronted Lincoln before he issued this proclamation had much in common with the problem which confronts every officeholder in government, even today: should an elected official be the servant of his constituents or should he lead them? Obviously he must please them if he is to continue in office, but should he always do what the voters want even when he knows it is not right?

Abraham Lincoln was faced with this dilemma many times and he never solved it more skillfully than he did when he issued the Emancipation Proclamation. Today we all admit slavery to be evil, but in Lincoln's time many people considered it good or tolerable or vital. Some, who disapproved of it in principle, did not favor abolition. Freeing the slaves meant confiscating millions of dollars' worth of property as well as wiping out the labor

231

supply in a large area of the country. To advocate such an economic revolution seemed dangerously radical.

Certainly Lincoln was not an abolitionist, although he disapproved of slavery. However he had been elected on a platform pledged only to restrict it to the states where it already existed and to prevent it from expanding into the territories. Lincoln admitted that this restriction might eventually let slavery wither and die. He hoped so. But in 1861 he was unwilling to do anything more radical than his party's platform recommended. Moreover when Lincoln became President he had no constitutional authority to free the slaves even if he wanted to. As soon as he was elected, however, some slave states seceded from the Union and the war began. This gave Lincoln new authority. As Commander-in-chief of the Army he was given powers which automatically permitted him to free the slaves in rebellious states. Northern abolitionists insisted that he do so at once, but Lincoln hesitated. He was confronted with the old question: was he the servant of the people or was he their leader? Certainly he had been elected to uphold the Union. Would abolition do that or would it divide the states irreparably? Preserving the Union was his primary consideration.

Lincoln worried first about retaining the border states in the Union. They permitted slavery but their citizens were also loyal to the Federal Government. Lincoln must hold this loyalty, for if he lost these states a restoration of the Union became much more difficult, perhaps impossible. Therefore when abolitionists came to the White House and told Lincoln that God would be on his side if he would only free the slaves, he told them that he certainly wanted God on his side but he must have Kentucky.

By 1862 the danger of losing Kentucky had passed and the demand for emancipation was more insistent, especially among liberal-minded people abroad. World opinion was as important then as now. Lincoln decided that he must use his war powers and abolish slavery. He discussed the question with his Cabinet. They argued against his doing so. The war was not progressing successfully, they said, and to emancipate the slaves now would be considered a "last *shriek* in retreat."

Lincoln waited all summer for a military victory. Finally, in September 1862, the Confederate army was checked at Antietam. It was not a signal triumph for the Union, but Robert E. Lee was forced to withdraw from Northern territory. Lincoln summoned his Cabinet members to a meeting. He did not tell them its purpose. He merely asked them to come to the White House at noon on September 22.

Lincoln's office was a small room on the second floor. In the center, almost filling the room, stood a baize-covered table. Around it the members of the Cabinet took their places. At Lincoln's right sat Secretary of State Seward. Beyond him, in the other chairs, sat Secretary of War Stanton and the Secretaries of the Navy, the Treasury, and the Interior, along with the Attorney General and Postmaster General. All waited for the President to speak. Lincoln held up a book. He said it was very funny and had been sent him by the author, Artemus Ward. The President opened the volume and began to read. The Cabinet members, all busy men, laughed dutifully at the amusing passages, and all probably wished to be back at their desks. Secretary of War Stanton even showed impatience, but Lincoln read to the chapter's end. Then he put the book down.

"Gentlemen," he said gravely, "I have, as you are aware, thought a great deal about the relation of this war to slavery. . . . I have thought all along that the time for acting on it might very probably come. I think the time has come now. . . . I have got you together to hear what I have written down."

Lincoln took a long document from his pocket and read the Emancipation Proclamation. He did not call for a vote on it. He knew that his Cabinet members were opposed and he saw no reason for starting an argument. Lincoln had made up his mind to act. Today he was the leader, not the servant, of his Cabinet.

This proclamation of September 22, 1862, did not free a single slave. Instead Lincoln merely warned the rebellious states that their slave property would be confiscated if they failed to rejoin the Union before January 1, 1863. Slavery was not to be disturbed in the states which had remained in the Union. Thus the Southerners, as well as proslavery Northerners, had over three months to consider emancipation, and during that time Lincoln might still withdraw from his position. In short he was acting like the servant of the people now, watching to see their reaction, but he was also ready to be the leader if they approved.

In November the elections went against Lincoln's party. Politicians said the voters disapproved of his proclamation. Once more Lincoln had to make a decision between doing what he was sure was right and what the voters wanted. He appealed to them again on December 1 in his annual message to Congress. He explained to Northerners that purchasing all the slaves would be cheaper than continuing the war. He told Southerners that he would let each state emancipate its own slaves in its own way, provided only that it be accomplished by 1900. Few, if any, of the present-day planters would still be alive at that distant date. With this explanation before the people, both North and South, Lincoln waited another month. "I am a slow walker," he said, "but I never walk back."

On New Year's Day, 1863, a big reception was held in the Executive Mansion. Handsomely dressed ladies in their hoop skirts, men in frock coats, officers in blue and gold uniforms filed into the White House to be greeted by President and Mrs. Lincoln. After the guests departed Lincoln walked upstairs to his office where the official Emancipation Proclamation awaited his signature. His arm ached from shaking hundreds of hands and he was not certain that the majority of the voters wanted him to emancipate the slaves, but he had made up his mind. He was a leader, not a servant, of his constituents. "If my hand trembles as I sign my name," he said, "people will say that I was afraid."

Lincoln's hand did not tremble, and he signed duplicates, one to be sold at a fair for the benefit of the Sanitary Commission. Days later a friendly politician called at the White House. He knew that the President enjoyed funny stories and asked if he had heard the one about his proclamation being discussed at a Negro camp meeting.

Lincoln said he had not, so the politician told this story in dialect. A Negro preacher informed his congregation that Lincoln's act was only a war measure. The President did not really care about the colored people. At the back of the assemblage a patriarch with white, kinky head rose to his feet. "Bredren," he shouted, and his voice had an earnestness which made everyone listen, "you don't know nothing what you talkin' about. Now you jest listen to me. Mas'r Linkum he everywhar. He know eberyting. He walk de earf like de Lord."

The politician looked at the President, expecting a laugh, but Abraham Lincoln did not even smile. Instead he got up from his chair and walked back and forth in the room. At last he said, "It is a momentous thing to be the instrument under Providence for the liberation of a race."

J. Monaghan

40

ABRAHAM LINCOLN: MASTER POLITICIAN

by Roy F. Nichols

It was summer of 1832 and out in Illinois, where woodland and prairie once met, electioneering was in the air. Abraham Lincoln, just turned twenty-three, was running for the legislature. He had announced, ". . . if elected . . . I shall be unremitting in my labors . . . if the good people in their wisdom . . . keep me in the background, I have been too familiar with disappointments to be very much chagrined." At such an early age he had gained humility and a disciplined capacity to suffer failure without loss of confidence, an invaluable lesson for a politician.

That same season of contest, in the first printed address issued to the constituents he hoped would be his, Lincoln demonstrated his understanding of the essence of real politics. "Every man is said to have his peculiar ambition. . . . I have no other so great as that of being truly esteemed of my fellow men, by rendering myself worthy of their esteem." Here is the revelation that he comprehended the great political axiom; the basic factor in politics is personal. He believed that success for a politician rested largely on reputation. He must be morally convincing.

by Roy F. Nichols

Lincoln, in an early appeal to voters, showed himself possessed of still a third talent—his capacity for clear, simple statements. He could define issues with a minimum of words and in language which could not be mistaken. "My politics," he reportedly said, "are short and sweet, like the old woman's dance. I am in favor of a national bank. I am in favor of the internal improvement system, and a high protective tariff." Few who heard this statement could doubt where Lincoln stood.

Such talent had come to him as the fruit of unusually precocious diligence, of which he once gave an intriguing description: "I remember . . . when a . . . child, I used to get irritated when anybody talked to me in a way I could not understand. . . . I can remember going to my little bedroom, after hearing the neighbors talk of an evening with my father, and spending no small part of the night . . . trying to make out what was the exact meaning of some of their, to me, dark sayings. I could not sleep, although I tried to, when I got on such a hunt for an idea until I had caught it; and when I thought I had got it, I was not satisfied until I had repeated it over and over; until I had put it in language plain enough, as I thought, for any boy I know to comprehend."

Following this start, his formal political primary education was acquired during four terms of laboratory work as a member of the Illinois legislature. Here he learned the intimate relation between government and the community in a democracy in legislating on land titles, surveys, roads, canals, bridges, banks, debts, and paper money. He became acquainted with the intricacies of personal politics and patronage.

His definition of his democratic responsibility was couched in these words: "I go for all sharing the privileges of the government, who assist in bearing its burthens. Consequently I go for admitting all whites to the right of suffrage, who pay taxes or bear arms, (by no means excluding females). . . . While acting as [the] representative [of my constituents], I shall be governed by their will, on all subjects upon which I have the means of knowing what their will is; and upon all others, I shall do what my own judgment teaches me will best advance their interests."

In pursuing his ambitions as a politico he held his reputation high. When a fellow politico insinuated that he knew things that would destroy Lincoln's prospects in an election the latter forthwith challenged him to reveal them to the public. "If I have . . . done anything . . . which if known, would subject me to a forfeiture of . . . confidence, he that knows of that thing, and conceals it, is a traitor to his country's interest." As a campaigner he had become so effective that a local Whig paper commented, "A girl might be born and become a mother before the [Democrats] will forget Mr. Lincoln." He was Honest Abe.

After his education in this political laboratory he took a postgraduate course in Washington as a one-term member of the House of Representatives. Then fate forced upon him a period of patient waiting. He realized, as any perceptive politician must, that he had to bide his time until just the right moment. It came in the 1850's when the slavery issue revived and he joined with its foes. His leadership was recognized, and twice he sought a seat in the Senate. Twice he failed, but by the tactics of his failures he established his political availability. It was this availability that made him the Republican presidential nominee in 1860 and which was, in large part, responsible for his election.

Thus in 1860-61 he had achieved one great success, but it was a success that might almost be classified as a failure. His election initiated a series of secessions which shattered the nation and brought it to the brink of fratricidal war. This conflict he could not avoid. He was too convinced of the value of American democracy, in a world then largely dedicated to monarchy and privilege, to surrender to the demands of the "slave power." So the war came and in the white heat of this conflict his powers as a master politician were refined and perfected.

This contest which he must direct was as much political as it was military, for the President must fight three opponents on a civilian front. He must combat the Copperhead Democrats, the

by Roy F. Nichols

Radical Republicans, and a shifting group of amoral operators out for the profits possible in the danger and confusion. These foes in his own household had to be conquered as well as the Confederacy. To do this he had to mobilize not only armies and a navy but a political party. Without the latter he could never acquire the means to lead the former.

In carrying out his responsibilities of leadership Lincoln labored under a severe handicap. He was at the head of a new, inexperienced, and untried party which, in fact, was but a league of uneasy factions, some of which appeared to the almost incompatible because of previous long-standing hostility. His first task, which nearly ended in the wreck of his Administration before it began, was the creation of a Cabinet. This he finally achieved in the form of a coalition which embraced Whigs and Free Soil Democrats, Eastern and Western factions, New England and border-state elements, as well as some ill-advised and probably unnecessary commitments made by his somewhat anxious agents at the nominating convention. That the structure held together any length of time was a tribute to his masterly political capacity.

Organizing a Cabinet was soon to appear as child's play compared to dealing with Congress. The outbreak of war made it necessary to call a special session and to work occasionally within sound of enemy guns and sometimes with the Confederate flag in sight. Here his party proved an uncertain asset. Within its ranks was a zealous group determined to destroy slavery and the political power of the South. Ben Wade, Zach Chandler, Thad Stevens, Charles Sumner, and certain of their associates were so dramatic in their fanaticism that they were called Jacobins, reminiscent of the most violent of the French revolutionaries.

These Radicals demanded that the President proclaim the war a conflict to abolish slavery. Lincoln, on his part, had already salvaged four of the slave states and part of Virginia; he hoped to bring the rest back to their allegiance on a plea to their love of the old Union and its paramount significance in the cause of democracy. So he announced to the world that it was a war to save the Union, to salvage the democratic experiment.

To achieve this end he not only must discover military leaders adequate to combat the cream of West Point now in gray uniforms but had to mobilize a congressional coalition of moderate Republicans and War Democrats, against Jacobins and Copperheads on their flanks. This he did by enlisting Democrats like Edwin M. Stanton, whom he made Secretary of War, and certain Democratic generals, like George B. McClellan.

His warfare with the Jacobins particularly sharpened his political skill. These radicals believed that the Secretary of the Treasury, Salmon P. Chase, was better fitted to be President than Lincoln, and they were particularly resentful of the influence of William A. Seward, the Secretary of State. Lincoln therefore must engage in a series of political maneuvers against these "Republicans," which, to their great chagrin, bested them in most instances and left him generally master of the situation. For nearly four years he kept both Chase and Seward.

These two secretaries, together with Stanton and the President himself, made a political administration and high military and diplomatic command which organized conquering armies, and a superior navy and commanded the respect, if not the affection, of European chancellories and world opinion. No foreign power recognized the Confederacy. Slavery was abolished under circumstances most advantageous to the struggle to preserve the Union. The Confederacy was first blockaded and then conquered by the giant nutcracker operation of Grant and Sherman.

In all this turmoil the political master stroke was Lincoln's reelection in wartime. The way was difficult. He had first to checkmate an attempt by the Jacobins to nominate Chase for his place, and then to defeat the man most popular with the Army, General George B. McClellan, whom the Democrats nominated to oppose him. Lincoln's tactics included first the creation of a series of Union Leagues and then the replacement of the Republican party by a new organization, the Union party. He and a uniquely loyal

Southern Democrat, Andrew Johnson of Tennessee, headed its ticket. With the aid of Sherman's victory at Atlanta and the soldier vote, cleverly organized, Lincoln and Johnson were triumphant. Lincoln turned finally to reconstruction, but the assassin's bullet prevented him from putting his superb powers to this great test.

Lincoln's greatest political skill was his power of utterance. His early promise came to fulfillment. He was the man who in these trying years proclaimed his faith in a government "which gave promise that in due time the weights would be lifted from the shoulders of all men, and that all should have an equal chance." He was likewise the leader who had defined the war as "essentially a people's contest . . . for maintaining in the world that form and substance of government whose leading object is to elevate the condition of men." He was the spokesman who believed that the "nation, conceived in Liberty, and dedicated to the proposition that all men are created equal . . . [was to have] a new birth of freedom. . . ." And finally the President was the prophet who announced that "With malice toward none; with charity for all; . . . [he was prepared] to bind up the nation's wounds; . . . [and] to do all which . . . [was needed to] achieve and cherish a just, and a lasting peace, among ourselves, and with all nations."

By words such as these he showed himself to be complete master of the political arts. For the supreme political art is the capacity to speak the people's thoughts in such terms that they can recognize them as theirs. Such master politicians truly belong to the ages.

241

41

LINCOLN: COMMANDER-IN-CHIEF

by Ulysses S. Grant, III

After taking the oath of office as President on March 4, 1861, Lincoln was to find that probably the most onerous duty he had undertaken was that prescribed by Section 2 of Article II of the Constitution; namely: "The President shall be Commander-in-chief of the Army and Navy of the United States." Practically self-educated, experienced only as a lawyer, politician, and member of Congress for one term, he had no knowledge whatever of the theory of war. He had no military experience except the short period of duty as captain of a militia company and as a private in the Black Hawk campaign. Nevertheless his natural sagacity, good common sense, and a certain innate ability to see any problem as a whole and to pick the crux of every situation made of him a better strategist in the varying crises of the Civil War than many of his generals.

Certainly the wise men who drafted our Constitution in Philadelphia in 1787 had no idea or intention that the President should assume personal command of either the Army or the Navy. Indeed it was but a recognition of the fact that in war all the power

and resources of the nation—military, naval, political, and economic—must be directed in unison for the winning of the war.

Possibly President Lincoln's major claim to greatness is the consummate skill with which he was able to direct and guide the
resources and patriotic efforts of the North. In spite of personally
ambitious and jealous generals, political opposition, economic and
legal problems of the most serious kind, he proved equal to the
task. He was able to drive the often balky and sometimes hostile
members of the team upon which he had to depend to achieve
the final victory.

Some of President Lincoln's generals complained that he inter-
fered with them and intervened in their operations unduly and to
their embarrassment. Careful study of these complaints shows
they were not justified. His intervention in each case was necessary and a performance of the function for command which the
Constitution had imposed upon him. Major General George B.
McClellan was certainly the foremost complainer, and perhaps
with the least justification.

Lincoln was at a disadvantage compared to the Confederate
President. He had no personal acquaintance with or knowledge of
the officers of the Army, and moreover had to choose his generals
from among men in the regular establishment who had achieved
relative rank, or from political leaders. Jefferson Davis, having
met many of his officers in the war with Mexico and having been
Secretary of War, possessed this knowledge to a great extent.
Being engaged in organizing a new army for a newly established
government he had more freedom to make selections, according
to his personal judgment of the fitness of each, without equal risk
of creating jealousies and internal friction. However President
Lincoln's judgment of men by their actions and his fairness and
ability to estimate the personal equation of each with experience
made up for this deficiency as time went on.

When the bombardment of Fort Sumter forced on him a shooting war General Winfield Scott, the old hero of the Mexican War,
was commanding general of the Army and naturally the Presi-

dent's chief military advisor. Prevented by age, overweight, and other physical afflictions from taking the field in person, he offered command of the field army to Robert E. Lee. The latter refused it after mature consideration, feeling he could not bring himself to take up arms against his own neighbors and state. In the meantime the President with admirable decision and energy took the military measures that were possible: on April 15 he called out seventy-five thousand militia under the authority of an old law of 1795 and convoked a special session of Congress for July 4. On April 19, by proclamation, he declared a blockade of the Southern ports, a strategic step of great importance. For some days Washington was isolated from the rest of the country by the cutting of both the railroad and telegraph. However the newly raised troops began seeping into the capital by April 25, and the little stream rapidly grew into a flood. On May 14 Major Irvin McDowell, who had been mustering and inspecting the troops as they arrived in Washington, was promoted to brigadier general and placed in command of the new Department of North Eastern Virginia. General Scott had said, with much wisdom, ". . . the great danger now pressing upon us—is the impatience of our patriotic and loyal Union friends. They will urge instant and vigorous action regardless, I fear, of consequences. . . ."

Indeed the popular demand "On to Richmond" was so universal and irresistible that McDowell led his raw levies to attack the Confederate troops near Manassas. Confederate General Joseph E. Johnston's skill in evading General Robert Patterson in the Shenandoah Valley and joining General Beauregard at Manassas resulted in the rout of McDowell's army, though the Confederate force itself was too shaken to exploit the success. General Mc-Clellan, who had invaded what is now West Virginia with considerable success, was accordingly brought to Washington and placed in command of what was soon to become the great Army of the Potomac. Young, handsome, energetic, intelligent, and ingenious in proposing plans, with the success in western Virginia reputedly to his credit, he soon became "Young Napoleon" to the press and populace and proved most efficient and hard-working in organizing and training the volunteer army under his command. Soon McClellan was irritated by having to deal through General Scott, and was elated when the latter's request for retirement was granted and he was promoted to the position of commander-in-chief. McClellan evolved no general strategic plan for winning the war, however, and concentrated his own efforts on the training and reviewing of the Army of the Potomac. He gave to the Army commanders in other theaters of war but occasional and intermittent guidance.

The President, properly intent upon winning the war, kept urging his young general, with the tact and consideration of which he was such a master, to lead his great army against the enemy, to take some action. McClellan's egotism grew, and, as one writer phrased it, he seemed to think himself "a superman with a mission" whose "inflated self-esteem required that he should not be crossed or even questioned." Finally the country's and the President's patience was exhausted. On January 31, 1862, the latter exercised his prerogative as over-all Commander-in-chief and issued the President's Special War Order No. 1, directing a forward movement on or before February 22. McClellan still did not move; he disapproved of the plans the President kindly suggested for his consideration, and finally secured approval of his own plan, which resulted in the Peninsular Campaign, April to August 1862.

So, "Little Mac" blamed the President's action for his own failure to defeat Lee, who had replaced the wounded Joe Johnston, and to take Richmond. The Army of the Potomac was ordered back to Washington, and arriving just after Pope's defeat at the second battle of Bull Run, McClellan was put in command of Pope's beaten troops as Lee marched north through the Shenandoah Valley. Here his popularity with the soldiers and his organizing skill did bring order out of chaos and enabled him to lead the reconstituted Army of the Potomac to meet Lee at Antietam and win an indecisive victory, failing because of his innate lack of enterprise and will to destroy the enemy.

Upon McClellan's taking the field for the Peninsular Campaign he was relieved as commander-in-chief by presidential order, so that from then until the arrival of General Henry W. Halleck from the West, Lincoln, with Stanton's assistance, actually acted as the high command. As commander-in-chief of the Army General Halleck lacked the stamina and self-confidence to make crucial decisions, but did give the President advice that was replete with military learning and often sound, and as an administrator his services were necessary. However it cannot be said that any over-all strategic plan for achieving final victory was devised by him or by Lincoln. Other generals were tried in command of the Army of the Potomac, only to meet defeat. With all his commanders, East and West, Lincoln exercised the same patience and consideration, made sensible suggestions as to stragetic objectives, and urged energetic action. One only, General Grant, in the Western theater, was inspired by the same spirit and energy, and in spite of attacks on his character by the jealous and malicious, the President supported him saying, "I can't spare this man, he fights."

Finally Congress passed an act reviving the rank of lieutenant general, properly leaving to the President the choice of the general who should be promoted to this grade and given command of all the armies. However it was generally recognized that the new position was intended for General Grant, who had won the inspiring victories of Donelson and Shiloh in 1862, and had captured Vicksburg, the "Gibraltar of the Confederacy," after a brilliant campaign. By this victory he sealed the fate of secession, cutting the Confederacy off from the supplies west of the Mississippi in 1863. He had more recently released the Union Army besieged in Chattanooga and there inflicted a disastrous defeat on Bragg's Army of Tennessee. The President concurred and called General Grant to Washington to receive his new commission.

The President and General Grant had never met before the latter was handed his commission as lieutenant general, but through the years Grant had earned Lincoln's approval and backing by the skill and energy with which he had pushed his operations and by his readiness to assume responsibility. Mutual confidence and intimacy of sorts were established between the two almost immediately. The President slowly realized that he had been relieved of his heavy burden as Commander-in-chief, and could say, "Grant is the first General I have had." Of course Lincoln's interest and constant following of the operations in the field never ceased, and although not bothered with military decisions he was kept constantly informed of what was happening and of changes in the situation and plans.

The new commanding general now made an over-all strategic plan, which he knew from their conversations would have the President's concurrence, and issued his orders accordingly for the co-ordinated action of all the armies in different theaters. In spite of the skill of the enemy and the failure of many local commanders to execute their parts promptly and effectively, it won the war. It took longer and involved heavier losses than had been hoped; but on April 9, 1865, the greatest of the Confederate generals, Robert E. Lee, surrendered his army at Appomattox. The terms of surrender were so magnanimous and considerate that not only was the country ultimately reunited politically but real unity was achieved. The sons of the men who fought on both sides have since fought shoulder to shoulder in four foreign wars, some of the Confederate veterans themselves having worn the reunited country's uniform in the war with Spain.

42

GETTYSBURG AND THE FEW
APPROPRIATE REMARKS

by Norman Corwin

The Gettysburg Address is so familiar to so many people that one feels almost apologetic in bringing it up again. Yet it is like a gram of radium whose energy is out of all proportion to its size and whose radiations are steady and persistent.

Ten sentences, that's all. But they're a national treasure and one of the monuments of world history. The speech, like Abraham Lincoln himself, long ago passed beyond the need for praise; now it remains only to be marveled at, enjoyed for its beauty, and cherished for its substance.

Still, new things are always being discovered about it, and perhaps this is one: the address and the events surrounding it make an almost perfect small-scale model of Lincoln and his times. If, by some unfortunate mandate, it became necessary for us to reduce volumes to paragraphs and murals to the size of postage stamps, we could learn enough from just the Gettysburg episode in Lincoln's career to understand a great deal about the man, about his era, his cause and his country.

We would learn not only the obvious things—that Lincoln had a novel cast of mind, that he was humane, that he had a deep sense of the sanctity of life together with a compassion for those in travail, and a touching respect for the honored dead. We would also learn that Lincoln was modest, hard-working, and patient; that he fussed about his writing; that he was gracious to a point of gallantry; that he tended to run down his own accomplishments, and had a generally pessimistic view about the chances of anything he did amounting to much or shaking the world; that Americans were capable of being touched by his words, and were in every way worthy of them; that there were present in the land men of such ill will and hostility that they were violently offended by the Gettysburg Address; and that there were also men of clear vision who within twenty-four hours of the occasion reached the same estimate of the greatness of the speech that we all concur in some ninety-seven years later.

Now you may ask how Lincoln's modesty was involved. In the first place the program dedicating the national soldiers' cemetery at Gettysburg was not built around the President at all. He was invited as an afterthought. The main part of the program had been arranged for almost two months before Lincoln was asked to make "a few appropriate remarks" toward the end of the exercise. The feature of the program was to be an oration by Edward Everett, a polished speaker who had rounded off his style and manner as United States Senator, governor of Massachusetts, and president of Harvard. Obviously the man for the job.

A vain Chief Executive and Commander of the Armed Forces might have felt slighted to be invited late, to find himself journeying to Gettysburg to sit on a platform for hours, listening to the speaker of the day and the Baltimore Glee Club, only to get up at the close and make a few appropriate remarks to an audience that by this time was tired of standing. But not Lincoln. He accepted and went. He worked hard on his few remarks. The first drafts were written in Washington, and these and others were made without the help of a ghost writer. And he kept revising the speech right up to the moment he delivered it. In fact he made changes after he got to his feet.

Notwithstanding all the work he had put into those ten sentences he was not satisfied. Just after he finished making the speech he told a friend that it wouldn't come off cleanly—called it a flat failure and said he was sure people were disappointed by it. Here Lincoln was true to his pattern. Hadn't he said during a campaign for the Senate that the job was too big for him? Hadn't he prophesied that he would never be President. Hadn't he announced following his defeat for the senatorship that he would now sink out of view and be forgotten? In the Gettysburg Address itself he did it again—made a wrong prophecy about himself. "The world," he said, "will little note, nor long remember, what we say here."

There were those who were only too happy to agree with him. A Pennsylvania paper dismissed his address as a series of "silly remarks" and hoped that "for the credit of the nation, the veil of oblivion shall be dropped over them, and that they be no more repeated or thought of."

The Chicago *Times* said Lincoln had "foully traduced the motives of the men slain at Gettysburg," and was deeply mortified in behalf of the country: "The cheek of every American must tingle with shame as he reads the silly, flat, and dish-watery utterances of the man who has to be pointed out to intelligent foreigners as the President of the United States."

We had that type of journalism then as now. But others took a quite opposite view. There were those who overnight were able to size up Lincoln's few remarks as being appropriate for, and worthy of, the attention of posterity. A reporter for the Chicago *Tribune* wired back: "The remarks of Lincoln will live among the annals of man." The Cincinnati *Gazette* found the speech "perfect in every respect"; the Springfield (Massachusetts) *Republican* commended it as "worthy of study as a model speech."

The Lincoln legend has been long on his craggy humor, his sufferings and melancholy, his lofty sentiment, his kindliness, and many other attributes, but less often is there recalled his charm and graciousness. Here again the Gettysburg occasion gives us a glowing example. Following the exercises at the cemetery, Everett, whose two-hour address had been turned out with considerable thought, wrote to Lincoln:

"I should be glad if I could flatter myself that I came as near the central idea of the occasion in two hours as you did in two minutes."

What did Lincoln reply to this? What would *you* have replied to such a compliment from a speaker with whom you had shared a program? Listen now to the sheer genius of Lincoln's brief answer, as beautiful an example of tact and the return of a good word as there exists in the language:

> In our respective parts yesterday, you could not have been excused to make a short address, nor I a long one. I am pleased to know that, in your judgment, the little I did say was not entirely a failure.

So far from a failure was the little Lincoln did say that we continue to read and speak it across the decades, enshrining it with familiarity, yet always learning from it, and doing our best, most of the time, to live up to it.

Norman Corwin

43

PRESIDENT LINCOLN AND WEAPONS POLICY

by Robert V. Bruce

"What would you do in my position?" Abraham Lincoln asked an advocate of softer measures in the desperate and bloody mid-summer of 1862. "Would you drop the war where it is? Or, would you prosecute it in future with elder-stalk squirts, charged with rose water? Would you deal lighter blows rather than heavier ones? Would you give up the contest, leaving any available means unapplied." Lincoln left no doubt of his own answer: "I shall do *all* I can to save the government."

From the beginning Lincoln had been applying means both subtle and stern. Of the latter type was one implied by his mockery of "elder-stalk squirts charged with rose water": the search for more effective weapons (which in the long run would be more sparing). In the decisive years from Sumter to Gettysburg, Abraham Lincoln stood in his own person as the Union's closest approach to a weapons research and development agency.

One motive in this was his long-standing personal interest in science and technology, wherein Lincoln shared the spirit of his nation and his times as he did in so much else. He had worked

as a surveyor, had studied mathematics for love of it, had kept up
with the latest developments in science, had given a lecture on
"Discoveries and Inventions," had even taken out a patent of his
own. As a successful lawyer, he had handled many patent cases
for others, and had done much work for the Illinois Central Railroad, thereby coming to know both the workings of machines and
their impact on human affairs. His legal training had also developed and refined the inherent lucidity, penetration and power of
his mind.

Another motive, somewhat akin to the first, was his need for
relaxation. The many weapons trials conducted before Lincoln at
the Washington Arsenal or the Washington Navy Yard were
dubbed "champagne experiments" by impatient ordnance functionaries. Whoever coined the phrase spoke more aptly than he
knew. The outings did indeed serve the careworn President as a
tonic and stimulant. In the absorbing novelty of some warlike
device, in the sharpening of logic and wit as he sought to master
its intricacies and expose its flaws, in the wind, air, sun, and sound
of the proving grounds, in the sober, precise talk of technical experts, Lincoln found refreshment of mind and renewed steadiness
for the grinding days ahead.

But primarily Lincoln shouldered his fateful responsibility for
weapons development because it promised to shorten the war and
because no one else in the government would take the job.

The job was, in fact, belligerently declined by its logical claimant, Brigadier General James W. Ripley, a stiff-necked, irascible
veteran of forty-six years in the regular army, who served as Chief
of Ordnance from April 1861, to September 1863. Though hard-
working and devoted to duty, he resolved at the start to oppose
the introduction of any new weapons during the Civil War, and
he never weakened in his stated purpose. Ripley's attitude did
not arise solely from age and inborn conservatism. He believed,
like many another, that the war would be short; and his leading
role in the adoption and production of the muzzle-loading Springfield rifle during the 1850s had deeply impressed him with the

time, money and output lost in weapons changes. He wanted to be first with the most, not last with the best. The reasoning was plausible, but its premise turned out to be false.

Lincoln feared as much almost from the beginning. After a few months he tried to replace Ripley. But he could find no one willing, qualified, and available to take the job, and so he had to go on doing what he could personally to counterbalance Ripley's fierce conservatism. The struggle was one of the most remarkable campaigns of the Civil War, nonetheless so for being waged largely along the line of Seventeenth Street in Washington.

Lincoln's earliest ventures in the making of ordnance policy happened to be in procurement and distribution. His prodding hastened the purchase of foreign arms, carried by more than half the Union regiments that went into battle before the fall of 1862. He also saw to it that arms went to the hard-pressed Unionists of his native Kentucky, the loss of which he felt would be fatal to the Union cause. Both these moves paid off handsomely. But he and General Ripley clashed most often in the matter of new weapons.

During the summer and fall of 1861 Lincoln developed his role. Hundreds of inventors wrote to him because of his reputation for kindliness and accessibility, and because they either did not know the proper agency to address or else had been rebuffed by it. Lincoln personally screened scores of such proposals and, in the case of those he deemed promising, arranged "champagne experiments" by the unwilling Army Ordnance Department or the less overworked and more sympathetic Navy Ordnance Bureau. He spent much time, for example, in testing a new elevating and traversing mechanism for heavy guns, in watching trials of breech-loading and rifled cannon, even in cranking a centrifugal gun, one of the wilder notions of the time. A Cabinet meeting was enlivened by an inventor who demonstrated the model of a breech-loading cannon on the table. Early that summer Lincoln gave the push which put Professor Lowe's reconnaissance balloons into useful service. Later he gave a similar push to John Ericsson's plans for the *Monitor*. In October he tried out a new bullet intended to give the Union's smoothbore muskets the effectiveness of the rifles which had just done deadly service for the Confederates at Ball's Bluff. Most of all Lincoln became an active tester and partisan of the breech-loading rifles which were just then becoming dependable and effective.

By then Lincoln had found an expert on whom he could rely for technical guidance: Captain John A. Dahlgren, the wiry, ambitious, brilliant chief of the Navy Ordnance Bureau. In one case or another Lincoln turned to General Totten of the Engineer Corps or Joseph Henry of the Smithsonian Institution, but in the end he always came back to Dahlgren.

As the summer and fall slipped by, Lincoln grew more impatient and peremptory. In September he took it upon himself to purchase twenty small breech-loading cannon, the so-called "Ellsworth guns," for trial in service. This order turned out to be the largest and, except for one imported Whitworth, the only Federal purchase of breech-loading cannon during the war; for the little Ellsworth guns fell into enemy hands before they could prove their value—if any.

Lincoln made other purchases of new weapons, but the most epochal were of machine guns and breech-loading rifles. In October and December 1861 he bought sixty "coffee mill" machine guns, the first such transaction known to history. These had only moderate success in battle. Nevertheless the ice was broken, and the Gatling gun probably found quicker acceptance as a result.

In October 1861 Lincoln gave the war's largest order for breech-loading rifles: twenty-five thousand of the Marsh single-shot model. Ripley's brilliant bureaucratic footwork kept the order from being filled. But in December 1861 Lincoln ordered ten thousand Spencer repeaters, which not only saw important action but also opened a way for the breechloader in the armies of all the world.

That month brought the strain of the *Trent* crisis. In this near collision with Great Britain, Lincoln's decision to sheer off must have been strongly reinforced by his knowledge of ordnance. Sitting in on a "Military Armament Board" appointed by General McClellan, Lincoln had learned of the uselessness of the Union's smoothbore coastal guns against British ironclads. Dahlgren and Secretary Seward had further impressed Lincoln with the Union's dependence on British India for niter, a principal ingredient of gunpowder. It is not surprising that Lincoln chose to yield the point at issue.

A few months earlier, a plan had been conceived to mount siege mortars on small craft for use against river forts. Lincoln had taken up the idea enthusiastically with special thought for the forthcoming Tennessee River campaign. But the indifference of field commanders and the Navy's preemption of mortars left the mortar boat flotilla unfinished. Lincoln found this out early in January 1862. "Now," he said grimly, "I am going to devote a part of every day to these mortars and I won't leave off until it fairly rains bombs." Day after day for weeks, Lincoln followed every detail of production, shipment, and mounting. The boats missed out on the Tennessee campaign, but did good service at Island Number Ten in April.

During 1862 and 1863 attempts were made to set up independent agencies for research and development, but the fulfillment of that idea had to wait for World War II. Lincoln therefore kept on listening to inventors and watching trials. He was less inclined, however, to make actual purchases of new weapons on his own responsibility, probably wanting to see how his earlier projects worked out in battle. Except for the breechloaders, field indifference and bureaucratic foot-dragging made the reports disappointing. As the end came visibly nearer, Lincoln concentrated on weapons that could be put into production quickly if adopted: flame throwers, incendiary shells, a new gunpowder not dependent on British niter, new types of ammunition for small arms and artillery. After the Union victories of 1863, Lincoln confined himself to winding up the weapons projects already under way.

by Robert V. Bruce

Early in 1865, with victory being hastened on more than one front by the breechloaders Lincoln had backed, a *Scientific American* reporter interviewed the President. "Himself an inventor and patentee," wrote the correspondent, "he readily discerns the intrinsic value of all good inventions, not only to the public service, but also in their application to the industrial arts generally, and he will do all in his power to encourage and to promote the progress of these arts, by sanctioning all wise legislation in behalf of inventors." Lincoln, in short, foresaw the contributions peaceful technology would make in future years to the realization of his long-cherished dream: "the progressive improvement in the condition of all men everywhere."

And though he did not live to share in that peaceful work, his part in sharpening the tools of war may have served to advance it. If, as seems presently possible, the very power of weapons enforces a lasting peace among nations, then Abraham Lincoln will have helped, in more ways than he knew, to keep alive the last best hope of earth.

Robert V. Bruce

44

LINCOLN AND THE NAVY

by Joseph T. Durkin, S.J.

Lincoln once remarked to Gideon Welles, his Secretary of the Navy, "I know but little about ships." This was true, but he possessed a compensating virtue. In any field he was quick to learn. He had a keen sense for a good thing, and the newness of an idea did not scare him away from it. Consequently he accepted at once a naval strategy which, though not essentially original, had never been applied as thoroughly before. The principle was that the naval arm was to be used not only as an independent striking force but chiefly as an aid to the ground troops. The Navy was to be employed to win victories not only on the water but, more often, on land.

This would be accomplished in two ways: tactically, as at Forts Henry and Donelson, where the Navy hammered the enemy positions from one direction while the Army closed in from the other. And logistically, as demonstrated in nearly all the campaigns of the West.

Poring over the maps of the states that bordered both shores of the Mississippi, the President perceived two basic features of the terrain. The area was vast. And it lacked suitable wagon roads and railroads. From these two facts there followed a highly important military corollary: the supply line of an army invading the area would be dangerously long.

The Army of the West could not "live off the country." The region was not sufficiently fertile in crops and cattle, and the army's demands were too great. Nor could the army, as it advanced southward, be adequately supplied by land transport.

To provision an army of 50,000 men, at two days' march from its base, required 400 wagons. Another 400 vehicles were needed to carry the fodder for the 8000 horses that such an army would ordinarily include. About 4800 mules or draught horses pulled these wagons. To supply the fodder for these animals 180 more wagons had to be employed, with over a thousand more mules or horses to move them. As the army lengthened its lines of communications the required number of wagons and animals greatly increased.

There was a further difficulty. The roads in the Western theater of war were mostly abominably poor. Moreover a long caravan of lumbering wagons had to be protected by troops, preferably cavalry. This constituted another drain on the army's manpower. Maintenance, repair, and veterinary problems would be a worry for the generals.

It must be stressed that if the army's supply line was seriously hampered the army was shackled. The condition of fifty thousand men would be that of the population of a city the size of Hartford cut off from its vital services.

It might be asked, could not the supply service have used the railroads? But the difficulties of rail transport in a Western combat area in the Civil War were immense. The "iron roads" could be torn up by the enemy. Railroad bridges could be blown up. Even when the railroads were in operation they were then highly inefficient for carrying freight. The Confederate commanders in the West found that out.

What, then, was the only effective means of supplying the land forces of Grant and Sherman as they pushed southward? In retrospect the answer is obvious. But it took a mind like Lincoln's to perceive that obvious answer at the time.

He saw at once that the army's lines of supply must be based on the great rivers. A river was a protected and smooth highway that could keep pace with an army in motion. A river could carry the army's supplies in ships, with less expense of men, vehicles, and time. Only two conditions must be met: the streams must be closed to the enemy, and the army must not move too far from the streams. The first condition the Union Navy took care of. The second condition was easily made a part of the strategy of the army's commanders.

Just as truly as an army travels on its stomach the Army in the West traveled on its ships. The Navy took an essential part in all the land movements of the Federals in the Mississippi area. At Vicksburg the services of the Federal Navy were of the utmost importance. There Admiral Porter so disposed his ships that Grant could have a base below Vicksburg. From there the General's supplies could reach him by river, and by the western shore, and from there he could communicate with General Banks below. There was another depot at Haynes' Bluff, where his food and reinforcements could come directly from the North. Grant paid earnest tribute to the naval support at Vicksburg. "The Navy," he said, "was all it could be during the entire campaign. Without its assistance the campaign could not have been successfully made with twice the number of men engaged."

Equally important was the Navy's function in transporting large bodies of troops. Grant's forces were ferried from the west to the east shore of the Mississippi at the beginning of the crucial phase of the Vicksburg campaign. Again and again the Army was at the right spot at the right time because the Navy had put the Army there. The mobility of the land forces would have been cut by at least one half if they had had to depend on land transport.

The utilization of such naval potential was most clearly called for. On what grounds, then, is Lincoln to be praised for recognizing a necessity that the facts practically shouted into his ears? The reply is that not always has a civilian leader been so ready to learn from his generals and to subordinate his thinking to their own. It was the greatest of Lincoln's field commanders who taught him this lesson about the Navy. A mark of Lincoln's greatness is that he caught on at once and co-operated with Grant to the limit.

There are a few other aspects of the story of Lincoln and the Union Navy. In dealing with naval affairs the President displayed, in three directions, an attitude that was completely modern.

For instance he had a keen appreciation of the value, for the naval service, of efficient machinery. When he heard that the Confederate ironclad *Virginia* (previously called the *Merrimac*) had sunk the Union frigates in Hampton Roads his first questions were about her tonnage, gun power, armor, and engines. Jefferson Davis would never have thought of those things. It is evident that Lincoln thought in terms of technics, and in doing so showed himself to be a man of the new industrialized and scientific America.

Allied to this viewpoint was Lincoln's belief that a navy was, properly, a professional service to be officered by professionals. His idea of a naval officer was, again, a scientific one. The naval officer must of course be a fighting man. But, Lincoln thought, he must also be a technician and an engineer. This admirable professionalization of the service was displayed in men like Admiral Dahlgren, the ordnance expert, in Porter, and in Benjamin Isherwood, the Navy's engineer-in-chief.

Finally, as Lincoln directed the Union Navy in a broadened concept of amphibious warfare, so by his famous blockade of Southern ports he anticipated the modern method of total war. He was one of the first of the nineteenth-century political leaders to think of war on the plane of economics. He saw that the South would be more surely defeated by halting her sea-borne commerce than by halting her armies.

So Lincoln, who by his own admission did not know much

about ships, used his common sense to learn a great deal about their use from men who did know. He was not a jack-of-all-trades but he had the knack of listening to an expert and catching the core of his argument. It was this facility that led him to sound, daring, and imaginative thinking about the deployment of the American Navy in the war to keep America united.

Joseph T. Durkin, S.J.

"WORK, WORK, WORK, IS THE MAIN THING."

45

WHITE HOUSE ROUTINE UNDER LINCOLN

by Lloyd A. Dunlap

His lank figure was sometimes seen in the gray Washington dawn, walking alone, seeking a newsboy. For Abraham Lincoln slept lightly and rose early. His day began, as it ended, with work and the search for an answer—how was it with the divided nation he led?

By eight o'clock he had been working one or two hours. Breakfast was served at this hour—for Lincoln, a cup of coffee and an egg. Sometimes he refused even this, and Mrs. Lincoln often invited old friends to make sure that he would appear at the table.

After breakfast he walked to the War Department office to read the telegrams which had come in during the night. Special copies were set aside for him (sometimes, it was rumored, certain messages were withheld), and the worried Lincoln was here early and late, perhaps occasionally the night through. One of his messages was written at four A.M. A talk with General Henry W. Halleck, Chief of Staff, ended his morning business here.

By nine o'clock Lincoln was in his second-floor office in the East Wing of the White House. In the words of an observer, "the furniture was not exactly what it should be." On the walls were framed maps, an old engraving of Andrew Jackson, and a photograph of John Bright, the English liberal leader. In the room were two plain sofas, a fireplace with a marble mantel, a large table for Cabinet meetings, a smaller table where Lincoln wrote, a few straight-backed chairs, and a tall pigeonhole desk for filing. A visitor noted that one opening was labelled "W & W." Lincoln explained: "That's Weed and Wood. Thurlow and Fernandy." Then the President added, "That's a pair of 'em," thinking of his trials with these New York politicians.

The office staff consisted of John G. Nicolay, the secretary, and John Hay, his assistant. A third secretary was added later. Two doormen brought in visitors' cards, carried messages, and tried to control the crowds which daily swarmed through the halls. In 1864 a few plain-clothes men were detailed to the White House as a security measure.

From nine to ten Lincoln went over his mail, previously sorted and classified as personal or political. Nicolay and Hay had summarized the contents of each document. Some letters Lincoln kept to answer himself; he directed the reply he wished made to others; many were routed to the departments. To these he sometimes added an endorsement. Occasionally these had a distinct Lincoln flavor: "Greel[e]y, Opdycke, Field & Wadsworth, in favor of having the two big puddings on the same side of the board," or, "Submitted to Mars and Neptune."

The secretaries answered some letters in his name, beginning them, "The President directs," and then signing the reply they were instructed to make. On occasion Lincoln drafted letters which were signed by Nicolay or a Cabinet member.

He personally composed almost all of the letters which bore his signature. He wrote slowly and carefully, sometimes pronouncing words or sentences aloud before writing them. Important letters and documents were revised and edited with care. Draft copies were usually retained for the files, but occasionally he took the time to prepare a file copy in his own handwriting.

264

Only the most interesting and important letters came to his attention. When Judge David Davis, an old friend, protested that Nicolay withheld letters from the President, the secretary replied, with Lincoln's approval: "Of a hundred miscellaneous letters, there will be a large proportion which are obviously of no interest or importance. These the President would not read if he could." There were times when Lincoln refused to read extremely long letters or those which he understood were ill-tempered in tone. Abusive and threatening letters were discarded.

At ten o'clock the doors were opened to visitors, and Lincoln's "public opinion baths," as he called these visits, began. People came in a steady stream, everybody wanting something—an office, a favor, sometimes a life. Many requests were beyond his power to grant, and when he contracted a mild form of smallpox he remarked wryly that at last he "had something he could give to everybody."

His usual greeting was simply, "How do you do?" or, "Well, friend, what can I do for you?" He received strangers with kindness, an innate casual dignity, and uniform courtesy. His sense of humor was generally present, and disliking to give an outright no he sometimes used his anecdotes to point out the impossible nature of a request.

When he could act he sent short, decisive notes: "Mr. Secretary, please see and hear this man." Or, "The lady—bearer of this—says she has two sons who want to work. Set them at it, if possible. Wanting to work is so rare a merit, that it should be encouraged."

Lincoln at first refused to limit visiting hours, and three quarters of his time, his secretaries estimated, was taken up by people. These young men complained that the President "would never take the necessary measures to defend himself," and that he "disliked anything which kept people from him who wanted to see him." Lincoln recognized soon that some restrictions were necessary and limited visiting hours from ten to three. Later they were further shortened from ten to one.

Leaning forward, his long legs crossed, Lincoln listened to the people and made their cares his own. A reporter described him during one of these visits: "Care and anxiety have furrowed his rather homely features, yet occasionally he is 'reminded of an anecdote,' and good-humored glances beam from his clear, gray eyes, while his ringing laugh shows that he is not 'used up' yet. The simple and natural manner in which he delivers his thoughts makes him appear to those visiting him like an earnest, affectionate friend."

From the cards on his desk Lincoln selected the persons to be ushered in, usually giving precedence to Cabinet officers, Senators, and Congressmen. Still, many people of more humble status gained access to him, and Senators found it easier to enter his office in groups rather than alone. He often overstayed his time to listen to an anxious old lady, and occasionally generals waited while he talked with a young private. Lincoln especially liked to hear eyewitness accounts of recent battles. Inventors were sure of an attentive listener in him, and he liked to watch demonstrations of new weapons. He was fond of quoting the rural inventor who believed that "a gun ought not to rekyle, but if it rekyled at all, it ought to rekyle a little forrid."

On Tuesdays and Fridays the Cabinet generally met and the doors were closed at noon. On Mondays a public reception from one to two usually caused him to miss his lunch. On other days, about noon, he ordered the doors thrown open and the crowd surged into his office. Some presented their cases publicly, while others lingered, hoping to be the last to see the President. Until 1864, when a door was cut from his office to the family quarters, Lincoln ended these mornings by running the gauntlet of people who still remained in the halls. In hearing these constant demands and pleas he seldom lost patience. "If I do get up a little temper," he wrote, "I have no time to keep it up."

Lunch was at one and, like breakfast, it was simple—perhaps only fruit and milk. After lunch he read briefly, sprawled in a chair in his stocking feet until Mrs. Lincoln noticed and ordered his slippers brought.

by Lloyd A. Dunlap

In the afternoon there was more work until four o'clock. That was the hour for his daily ride with Mrs. Lincoln in her carriage. Usually a visit to a hospital ended the day. The President was fond of riding, and in the summer, when the family lived at the Soldiers Home in the suburbs, he varied his routine by riding to and from the office on horseback.

Dinner was at six; usually a friend was present. Once a week, except in summer, there was a reception; but if no formal events were scheduled coffee was served in the crimson drawing room. Here Lincoln occasionally spent the evening, reading aloud if only one or two outsiders were present. Other diversions were concerts on the lawn by the Marine Band, private performances by actors and entertainers, and trips to the theater.

Evenings usually were spent back in his office, where Lincoln signed papers or reviewed courts-martial sentences while insects swarmed through the unscreened windows. Here, too, he spent much of his leisure, talking with friends who dropped by. In this informal atmosphere only the approaching thump of the gold-headed cane carried by the elegant Senator Charles Sumner could bring Lincoln's feet off the desk and back to the floor. Here he was, in the words of John Hay, "once more the Lincoln of the Eighth Circuit, the cheeriest of talkers, the riskiest of story tellers." Perhaps it was here that he gave his personal opinion of the Presidency. It reminded him of the man who was being ridden out of town on a rail and who remarked that "If it wasn't for the honor of the thing, I think I'd rather walk."

When the yarns had ended and the friends had gone the lank figure was again seen walking, ending his day with another visit to the War Office. There were more telegrams to read, more answers to seek. Where was Sherman? How was it with Grant? How was it with the bleeding nation he loved?

Lloyd A. Dunlap

46

PRESIDENT LINCOLN AND GENERAL GRANT

by E. B. Long

On a day in March 1864 a scrubby, unobtrusive man with a cigar in his mouth checked into Willard's Hotel in Washington, his fourteen-year-old son Frederick by his side. A short time later the same man, in a disheveled major general's uniform, appeared at a White House reception. Here the President and the General met for the first time. Newly created Lieutenant General and Commander of the Armies of the United States, Ulysses S. Grant was received briefly by Abraham Lincoln. In the East Room cheer after cheer greeted Grant until, greatly embarrassed, he was forced to climb up on a sofa and shake hands with his admirers.

Grant received his formal commission the next day. A new military commander was in charge.

Lincoln had called the victor at Fort Donelson, Vicksburg, and Chattanooga because, after three years of struggle, the Civil War in Virginia was languishing, while the campaign in the West, under Grant's direction, was steamrolling smoothly. He needed the man who was doing that job.

Grant had been warned about the "buffets of intrigue" at the

by E. B. Long

capital even by General Sherman, who feared that if Grant went East he would suffer the fate of his predecessors—McDowell, McClellan, Burnside, Hooker, Pope, Meade, and Halleck. But Grant did not plan to be an armchair general entrapped in Washington. The capital to him was a place to receive his instructions—and leave.

Grant said the President never professed knowledge of military affairs or of how campaigns should be conducted. Lincoln had, however, been forced to interfere more than he might have wished because of procrastination on the part of his commanders and pressure from Congress and the people of the North. Lincoln did not know whether all his military orders had been wrong but he admitted to Grant that he knew some of them were. Grant maintained that all Lincoln "had ever wanted was some one who would take the responsibility and act, and call on him for all the assistance needed." So Grant simply assured Lincoln that he would do the best he could with what he had at hand. The Commander-in-chief did not attempt to tell the new general what to do or how to plan the forthcoming spring campaign. Nor did Grant communicate his ideas to the President or anyone else. He soon left Washington, made his headquarters with the Army of the Potomac, and went to work.

The campaign under Grant in Virginia at the Wilderness, Spotsylvania, Cold Harbor, and Petersburg cost lives aplenty and caused Lincoln much anxiety, but it ended in the final victory at Appomattox. Sherman in the West captured Atlanta and foraged on to the sea. The war was won. It probably would have been won without Grant in charge, but certainly not so soon. Things were vastly different in the nation after March 1864. Lincoln had called on the right man at the right time for the right job.

Lincoln undoubtedly heard of Grant in mid-1861, the first year of the war, when in July he appointed the Westerner brigadier general of volunteers. But in February of 1862 Grant's name became known to everyone in the nation after the unconditional surrender of Fort Donelson in Tennessee. Then came two desperate April days on the banks of the Tennessee River at Shiloh Church. Wild charges were bandied about in an effort to account for the Federal near-disaster. Congressmen, newspapers, citizens railed against Grant. The President was asked to remove Grant from command. But Lincoln steadfastly refused.

Thus Lincoln saved a general for future victories. Grant did not fully realize Lincoln's strong support of him after the battle of Shiloh. Apparently he was not entirely aware of it until after Lincoln's death.

As the war took unfortunate turns in the East there were at least some hopeful events in the West. Vicksburg, the last vital bastion of the beleagured Confederacy on the Mississippi River, became the objective, and Grant plodded toward that goal, trying first one method and then another. Here, too, he was hindered by political machinations supported to some extent by Lincoln. In one of the most masterful campaigns ever executed Grant won Vicksburg on July 4, 1863, the day after the battle of Gettysburg in Pennsylvania.

The clarion of victory had been rung in the West and was to reverberate at Chattanooga, Lookout Mountain, and Missionary Ridge. Lincoln began to realize the kind of man he had in Grant. He had had much discouragement from his generals—had been forced to cajole, persuade, order, and practically cudgel them into action. He had pestered Grant, too, with letters and telegrams. But when he summoned Grant to Washington the President gave his general full authority to plan his over-all strategy. Grant did call the plans, but not in careless disregard of his chief. During the spring of 1864 he visited Washington weekly and was in constant touch with Lincoln.

Lincoln, both in Washington and during his visits to the army on the James River, probably saw more of Grant than he had of any of his other major commanders. This did not mean interference; it meant co-operation. One sees a great difference in the communications between Lincoln and Grant from those between the President and other generals. No longer does the General complain constantly of the lack of men and material while the enemy towers over him in numbers like a giant. Grant takes what he has and does the job. In return he receives the support he needs, particularly the manpower.

There grew up a fond understanding between the two men which amounted to silent recognition of their faith in each other. Lincoln, the President, had to defend Grant, the General, against charges of being a butcher. This he did. He had to defend Grant against accusations of moral turpitude. Whether or not Lincoln ever sought to learn what brand of liquor Grant drank so he could furnish it to his other generals, to make them win as Grant did, is unimportant. What is vital is that Lincoln, the ever-so-human being that he was, expected perfection of no one. So what if Grant took a drink occasionally? Lincoln felt assured this would never happen when it mattered, when the nation's fate was at stake in battle.

Here were two men who had found each other. They had similarity in the earth itself; in their basic integrity; in their quiet, undemonstrative attachment to a task to be done. History had touched each, crowning him with a bright fame gained at an undesired cost in blood and agony.

Lincoln, perhaps the most astute politician in the history of the world, far exceeded Grant in his ability to mold and direct the political situation. Lincoln's deft touch in this regard was not Grant's. But the General had an ability to discern the military value of a man, and those around him felt the staunchness of his confidence.

Grant never received the shouts and emotional, almost hysterical, plaudits that the Army gave McClellan. But in Grant the Army of the West and Army of the Potomac soon found they had a leader who needed no cheering but for whom they would fight. They found a pillar to uphold them in time of battle, whose only direction was "Forward."

As the armies discovered this so did Lincoln. The President often wondered about Grant's strategy, but had learned the danger of the do-nothing element in Washington and warned Grant that nothing would "be done or attempted unless you watch it every day, and hour, and force it." Force it Grant did, until the end when, in the magnanimity that brought Lincoln and Grant even closer together, the Confederate Army of Northern Virginia was given the honorable terms of a noble foe.

To Lincoln and to Grant and to all the nation enough lives had been sacrificed. The Cabinet met at Lincoln's request to "act in the interest of peace." Grant, advising at the meeting, heard the President relate a prophetic dream in which Lincoln had moved in an indescribable vessel on a river toward a dark and mystic shore. The President believed that dreams had special meanings, perhaps prophetic warnings, and this dream puzzled him. Grant finished his report and departed to visit his sons in New Jersey. The same day, in Charleston Harbor, impressive ceremonies marked the fifth anniversary of the surrender of Fort Sumter. In the evening, in Washington, the President went to the theater. The day was Friday, April 14, 1865.

Grant heard the news in Philadelphia. The man whom he had known so intimately for one short year was dying of an assassin's bullet.

Years later Grant would write of Lincoln, as might well have been said of himself: "I knew his goodness of heart, his generosity, his yielding disposition, his desire to have everybody happy, and above all his desires to see all the people of the United States enter again upon the full privileges of citizenship and equality among all."

It was this similarity, almost oneness, of character that enabled Lincoln and Grant, together, to win the war for the Union of States and to preserve for posterity the American experiment.

C. B. "Pete" Long

47

THE WAR POWERS OF PRESIDENT LINCOLN

by Fred Schwengel

During the agonizing war years Abraham Lincoln heard himself called, by important people in the country and powerful spokesmen in his own party, both a despot and a tyrant. There were complaints charging that under him, and against the basic law of the land, the personal power of the President became greater and greater and the power of Congress, unconstitutionally, smaller and smaller.

Were these complaints just?

It is a fact that no President in our history, before or since, has cloaked himself with more power than did Lincoln. But as we look at history from the cool and objective vantage of almost a hundred years' perspective we know that in the whole dictionary of our language no words are so ill suited to describe Lincoln as "despot" and "tyrant."

The verdict of history is that Lincoln's *use* of power did not constitute usurpation or abuse. It was always a firm and wise emergency grasp of the helm of government, according to the

273

needs of a desperate hour and with a thorough understanding of the philosophy of representative government. Had Lincoln actually distorted and misapplied his authority, against the Constitution, it is not too hard to imagine that the whole course of history would have been altered against the current of human freedom.

Well, then, what really happened?

On the eve of war Alexander H. Stephens, Lincoln's colleague in Congress twelve years before, who was to become Vice President of the Confederacy, felt that the South held Lincoln captive in the Congress. He predicted:

> The President is no emperor, no dictator—he is clothed with no absolute power. He can do nothing unless he is backed by power in Congress. The House of Representatives is largely in the majority against him. In the Senate he will also be powerless.

Stephens had served in the Congress from 1843 to 1859. He knew most of the strong, able, effective, and determined leaders in both houses, all of whom had had much more legislative experience than had the President. Stephens also knew the caliber of the twenty-two Senators from the twelve seceding states who withdrew or were expelled, as well as most of the representatives from those states.

As Lincoln took the reins of government he must have been keenly aware of the fact that he must drive carefully and guide intelligently, for emergency was already upon him. Secession began when his election was assured.

By the time of his inauguration on March 4, 1861, seven Southern states had already seceded from the Union. But Lincoln played a waiting game and made no preparation for the use of force until his sending of provisions to Fort Sumter in Charleston Harbor, a month later, excited its bombardment by the Confederacy.

Now began the period of executive decision. Congress was not in session at the time (nor would it meet until the special session

by Fred Schwengel

of July 4), even though it was basic to the Whig-Republican theory of government that Congress had the ultimate power.

By presidential proclamation on May 3, 1861, he increased the regular Army by 22,714 officers and men and the Navy by 18,000. He called for 42,034 volunteers for three years.

Lincoln knew as well as the Congress that it was the constitutional prerogative of Congress to "raise and support armies." Senator John Sherman, a loyal Republican, complained, though without rancor: "I have never met anyone who claimed that the President could, by proclamation, increase the regular Army."

Those who defend this action believe that Lincoln was acting according to the "spirit of the Constitution" rather than its precise clauses, in an attempt to avoid further confusion in public opinion. The attack on Fort Sumter had solidified opinion in the North. Not until even weeks later did the Congress meet, convened by Lincoln's proclamation of April 15.

Lincoln's message to Congress on July 4, 1861, was revealingly candid, proving that he knew exactly what he had done. He asked simply and blandly that the Congress retroactively endorse his extraordinary assumptions of authority. He said:

> These measures, whether strictly legal or not, were ventured upon, under what appeared to be a popular demand, and a public necessity; trusting, then as now, that Congress would readily ratify them. It is believed that nothing has been done beyond the constitutional competency of Congress.

About a month later the Congress replied: ". . . all the acts, proclamations, and orders of the President respecting the Army and Navy of the United States, and calling out or relating to the militia or volunteers from the United States are hereby approved and in all respects made valid . . . as if they had been issued and done under the previous express authority and direction of the Congress of the United States." This endorsement could not have been more explicit or more complete.

275

Again in 1863 Lincoln issued a general order setting up rules governing Federal armies in the field—a function clearly defined in the Constitution as belonging solely to Congress. He ordered the Secretary of the Treasury to furnish two million dollars to three private individuals for defense and government support purposes. This in spite of the clause in the Constitution which commands that "No Money shall be drawn from the Treasury but in Consequence of Appropriations made by Law. . . ."

Because of the breathless sweep of power that Lincoln gathered into his own hands, and other dissatisfactions, Congress appointed, on December 20, 1861, a Joint Committee on the Conduct of the War.

Debates flared up in Congress. Senator Charles Sumner of Massachusetts held forth that the President was "only the instrument of Congress under the Constitution of the United States." Senator Trumbull from Illinois argued that the President "is just as much subject to our control as if we appointed him, except that we cannot remove him and appoint another in his place."

Senator Orville H. Browning of Illinois defended the President, citing Supreme Court decisions, and saying that Congress could call the Chief Executive to account for his actions but that Congress could not be called to account if it committed usurpations. Browning also insisted that the President enjoyed great powers as Commander-in-chief of the Army and Navy, powers necessary to "a full, faithful and forceful performance of the duties of that high office. . . ."

To all of this Lincoln made no reply. He went ahead and proposed compensated emancipation of the slaves, preparing a veto message in advance to keep anticipated objectionable features from getting into the bill. He kept his Cabinet intact against demands of the radicals in Congress. On the question of the Emancipation Proclamation and a parallel measure presented by Congress, known as the Wade-Davis Bill, he observed: "I conceive that I may, in an emergency, do things on military ground which cannot constitutionally be done by Congress." He gave the Wade-Davis Bill a pocket veto.

To sum up his so-called "unconstitutional" acts, Lincoln:

Assumed for himself the power to increase the Army and the Navy beyond the statutory limits.

Paid out two million dollars from unappropriated funds in the Treasury to persons unauthorized to receive it.

Closed the Post Office to what he termed "treasonable correspondence."

Subjected travelers to and from foreign countries to new passport regulations.

Proclaimed a blockade of Southern ports.

Suspended the writ of habeas corpus as he saw fit, and caused the military arrest and detention of persons "who were represented to him . . . as being engaged in or contemplating . . . treasonable practices."

How did Lincoln justify this massive seizure of power? The answer comes from a letter he wrote on April 4, 1864, to A. G. Hodges. He wrote:

> . . . my oath to preserve the constitution . . . imposed upon me the duty of preserving, by every indispensable means, that government—that nation—of which that constitution was the organic law. Was it possible to lose the nation, and yet preserve the constitution? By general law life *and* limb must be protected; . . . but a life is never wisely given to save a limb. I felt that measures, otherwise unconstitutional, might become lawful, by becoming indispensable to the preservation of the constitution, through the preservation of the nation. Right or wrong, I assumed this ground, and now avow it. I could not feel that, to the best of my ability, I had even tried to preserve the constitution, if, to save slavery, or any minor matter, I should permit the wreck of government, country, and Constitution all together.

The logic is complete and unanswerable. Abraham Lincoln ignored Congress and roughed up the Constitution in the face of emergency, *but he saved both.* He also saved the Union. Lincoln had prayed "that this nation, under God, shall have a new birth of freedom." It came to pass, and Lincoln's unorthodox actions opened doors to presidential actions which have saved the nation time and time again.

Fred Schwengel

48

LINCOLN AS A LIBERAL STATESMAN

by Ralph W. Yarborough

The word "liberal" comes to us from the ancient Latin *liberalis*, meaning "free." A liberal man therefore is one who is free of prejudice, bigotry, dogma; one not bound by established forms in political or religious philosophy; a man independent in opinion and generous in action. A liberal policy is one pertaining to—or befitting—a freeman.

Does Abraham Lincoln qualify according to these meanings? The answer is in his character as read in his words and his actions.

Upon the bedrock of human freedom Lincoln based his career. His words "pertaining to a free man" are almost unparalleled in their eloquence and simplicity. But Lincoln could interpolate, too.

To an Illinois audience he said: "Our reliance is in the *love of liberty* which God has planted in our bosoms. Our defense is the preservation of the spirit which prizes liberty as the heritage of all men, in all lands, everywhere."

He put it another way to a man in Massachusetts to whom he wrote: "This is a world of compensations; and he who would *be* no slave, must consent to *have* no slave. Those who deny freedom to others, deserve it not for themselves; and, under a just God, cannot long retain it."

On the eve of his debates with Stephen A. Douglas Lincoln told a Chicago audience: "I believe each individual is naturally entitled to do as he pleases with himself and the fruit of his labor, so far as it in no wise interferes with any other man's rights." Four years earlier he had said, "No man is good enough to govern another man *without that other's consent.*"

Upon these beliefs, this credo, Lincoln based and built his statesmanship. Toward the acceptance of this philosophy and its *enactment into law* he directed his every public act from the time of the great debates to the end of his life.

His purpose was not easily apparent at the time, though his words were clear enough. During his Presidency, and the war which his election did not cause but precipitated, he was condemned by some as a bloody tyrant who flouted the Constitution and joked as he led the country to ruin. He was assailed by others as a vacillating weakling and hopeless incompetent. Even friends spoke patronizingly of his poor ability to cope with the tremendous problems which confronted him. It was bad enough so that Lincoln once wrote wistfully, "I have endured a great deal of ridicule without much malice; and have received a great deal of kindness not quite free from ridicule."

But the people, the mass from which he had sprung, seemed to understand that Lincoln had but one aim—to preserve and promote the principle of popular government. On taking office he had spoken: "In *your* hands, my dissatisfied fellow countrymen, and not in *mine*, is the momentous issue of civil war. . . . *You* have no oath registered in Heaven to destroy the government, while *I* shall have the most solemn one to 'preserve, protect and defend' it."

To Congress he wrote that he was struggling to maintain "that form, and substance of government, whose leading object is, to elevate the condition of men—to lift artificial weights from all shoulders—to clear the paths of laudable pursuit for all—to afford all, an unfettered start, and a fair chance, in the race of life. Yielding to partial and temporary departures, from necessity, this is the leading object of the government for whose existence we contend." And on a hill in Pennsylvania he had spoken of "government of the people, by the people, and for the people."

By and large the people understood this. But there were critics who did not or would not. They said he was a drifter, that he had no policy. He answered the accusation by informing his secretary, "My policy is to have no policy." In the shifting events of war no ironclad "policy" could be laid down which would meet all emergencies. These were not the hasty words of the drifter. Lincoln spoke in full recognition of the fact that precedent was not so important as the principle for which he strove. Guided always by his lodestar, the Declaration of Independence, he had to put first things first. In the dark and bitter December of 1862 he told the Congress that crisis called for boldness.

"The dogmas of the quiet past," he declared, "are inadequate to the stormy present. . . . As our case is new, so we must think anew, and act anew. We must disenthrall ourselves, and then we shall save our country."

Gradually from his acts there emerged a pattern and an image of a man who would not permit freedom to perish because of a too-strict interpretation of the rules. Denounced for arbitrary arrests and his suspension of the writ of habeas corpus, Lincoln defended himself by asking, "Must I shoot a simple-minded soldier boy who deserts, while I must not touch a hair of a wily agitator who induces him to desert?"

Lincoln considered the Constitution of the United States as sacred, just as his predecessors in the Presidency had done. He had taken a solemn oath to defend it. But a too literal view of the document could bring about its destruction and that of the creed from which it came, the Declaration of Independence.

The preservation of the Union, and with it human freedom within the law, was the cause. The form of action could not be held sacrosanct. To a war governor who too jealously guarded his own prerogatives Lincoln wrote, ". . . please do not ruin us on *punctilio.*" For petty regulations he had little patience. He could cut through yards of red tape with notes like: "This man wants to work—so uncommon a want that I think it ought to be gratified," and, "Wanting to work is so rare a merit that it should be encouraged."

Fully cognizant of the dignity of his office, Lincoln still had little regard for protocol. One of his duties, as he saw it, was to keep himself available to the people. Not only that, he had to know what they were thinking. So Congressmen and generals often fretted in the corridor outside his study while he talked with farmers and privates in the Army, who had come all the way to Washington for just that purpose.

A man of paradox was Lincoln. And yet there was no paradox in his basic creed: "Stand with anybody that stands right. Stand with him while he is right and part with him when he goes wrong." And so he could use politics and men with seeming ruthlessness, could prosecute the bloodiest war in history, could take freedom from thousands—to give it to millions.

"To keep the jewel of liberty within the family of freedom"— that was his dedication. When the preservation of the jewel of freedom demanded that old values be discarded he was without hesitation. When boldness was needed he was bold. When caution was called for he was cautious. In some quarters he was a dangerous radical, in others he was considered hopelessly conservative. For some he moved too rapidly, for others too slowly. But through all his actions there shines his abiding faith in the ability of the people to govern themselves. In Illinois he had expressed that faith: "*Most governments* have been based, practically, on the denial of equal rights of men . . . *ours* began, by *affirming* those rights. *They* said, some men are too *ignorant*, and *vicious*, to share in government. Possibly so, said we; and, by your system, you would always keep them ignorant, and vicious. We proposed to give *all* a chance; and we expected the weak to grow stronger, the ignorant, wiser; and all better, and happier together. We made the experiment. . . ." The war was fought to preserve and continue the experiment and, as far as Lincoln was concerned, for no other reason.

A later President, who also went down in history as a liberal statesman, once spoke of Lincoln. Not of Lincoln's party but surely of his political faith, Woodrow Wilson asked this question fifty years ago: "Can we have other Lincolns? We cannot do without them. This country is going to have crisis after crisis. God send they may not be bloody crises, but they will be intense and acute. No body politic so abounding in life and so puzzled by problems as ours is can avoid moving from crisis to crisis. We must have the leadership of sane, genial men of universal use like Lincoln to save us from mistakes and give us the necessary leadership in such days of struggle and difficulty."

Leo Tolstoy, the great writer of *War and Peace*, put it in fewer words. "As broad as humanity itself," he described Lincoln.

History itself has written the verdict. The paradoxes fall into place. The inconsistencies, so poorly understood at the time, make a pattern which is clearly distinguishable. Lincoln emerges not only as a liberal statesman but as the most liberal statesman we have had. For his every act was directed toward the freedom of men.

Ralph W. Yarborough

49

ABRAHAM LINCOLN AND JEFFERSON DAVIS

by Frank E. Vandiver

Abraham Lincoln and Jefferson Davis were born within one hundred miles of each other, and in age were only some eight months apart. They were both to achieve renown at the same time, but beyond these vital statistics the similarity ends, for history and fate marked them for divergent roles.

Humbly born and humbly raised, Lincoln followed a path that took him from a back-country law office and politics to the United States Congress, finally to the Presidency and a place "in the hearts of the people for whom he saved the Union." Always there was a grandeur about him, whether in his earthy and humorous stump-speaking, in his struggle for recognition, in his calm choice of political roads, in his two minutes at Gettysburg, or in his firm dedication to politics free from malice. There was grandeur in the way he looked. His long, tragically etched face seemed to capture all the suffering of all his people, and his gentle eyes spoke compassion.

A few things he did during the Civil War to save his country angered his political foes and now and then frightened his friends, but in the end the Union was preserved. If sometimes the Constitution bent under a strong executive hand the Constitution somehow survived. Lincoln's warm human dynamism, which never left him even during the most fearful moments of the war, seemed forged out of a vigorous young industrial nation. A country with a limitless future had little time for the trammels of tradition, and Lincoln held few traditions sacrosanct. The future had to be saved at the expense of the past. So he suffered the agonies of four bloody years. But not without cost. The face grew more tragically etched, the eyes wiser in the ways of suffering.

Problems Lincoln faced would have shattered most men. His country had divided views on the virtues of the war; bankers feared financial disaster if the South departed the Union; the Army was small and appallingly scattered; the Rebels seemed united and determined to gain independence. Bull Run in July 1861 proved Rebel sincerity, and Lincoln settled down to the rigors of hard war. Now he had the people with him, at least, but apparently he had no generals. Union boys were willing to die for the Union, but their leaders could not give them victory. Faced with incompetence in his high command, Lincoln had to be his own general for some time. Groping for a command system adequate to wage a modern, virtually total war, he tried one man after another and found them uniformly wanting. Not until the miracle worker of the West, Ulysses S. Grant, gained prominence did the President have a general who could handle the military end of the war while Lincoln went about the business of organizing behind the lines. With Grant in charge after March of 1864 military affairs progressed rapidly to the climax of April 1865.

For his own part Lincoln had winked at political arrests, played politics with the shrewdness of a veteran to hobble the rambunctious Radicals in his party, shaved the law here and there, but had kept the shining vision of Union and freedom always in sight. The cause amply justified the measures. Lincoln never held himself infallible; that he did some things which alienated strict constitutionalists he was the first to concede. But he felt no compulsion to be sorry. When the last gray man with Lee laid down his arms at Appomattox all the terror, the dying, the agony, the wanton destruction, the heroism had meaning at last. The men in blue who fell along the ridges at Cemetery Hill and who lay sprawled across Georgia and the Deep South had not died in vain. The tall man in the stovepipe hat could walk the ruins of Richmond sure in the knowledge that his own personal nightmare had been worth the price. Now all that remained was to "bind up the nation's wounds," and this he had set himself to do with no hatred in his heart.

In the end he went to apotheosis at Ford's Theater. His friends, his enemies, his countrymen, and the world would remember the Great Emancipator for what he surely was—the giant of his age.

Jefferson Davis is remembered, too, but not in the roseate light of his Northern adversary. Proudly born and proudly raised, he had the natural hauteur of an aristocrat. In the time-honored tradition of the Old South Davis gained military education at the United States Military Academy and martial glory in the Mexican War. Tempered by tragedy when his first wife (a bride of a scant few months) died, he devoted years to lonely study of political problems. At length his breeding and training charmed the fates, and Davis rose to fame in the United States Senate and earned deserved prestige as Secretary of War in Franklin Pierce's Cabinet.

Not a "fireater," Davis nonetheless consciously guarded the shade of John C. Calhoun and finally came to have a major voice in Southern policy. There was nothing of the common man about him and very little of social magnetism. He was almost as tall as Lincoln, equally emaciated, and his face, too, showed the ravages of suffering—physical suffering. Jefferson Davis could feel human compassion but the caste mark of reserve debarred him from showing it. Around him clung a phantom chillness, a stoicism, an intellectual detachment which alienated many. A few close friends he had, and they saw beneath the armor of aloofness. But to those who saw only the exterior he was a cold, unbending martinet.

History played a fell trick on Davis when it elevated him to the Presidency of the Confederate States of America. Doomed to lead a lost cause against a nation headed by one of the warmest of human beings, Davis had little chance for appreciation by history. As Confederate President he fought states' righters and growing factions within various states and in the Southern Congress, and garnered enemies in droves as Confederate fortunes faded.

At first everything seemed to go his way. The confident Confederates marched to triumph at Bull Run, and the Yankees seemed to pose no serious threat to the Southland. But the North dug in for a long, grim struggle. And that kind of war was just the sort the South could not fight. Below Mason and Dixon's line were few factories, scant sinews of war, limited manpower reserves. Quick victory was the only real way for the South to prevail. Each month of attrition brought the Confederacy lower while the Union rose in strength. And as the war dragged on its character changed. To wage it Davis and his Rebels had to change traditional attitudes. A collection of intensely self-conscious states found it hard to submit to the regimentation required in a total conflict. Davis, who learned the hard way, fought to forge a centralized war administration, but his inability to win confidence, to attract the wholehearted support of his Congress, his people, and even of his Cabinet, brought him hatred for his pains.

Like Lincoln, Davis had to evolve a command structure for his armies. He had special problems, of course, problems born of states' rightism. Each state wanted its borders kept inviolate. Few of them parted willingly with men to aid sister states, and none would submit to a central directing agency—a general staff. Not until 1865 did the Confederacy admit the need for a general-in-chief, and meanwhile Davis had had to grope toward a system of command compatible with Confederate needs, resources, and predilections. His experimentation with departmental command, a system not unlike that used by the United States in World War II, stamped him an original strategist, a bold and daring one. But in the end his armies lost, so he would be rated by posterity as a poor war leader.

There have been better war leaders who made fewer mistakes, but Davis yielded to none in courage, in devotion to the Confederacy, and in personal bravery. He showed, too, that he could grow with his job, but perhaps long experience in a military milieu made him less pliable than Lincoln. Still, when the end came it could be said of Davis that he stayed steadfast to the last and held together the separatist Confederate States beyond the limits of their endurance.

The nobility of Lincoln's humanity, his wisdom, and his understanding lifted him to Olympus—we have produced none greater. But in Davis' tragedy there also is nobility, for he remained true to himself, to his cause, and to history. For him defeat was the ultimate degradation, yet he bore it with a fortitude which stamped him a product of Lincoln's mold.

Abraham Lincoln and Jefferson Davis—poles apart they were, but men of virtue and much valor. Each typified a special strength in the American character.

Frank E. Vandiver

50

LINCOLN AND THE COPPERHEADS

by Wood Gray

January 1861. South Carolina, followed by six other states of the lower South, is attempting to withdraw from the Union and organize a new slaveholding Confederacy.

A state convention of the Democratic party in special session officially resolves that "we distinctly deny that the Federal Government has any constitutional power to call out the militia to execute . . . laws within the limits and jurisdiction of any state except in aid of the [state's] civil authorities." The state is not South Carolina or Virginia but Illinois, and the meeting place is President-elect Lincoln's own Springfield. Similiar resolutions are being adopted by conventions in Indianapolis and Columbus, Ohio.

Southern leaders meeting in Montgomery, Alabama, to organize the Confederacy were pleased to receive such news. But they were not surprised. In plotting the disruption of the Union they had been confident that if they were forced to fight for their independence three things would insure victory for the South. First, from a purely military point of view, they believed that a geography well suited to defense and a people accustomed to hunting and an outdoor life would counterbalance the Northern advantages in population and manufacturing. Second, they expected the ruling classes of England and France, dependent upon Southern cotton for their textile factories and eager to see the destruction of democratic government, to come to their aid even to the extent of entering the war. Third and fundamentally, they were confident that the Northern people or a sufficiently large proportion of them would either refuse to fight to preserve the Union or would be so discouraged in the face of prolonged Southern resistance that they would sue for peace.

They expected some help from old allies in trade and politics in the Middle Atlantic states of the North and even in New England. But they were even more confident of the Midwest, particularly the three states of Ohio, Indiana, and Illinois that bordered on the Ohio River. The Mississippi River sytem had tied the trade of these states closely to the South before canals and railways were built to bind the Midwest and Northeast together. The influence of that tradition was still strong. Southerners had led in the early settlement of this area, and they and their descendants were still numerous and devoted to memories of their ancestral homes. And many of the poverty-stricken immigrants who had come in more recently from Ireland and Germany were fearful that war might set the Negroes free to move North to compete with them for jobs.

After the Civil War began many of its opponents in the North wore lapel badges made by cutting out the head of the goddess of liberty that then appeared on the copper penny. These badges served as silent protests against the policies of conscription and suspension of habeas corpus adopted by the Federal Government in the conduct of the war. Supporters of the war retaliated by calling their opponents Copperheads, suggesting the name of a common species of venomous snake.

Southern expectation of Copperhead help suffered a great setback when the firing on the American flag at Fort Sumter in

April of 1861 united the great majority of the Northern people, regardless of political party, in a determination to restore the Union by force of arms. The South had also overlooked the hidden powers of statesmanship, the political skill, and the understanding of the American people that President Lincoln would bring to bear in rallying support for the Union.

Nevertheless Southern hopes and Union danger continued almost to the end of the war, even after the fading of hopes of European intervention and of outright military victory in the field. If Abraham Lincoln's old friend and political opponent, Stephen A. Douglas, Senator from Illinois and leader of the Democratic party in the Midwest, had lived, the Copperhead movement might have been strangled in its infancy. He had rallied men of all parties with the cry, "There can be no neutrals in this war, *only patriots—or traitors!*" But his death in the summer of 1861 opened the way for the rise of a very different sort of Democratic leader, Congressman Clement L. Vallandigham of Ohio. Vallandigham was brave, magnetic, narrow-minded, and unrelenting in his opposition to the war. In a defiant speech in Congress early in the year 1863 he declared, "Defeat, debt, taxation, sepulchers, these are your trophies. . . . The war for the Union . . . is a most bloody and costly failure. You have not conquered the South. You never will."

The combination of persistent minority opposition to the war, shortsighted partisanship, and discouragement over repeated defeats suffered by the Army of the Potomac at the hands of General Lee twice brought the North toward the brink of abandoning the war.

The first of these periods came in the winter and spring of 1863. Public disgust over military failures, resentment toward conscription and arbitrary arrests, and fears as to the results of the Emancipation Proclamation had enabled the Peace Democrats to win control of the legislatures of Indiana and Illinois in the autumn elections of 1862. Once in power they threw off the masks with which they had earlier concealed their intentions. In February 1863 the Illinois House of Representatives declared, by a vote of 52 to 28, "The Constitution cannot be maintained, nor the Union be preserved by the . . . exercise of coercive powers"; and the Indiana legislature threatened that "Indiana will never voluntarily contribute another man or another dollar" to the further prosecution of the war.

In the background was a secret Copperhead organization of armed men, formed originally in the South to promote secession and to seize a circle of lands all around the Gulf of Mexico and Caribbean Sea for a slave empire, calling themselves the Knights of the Golden Circle. They were pledged to resist conscription and to aid deserters. A number of recruiting officers were murdered while carrying out their duties. The outlook appeared so black that Joseph Medill, one of the owners of the Chicago *Tribune*, wrote to a friend in Congress that it would be necessary to ask for an armistice. After a call at the White House a Massachusetts Senator confided to a Columbia professor, "The President tells me that he fears 'the fire in the rear'—meaning the Democracy (that is, the Democratic party) especially at the Northwest—more than our military chances."

But then it appeared that fate had dealt the Copperheads three bad cards that were, for the time being, sufficient to save the Union. Unlike most states of the time both Indiana and Illinois elected their governors for four-year instead of two-year terms, and Ohio held its state elections in odd-numbered instead of even-numbered years, and thus had a carry-over Republican governor and legislature elected in 1861. The Republican governors of Indiana and Illinois each used a parliamentary maneuver to send their legislatures home and refused to recall them until the end of their elected terms, ruling their states and raising taxes by extralegal means. In Ohio, where the Peace Democrats had the ablest and most determined leadership, they could only hope to win control of their state in the autumn election of 1863. And President Lincoln quietly promoted the growth of the Union League, originally formed by men loyal to the Union in eastern

Tennessee, as a counterweight to the lodges of the Knights of the Golden Circle.

The victories of Grant at Vicksburg and Meade at Gettysburg gave renewed hope to the Union, and for a year the Copperheads, both political and revolutionary, remained relatively quiet. Vallandigham was defeated for the governorship of Ohio by a combined ticket of Republicans and War Democrats, even though he drew more votes than any previous Democratic candidate for that office had ever received.

Then suddenly, during the summer of 1864, the success of Lee and Johnston in frustrating the efforts of Grant and Sherman's armies to capture Richmond and Atlanta caused a wave of defeatism and war weariness to sweep the North. Vallandigham succeeded in getting the Democratic National Convention to adopt a platform declaring that the war was a failure. President Lincoln wrote a secret memorandum expressing the belief that he would be defeated for re-election and the war abandoned. The Confederates sent army officers north in civilian clothes with a half million dollars to organize a revolt which would set free and rearm Confederate prisoners. These prisoners and the former Knights of the Golden Circle, now reorganized as the Order of American Knights or Sons of Liberty, with Vallandigham as supreme commander, would then seize control of the state governments. The Democratic candidate for the governorship of Illinois accepted forty thousand dollars to become a member of this plot. The Confederacy seemed to have gained one last chance.

This time it was not fate but Jefferson Davis who intervened. He decided to remove his old enemy Joe Johnston from command and replace him with the impetuous General Hood, who quickly proved himself no match for Sherman. Atlanta fell and other Union victories followed. Northern confidence returned and defeatism spread over the South. President Lincoln was re-elected and military victory was only a matter of time. The Sons of Liberty lost their courage, and those who were not apprehended by the Federal authorities slunk off to their homes.

The Union was thus restored. But how narrow and uncertain, as we look back, had been the margin of victory. Lincoln's genius, Douglas' patriotism, timely military victories, and the chance fact that of the three key states of the Midwest two elected their governors for four-year terms and the other had its state elections in odd-numbered years, all may well have constituted the crucial measure of that margin.

51

LINCOLN AND THE STATESMEN OF REBELLION

by Robert D. Meade

On April 4, 1865, Abraham Lincoln made a memorable visit to Richmond, Virginia. It was only two days since the Southern government had evacuated the capital, and in the pillared Confederate White House Lincoln had an interview with John A. Campbell, the most prominent Confederate who had remained in the city. Campbell, a former Justice of the Supreme Court and now Assistant Secretary of War of the Confederacy, came to Lincoln to urge a moderate policy toward the South. " 'When levity and cruelty play for a kingdom the gentler gamester is the soonest winner,' " Campbell quoted.

Lincoln made no immediate reply. But sitting in Jefferson Davis's chair, before his conference table, Lincoln could reflect on the fate of Davis and the other statesmen of the dying Confederacy.

Here, in the Confederate capital, had been the center for the civil leaders of the rebellion—Davis, Stephens, Toombs, Hunter, Benjamin, Seddon, and the rest. Here, leaving memories still only days old, had lived and worked the Southern statesmen against whom Lincoln and the Union government had been pitted in the long and bloody war. And to add a curious twist so often found in civil war, several of these Confederate statesmen had been Lincoln's political associates, and one, his admired friend.

Precisely what had there been, during the war or earlier, to connect Lincoln with these Southern leaders? His only personal contact with Jefferson Davis appears to have occurred when they served together in Congress. Lincoln was then a new member of the lower house, and the slender, dignified Davis, a new Senator from Mississippi. For his estimates of Davis when they were heads of rival governments Lincoln had to rely largely on the advice of other Northern men who had been associated with him in the Washington government before 1861.

With Robert Toombs, Alexander H. Stephens, and R. M. T. Hunter, Lincoln had in the late 1840's served his one term in Congress. He and Bob Toombs, then a rising Whig Congressman from Georgia, had been on friendly terms. Later Toombs became a leader of the Southern states' rights party, and after the formation of the Southern Confederacy was appointed its Secretary of State. But the talents of the vigorous and capable, though choleric, Georgian lay largely in finance. At odds with Davis and unhappy in his civil post, Toombs resigned in July 1861 to become a brave but none too tractable brigadier general.

R. M. T. Hunter had been a United States Senator when Lincoln was a member of the House of Representatives. A Virginia politician of long experience and recognized capacity, he was appointed Confederate Secretary of State to succeed Toombs. The temperamental Georgian was said, with some truth, to have "carried the State Department in his hat." Through his organizational efforts Hunter laid much of the framework for the Confederate State Department which Lincoln and Seward opposed during the war.

Curiously, between Lincoln and Alexander H. Stephens, the Confederate Vice President, there had been a long-time friendship. "Little Alec," a Georgia Whig of outstanding ability and character, had served with Lincoln in the House of Representatives. Lincoln admired Stephens' successful struggle against difficulties and soon found further reason to like and respect him. As early as February 2, 1848, Lincoln wrote his law partner, William H. Herndon: "I just take up my pen to say, that Mr. Stephens of Georgia, a little slim, pale-faced, consumptive man, with a voice like Logan's has just concluded the very best speech, of an hour's length, I ever heard." And the then youngish Lincoln added, "My old, withered, dry eyes, are full of tears yet."

A decade later opinions North and South had formed on harder lines. In a speech at Columbus, Ohio, on September 16, 1859, Lincoln expressed his fear of "Jeff. Davis and Stephens and other leaders of that company" being given an opportunity "to sound the bugle for the revival of the slave trade." But on December 18, 1860, after his election as President, Lincoln asked John D. Defrees, chairman of the Indiana State Republican Committee, if "Scott" a Virginian, (he did not specify whether he meant General Winfield or Robert E., both of whom were being mentioned for the Cabinet), and Alexander H. Stephens would be willing to go into his Cabinet. Lincoln did extend a Cabinet bid to John A. Gilmer, a strong North Carolina Unionist, but it was declined.

In late December 1860 Lincoln also established a direct contact with Stephens. On November 14, 1860, Stephens, with characteristic courage, had made a pro-Union speech before the Georgia legislature. Lincoln, the President-elect, asked Stephens for a revised copy of his speech. He then wrote confidentially to Stephens as "once a friend, and still, I hope, not an enemy," to assure the South personally that the Republican Administration would not interfere with its slaves. Stephens replied to Lincoln in terms of mutual respect. But he expressed dissent from the opinion of Lincoln and "perhaps a majority of the North" that slavery was morally and politically wrong. And he entreated Lincoln not to be deceived into believing that "conciliation and harmony" could be established by force.

After Stephens became the Confederate Vice President early

in 1861 Lincoln might have had some glimmering hopes that, as a statesman in the Confederate inner circle, he would offer a contact for political negotiations. But Stephens, as sincere and at times as dogmatic as Jefferson Davis, was by early 1862 at odds with the Confederate administration. He now had little influence on Confederate policy, and Lincoln's only noteworthy contact with him thereafter was when Stephens was a Confederate delegate to the abortive Hampton Roads Peace Conference of February 1865. Then Lincoln and Seward agreed to confer with Stephens, Hunter, and Campbell, but Lincoln would consider no terms that did not allow for restoration of the Union and abolition of slavery. Stephens wanted to continue the negotiations, but his proposal was vetoed by Jefferson Davis.

There were some more men of outstanding ability in the Confederate civil administration such as James A. Seddon of Virginia, Secretary of War from late 1862 to early 1865, and Josiah Gorgas, the Pennsylvania-born West Pointer who brilliantly directed the Confederate Ordnance Department. In general, however, the best brains and character in the South were attracted to the army. Moreover, the advice of the Confederate generals was not sought in civil policy-making, with occasional exceptions for high officers such as Robert E. Lee and perhaps Braxton Bragg.

As reputations were made and broken in the stress of war it became more evident that none of the Confederate civil leaders could equal the brilliance and inexhaustible energy of Judah P. Benjamin or the influence he had obtained over his President. He became Jefferson Davis' "chief reliance among men," a position that was heightened by his congeniality with the clever and strong-minded Mrs. Davis. Selected as Attorney General of the original Confederate government at Montgomery, he quickly rose to be Secretary of War and then Secretary of State.

Only in democratic America, among the great powers, were two statesmen of so obscure origin as Lincoln and Benjamin then likely to rise to top rank in political power and responsibility. The stoutish, dark-haired Benjamin, an exotic figure in a Christian-

by Robert D. Meade

Occidental milieu, was derived from a family of poor Hebrew tradesmen though with the cultural heritage of the Spanish Jews. Born in the Virgin Islands, he spent his early youth in the Carolinas, had a truncated career at Yale, and sought his fortune in the fast-developing port of New Orleans. Here he rose to be one of the eminent American lawyers, a United States Senator, and a leader, after Jefferson Davis, in the Southern Democratic party. His imagination had been caught by the vision of a united America, and he joined the secession movement reluctantly.

As a Cabinet officer Benjamin saw the problems of the Confederacy with a cool detachment. In early 1861, before the establishment of the Northern blockade, he made an unsuccessful effort to have the Confederacy send a large quantity of Confederate cotton abroad to be used for the purchase of arms and as a basis for credit. As Attorney General he then concentrated on being competent and agreeable, especially to his former senatorial colleague Jefferson Davis.

During the last three years of the war Benjamin was Lincoln's most formidable opponent, after Davis, among the Confederate civil leaders. While he was Secretary of War from September 1861 to March 1862 his energy and efficiency were in no small measure responsible for the Confederate victories in the following years. He was none too tactful, however, and there were demands for his removal. But Davis promoted him to be Secretary of State, in the teeth of the criticism.

Here was a position in which Benjamin could make full use of his intellect and experience. He offered Louis Napoleon large tariff and cotton concessions in exchange for recognition of the Confederacy by France, and toward the last favored arming the slaves and emancipating them.

Even his most resourceful plans were doomed to failure, largely due to the diplomacy of Lincoln and Seward and the eventual failure of Southern arms. But a brilliant man whom adversity could never keep down, Benjamin escaped to England with a price on his head and became a leader of the English bar.

All of these Confederate statesmen were more favored at birth than Lincoln. They were better trained, more widely experienced, more knowledgeable in the ways of the world and of nations than he. How, then, was Lincoln able to defeat them all? Was it that the North was morally right and so had to win? Lincoln himself believed so. Was it only the economic superiority of the North that turned the tide? The South thought so. Did Lincoln simply outwit all opponents with a shrewd but untutored backwoods instinct? His enemies on both sides believed that. But the truth of the matter is probably that Lincoln knew men—their ways, their thoughts, their emotions—better than any of them. And so he proved himself the master of them all.

Robert D. Meade

52

LINCOLN REMAKES THE SUPREME COURT

by Irving Dilliard

Harvests were bountiful in that year of 1861. They were so abundant that President Lincoln in the first sentence of his annual message to Congress, on December 3, told his "Fellow Citizens of the Senate and House of Representatives" that "we have cause of great gratitude to God." But the country was also, as the hard-beset Chief Executive said, "in the midst of unprecedented political troubles." A portion of the people had been engaged during the year, so he phrased it, in "an attempt to divide and destroy the Union." The consequences reached throughout the government and into every area of American life.

One of the most eminent of these areas was the United States Supreme Court. Early in his message the President directed the urgent attention of the Union's lawmakers to the precarious state of the highest bench. He described in detail the adverse affect of the war on the judiciary. A third of the Supreme Court's nine seats were vacant, two by death and one by the resignation of an extremely able Justice from the Deep South who chose reluctantly to follow his home section in secession.

The chair of that onetime duelist and scholar Justice Peter Vivian Daniel of "Crows' Nest," Stafford County, Virginia, a Van Buren appointee, had gone unfilled since the death of the unswerving scholar, in the last year of Buchanan's Presidency. The cautious, slow-moving Pennsylvanian then in the White House had preferred to keep the seat empty rather than decide whether or not to appoint a Southerner, as many Democrats from below Mason and Dixon's line were demanding.

In the month following Lincoln's inauguration two more Supreme Court vacancies developed. Dignified, mannerly Justice John McLean of Ohio, a Jackson appointee courageous enough to be one of two dissenters in the inflammatory Dred Scott case, died after thirty years of painstaking service. Then hard-working Justice John Archibald Campbell of Alabama, a Pierce selection who had freed his own slaves in 1853 on assuming his judicial duties, ended weeks of soul searching, quit the bench on which he had been so happy, and cast his troubled lot with his homeland South.

Why had Lincoln allowed these important seats to remain vacant so long? In his first year, when the Supreme Court was not sitting, he had forborne making appointments, he told Congress, in large part because two of the three late justices lived in states overrun by revolt, so that if successors had been appointed in the same localities the new judges could not have served on their circuits.

Moreover, as the President said, many of the most competent men probably would have rejected the personal hazard of accepting service. And he was unwilling, Lincoln continued, "to throw all the appointments northward," thus disabling himself "from doing justice to the south on the return of peace." But as the Civil War went into its second year it became grimly evident that appointments would have to be made from the North if the Supreme Court was to function in the wartime crisis.

Lincoln knew a lot about the Supreme Court. First of all he was a lawyer. From his mid-twenties in New Salem the law had been his profession, its practice his livelihood. Then the Supreme Court had come inevitably into the spreading struggle over slavery, but with more impact on the prairie circuit rider in central Illinois than on most of his brethren at the bar. The Dred Scott decision of 1857, which held that a Missouri slave was not a citizen and hence did not have the constitutional right to sue for his freedom in a Federal court, embodied a futile effort at settling the controversy as undertaken by the octogenarian Chief Justice Roger Brooke Taney.

Instead of calming the storm the Supreme Court's entry into the conflict provoked the abolitionist press and hostile politicians to attack the supreme tribunal with invective and bitterness unparalleled in its history. The Taney opinion was hotly debated in the Illinois senatorial campaign of 1858 when an angular, beardless, aggressive Lincoln tried to unseat the Little Giant, Stephen A. Douglas. The challenger unhesitatingly criticized the decision and called for its review and eventual reversal.

In hardly more than two years from his oratorical encounter in Illinois with state sovereignty's ablest spokesman, Lincoln was confronted with grave conflict with regard to the Supreme Court. He was now not only head of one of the three co-ordinate branches of the Federal Government but also military Commander-in-chief, confronted with wartime disloyalty in the North. Exercising extraordinary emergency powers the President suspended the writ of habeas corpus in order to prevent the release of Southern agitators of whom John Merryman, imprisoned Maryland secessionist, was typical.

The commanding officer at Fort McHenry followed Lincoln's directive and refused to comply with a writ for the release of Merryman, issued by Taney. Thereupon the Chief Justice wrote a strong opinion holding that the historic protection of the individual citizen could not be suspended by the President but only by Congress. The North denounced the Merryman decision, and its only effect on Lincoln was to resolve him the more firmly in his policy of prosecuting the war as effectively as possible. He yielded not an inch, and neither did Taney, who was no less determined to maintain the equal role of the Supreme Court, even during civil war. Thus was the issue joined in the early weeks of 1861 between the new President from free Illinois and the old Chief Justice from largely proslavery Maryland.

With the seats of Justices Daniel, McLean, and Campbell still unfilled the Supreme Court divided in general three-to-three on support of the Lincoln Administration. Gloomy, pessimistic Justice Samuel Nelson of New York, a Tyler appointee, and deeply perplexed Nathan Clifford of Maine, a Buchanan choice, joined Taney in dislike for Lincoln's policies. Three Justices saw the issues much as Lincoln did: two Southerners, Justice James Moore Wayne of Georgia, a Jackson nominee, and Justice John Catron of Tennessee, chosen by Van Buren; and Pennsylvanian Robert Cooper Grier, named by Polk—staunch Unionists all. If this state of judicial affairs was both frustrating and dangerous it reflected as well the seemingly even balance in the dismembered Union.

Many of his advisors urged the President to take control of the Supreme Court with a firm hand, even to the point of creating additional seats to ensure a comfortable pro-Administration majority. Yet Lincoln was a model of patience. Fighting rebellion, he was as restrained as circumstances would permit. Notwithstanding pressures for this candidate and that, the President waited until January 1862 before he filled the first of the three vacancies. The choice was Noah Haynes Swayne of Ohio, whose basic qualification, as was that of all five of Lincoln's appointees, was intense belief in the Union cause. Swayne had moved from his native Virginia in protest against its slavery. Although he could help the struggling Administration politically, Swayne was so little known outside Ohio that leading Eastern newspapers persisted in misspelling his name.

Swayne's energy and industry provided some relief for the aged, illness-stricken, overworked supreme bench, but a heavy burden remained and six months later Lincoln made his second choice, Samuel Freeman Miller of Iowa. The ex-Kentuckian was the first Supreme Court appointee from west of the Mississippi and a frontier physician turned lawyer. He was a striking man with a massive head and clear-cut features. Although he had not held any public office he was an active Lincoln supporter and on the high bench at once became a tower of strength for the interests of the Federal Government. But Justice Miller also had a streak of independence and concerned himself with the rights of both states and citizens.

Then for his third appointee, in December 1862, Lincoln turned to Illinois and David Davis, an old and portly friend. Davis was a native of Maryland and a prairie circuit judge before whom Lincoln had practiced. In 1860 Davis had managed the shouting forces that nominated Lincoln for the Presidency in Chicago's "Wigwam."

These Lincoln Justices settled into their seats none too soon. In March of 1863 the full bench, in the historic "Prize Cases," upheld by the hairline majority of five to four the President's exercise of emergency powers—calling for volunteers, enlarging the Army, blockading Southern ports, suspending the habeas-corpus writ—without previous authorization by Congress. The three Justices appointed by Lincoln, plus Grier and Wayne, sustained the blockade proclamation and along with it the subsequent capture of merchant vessels that were seized in their attempt to reach Confederate ports. Chief Justice Taney and Justices Nelson, Clifford, and Catron, in sharp dissent, held that since Congress did not recognize the existence of war until July 13, 1861, the President had no war powers before that date. By this thread was Lincoln spared grave embarrassment at the hands of the Supreme Court in the floodtide war year that was to see Chancellorsville, Gettysburg, Chickamauga, and Vicksburg.

With the President's approval Congress now completed its reorganization of the Supreme Court circuits and in doing so created a tenth seat. To this new seat the President appointed from the Far West ex-Democrat Stephen Johnson Field, a native of Connecticut who had settled in California in the Gold Rush year of 1849. Despite his involvement in a feud that produced two disbarments for him and a hitch in jail the two-fisted Field had risen to the California Supreme Court.

Still once more was Lincoln called on to fill a Supreme Court seat. That was when Chief Justice Taney died in his eighty-seventh year in 1864. Seemingly the highest judicial office could go to only one man—ambitious, vain, proud, New Hampshire-born Salmon Porter Chase of Ohio. He had been Lincoln's Secretary of the Treasury for three crucial years during which he regarded himself as infinitely superior to the President. By 1864 he was a prospective rival of Lincoln in the approaching re-election campaign. Although the elevation of Chase was virtually by prearrangement Lincoln made the appointment with deep misgivings, and in part to place the troublemaking Chase in a restricting position and under obligation to the President.

With a new Chief Justice sworn in Lincoln had remade the Supreme Court. A tribunal that was Eastern and Southern in 1860 four years later was Western for the first time. It was a bench that would project itself beyond Appomattox and far into the future—Chase to 1873, Davis to 1877, Swayne to 1881, Miller to 1890, and Field to 1897 and the eve of the Spanish-American War. Thus did Lincoln's tall shadow slowly lengthen across a third of a century of the deliberations of the Supreme Court of the United States.

Irving Dilliard

53

THE UNPOPULAR MR. LINCOLN

by Robert S. Harper

He was the most unpopular man ever elected President of the United States. Almost five million men voted, but he received nearly a million votes less than the total cast for his three opponents.

When he entered the White House they said he was an illiterate, a barroom witling, a crude fellow, a charlatan, a wretched imbecile, a pettifogging demagogue, a half-witted usurper, a simple Susan.

His name was Abraham Lincoln.

When the disunion he inherited with the office blazed into frightful civil war they called him a second Benedict Arnold, a blunderer, a lunatic, a perjured traitor.

His name was Abraham Lincoln.

When he marshaled the men and resources of the Northern states to preserve the union they charged he was a tyrant, a dictator, a despot, a subservient tool of designing men.

His name was Abraham Lincoln.

When he prayed with the nation at Gettysburg that we highly resolve that these dead shall not have died in vain and that this nation, under God, shall have a new birth of freedom, they scoffed at his words as silly remarks, dishwatery utterances, totally inadequate and ludicrous sallies.

When he sought a second term they called him a ridiculous joke, a compound of cunning and heartless folly, a betrayer of liberty, a politician but never a statesman, a vulgar and swaggering storyteller. They said he was weak intellectually, false to the cause of freedom, controlled by dishonest interests, guilty of damnable blunders, and that the country was doomed unless he was turned out of office.

They plotted to force him out of the presidential race and they tried to produce a rival candidate to run against him. His own trusted advisors told him there was no hope for his re-election.

A circular listing ten reasons why Lincoln should not be elected was published. Number one accused him of failing to keep his oath to support the Constitution and of trampling it underfoot.

Embittered because they could not control him, two powerful Northern political leaders issued a manifesto to charge that he had usurped the powers of Congress, and that his emancipation policy was weak and was but a scheme to win support of Southern delegations for his renomination.

The haggard, war-racked President sadly remarked: "To be wounded in the house of one's friends is perhaps the most grievous affliction that can befall a man."

The days grew even darker, and to Lincoln it seemed he had not a friend in the world. He wrote a little note saying it appeared improbable the Administration would be re-elected.

"Then," he penned, "it will be my duty to so co-operate with the President elect, as to save the Union between the election and the inauguration; as he will have secured his election on such ground that he can not possibly save it afterwards."

He folded the paper, pasted it, and asked his Cabinet members to endorse it, before putting it away in his desk.

by Robert S. Harper

Lincoln's fears proved groundless. A surprising ground swell of support from the people all over the North installed him for a second term.

When, the next March, Lincoln took the oath a second time ultimate victory for the Union was apparent. Then in a sudden tragic flash, at the moment victory bells were ringing in the North, Abraham Lincoln was dead, struck down by an assassin. Telegraph wires carried the news to the people across the mountains, over the plains, into the cities and villages, and finally to every home. All the land wept.

A stunned nation, both North and South, gasped at the hole in the sky where the giant had stood. Suddenly it seemed as though the whole world realized there had passed a man whose like it might never see again. It was as though even those who hated Abraham Lincoln had known all along of his greatness and had stubbornly refused to admit it. Never was such high tribute paid to a human being.

Thus was born a paradox of history: the most unpopular man ever elected President of the United States became the most popular name of all the nation's great.

There is an explanation for it. Abraham Lincoln's popularity was no sudden thing that blossomed overnight with his martyrdom and left us with the heroic image we have today. He was taken into the hearts of his countrymen while he lived. His popularity had been building up for months previously, but the politicians were not aware of it.

In some manner, despite the shouts of his critics and the roar of presses pouring out millions of words against him, an understanding of Lincoln's love of his fellow man and his desire to be loved in return got through to the people.

They wrote letters to him, these little people, as they would have written to a dear friend or to their father. They called him Father Abraham and they told him of their troubles, for they knew he understood.

That was the way Lincoln wanted it to be. Desire to be a man of the people was the ruling passion of his political life. Nevertheless he refused to sacrifice his ideals—the ideals that held him to the course that preserved the Union—to gain public favor. Consequently he would suffer temporary damage to his popularity until the people understood his position and time proved him to have been right.

Such popularity as he enjoyed was a prideful thing to him. Almost boastfully he could recall how popular he was as a young man in New Salem. When he ran for the Illinois legislature he was encouraged to do so, he said—these are his exact words—"by his great popularity among his immediate neighbors." He was beaten, but that mattered little. What really counted, as he later pointed out, was the fact that he won all but seven of the votes in his precinct.

After four terms in the legislature and marriage to well-born Mary Todd of Kentucky Lincoln went after his party's nomination for Congress. The convention passed over him. Brooding over the setback he thought his marriage might have hurt his popularity with the people, and he felt that he had lost ground politically.

It was astonishing, he said, that he had been put down "as a candidate of pride, wealth, and aristocratic family distinction."

He made a promise. "I am now and always shall be the same Abraham Lincoln that I was."

When later he won the nomination for Congress he was elected with an unprecedented majority, the only Whig in the Illinois delegation. The war with Mexico, which he opposed in principle, was in its final stages. Contending that the war was unnecessarily begun, he boldly offered a set of resolutions challenging President Polk to point out just where was the spot the first American blood was shed. Three weeks later he spoke for his resolutions. The people back home in the Seventh District, many of whom had boys in the fighting, disowned him and called him a disgrace to Illinois. They gave him the nickname "Spotty" Lincoln, which plagued him for years. He was not a candidate for re-election, and the Whig who attempted to succeed him was defeated.

Sick at heart because his policy had been rejected by the people, Lincoln went back to the circuit. Ten years more and again he was the popular idol of Illinois, the underdog battling Stephen A. Douglas for the Senatorship. His party's candidates won the popular vote, but an outdated apportionment law cost him the election in the legislature.

He carried his home city of Springfield, where he lived for a quarter of a century, the last two times he was a candidate, in 1860 and again in 1864, by only the narrowest of margins.

"Mr. Lincoln," wrote his faithful law partner Billy Herndon, "was not appreciated in this city, nor was he at all times the most popular man among us. The cause of the unpopularity, or rather the want of popularity here, arose out of two grounds: first, he did his own thinking, and second, he had the courage of his convictions and he boldly and fearlessly expressed them."

No finer tribute was ever paid to Abraham Lincoln.

Robert S. Harper

54

THE ELECTION OF 1864

by Howard K. Beale

In many ways the election of 1864 was the most critical (and important) in all American history. It was the only presidential election ever conducted in the midst of civil war when the continuance of democracy and the very existence of the nation were endangered. The contest was fought over some old issues and many new ones. Democratic and Republican (Union) parties battled each other for control of government. But the traditional North-South struggle within parties had broken into bitter civil war and was not a part of the campaign. In the place of Southern Whigs, destroyed by the slavery issue, a newborn Republican party was trying to establish itself. In the North both Democrats and Republicans were divided as they always are into rival sectional interests, but also into factions split wide apart by war issues, postwar plans, race attitudes, and economic interests. And all of the bitterness of factional feuds was heightened by the emotion of civil war and the destruction of property and loss of life that war brought.

As the incumbent seeking re-election Abraham Lincoln was

attacked for almost everything. Democrats denounced him for breaking up the Union by making it impossible for Southerners to stay in it, for fighting the war at all, for stern measures against Northerners who supported the effort to overthrow the government, for autocratic exercise of war powers that endangered traditional American freedoms, for his reluctant freeing of slaves as a war strategy, for not ending the war on almost any terms, for his removal of General McClellan—whom Democrats made a popular hero and in 1864 nominated for the Presidency. Even leading members of his own party denounced Lincoln and tried to break his leadership.

Lincoln's conduct on the slavery issue displeased many. He had initially been a compromise candidate and as such had satisfied neither the extremists who wished to destroy slavery even in the South nor the moderates who did not care about slavery and wanted concessions made to the South to keep it within the Union. Lincoln had no midtwentieth-century desire for integration or equality of Negroes and whites. From the first he had held together the great mass of moderate Republicans and moderate Northern Democrats in support of the government by refusing to fight to free the slaves, and by insisting on keeping the conflict a war solely to preserve the nation and prevent the overthrow of its government. When he freed the slaves of those still in rebellion—but only those slaves—he did it as strategy of war under his war powers and insisted that the Federal Government had no authority to free further slaves except by constitutional amendment. While this moderate position held the nation together and won the support of moderate War Democrats it alienated many men of Lincoln's own party. Old abolitionists and humanitarians concerned about the Negro opposed him because he did not take a vigorous stand for Negro freedom and protection of Negro rights. He was attacked, too, by Republican extremists who hoped to use enfranchised Negroes to break the power of the agrarian South and establish Northern business control. Opposition came likewise from congressional leaders, particularly in his own party, who resented a strong President and wished power to remain in the hands of congressional party leaders.

Lincoln's conduct of the war led to further attacks. Some blamed him for the length and costliness of the war. McClellan, popular with his soldiers and with Democrats, had a great following that turned on Lincoln when he relieved McClellan of command. Removal from the field of Frémont and of several lesser generals of German background made German-Americans hostile. He was blamed for the failures of earlier generals and then denounced for the terrific cost in human life of Grant's successes.

Republican unity, endangered by party attacks on Lincoln, was further complicated by conflicting economic interests. In general Northeastern and Middle Atlantic States Republicans favored and Western Republicans opposed the new national banks, a high protective tariff, the national-bank currency, and floating bonds by paying high profits to bankers for disposing of them. While Westerners favored, Easterners opposed internal improvements and inflation through depreciated state-bank notes and Federal greenbacks. Everywhere many resented conscription that Lincoln considered necessary. Poorer people denounced Lincoln for drafting men unable to hire others to fight for them, while permitting prosperous people to buy their way out of Army service by paying substitutes. In this complicated situation it was hard to draw up a platform or hold the Republican party together.

Republican success in 1864 was jeopardized by jealousy toward Lincoln on the part of some of his 1860 party rivals and by the aspirations of ambitious party leaders who thought they could run the Presidency better than he did. William H. Seward, Edward Bates, and Salmon P. Chase, among those considered for the Republican nomination in 1860, had been invited into Lincoln's Cabinet. Seward and Bates had become devotedly loyal to him, but Chase, eager to be President and always convinced that he was far abler than Lincoln, schemed constantly with malcontents who he hoped would put him into Lincoln's place. And another 1860 rival, Frémont, was jealous of the influence of Lincoln's friends the Blairs in his own state of Missouri and in Washington, angry over Lincoln's lack of appreciation of him in the Army, and opposed to Lincoln's policy for the South. He therefore became the center of another effort to depose Lincoln. German friends of Frémont in Illinois and Missouri and New England abolitionists combined to call a convention in Cleveland to nominate Frémont.

Among those opposed to Lincoln were leading Republican newspapers, powerful men in the party, and clergymen. Republican leaders wished to replace him: men like Chase in his Cabinet; Republican United States Senators like Charles Sumner and Henry Wilson of Massachusetts, Zachariah Chandler of Michigan, Samuel C. Pomeroy of Kansas, Benjamin Wade of Ohio; Republican Congressmen like Henry Winter Davis of Maryland and Thaddeus Stevens of Pennsylvania; and Republican governors like John A. Andrew of Massachusetts and Oliver P. Morton of Indiana.

A campaign of vilification was organized against Lincoln. He was "a vulgar joke," "a joke incarnate." Stories were circulated about an insensitiveness to suffering and grief for the dead that led him to tell crude jokes in the midst of the dead and dying on visits to the front. He was denounced as a representative of the money power. He was described as a tyrant, a scoundrel, the "railsplitting buffoon." In his own campaigning Lincoln seems to have been a model of fairness. Faced with possible—many thought certain—defeat by McClellan, he would never allow McClellan's loyalty to be questioned. He never used vilification against his enemies. He refrained from using electoral votes of his newly reorganized states of Arkansas and Louisiana, and hesitated until the last minute before he issued the proclamation of statehood for Nevada, a state with little population but with three certain additional electoral votes.

Perhaps the most serious cause of attacks upon him by members of his own party was his policy of conciliation toward the

South, his obvious unwillingness to let extremist members of his party use Negro votes, political disqualification of Southerners, and prolonged military rule of the South in order to keep it subordinate until it could be made Republican. Indeed as early as December 1863 he had made his proposal of presidential restoration of the South: to forget the past, and to recognize new state governments whenever 10 per cent of the voters of 1860 in any rebelling state should have taken an oath of future loyalty and should have set up a new state constitution and government that would recognize freedom for the Negro. Frémont's platform, on the other hand, called for taking reconstruction powers away from the President and giving them to Congress, and for confiscation of the land of all Southern Rebels. Just before adjournment Congressman Henry Winter Davis of Maryland and Senator Benjamin Wade of Ohio combined to get a reconstruction bill passed by Congress. It repudiated the doctrine on which the North had stood at the outbreak of war, that states could not leave the Union, and insisted that Southern states were out of the Union and should be treated as conquered provinces. Only Congress, it said, could reorganize them. Fifty per cent of 1860 voters must first take an oath of loyalty, but then all of these that had voluntarily supported rebellion or given it aid and comfort should be disqualified from voting or holding office. Under pressure to sign the bill on the last day of the session, Lincoln refused and then pocket-vetoed it, issuing a proclamation criticizing the bill and arguing for his own views. Wade and Davis responded with a manifesto denouncing him. Stevens and other extremists wanted to go even beyond this bill to Negro suffrage and confiscation of large planters' lands, but failed to carry their Northern fellow Congressmen to this extreme.

The summer of 1864 was militarily depressing. Early's Confederate troops raided the northern suburbs of Washington itself, and the casualties in Grant's army reduced many Northerners to anguish and despair. As war prospects became gloomier Lincoln's chances of re-election seemed to decline. Lincoln and his friends feared political defeat.

Out of the despair of the summer, political victory was ultimately won. The tide of battle turned, with military successes like the heartening fall of Atlanta. Grant's grim and bloody campaign pushed forward. The Democrats lost many votes by confusing issues through combining a candidate, McClellan, who promised to continue the war to victory, with a peace platform that called for cessation of hostilities. Republican leaders, sensing Lincoln's popularity, hesitated to support his rivals openly. The masterful politicianship of Lincoln overcame opposition. For example, the Chase bubble had burst by March 1864, and in his embarrassment Chase offered his resignation from the Cabinet. Lincoln shrewdly declined to accept it then, but the next summer, when Chase again resigned in a controversy over New York patronage, Lincoln surprised him by accepting his resignation in time to turn large numbers of Treasury employees from opponents into supporters. Again, Frémont's candidacy was withdrawn in September in return for Lincoln's accepting the resignation, long in his hands, of his friend Montgomery Blair, who was devoted enough to help Lincoln by stepping out of the Cabinet while continuing support. Leaders in state after state fell into line rather than risk Democratic victory through a Republican split. The soldier vote helped Lincoln. And all along the masses of the common people wanted Lincoln's re-election. Yet in spite of a large electoral majority Lincoln's victory was by a narrow margin in a number of states, and some think the soldiers' ballots carried the election.

One important result of the election was the notice it gave that once the war was won Lincoln's plan of speedy restoration would face bitter opposition in his own party; that Congress dominated by his party would contest his right to reorganize the defeated states at all. Powerful Republican leaders would try to move on to the confiscation of Southern lands, the disfranchisement of white Southerners, and the maintenance of Republican power in the nation by keeping control of the South through Negro votes.

Though later the dead Lincoln was to be useful to Republicans in winning elections the 1864 campaign showed that he was hated by the leaders of his own party. Privately many leading Republicans were relieved at his death. They saw an act of Providence in his assassination; they thanked God and took courage because Lincoln's death ended what they considered "criminal clemency to traitors" and "milk-and-water" as a remedy for treason. A caucus of Republican leaders felt that Lincoln's death "would prove a godsend to the country."

Perhaps the most important fact about the election was that democracy stood the test of crisis. In the midst of bitter civil war, with the existence of the nation threatened, with many Democrats demanding peace and many Republicans wishing to turn their own leader out of office, Lincoln resisted temptation, to which many leaders in other times and places have succumbed, to save the country and maintain himself in power by suspending democratic processes. And at the height of the worst crisis in American history the American people conducted an election through normal democratic machinery. This election proved to a skeptical world that democracy could and would survive even great peril to the nation.

Howard K. Beale

55

THE PHOTOGENIC MR. LINCOLN

by Roy Meredith

To many Americans the photographs of Abraham Lincoln are more than merely antique likenesses of the great Civil War President. Each newly discovered photograph or plate fragment, from some dusty garret or other remote hiding place, brings with it the thrill of discovery to finder and viewer alike.

To weigh the relative artistic and technical merits of the Lincoln photographs one must temporarily cast aside his love for the Lincoln legend; forget completely the vast panorama of dreadful events linked so closely with each picture; and look upon them as would the chief restorer at the Louvre judging a rare painting—in a raking light which strikingly reveals every defect and brush stroke. But this kind of criticism would be unfair.

More important than artistic and technical judgments is the drama behind the scene in these pictures, for each of these wonderful photographs—ambrotypes, daguerreotypes, and tintypes— represents an important milestone in the life of Abraham Lincoln.

Abraham Lincoln was perhaps the most photographed man of his time. More than twenty photographers of varied technical skill, at one time or another, from the prairies to the White House, gazed on, marveled at, and aimed their cameras at "the unfathomable face." Today the sum total of Lincoln photographs, owned by private collectors and educational institutions, is an impressive figure, well over a hundred.

This flood of Lincoln photographs tends to divide itself into two groups: Lincoln the lawyer and Lincoln the President. The most dramatic of these pictures, made by the master photographers Mathew Brady and Alexander Gardner, begin with Brady's first official preinaugural photograph and end with Gardner's stunning portrait of the President taken on April 10, 1865, four days before Lincoln's assassination.

Almost every dramatic element in the human experience is embodied in these pictures. There is even some wry humor in the taking of the preinaugural photograph. Oddly enough, after sixteen years of posing the chins of the great and near-great of Europe and America, Brady, the world-renowned portrait specialist and winner of gold medals for his magnificent work, was unsure of himself when confronted with posing the President-elect. Lincoln was not an easy subject for photographers or artists, according to John G. Nicolay, the President's secretary. "Lincoln's features were the despair of every artist who undertook his portrait," he said. The arrival of Lincoln and his friend Ward Hill Lamon at Brady's gallery caused more than consternation—even Brady panicked.

Maturity, immense mental stature, and a quiet inner power had come to Abraham Lincoln. The newly bearded President-elect who quietly took his place before the camera was probably haunted by the thoughts of silent enemies among the spectators at the forthcoming inaugural ceremonies and the possibility of war.

George Story, an artist, later curator of the Metropolitan Museum of Art, fondly recalled that Brady rushed into his studio, on the floor above the gallery, and begged for assistance in posing Lincoln. Story agreed to help, and artist and photographer hurried back to the gallery only to find Lincoln already seated under the skylight, "relapsed into his melancholy mood," a pose long familiar to young Robert Lincoln, his son.

Seeing Lincoln thus seated brought out the artist in Story. "Pose him?" he cried. "No! Bring the camera at once!" And the picture was made. Story had realized something Brady had not. It was unnecessary to pose Lincoln. The pictures made by Brady at this sitting contain drama of expression, photographic interpolation, and depth of feeling, all essentials of good photography.

More dramatic even are the pictures made of the President on the battlefield of Antietam in October of 1862. The war had been going badly for the Union, and Lincoln was painfully aware of it. That year numerous pictures were made; awesome in their great silence, to feel their full impact is to know the story in the shadows behind them. Lee had all but annihilated the Army of Virginia under Pope at Second Manassas, in August, just two months before. Emboldened by his unbroken string of victories, Lee attempted an invasion of the Northern states. To halt it Lincoln, in desperation, returned his wavering field commander, General George B. McClellan, to command. McClellan met Lee head on at Antietam Creek, in Maryland, in the bloodiest single day's action of the war. A lost order of Lee's, revealing his troop dispositions and found by one of McClellan's soldiers, gave the battle to the Federal general. But McClellan failed to follow up his advantage and let Lee get away. Chided for his inaction McClellan wrote to the President, blaming his failure to pursue Lee on the condition of his horses. The President replied: "Will you pardon me for asking what the horses of your army have done . . . that fatigue anything?"

Lincoln visited the army in early October and was photographed with General McClellan in the latter's tent, both men looking very grim. Later several group photographs of Lincoln, McClellan, and his staff officers were made. In these pictures Lincoln's face is a study in exasperation and disappointment.

The soft fall light at Antietam modeled the towering figure of

Lincoln and his shorter generals, a picture which has not exhausted, nor ever will exhaust, its message. It is the same with all pictures made at Antietam. There, captured for all time, are the tensions and emotional frustrations of the President and his men at war.

Lincoln returned to Washington finally satisfied that McClellan was not the man to command the army. "I said I would remove McClellan if he let Lee get away," he said, "and I must do so." These pictures are perhaps the most important of the entire Lincoln collection. Strangely enough no pictures were made at City Point, Virginia, when he visited General Grant at the close of the war. The only pictorial representation of this event is an on-the-spot drawing by Winslow Homer, an enterprising artist for *Harper's Weekly*.

Sometime in August of 1863, a month after the battle of Gettysburg, Lincoln sat for Alexander Gardner. The battle had been nearer a draw than a victory to both Lee and Meade, but Lee had again gotten away to prolong the war another two years. Gardner's picture reflects the anguish and mental torment Lincoln was undergoing. The astronomical losses in life at Gettysburg, and the fact that General George Gordon Meade had not come up to expectations, saddened the President and caused him great concern.

In November of that year President Lincoln delivered his immortal address at Gettysburg. There is no more explanation of why Brady and Gardner or their photographers weren't present on such an important occasion than there is accounting for the fact that no photographers were present at Lee's surrender at Appomattox two years later. It was left to local photographers to perpetuate the event. The photographers, troubled by the weather and the large crowd and unable to get close enough to the speakers' platform, had to be satisfied to place their cameras wherever they were. The existing picture, taken from a great distance, is inadequate to the occasion, and no amount of detailed enlarging will improve it.

by Roy Meredith

Gardner made several pictures of Lincoln in 1863; most were made in the gallery in early August in seated pose. Another was made three months later with Lincoln's secretaries, John Nicolay and John Hay.

The stories behind the taking of the Lincoln photographs are legion. There is the story of little Tad, the President's son, locking Brady's men in the closet when he disapproved of their using his playroom for a darkroom, with the President quietly coaxing the boy to let them out. There is the fact that Mary Todd Lincoln was never photographed with her husband.

With few exceptions the photographs of Abraham Lincoln reflect the sadness he felt toward the great tragedy of the war. Everything in these pictures is significant: small joys, some bitterness, much sadness and personal heartbreak are intermingled with each day's hard, relentless routine. Only in the last picture, made of Lincoln by Alexander Gardner on April 10, 1865, is there the trace of a smile. Lee had surrendered the day before and the war was over.

As for the artistic and technical properties of the photographs of Abraham Lincoln this can be said: in each of the Lincoln portrait photographs there is an absence of photographic refinements. Only a table, or in some a plain chair or a single column, forms the background. Lincoln himself made the picture. Some of the Gardner pictures show poor composition, an awkward posing of Lincoln. In these the President is seated before the camera in an uncomfortable straight-backed chair too small for his long legs; the pose and very stiff facial expression reflect his discomfort.

Of course the picture made in the Brady studio, called the Five Dollar Bill portrait, is one of the finest of the lot. Only the plain background is used, which is proper for nearly all portrait photography. The handsome chair is the famous "Brady chair," hallmark of Brady's portraits. For the most part the Lincoln photographs are wonderful examples of photographic composition. Many others are poor attempts at portraiture.

One fact is certain. The discriminating eye of the camera did not record in the plain backgrounds the triple specters of violence, bloodshed, and immeasurable personal loss. Yet they are forever there in the face of the man who has rightfully become, through the years, all that can be truly termed American.

56

LINCOLN AND HIS HOPE
FOR A JUST AND LASTING PEACE

by Carl Haverlin

To Abraham Lincoln and to some, at least, of those who heard the noble peroration of his Second Inaugural Address the phrase "achieve and cherish a just, and a lasting peace" had overtones and meanings that succeeding generations find increasingly difficult to sense.

To him these words meant a restoration of the perfect Union even more than an end to war, for despite his innate humanity he mourned the dismembered nation above the dead and their bereaved of both the North and South. After many years of unity we have come to take the Union as a matter of course. We must strive to remember that to Lincoln, in that time and in that place, the Union had been but newly won and twice, within his own memory, nearly lost. He had known men who bore the scars of Revolutionary battles and remembered, "like a firebell in the night," the national tension before the admission of Missouri, and South Carolina's first threat of secession in 1832.

With the passing of the years it becomes difficult to keep our past in focus. The canvas of Lincoln's time, shadowed emotionally for him by our nation's beginning, today seems to us so full and busy that even his commanding figure sometimes fades into the men and events around him. When he does stand out clearly and speak for himself some do not comprehend him fully due to their preconceptions and because the words of an oft-told tale tend to lose edge and meaning with repetition.

His long and stubborn stand against the extension of slavery to the territories is so well known that it may obscure, as it did for some of his contemporaries, his equally firm stand for the constitutional protection of slavery where it was legal and his open adherence to the operation of the Fugitive Slave Law—though it and slavery were personally repugnant to him. Only those who read his writing in the *Collected Works* can fully grasp how desperately he struggled, between his nomination and his departure for Washington, to keep the peace and maintain, intact, the Union. Only his own words, day by day, can make clear how careful he was, then and during the war that followed, to avoid excess of word or deed and the taint of the doctrinaire.

Through all this troubled period, and indeed from 1854 to the end of his life, he made it crystal clear in his letters, speeches, and messages "how fondly he hoped and fervently prayed" for the Union and for the peace that would restore it. But he found the communication and understanding of his views to be difficult, and learned early that there are none so deaf as those that will not hear. To a friend, William S. Speer, he wrote in part on October 23, 1860, "Those who will not read, or heed, what I have already publicly said, would not read, or heed, a repetition of it. 'If they hear not Moses and the prophets, neither will they be persuaded though one rose from the dead.'"

In a letter dated February 14, 1860, explaining a paragraph in the House Divided speech, he wrote: "That is the whole paragraph; and it puzzles me to make my meaning plainer. Look over it carefully, and conclude I meant all I said and did not mean anything I did not say, and you will have my meaning."

Lincoln was assuring his correspondents, and those of us who will hear him, that he thought before he spoke or wrote. To him his words were weapons in his battles for the Union, before and after the outbreak of the war. He thought with the exquisite precision of a great advocate, and with necessity he could write with the emotional intensity of a major poet. From his nomination to his death he devoted this precision and this emotion to the maintenance of the Union and, when it was threatened, to its restoration.

The measure of his stability was never more clearly demonstrated than during the crumbling away of the Union through the fateful 119 days between his election and his inauguration. While in Springfield he resisted steadfastly the pressure upon him from both friends and foes alike for public declarations and refused to be drawn into statements, explanations, or promises.

He believed that the Republican platform upon which he had been elected and his own printed speeches, particularly the volume of the debates with Douglas, explained his principles, and those of his party, in full. He feared that any attempt to expand upon them or explain them would satisfy neither his friends nor his opponents and indeed might be considered a sign of weakness and withdrawal by both.

Writing confidentially on December 15, 1860, to John C. Gilmer of North Carolina, to whom he later offered a Cabinet post, he asked: "Is it desired that I shall shift the ground upon which I have been elected? I can not do it. You need only to acquaint yourself with that ground, and press it on the attention of the South. It is all in print and easy of access. May I be pardoned if I ask whether even you have ever attempted to procure the reading of the Republican platform, or my speeches, by the Southern people? If not, what reason have I to expect that any additional production of mine would meet a better fate? It would make me appear as if I repented for the crime of having been elected, and was anxious to apologize and beg forgiveness. . . . On the territorial question, I am inflexible, as you see my position in the book. On that there is a difference of opinion between you and us; and it is the only substantial difference. You think slavery is right and ought to be extended; we think it is wrong and ought to be restricted. For this, neither has any just occasion to be angry with the other."

In dwelling upon the continued requests for him to speak out, it is both ironic and touching to realize that on the trip to Washington he did not deliver the one address he most wanted to make because the one invitation he most wanted to receive—from Kentucky—was never extended. But had he been asked to cross the Ohio we know what he would have said, in part at least, for in the Library of Congress is a five-page manuscript, "Fragment of Speech Intended for Kentuckians." He would have delivered it on February 12.

"I am grateful," it opens, "for the opportunity your invitation affords me to appear before an audience of my native state." (And here it is tempting to speculate whether he did not decide, on or about January 26, to leave Springfield four days earlier than planned and thereby emphasize his kinship with the people of this pivotal border state, so far uncommitted to the Confederacy, by pointing out that he spoke on his native soil on his fifty-second birthday. A compelling reason for his visit was that it would offset, to some degree, a story the New York *Herald* had printed in August that inferred Lincoln was afraid he might be lynched in Kentucky.)

"During the present winter it has been greatly pressed upon me by many patriotic citizens, Kentuckians among others, that I could in my position, by a word, restore peace to the country. But what word? I have many words already before the public; and my position was given me on the faith of those words. Is the desired word to be confirmatory of these; or must it be contradictory to them? If the former, it is useless repe[ti]tion; if the latter, it is dishonorable and treacherous. . . . Who amongst you

by Carl Haverlin

would not die by the proposition, that your candidate, being elected, should be inaugerated, solely on the conditions of the constitution, and laws, or not at all. What Kentuckian, worthy of his birthplace, would not do this? Gentlemen, I too, am a Kentuckian."

Since he was not asked to speak in Kentucky he was forced to speak to it and, hopefully, to all the disaffected states, whether he was reported there or not, from the balcony of the Burnet House in Cincinnati. In doing so he first repeated a portion of an address, directed to Kentucky, that he had made there in 1859, and then, directly: "Fellow Citizens of Kentucky—friends—bretheren, may I call you—in my new position, I see no occasion, and feel no inclination, to retract a word of this. If it shall not be made good, be assured, the fault shall not be mine."

In closing he trusted to "the good sense of the American people, on all sides of all rivers in America, under the Providence of God, who has never deserted us, that we shall again be brethren, forgetting all parties—ignoring all parties. . . ."

Is it too much to think that in this undelivered address and in his Cincinnati speech are to be found the stark and simple outlines of his future course?

He never lost confidence in the American people "on all sides of all rivers"; to the very end he continued to invoke the Providence of God and the sanctity of the Constitution; he forgot parties in his selection and employment of men to help bring peace and restore the Union.

Despite his experiences since the election Lincoln could not have fathomed how bitter would be the storm after he took office and the crises developed. Then, added to the prevailing but always conflicting winds of public opinion, would blow the sharp hurricane gusts of congressional differences and from every quarter the whistling gales of the editorial lash. Worst of all, in the very eye of the storm, where he stood, he would feel the bitter and icy vacuum of a growing sense of his own insufficiency for the task he faced. It would be then that he knew himself un-

329

guyed except for the cables of his conviction. It would be then that he would learn that the power of the Chief Executive, though guaranteed by the Constitution, in a time of stress is no stronger than his own resolution to withstand all arguments, from whatsoever source, that do not accord with his own deepest convictions.

In his times of loneliness and distress he must have been deeply tempted to yield, in some part, his granite reserve; to waver in his determination to say nothing and do nothing that could, by any possibility in the future, delay or prevent the healing of the breach. It would have been easy for him, who had mastered the art of swaying men by logic and through emotion, to win the quick and easy affirmation of the crowd and soften, if not eradicate, the powerful antagonisms of individuals who troubled him, at times, more than the armor of the South. But by instinct or design, and probably by both, even in times of real desperation he kept his own counsel and refrained from any unnecessary word or deed that would inflame the South or its friends.

Though all of his presidential addresses and his messages to Congress were the careful works of a great propagandist whose faith was the Union, it was not until he created the compact miracle of the Second Inaugural Address that we see this aspect of Lincoln at its height. After four years he knew the time was ripe for a supreme effort. In this address his "steel and velvet" (to use Carl Sandburg's admirable phrase) are for the first time brought into direct and dramatic opposition. In its final 160 words we hear first the thunder of drums and the blast of the trumpets of Armageddon, and then, over their reverberating echoes, falls the soft, the gentle, the velvet murmur of all that is compassionate.

Though in the opening of the address Lincoln specifically refused to predict the outcome of the war, his complete conviction that it was won shone through every luminous phrase. And it is not beyond belief that what he said on the Capitol steps hastened the end, for it must not be forgotten that he was noted for his careful choice of words. His announcement of so grim a determination to win the war, at whatever cost in blood and treasure, must have had a more chilling effect in Richmond than the appearance of a new army before its defenses. Yet he did not let slip on that day, as he had not on any previous day, one word that could give personal apprehension to any individual in the Confederacy. Even at this grave moment, with victory in his grasp, he refrained from boast or acrimony, reserving himself for the work of restoration that he would not live to see.

"Fondly do we hope—fervently do we pray—that this mighty scourge of war may speedily pass away. Yet, if God wills that it continue, until all the wealth piled by the bond-man's two hundred and fifty years of unrequited toil shall be sunk, and until every drop of blood drawn with the lash, shall be paid by another drawn with the sword, as was said three thousand years ago, so still it must be said 'the judgments of the Lord, are true and righteous altogether.'"

"With malice toward none; with charity for all; with firmness in the right, as God gives us to see the right, let us strive on to finish the work we are in; to bind up the nation's wounds; to care for him who shall have borne the battle, and for his widow, and his orphan—to do all which may achieve and cherish a just, and a lasting peace, among ourselves, and with all nations."

57

LINCOLN AND THE THIRTEENTH AMENDMENT

by Justin Miller

"Neither slavery nor involuntary servitude, except as a punishment for crime whereof the party shall have been duly convicted, shall exist within the United States, or any place subject to their jurisdiction." So reads the Thirteenth Amendment, which became a part of the United States Constitution in December 1865. And so ended the institution of human slavery which had plagued this country since its beginnings and which had caused the war between the states—the most bloody and devastating war in history. The one man to whom credit is due, above all others, for destroying this vestige of barbarism is Abraham Lincoln. And the history of this Thirteenth Amendment is, in large measure, the life story of this great American.

As he reached adult years, became a lawyer, and participated actively in public affairs, slavery became one horn of the great dilemma of Lincoln's life; a preponderating problem which went with him through every campaign, into every public office he held, and particularly throughout the years of his Presidency. Lincoln's dilemma arose from his repugnance to slavery—as the *by Justin Miller*

dispassionate conviction of a civilized man, upon the one hand and, on the other, from his loyal adherence to his country and to the Constitution, which at least by implication sanctioned slavery.

In 1854 Lincoln made one of his greatest speeches, opposing the Kansas-Nebraska Bill. In the Ordinance of 1787 Congress had provided for the government of the Northwest Territory and had decreed therein that "There shall be neither slavery nor involuntary servitude in the said Territory, otherwise than in punishment of crimes, whereof the party shall have been duly convicted." Stephen A. Douglas was the proponent of the Kansas-Nebraska Act, which reversed the policy of the Ordinance and opened to slavery new states which were being formed west of the old Northwest Territory. Lincoln, opposing him, called attention to the fact that Thomas Jefferson was the author of the Ordinance, that its adoption was concurrent with the Constitution itself, and that it represented the real sentiments of the Constitution-makers concerning the institution of slavery. During the next ten years Lincoln's thinking crystalized into a constitutional amendment which would speak in language almost identical with the great Ordinance of 1787.

Lincoln's election in 1860 put him in position to exercise the power of his office in favor of the desired amendment. But the events of history were running strongly against him. The South had already seceded when he took office in March 1861; President Buchanan had done nothing to check it; indeed in Lincoln's opinion secession was "being fostered rather than repressed"; many Northerners welcomed secession as the only possible solution of the slavery question, and Lincoln was urged to accept the Confederacy as a new nation rather than risk the devastation of war.

Lincoln made a deliberate choice to preserve the Union and to bypass the slavery question. In his inaugural address he said: "I have no purpose, directly or indirectly, to interfere with the institution of slavery, in the States where it exists. I believe I have no lawful right to do so, and I have no inclination to do so."

Then he went on to say: "I hold, that in contemplation of universal law, and of the Constitution, the Union of these States is perpetual. . . . I therefore consider that, in view of the Constitution and the laws, the Union is unbroken; and, to the extent of my ability, I shall take care, as the Constitution itself expressly enjoins upon me, that the laws of the Union be faithfully executed in all the States."

During the first two years of the Civil War Lincoln was fearful that Missouri and Kentucky would join the Confederacy. He urged representatives of these border states to take action leading to gradual emancipation and argued that compensation be paid at the rate of four hundred dollars per head for slaves freed by such state action. His proposals met with little favorable reaction. The border states were not interested in emancipation under any circumstances; the abolitionists of the North bitterly objected to compensating the slaveowners; Congress was not impressed by Lincoln's reasoning. If the South had been willing to abandon secession in return for such a program of gradual emancipation and compensation, Lincoln might have been able to effect such a compromise. But the South rejected his overtures with scorn.

By the end of the summer of 1862 Lincoln had become convinced that his ideas of compromise were hopeless. He had also become convinced that his wartime powers under the Constitution and authority given him by recent legislation were sufficient to warrant emancipation as a matter of military strategy. This was the background against which the Emancipation Proclamation was issued, effective as of January 1, 1863.

On its face the Proclamation was so limited as not to apply to slaves in the border states or to those parts of the Confederate states which already had come under control of the Union armies. Moreover the President knew that when the war ended, and with it his wartime powers, the grim specter of slavery would still be present; there would be many unsettled questions and a multiplicity of lawsuits concerning slave ownership.

The Emancipation Proclamation, however, produced amazing psychological results. It brought worldwise praise and commendation to the President. It brought immediate and far-reaching havoc in the economy of the Southern states as the Federal armies advanced; it brought realization to many neutral Northerners that here was a wartime weapon which, if timely use was made of it, could end the slavery controversy forever. All that was needed was to heed Lincoln's advice and go forward with the adoption of a constitutional amendment which would clinch, for all time and beyond all question, the emancipation of the slaves throughout the nation.

Lincoln took full advantage of the situation. He encouraged the introduction in Congress of a resolution proposing such an amendment. The proposal passed the Senate, but in the House the Democrats had sufficient strength to defeat it. But this was only the beginning of the campaign. Lincoln urged privately that the National Union platform should call for an "amendment of the Constitution abolishing and prohibiting slavery forever." Accordingly the platform stated that slavery was the cause of the rebellion, that the President's Proclamation had aimed a death blow at "this gigantic evil," but that a constitutional amendment was necessary to "terminate and forever prohibit" it.

Here at last Lincoln was able to bring together the two horns of the old dilemma, without need of a compromise. His re-election quieted his critics and convinced him, as well as Congress, that he spoke for the people of the country. Moreover so many Republican candidates for Congress were elected that the necessary two-thirds majority was assured to make certain the adoption of the resolution. Increasing successes of the Union armies and the obvious deterioration of Southern strength increased the psychological advantage of the President.

When the lame-duck Congress met in December 1864 Lincoln urged immediate action. In his message he noted that a proposed amendment had passed the Senate at the preceding session but

335

had failed in the House. He called attention to the intervening election and the certainty that the next Congress would pass the measure. "May we not agree," he urged, "that the sooner the better." Following this message, Lincoln invited a number of Congressmen, especially Democrats, to the White House for individual interviews. Several prominent Democrats, impressed not only by the election results and some expert political maneuvering by the President but also by the fact that the amendment promised a way out, respecting an issue which had split the party disastrously, changed their votes; and on January 31, 1865, the resolution was adopted.

Lincoln's home state, Illinois, was the first to ratify the amendment, on February 1, and others followed quickly. Ironically Kentucky, Lincoln's native state and the one of whose interests he had been so solicitous in all his efforts to secure compensation for slaveowners, refused to ratify and never did so.

Five days after Congress acted upon the resolution Lincoln made a final gesture of friendship to the Southern states. On February 5, 1865, he presented to his Cabinet a message which he proposed to deliver to Congress, recommending the passage of a joint resolution authorizing him to pay four hundred million dollars to the slaveowners, conditioned upon immediate cessation of resistance and upon the ratification of the Thirteenth Amendment by the Confederate states. The members of his Cabinet—who knew that previous similar suggestions had been scornfully rejected by the South, and who also knew the hostility of Congress toward any such concessions—unanimously opposed Lincoln's proposal, and he abandoned it.

Lincoln died on April 15. He did not live to see the Thirteenth Amendment finally ratified, as it was not until the following December that it became a part of the Constitution. But no one could doubt that it was a Lincoln masterpiece. William Lloyd Garrison, violent abolitionist and at times hysterical critic of Lincoln, paid him the final tribute: "And to whom is the country more immediately indebted for this vital and saving amendment to the Constitution than, perhaps to any other man? I believe I may confidently answer—to the humble railsplitter of Illinois—to the Presidential chainbreaker for millions of the oppressed—to Abraham Lincoln!"

Justin Miller

58

LINCOLN AND MUSIC

by Kenneth A. Bernard

When the name of Abraham Lincoln is mentioned varied thoughts may come to your mind. You may think of the boy in a Kentucky cabin or the youth on a flatboat on the Mississippi. You may remember the young storekeeper in New Salem or the lawyer in Springfield. You may recall the railsplitter President who saved the Union and emancipated the slaves. But you probably do not associate Lincoln's name with music.

Yet Lincoln has been the subject of more musical effort than any other President, and he likely heard more music than did any other President.

The Civil War was a singing war, and throughout the four long years of conflict the harshness of strife was softened by the sound of music—music which even reached the White House where the tall, gaunt, sad-faced man liked to listen to it whenever he had an opportunity.

Lincoln, as his close friend Noah Brooks said, had a love of music that was something passionate. And although he could neither sing nor play an instrument (except the harmonica) his interest in music was constant throughout his life.

Lincoln's fondness for music began when as a youth in Indiana he first came to know and enjoy the folksongs and ballads of the frontier—"Barbara Allen," "William Reilly," "The Turbaned Turk," and "John Anderson's Lamentation." Here also he became familiar with the favorite hymns of the frontier—"There Is a Fountain Filled with Blood" and "When Shall I See Jesus and Reign with Him Above." When the young people gathered for a good time they sang and danced to "Weevily Wheat," "Skip to My Lou," and "Way Down Yonder in the Paw Paw Patch."

It may be also that in New Salem, Illinois, the young man Lincoln became acquainted with the songs in the popular work *The Missouri Harmony Songbook.*

In 1837 Lincoln went to the small but growing town of Springfield, Illinois. Springfield had a busy social life which included parties, balls, and concerts. Artists of local and national reputation gave programs there. Lincoln attended many of these events, and while he may not have danced much he did have an opportunity to hear much music, vocal and instrumental, amateur and professional.

Lincoln found his chief musical delight on the circuit with his lawyer associates. Traveling from one county seat to another, by horseback or wagon, the lawyers often whiled away the hours by singing. If Lincoln's friend Ward Lamon was in the party the music was especially lusty, for Lamon loved to sing. How he would sing that buzzing ballad "The Blue-Tail Fly" or, in contrast, that song of tender memory "Twenty Years Ago"!

After a long day in court the judge and lawyers gathered in the local hotel. There they discussed politics and law. There they also sang—perhaps a favorite comic song, "Hoosen Johnny."

Sometimes concert artists on tour were in town at the same time that court was in session. If a concert was scheduled for the evening Lincoln would leave his lawyer friends and go alone to hear the program. He rarely missed a concert, and during his years on the circuit he made the acquaintance of several of the traveling musicians.

Occasionally the concert artist or singing troupe and the lawyers stayed at the same hotel. Then everyone assembled in the parlor for an informal program in which the lawyers as well as the professionals joined.

At one informal concert Jane Martin, a well-known musician, played a number of long selections on a newly arrived piano. She then sang several popular songs including "The Ship on Fire" and "The Maniac." Then it was the lawyers' turn. They joined heartily in "Old Dan Tucker," and a trio sang "Rocked in the Cradle of the Deep" and "Kathleen Mavourneen."

Miss Martin concluded by singing a sentimental song that affected Lincoln deeply. It was entitled "He Doeth All Things Well." When she had finished Lincoln said, "Don't let us spoil that song by any other music tonight."

At another gathering everyone contributed in some way to the music of the evening. That is, everyone except Lincoln. He was urged to do his part. Not being able to sing he finally offered to recite his favorite poem.

Standing in the doorway of the parlor, his six feet four inches practically filling the frame, he recited William Knox's lengthy and melancholy poem "Mortality":

> O why should the spirit of mortal be proud!
> Like a fast flitting meteor, a fast flying cloud,
> A flash of the lightning, a break of the wave—
> He passes from life to his rest in the grave.

Lincoln wished that this poem, which he kept fresh in his memory, might be set to music. It was, but he never heard it. For ironically it was in the year of his death, 1865, that the poem was put to music, and by three different composers.

During his four years in the White House Lincoln was burdened almost beyond human endurance by the awful tragedies of the Civil War. Yet there was some time for music.

by Kenneth A. Bernard

In the hectic days of April and May 1861 Lincoln found time to enjoy the music of the band playing on the White House lawn, to attend a concert at the Navy Yard, and to hear Carl Schurz play the piano at a tea.

Throughout the summer months (except after the death of Willie Lincoln in 1862) bands played regularly on the south lawn. The President went out to listen whenever he could. In the winter the Marine Band played faithfully at White House receptions. The President heard very little of its music because of the great crush of visitors.

Real pleasure and relaxation came to the weary President, however, when musical celebrities visited the Executive Mansion. One of these was a charming young lady just returned from study abroad who sang "Casta Diva" from the opera *Norma*. Others were a Penobscot Indian princess from Maine whose voice was pleasant but somewhat thin; "Commodore" Nutt, the rival of Tom Thumb, who sang "Columbia, the Gem of the Ocean"; and a famous Western scout who favored the President with selections on a violin which he had made himself from the bones of his favorite mule.

At parades, troop reviews, and on visits to army camps Lincoln heard much band music. This he liked, especially if the "Soldiers' Chorus" was played.

Lincoln enjoyed programs given by patriotic organizations. He liked the serenades which loyal supporters gave outside the White House, and on numerous occasions he went to the opera.

What were Lincoln's favorite songs? Throughout his life Lincoln had a fondness for folk songs, ballads, and heart songs. In his later years he appreciated songs whose theme was the rapid flight of time and recollections of earlier days. Among his favorites were "Ben Holt," "Annie Laurie," "Old Robin Gray," and "Twenty Years Ago." This last piece often brought tears to his eyes. Of the religious music which he heard and knew, two hymns seem to have been favorites. These were 'Father, Whate'er of Earthly Bliss Thy Sovereign Will Denies" and "Rock of Ages."

341

Lincoln was much moved by the war songs which were played and sung everywhere. He heard "We Are Coming, Father Abraham" many times, once or twice in the White House. At the theater one night the entire audience, including the President, was stirred to patriotic heights by the singing of "Rally 'Round the Flag, Boys."

Two pieces very different in nature which Lincoln enjoyed were "Dixie," which he maintained was a Northern as well as a Southern song, and the "Marseillaise." One of his first requests after his arrival in Washington was for the "Marseillaise." On his return to the city after his final visit to the Army in 1865 he asked the band to play both the "Marseillaise" and "Dixie." The last piece that he requested before his death was "Dixie."

Lincoln was never more profoundly affected by music than he was during a great patriotic meeting at the Capitol one evening in 1864. A famous Methodist chaplain described his experiences in Libby Prison. He told how he endeavored to boost the morale of his fellow prisoners by encouraging them to sing. He recounted teaching them a new song and how they finally caught the spirit of it and sang with enthusiasm. Then he and a companion sang, their voices ringing throughout the hall, "Mine Eyes Have Seen the Glory of the Coming of the Lord."

When they had finished a voice called out: "Sing it again! Sing it again!" It was the President. They performed it again, the audience joined in the chorus, and how they all sang:

> Glory, Glory, Hallelujah,
> His Truth Is Marching On!

No wonder the President said later to the chaplain, "Take it all in all, the song and the singing, that was the best I ever heard."

Yes, Abraham Lincoln's life contained much music, and his musical tastes developed as he himself developed. His attendance at musical events and his acquaintance with prominent musicians broadened his musical horizon and gave him a source of unending satisfaction.

by Kenneth A. Bernard

There was room in his great heart for all kinds of music—music, which to him was unique, for unlike all other pleasures it had no utilitarian aspect. Music, he said, "was simply a pleasure and nothing more, and . . . he fancied that the Creator, after providing all the mechanism for carrying on the world, made music as a simple, unalloyed pleasure. . . ."

Kenneth A. Bernard

59

LINCOLN AND THE ADVENT OF PEACE

by Otto Eisenschiml

On the evening of March 23 Secretary of the Navy Gideon Welles made the customary entry in his diary, and on this occasion he managed to pack a great deal of meaning into few words. This is the way it read:

> The President has gone to the front. . . . There is no doubt [that] he is much worn down; besides he wishes the war terminated, and . . . that severe terms shall not be exacted. . . .

That Lincoln had gone to City Point to visit General Grant was known to many; that he was much worn down was attested to by the pitiful corrosion of his granitelike features; that he wanted to see the war finished quickly could be surmised; but that his main purpose was to offer the South conciliatory terms was a secret he had shared with only a select few. Washington harbored many radical politicians who opposed this benevolent course and wanted to see the South treated as conquered territory.

For the Confederacy the situation had become desperate. Lee and his army, besieged in Richmond, were starving; desertions took place daily at a steadily quickening pace. The trenches around the Southern capital had become no more than a fragile shell which might be shattered by the next blow. Lee's only chance for survival was to break out of the fortifications and join General Johnston, who was fighting a delaying action against Sherman in North Carolina. Together the two armies might yet stave off immediate disaster. But the roads, softened by heavy winter rains, were impassable, and Grant was watching every escape route Lee might use with never-relenting vigilance. During the next few days, however, the roads would dry out, and then fighting was bound to explode in what Lincoln hoped to be the final flare-up of a dying war. Before this happened he wanted to inaugurate a plan he had evolved, which was to prevent the Radicals from thwarting his determination to hold out a friendly hand to the beaten enemy.

Those who had seen Lincoln lately were shocked by the weariness which showed in his face and his movements. The President needed a rest, needed it badly. He might find it at City Point. Located near the confluence of the Appomattox and the James Rivers, City Point was a settlement born of the war and presented a crowded conglomeration of soldiers, hospitals, tents, huts, warehouses, and wharves. A hastily built, rickety railroad connected the place with the nearby battle zone. Here Grant had established his headquarters, and here he was anxious to receive his illustrious visitor, to whom he had extended a hearty invitation.

Soon after its arrival the presidential party was on the way to the front. Lincoln and Grant traveled by rail and horseback while their wives rode in an ambulance, accompanied by Adam Badeau, Grant's military secretary. The President wanted to judge for himself how matters stood, how close the country was to peace. A short inspection tour showed him that the goal was not far off and that the time had arrived to put his plan into effect. He had secretly summoned his three foremost military leaders, Grant, Sherman, and Admiral Porter, to a conference. It was to be held on board the *River Queen*, the dispatch boat which had carried the presidential party to City Point.

The President opened the meeting by saying that the crisis of the war was at hand, and inquired anxiously if further bloodshed could not be avoided. The officers declared that they could not give such a promise, as everything depended on what Lee would do. Sherman then asked a pertinent question: what was to be done with the enemy soldiers after they had laid down their arms? Lincoln was ready with his answer: all he wanted was to see them go home and start working again. Sherman asked another question: what about Jefferson Davis, the President of the Confederacy? Lincoln secretly hoped Davis would escape, and, as he often did in cases of a delicate nature, he gave his answer in the form of a story. A man who had taken the total abstinence pledge, he said, was offered a glass of lemonade, with the intimation that it would taste better with brandy in it. "If you were going to pour it in unbeknown to me," the abstainer grinned, "I could not very well object, could I?"

Everyone laughed, but Sherman was not through with his queries. How about the civil reorganization of the South? Lincoln assured him that her people would be guaranteed all their rights, and that chaos would be averted by leaving the civil functionaries in their places until permanent arrangements could be made and approved by Congress.

"When I left him," Sherman wrote afterward, ". . . I was more than ever impressed by his kindly nature, his deep and earnest sympathy with the afflictions of the whole people . . . his earnest desire seemed to be to end the war speedily, without more bloodshed. . . ."

The high officers then departed to their respective duties, but Lincoln did not leave for Washington until April 8.

On the ninth Lee surrendered. The terms Grant offered him were fully in line with the spirit of generosity and reconciliation which Lincoln had instilled within him at that memorable meeting on the *River Queen*.

When the news of Lee's surrender reached Washington the city went wild with joy. Strangers hugged each other on the streets, flags flew from every vantage point. The crowds sang, cheered, and danced. It would not be until fifty-three years later, at the end of World War I, that America would see anything like it again.

The morning of April 10 Lincoln made an impromptu speech to a crowd which had gathered on the White House lawn and clamored to hear him. Inasmuch as he had prepared an address for the following night he sidestepped the request by asking a nearby band to play "Dixie." He quipped that he considered the song now a fair prize of war, and those who had heard the jocular remark showed their appreciation by prolonged noisy cheers.

The evening of April 11 Lincoln made his formal address. Standing at an open window of the White House he held the manuscript in one hand, a candle in the other. This proved somewhat cumbersome, and after a while the journalist Noah Brooks held the candle for him while little Tad, the youngest of the Lincoln family, provided comical byplay by picking up each used sheet as his father dropped it on the floor.

The throng which faced Lincoln listened in solemn silence, feeling that they were witnessing the most important event which would ever come their way.

The President began: "We meet this evening, not in sorrow, but in gladness of heart . . . the surrender of the principal insurgent army, give[s] hope of a righteous and speedy peace whose joyous expression can not be restrained."

Lincoln then turned abruptly to the new difficulties with which the nation was confronted. The Confederacy had ceased to exist, its government was in flight, leaving no authority behind to help in the task of reorganization. To aggravate matters, the people of the North were by no means in agreement on how the task was to be handled. His own ideas, he added, were well known. Now that the seceded states were back in the fold they were to resume their former relations with all their political rights unimpaired. The question whether they had ever been out of the Union had become an academic one.

In conclusion the President called attention to the experiment he had undertaken in reconstructing the state government of Louisiana, where only twelve thousand white citizens, a small percentage of the population, had taken the oath of allegiance. Nevertheless this number had been considered sufficient to establish self-government. It was yet an egg, not a fowl, he admitted, but would it not be wiser to hatch the egg than to smash it? The voting privilege, if Lincoln had his way, would be conferred on intelligent Negroes, also on those of their race who were serving or had served in the Northern armies. He dwelt on the Louisiana plan at great length, then declared that he would make an announcement to the people of the South in the not too distant future. History has suffered greatly by our ignorance of what Lincoln had intended to say, for he died before he could make the promised proclamation.

The listeners had followed the speech with rapt attention, but the applause which followed lacked warmth. They had not expected to hear a discussion on one of the most controversial issues of the day. Many members of Congress had fought Lincoln's plan vigorously, and a sizable portion of his audience was not in sympathy with it.

As the crowd slowly dispersed some of those present afterward claimed to have noticed on its fringes two men standing in low-voiced conversation with each other. One of them was unusually handsome, and when he lifted his hat to someone he knew they observed his black silky hair, which harmonized well with his olive complexion. The other was a pimply youth with undistinguished features, who was listening in awe and admiration to these parting words of his companion: "This is the last speech Lincoln will ever make."

Three days later the dark man made his prophecy come true. He, too, went to Ford's Theater on the evening of April 14. His name was Booth.

60

LINCOLN AS A DRAMATIC SUBJECT

by Dore Schary

More than any American who ever lived, Abraham Lincoln is pursued by historians, novelists, biographers, and dramatists. George Washington, the father of the nation, and other great souls such as Thomas Jefferson, Andrew Jackson, Theodore Roosevelt, and Woodrow Wilson have been the source of much pen power —and certainly Franklin Delano Roosevelt will continue to spark the writing of many books and plays; but Lincoln and his destiny are classic tragedy, and he was cast ideally for the larger than lifesize part. His remarkable head, long and lean body, and deep, brooding eyes seem designed from the beginning for this prime role of heroic triumph and sudden and heartbreaking death.

Even Lincoln's personal interest in the theater reflects the undertones of tragedy. His knowledge of Shakespeare was thorough and thoughtful. He speculated much on the meaning and intent of the Elizabethan's drama. The Marquis Adolphe de Chambrun tells that one week before Lincoln's assassination, while the President was on the *River Queen* sailing on the Potomac with some friends, he was reading his favorite passage from *Macbeth*, which also happened to be his favorite play. As we look at the words of this passage we are struck again by the dark coincidence and circumstances that mark the life of Lincoln—for here are the words:

> Duncan is in his grave;
> After life's fitful fever he sleeps well.
> Treason has done its worst; not steel, nor poison,
> Malice domestic, foreign levy, nothing
> Can touch him further.

One week later Lincoln's "fitful fever" was over and he slept well.

He had attended the theater frequently and was attracted to theatrical personalities. Many people who knew him and listened to his readings were convinced that if he had so chosen he could have been a gifted and resourceful actor. Certainly we can tell from the language of his letters and papers that he knew well the value of timing and emphasis. A less astute public speaker, on the occasion of the appearance at Gettysburg, might have competed with Edward Everett with a long and orotund speech. Not Lincoln. He wrote out less than three hundred words, two thirds of them in one syllable, and in reading them made a permanent contribution to literature and the performing arts.

His choice of stories, jokes, and anecdotes always reveals his ability to sense the climate of a situation and either adjust to it or alter it to suit his purpose. A tall man, more self-conscious, might have abandoned the stovepipe hat; Lincoln maintained it. Truly great men are conscious of their place in the stream of history, and with that awareness comes (if they are compassionate) a deep sense of responsibility and obligation, along with a willingness to act—perhaps with doubt—but in any event act they must.

Examine, too, the circumstances of the day Lincoln was assassinated, and here again are the plottings and twists and delays and possible postponements and the on-again, off-again arrangements that mark the work of master dramatic writing. His birth and humble origin, his early failures and defeats, his sudden victory and rise over Douglas as a result of the debates, his elections, his tormented war years, and his death—all these are a story to be told again and again with new meanings, reawakened heartthrobs, and the blinding well of tears.

No wonder then that he, Lincoln, has been pursued by the writer. But who can, in the continued flow of writing, even after a hundred and fifty years since his birth, tell what now is the man? How much of him has the dramatist succeeded in capturing and distilling? Does one generation see Lincoln as Frank McGlynn the actor and John Drinkwater the writer created him—and is this a lesser or a truer picture than that presented some years later by Raymond Massey the actor and Robert E. Sherwood the playwright? And what of Walter Huston's Lincoln or Henry Fonda's young Lincoln?

And what of the plays before our time?

There was *The Royal Ape, circa* 1863, published in Richmond, Virginia. We can assume what *that* was.

Then there was a flood of melodrama: *Assassination* (1879), by D. C. Vestel; *Madame Surratt* (1879), by J. W. Rogers; and another account of the tragedy by W. A. Luby in 1880.

In 1876 *The Tragedy of Abraham Lincoln,* by Hiram Torrie, treated official Washington in the language of the Romans. There were others spaced through the years and in the 1920's a new tide of scripts that included Thomas Dixon's *A Man of the People,* Test Dalton's *The Mantle of Lincoln,* and Gamman's *Spirit of Ann Rutledge.*

All of these followed Drinkwater's 1919 play about Lincoln, and none of the former achieved the success of the latter.

Reading Drinkwater's play today, one easily understands why it proved effective theater, though it hardly stands up as great playwriting. It is fragmentary and illusory. "The Chroniclers,"

Drinkwater's device of a Greek chorus, while serving the purpose of theater in the grand style, does nothing to create the image of a man. The characterizations in the play proper are superficial, and the telescoping of events, according to today's sterner standards, seems arbitary and meretricious. But even so the spirit of Lincoln moves through the pages; the incorruptible force of his powerful personality is glimpsed through the gilt trappings and the heavy words of "The Chroniclers."

An audience brings to any representation of Lincoln many primary conclusions. The face emblazoned on the penny, the marble and bronze figures in every large city in the nation, and the soft and wise eyes staring down from countless walls in countless schoolrooms and offices are part of our image of America. And so each person brings to the theater something of his own to place into the crucible. Let an actor place a beard on his face, keeping his upper lip bare, and he is halfway home to a performance because the audience is already saying, "He's Lincoln." But when he starts to speak, the challenge for the actor and the writer begins. It is a challenge that few have met successfully.

It is in Robert Sherwood's play *Abe Lincoln in Illinois* that one begins to feel truth beginning to walk hand in hand with theater. Here the expert writing of an important American craftsman meets up with the character of the great President, and even without Massey and his moving performance we catch on the printed page the essence that makes us believe that this is the way Lincoln must have talked and this perhaps is what he must have been. For the first time, as Carl Sandburg has pointed out, a playwright working on this theme went to the main studies derived from basic source materials. Liberties are taken with text and chronology, but not from lack of knowledge of the subject but rather due to the requirements of effective drama.

Biography—dramatic biography, that is—can be excessively deluding. The dramatist, unless he is aware of his obligations to fact, can betray his subject and his audience. As a dramatist he will of course constrict events and create dialogue, but if he throws away restraint and convinces himself that he owes nothing to the truth held so dear by responsible biographers, then he is writing a fantasy and not a dramatic biography. Far from parenthetically Carl Sandburg not only has written a great biography in his *Abraham Lincoln* but has also moved the heart with drama. His chapter of Lincoln's death, "Blood on the Moon," would make a wonderful play.

No dramatist can be responsible, of course, for the physical image. There is nothing that can be done about the generations which grew up convinced that Disraeli looked like George Arliss; that Zola and Pasteur were ringers for Paul Muni; that Dr. Ehrlich and Edward G. Robinson were one and the same; and that Sergeant York, Lou Gehrig, and Dr. Wassell had one thing in common—they all looked like Gary Cooper. I suppose a new generation will be convinced that certain pictures of Franklin D. Roosevelt are phonies, because they bear no resemblance to Ralph Bellamy.

But the student goes beyond and behind the physical portrait, and these thin obstructions to fact are of little concern. In the instance of Abraham Lincoln we are constantly amazed at the amount of literature that has been, is being, and will be written about him. A biographer can, with the mass of collected material available to him, construct almost a daily log of the days of Lincoln's life. And yet the legends, the half-truths, and the illusions continue. Perhaps because Lincoln, like all men, did not expose all of his inner life. Perhaps because Lincoln, as does each man, hid some of his dreams, his insecurities, his frustrations, his passing hates and bitter thoughts and unspoken loves. Perhaps because there were darkened rooms and lonely nights when no one but Lincoln and God knew of the tears and torments and terrors that were never revealed.

But the search for the "real" Lincoln goes on. The portrait painting continues, and the artists are many. Who is to tell, who will ever know, the time to say, "That is it. That is he. That is exactly as he was. That is Lincoln"?

We only know now that he remains, as he has always remained, the most majestic, the saddest, the noblest, and the most compassionate and dramatic figure in the history of the American scene.

61

LINCOLN IN RICHMOND

by Clifford Dowdey

With all the descriptions of Lincoln's visit to Richmond none has ever satisfactorily explained why the President entered the still-smoking capital less than forty-eight hours after the Confederates evacuated it. No members of the government remained in an official capacity, no representatives of the military forces, and the ruins of the four-year citadel had been abandoned to starving mobs. Lincoln certainly did not enter Richmond in any spirit of the conqueror. The unannounced arrival of his informal little party bore all the appearances of an impulsive sight-seeing visit motivated by no more than very human curiosity.

The two men with him when he made the decision to go into Richmond disagreed as to his motives. Colonel Crook, his personal bodyguard, stated that Admiral Porter suggested the visit, while Porter claimed it was Lincoln's idea. The fact would seem to be that both felt they had engaged in a foolhardy stunt and neither wanted the responsibility. Most likely they all were curious to see the fallen capital. Lincoln, of course, made no explanations.

The release from the grimness of the four-year struggle created something of a holiday mood in the men on the scene. Lincoln had been at the Federal naval base and supply depot of City Point, Virginia, since late March, when Grant invited the President to be on hand for the climactic engagement which, for all practical purposes, would bring the war to a close. Except for a visit to the Army to celebrate his son's birthday Lincoln had taken no vacations while in office, and his few trips away from Washington had been in line of official business.

He journeyed to City Point on the *River Queen*, the boat on which he had met the Confederate peace commissioners in the February conference that foretold the coming of the end. Lincoln had come to Virginia several times before, for painful interviews with military commanders. His interview with McClellan had occurred across the James River from City Point, at historic Berkeley Plantation, the home of President Harrison and of a signer of the Declaration of Independence.

City Point, on the south side of the river in its huge loops southeast from Richmond, was in the center of the region that had spread from Jamestown and where later Revolutionary leaders gathered in the great James River mansions of the Virginia oligarchy. The President may have been aware of these associations with the nation's origins; assuredly he was aware that he was present on the eve of events which would make their own history.

At the City Point base Lincoln was situated at the center of the military activities directed by Grant, with the specific objective of the entrenchments around Petersburg. This city, twenty-two miles south of Richmond, connected the capital by rail with the rest of the South. There was general knowledge around City Point that the next push against Lee's thinly stretched lines would overrun the starved remnants of the once great Army of Northern Virginia. For Lincoln, accompanied by Mrs. Lincoln and their eleven-year-old son, Tad, victory long deferred would taste the sweeter.

The push began early Sunday morning, before daylight of April

2, and by nightfall Lee's lines were broken and his units fragmented.

During that night he managed the escape of his survivors to the west, but this move was recognized as a desperate and foredoomed flight.

His retreat served the immediate purpose of uncovering Richmond. Whatever the bemused Confederate administration believed, the Union forces knew that the flight of Lee's army and the fall of the Confederate capital marked the end of the war. On the scene Lincoln understandably was infected by the spirit of jubilation.

But Virginia's proud capital was not to be allowed the dignity of a capitulation with the honors of war after a heroic defense. Jefferson Davis refused to admit the end of the Confederacy's experiment in self-determinism. Without having made preparations for withdrawal the civil authorities left in hurried disorder between Sunday noon and ten o'clock at night. The bullion remaining in the treasury and in the Richmond banks went with them, along with oddments of records, though most of these were left. On fleeing the doomed city the authorities gave the senseless order to burn the supplies in the warehouses, burn arsenals, and fire the river gunboats. When the last Confederate troops crossed the bridge out of Richmond early Monday morning, the third, they looked back on a city in flames. With no military or civil authorities remaining the mobs of the war population took over to loot.

Meade's Army of the Potomac, under the personal supervision of Grant, had taken out after Lee on the road that led to Appomattox. North of the James River, Richmond had been threatened directly from the east by the Army of the James, commanded by General Ord. For Grant's last push against the works around Petersburg he had swelled Meade's numbers with the bulk of Ord's troops, leaving only one division of the Twenty-fourth Corps and a colored division of the all-Negro Twenty-fifth Corps. Commanded by General Weitzel these two divisions, accompanied by cavalry, entered Richmond during Monday, the third. These troops put out the fires that gutted one third of the city, including most of the business and manufacturing sections, established some order, and placed Richmond under military government. General Weitzel set up headquarters in the White House so recently vacated by President Davis.

On the next day, Tuesday the fourth, Lincoln and his small party started their impromptu trip up the James River toward Richmond. The U. S. Navy had been held at bay for four years by underwater torpedoes and obstructions that narrowed the channel to a slim passage directly under the guns of a river fort on Drewry's Bluff. With these shore guns at last silent, and floating torpedoes presumably cleared away, Lincoln's party transferred to the barge from Porter's flagship, *Malvern*, pulled by a tug. In a series of minor disasters which would have discouraged all but the stoutest heart the visiting party was finally reduced to being rowed ashore by twelve sailors.

The barge reached the landing at Rockett's, the shipping section on the eastern outskirts of the city, and the President stepped ashore accompanied by bodyguard Crook, Admiral Porter, three other officers, and eleven-year-old Tad. The tall figure, elongated by the black stovepipe hat, was immediately recognized by a group of Negroes who came crowding around Lincoln. Crook and Porter were under the impression that they were all slaves giving thanks to their deliverer, and this impression has been accepted. But Richmond had a large population of freed Negroes, and runaway slaves fled the city, usually seeking sanctuary in Union lines. It would be more accurate if less dramatic to assume that Lincoln, long recognized as a friend of the Negro, was welcomed as the friend of their race.

The ebullience of their welcome soon attracted attention and the crowd swelled, forming a dangerous press in the eagerness of the colored people to get near Lincoln. Alarmed, Porter formed his twelve sailors with bayonetted carbines in lines in front and back of the President's party, and in this formation the eighteen men and one boy pushed slowly westward through the smoldering ruins of Main Street.

They turned north one block and west again into Franklin Street, the crowd growing as they passed the sporting district where the Ballard and Exchange Hotels were connected by a balcony over the hilly street. The party again swung north, up the steep hill of Governor Street, winding by the back of the Governor's Mansion and Capitol Square. The grassy slopes of the Square were covered by dispossessed family groups who had fled from the flames and clustered, some with house slaves, about cherished objects they had saved from burning homes. The sick and aged lay on the ground, covered by shawls, and young Negroes, rushing to join Lincoln, ran whooping by them.

Between two and three o'clock of the warm April day Lincoln's party reached the White House four blocks from the Square on Clay Street. Between the climbing streets and the shouting crowds of Negroes, Lincoln was then perspiring and fanned his face with his tall hat.

Crook and Porter stressed sparsity of white people during this walk of less than one mile. Most of the residential sections were west and north of Capitol Square, and the majority of the apprehensive citizens, behind locked doors and shuttered windows, did not hear the cheering. Few who did hear knew what caused it. Weitzel's soldiers had been yelling and bands had been playing for twenty-four hours, the bedlam of the mobs had died down only the night before, and a fresh burst of crowd noise could not have interested the women, children, and old men left in the occupied city.

All observers, however, pointed out that the white people they saw looked on Lincoln's party with neither welcome nor animosity. Only a faint curiosity showed through their dazed stares.

At the finely proportioned White House, where the Davis family had lived, Lincoln seemed to relax for the first time. He revealed then his unaffected curiosity in looking over the high-ceilinged rooms of the three-storied house. After this tour Lincoln sat in the small downstairs reception room. Its floor was still covered by the white run on which Lee had placed his boots during winter visits with President Davis. General Weitzel and other officers joined Lincoln there and broke open a bottle left behind by the Davises. Lincoln did not join in the drinking or in the collecting of souvenirs from the personal belongings of the Davis family.

While there he was visited by Judge Campbell, recently Confederate Assistant Secretary of War. Judge Campbell was the former United States Supreme Court judge who had acted as intermediary between the Lincoln Administration and Confederate commissioners over a peaceable settlement of Fort Sumter, and had served in February on the Confederate commission that met Lincoln on the *River Queen* to discuss peace terms. He had elected to stay in Richmond when the government abandoned the city, and approached Lincoln as an unofficial commission of one toward the purpose of reconvening the Virginia General Assembly. This inconclusive interview was Lincoln's only communication with anyone trying to represent the Confederacy.

After this, Lincoln rode in an Army headquarters' wagon on a brief sight-seeing tour, pausing only at the columned capitol designed by Thomas Jefferson when governor of Virginia. Vandals had done a pretty thorough job of wrecking the chambers and a few farsighted ex-Confederates had made off with records which they were later to sell to the national government. By then, late in the afternoon, Lincoln showed no heart for tarrying.

Crook believed that the desolation depressed him. In the wake of his elation at victory he saw firsthand the tragic enormity of the road to reunion. At this time Lincoln held full knowledge of the vindictive and mercenary forces in his own government which planned to overthrow the policy summed up in his "with malice toward none."

by Clifford Dowdey

Of the moment that should have distilled the President's sense of accomplishment Crook said, "The revelation of the devastation of a noble people in ruined Richmond . . . wore new furrows in his face. Mr. Lincoln never looked sadder in his life than when he walked through the streets of Richmond."

Clifford Dowdey

62

LINCOLN AND THE WHOLE NATION

by Henry S. Commager

During one of the most critical periods of the war—it was the late fall of 1862, things were going badly on the battlefield and worse in the political arena—Lincoln sat down to prepare his annual message to the Congress. The heart of it was an appeal for compensated emancipation, and he was at pains to show that the country could well afford the cost, for it was growing in numbers and in wealth at an unprecedented rate. Just to drive home his point he submitted some population estimates: the population of 1860 (he included the South, of course) was some thirty-one million; by 1930 it would reach more than 250 million. He was prepared to look that far ahead—to a nation united and prosperous, a nation able to do anything it set its heart on.

That was what distinguished Lincoln from all of his contemporaries, even the ablest of them like Seward or Chase or Charles Francis Adams—or Jefferson Davis, for that matter: the habit of looking, and thinking, far ahead. The ordinary politician is content with scoring points, with winning immediate victories—at the polls or on the battlefield; the statesman thinks always of the ultimate consequences. The politician is content with the applause of contemporaries; the statesman is ever conscious of his responsibility to and his fiduciary relation to future generations.

Lincoln always saw the war, and the settlement to be made after the war, in these larger terms. We are engaged, he said, in his most memorable statement, in a great civil war, but it was not just a war to defeat the South; it was a war to test whether a nation dedicated to the proposition that men were created equal could long endure. No man in America was more determined to put down the rebellion, and no one less interested in punishing those responsible for it. He was going to save the Union, but he never forgot what kind of Union it was that he wanted to preserve. He was, it seems, incapable of hatred, and he scorned ever to advance his cause by whipping up hatred. He seldom called the Confederates "enemies," or the Confederacy "enemy territory": the South was still in the Union, and those who were attempting to destroy the Union were misguided, not wicked men. Strange that they should be willing to exploit their fellow men, but "let us judge not that we be not judged." Play "Dixie," he said to the band which came to serenade him a few days after Richmond had fallen—we have fairly captured it, and it is ours; and when he visited Richmond he is said to have found time to pay his respects to Mrs. George Pickett, wife of the Confederate general. He wanted no captures, no trials, no punishments, no bloodletting—how different from our modern civil wars, the Spanish or the Russian or the Chinese; he wanted no martyrs. What he wanted he made crystal clear: a restoration of the Union, an end to slavery—he was willing to pay the slaveholders for their slaves as late as February 1865—and as for the rest he expressed himself when he again took the oath of office on March 4, 1865. That was the whole of his platform.

This sense of the integrity of the Union, and of the interdependence of all its sections and peoples, was in part a product of his own background; it should be added that not all those with this background had a comparable sense of the integrity of the Union. He was born a Southerner; he married a Southerner;

his law partners were from the South; he could never think of the South as alien. But more, he was a child of the Great Valley. As a boy he had moved to Indiana and Illinois; as a young man he had floated down the Mississippi to New Orleans. This was the heart of the Republic, and this was indivisible. "Physically speaking," he had said, "we cannot separate," and again, "There is no line, straight or crooked, suitable for a national boundary upon which to divide." It was from the "great interior region . . . the body of the Republic" that he finally found his winning generals, Grant and Sherman, and his winning admiral, too, Farragut. And with his masterly instinct for grand strategy he saw what so many failed to see, that the Western theater of the war was crucial, and that control of the Mississippi was decisive. Nowhere is this more movingly expressed than in that eloquent letter to James Conkling, not long after the fall of Vicksburg:

> The signs look better. The Father of Waters again goes unvexed to the sea. Thanks to the great North-West for it. Nor yet wholly to them. Three hundred miles up, they met New-England, Empire, Keystone, and Jersey, hewing their way right and left. . . . The job was a great national one, and let none be banned who bore an honorable part in it. And while those who have cleared the great river may well be proud, even that is not all. It is hard to say that anything has been more bravely, and well done, than at Antietam, Murfreesboro, Gettysburg, and on many fields of lesser note. Nor must Uncle Sam's Web-feet be forgotten. At all the watery margins they have been present. Not only on the deep sea, the broad bay, and the rapid river, but also up the narrow muddy bayou, and wherever the ground was a little damp, they have been, and made their tracks. Thanks to all. For the great republic—for the principle it lives by, and keeps alive —for man's vast future—thanks to all.

"For man's vast future"! Was ever a statesman more conscious of the possibilities? What was that future to be? Lincoln wanted it to be a future rich alike for black and for white, for poor and for rich, and—for that matter—for Southerner as for Northerner.

He wanted to "lift the burdens from the shoulders of all *men.*" Labor, he said, comes before capital; let us guard the interests of labor. At the age of twenty-three he had asked election to the state legislature on an educational plank but was defeated; now he had a chance to sign the Morrill Land Grant Bill, setting aside land as endowment for state universities throughout the nation. It was to be a land for yeomen farmers, and he signed the Homestead Bill, which Buchanan had vetoed, providing free homesteads for actual settlers on public lands. It was to be a self-contained nation, and he signed the Morrill tariffs of 1862 and 1864—not for nothing was he a champion of the American system. It was to be a vast continental domain knit together by the iron ties of transportation, and he signed the Pacific Railway Bill setting aside public land to help build the transcontinentals. It was to be a nation of freemen, and not content with the Emancipation Proclamation he ceaselessly urged on Congress a constitutional amendment as a "king's cure," but he did not live to see that amendment put into the Constitution.

All this sounds nationalistic, and to many shortsighted Europeans the American Civil War seemed no different from other wars whereby empires put down rebellious minorities. But Lincoln's nationalism was the very opposite from chauvinism. From the beginning he saw the war as one significant to the cause of freedom everywhere. "And this issue," he said in his first message to the Congress, in July 1861, "embraces more than the fate of these United States. It presents to the whole family of man, the question, whether a constitutional republic, or a democracy . . . can, or cannot, maintain its territorial integrity. . . ." And again, from the same wonderful state paper:

> This is essentially a People's contest. On the side of the Union, it is a struggle for maintaining in the world, that form, and substance of government, whose leading object is, to elevate the condition of men—to lift artificial weights from all shoulders—to clear the paths of laudable pursuit for all—to afford all, an unfettered start, and a fair chance, in the race of life.

Nothing is more illuminating than the contrast between Lincoln's government and that of Davis in the struggle for English support. The Confederacy made out its case not on its merits but on necessity. One persistent note sounds all through Southern literature, like the refrain of the whippoorwill: Cotton is King, Cotton is King. Even the most infatuated Southerners knew that they could not hope to persuade the English that slavery was a good thing, and they did not seriously try. Lincoln put the case of the Union on the highest ground. Here, he said, is a contest not for empire but for freedom, for self-government, for the rights of men. Freemen everywhere, he insisted, had a stake in the preservation of the Union, for that Union was "the last best hope of earth," and when the workingmen of Manchester—as of London and Birmingham and Coventry—rallied to the Union cause, in the dark days of the war, Lincoln wrote them in proud confidence that "a fair examination of history has served to authorize the belief that the past actions and influences of the United States were generally regarded as having been beneficial toward mankind" and that English support was "an energetic and reinspiring assurance of the inherent power of truth and of the ultimate and universal triumph of justice, humanity and freedom." Lincoln felt that the Union was fighting for the freedom not only of the bondsman but of men everywhere; that it was fighting for the vindication of the principles and practices of self-government; and that upon the success of its struggle was staked the future of democracy in the Western world for years to come.

By his courage, his vision, his magnanimity, Lincoln saw to it that the war for union never degenerated into a war for conquest or a war for punishment; that it was so fought that it made possible a reknitting of the Union; that it brought with it a new birth of freedom and a new era of self-government.

63

LINCOLN AS A MAN OF LETTERS

by Roy P. Basler

During the ninety-odd years since his assassination Abraham Lincoln has probably been the subject of the most complete and widespread study ever applied to one man within an equal period of time. Yet what may in the future be considered his most important contribution has hardly been considered.

For Lincoln was above all an artist, and though his talents were not confined to literary expression his prose may still be recognized as his most permanent legacy to humanity. Even the most carping critic must admit this. The poet Edgar Lee Masters, author of the once heralded *Spoon River Anthology* and also of the most denunciatory biography of Lincoln ever written, gave his opinion that only Lincoln's literary accomplishments have "made him more important in history than William McKinley." That, coming from Masters, was tribute indeed. And certainly Lincoln's words will endure, longer perhaps than the marble and bronze upon which they have so often been engraved.

Though presently Lincoln's fame as a literary artist is not so widespread as his legendary and historical fame in the role of emancipator and savior of the Union of States, it is at least as complete, and seems to be growing far more rapidly. The probability of its permanence lies in the fact that its preservation must remain chiefly in the hands of those who study his works. Indeed it is not difficult to conceive of the time when much of what men know of the American Civil War will be derived largely from Lincoln's great speeches and letters, as the finest commentary and interpretation of the war.

It may be a bitter pill for the professional historian to swallow but the truth remains that rhetoric has time and again demonstrated its ability to outlive the facts that inspire it. "It is his poetical flashes," lamented Edgar Lee Masters, "that have stayed his fame against attack." Certainly today the popular conception of Lincoln is more the result of his Gettysburg Address and First and Second Inaugural Addresses than of his war policies—which few but historians understand. These words are part of the American bible.

No other oratory, not even that of Demosthenes or Cicero or Sir Winston Churchill, has so transcended the natural limitations of public speech as to infuse it with the simplicity and imagination and music of great poetry. It was well said by Lord Charnwood, the English biographer of Lincoln, that his great addresses are more like the speeches in tragic drama than like traditional oratory. This hardly clarifies their real quality but it does give some idea of their uniqueness. The more the magic of Lincoln's words is studied the more his works are recognized as masterpieces that cannot be catalogued or classified.

An examination of Lincoln's more important writing reveals just where this supremacy exists, as it has always existed in the works of the few indisputable masters of language. First, it lies in a superior vitality of imagination that was able to infuse the Civil War epoch with great poetic significance; and second, in an ability to employ language more effortless and yet more grandly beautiful than any of his contemporaries possessed, Whitman possibly excepted. That Lincoln took and made his own the thought and spirit of nineteenth-century America is so true that his subject matter, like that of Shakespeare, is his to a degree that is never met with in lesser literary genius. Though this matter was used often in his day and somewhat since, we can hardly think of it except as especially Lincoln's.

The tendency has been not so much to underestimate Lincoln's attention to style as to estimate it not at all. Here as elsewhere the legend of Lincoln the prophet and martyr has bedimmed the genuine achievement of a human mind at work, until a scathing critic like Masters, because of his knowledge of the craft of words, comes closer to the *why* of Lincoln's expression than all the idolators. Lincoln did not, of course, always preserve the extreme niceties of prescribed genius, but his genius was not the uncultivated accident of inspiration that has so often been supposed. Is it more reasonable to think that the man who gave English prose some of its finest balanced rhythm got no hint of style from his study of Sir Francis Bacon's essays and the King James Version of the Bible—or to recognize that he deliberately mastered a technique for what it was? It is true that as a rule Lincoln's words are the most austere simplicity, but it is equally true that his feeling for cadence is unfathomed subtlety.

It has been said that Lincoln's art was always applied art, utilitarian in purpose and held strictly to the matter at hand. Perhaps he did, even in the deep moving cadences and high imagination of the Second Inaugural Address, consider his prose only as a means to an end, but recognized that in an emotional crisis of national scope the truest appeal could not be made to the intellect alone. And because he had early learned to eschew the illusion of emotionalism—that bane of the swayer of multitudes, which sways the hearts of hearer and speaker alike with floods of mere rhetoric, he was able in his greatest moments to strike chords never before touched by oratory.

When we speak of originality in a literary artist we refer to a technique of expression rather than to his subject matter, for where one is individually his the other is universal. So it is less by his matter than by his technique that Lincoln is distinguished from the others above whom he looms, singular and lofty. His workmanship, even in many little known passages, is so individual that it cannot be imitated.

Even in his anecdotes his artistry is evident in application and point, in spite of the fact that most of them are retold in words remembered by others. And though as a humorist he was indebted to the mode and spirit of his time he displayed in his crude, sometimes bitter humor the touch which cannot be found in the works of lesser humorists of the age. Not the story, but how he told it, makes it a Lincoln story.

So it is that Lincoln, like the greatest literary figures of the past, becomes, as we study his works, more than a man. He is a creative consciousness in whom the enduring matter of Civil War America lives. As this subject matter is in Lincoln intrinsic and his expression of it inimitable so his works will endure, as something representative and symbolic, with singular completeness of the epoch which nurtured him. Even though some students of history may find him fallible as an ideal hero and President they must recognize that the most incontrovertible *fact* about Lincoln is his prose.

For nearly a century we have been taught to consider Lincoln primarily a political figure. But Lincoln belongs with our few literary lodestars. We must of necessity realize the significance of his literary accomplishment and perceive his dual role as artist-statesman without peer. Consider the profoundly moving truth uttered in the conclusion to his First Inaugural Address:

> I am loth to close. We are not enemies, but friends. We must not be enemies. Though passion may have strained; it must not break our bonds of affection. The mystic chords of memory, stretching from every battle-field, and patriot grave, to every living heart and hearth-stone, all over this broad land, will yet

swell the chorus of the Union, when again touched, as surely they will be, by the better angels of our nature.

Only a poet-statesman could have given so tersely and yet so completely the essential meaning of the American philosophy. In his words the stature of Lincoln will endure.

Roy P Basler

64

LINCOLN'S PLAN OF RECONSTRUCTION

by William B. Hesseltine

No legend of the American Civil War is more persistent than the belief that if Lincoln had lived the years of reconstruction that followed the conflict would have been different. The magnanimous Lincoln, so the legend runs, would not only have restored the Southern states to their "proper practical relation" to the Federal Government but would also have effected an emotional reconciliation between the members of the momentarily estranged American family that would have brought union and contentment to all.

The legend of course rests largely upon wishful thinking. It rests in part upon an understanding that Lincoln was a pragmatist and that he was relatively unaffected by the hate psychosis which characterized numbers of the so-called Radical Republicans. Perhaps, indeed, in the first days after Appomattox the Southern people wanted their sins forgiven, wanted to be welcomed back, and wanted to take a useful part in settling the difficulties which had divided the land. When they were disappointed they came to accept a "father image" of a Lincoln who, if he had lived, would have welcomed them back, forgiven the prodigals, and even set forth a feast to celebrate their return.

There is no doubt much reason to think that something like this could have happened. Reconstruction might indeed have been different if Lincoln had lived, and reconciliation might indeed have come sooner and more completely. But any speculation about the probable course reconstruction might have taken must rest upon an appraisal of Lincoln's policy and of the direction in which reconstruction was already going when John Wilkes Booth's insane bullet brought a change in the principal actors on the stage.

At the moment of Lincoln's death reconstruction was uppermost in every mind. A day or so later Generals William Tecumseh Sherman and Joseph E. Johnston met in North Carolina to make a "treaty" which Sherman alleged embodied Lincoln's final plan of reconstruction. Lincoln's last speech and his last Cabinet meeting dealt with the problems of reconstruction, while discussions among Congressmen and in the press concerned themselves almost entirely with the processes by which the Southern states could again become full-fledged members of the Union.

But of course reconstruction had always played a large part in men's thinking during the Civil War. Democrats, Republicans, Moderates, Radicals, social reformers, and tinkering theorists had long been concerned with it, and it is not incongruous to say that reconstruction had been a cause of the Civil War. It was a fear that incoming Republicans would "reconstruct" the Union, alter the social system, and destroy property that led the Southern states to secede. It was the search for acceptable formulae for "reconstruction" that occupied the attention of the nation from Lincoln's election to the firing on Sumter.

All the proposals for compromise before the war began were essentially plans for reconstruction, but each proposal that received attention called for a system of duality. Each proposed to recognize the South's special rights in the Union, to guarantee a separate and special position for the South's economic and social system. Against each proposal for a duality in the land Abraham Lincoln set his face. From the beginning Lincoln considered only means that would ensure a unified nation. But within the limits of a unified nation Lincoln's plans for reconstruction were pragmatic. He made adjustments to changing situations, and before the end of the war had adopted and discarded a number of plans by which the South might be restored to its proper practical relations in the Union.

From the beginning Lincoln tried to capture the support of Unionist elements in the Southern states. He first tried to use patronage, offering positions to leaders who could lead substantial groups of Southerners to remain loyal to the Union. He found a handful of such leaders, and by giving them military support he succeeded in saving the border states of the South for the Union. Although the path was difficult Lincoln managed to prevent the secession of Kentucky, Maryland, and Missouri. Had he been able to find leaders in the other states of the upper South he might have saved them for the Union.

Out of his experience with the border states there grew Lincoln's second plan of reconstruction. This was almost comparable to the governments-in-exile which proved useful during World War II. After the western counties of Virginia had declared themselves to be the "loyal" state of Virginia and then had given themselves permission to form a separate state, there remained—as the so-called "Restored Virginia"—four counties that recognized Francis Pierpont as governor. Lincoln showed no great enthusiasm for the movement that led to West Virginia's formation, but he protected and recognized Pierpont's "rump" government. He hoped that as the Federal armies advanced in Virginia more of the state's people would be brought under Pierpont's rule. The reconstruction of Virginia could therefore proceed smoothly until the entire state was in fact "restored."

Growing closely out of this plan was Lincoln's next plan of reconstruction. In April 1862, when Nashville fell before the advancing armies of Generals Ulysses S. Grant and Don Carlos

Buell, Lincoln appointed Andrew Johnson, the Tennessee Senator who had refused to follow his state into secession, as military governor and instructed him to organize a loyal government in the Volunteer State. But Johnson found the Unionists of Tennessee divided among themselves, and he postponed efforts to organize a government until he could be certain that the element known as the "Unconditional Unionists" could control the state. It was not until his own election as Vice President in 1864 that Johnson got a civil government under way.

In the meantime efforts at reconstruction were proceeding in other states. Lincoln appointed military governors for Arkansas and North Carolina, but neither of them could find a Unionist nucleus to organize. Somewhat more success came in Louisiana, where General Benjamin F. Butler, and after him General Nathaniel P. Banks, held elections for Congressmen in New Orleans and began the slow process of finding loyal citizens who would take over a state government.

Clearly experience showed that some other method must be used, and in December 1863 Lincoln announced a new, and this time formal, plan of reconstruction. He offered amnesty to Southerners who would abandon the Confederacy, and he provided that whenever 10 per cent of the voters of 1860 had taken an oath of allegiance they might organize state governments which he would recognize. The plan spoke volumes for Lincoln's practical approach to problems and for his humanitarianism.

But Lincoln's opponents both in and out of his party saw other things in it. Democrats immediately charged that Lincoln intended to make the Southern states into "pocket boroughs" which he could control easily with the Army, and which would be certain to give him their electoral votes. Radicals in Lincoln's own party saw in his plan an increase in executive power and a step toward making himself a dictator. In Congress Maryland's bitter and erratic Henry Winter Davis hastily concocted an alternate plan of reconstruction, and Ohio's fiery and vindictive Benjamin Wade hurried the bill through the Senate. The Wade-Davis Bill provided that 50 per cent of a state's voters must take an oath of allegiance before they could reorganize a government, and it prescribed a number of steps that would have to be followed in the process of reconstruction. The bill bore evidence of its hasty construction. As Professor Beale has pointed out, it rested on the theory that the Southern states were out of the Union and should be treated as conquered provinces. But most of all it revealed the animus of the Radicals against Abraham Lincoln. The President gave the bill a pocket veto, explaining as he did so that he was unwilling to be bound by any single plan of reconstruction but that he would accept any state which preferred to follow the course outlined in the Wade-Davis Bill. Incensed, Wade and Davis isued a manifesto denouncing Lincoln and asserting vehemently that the President must take a back seat in the work of reconstruction.

Thereafter the lines between President and Congress were sharp. When Congressmen from Louisiana appeared in Washington in Lincoln's last Congress, Senator Charles Sumner denounced the government that General Banks and President Lincoln had so carefully fostered. The Senator filibustered until the Louisiana question was laid aside in order to get on with other business before Congress. For the moment, at least, the Radicals had frustrated the President. And Lincoln was happy that Congress was not in session when Lee surrendered. He hoped that he would be able to work out a new plan of reconstruction before the contentious legislators met again.

In his conference with Generals Grant and Sherman he made it clear that he dreaded an interregnum in the South. Sherman understood that he intended to recognize the existing governments of the Southern states. In Richmond, after the city fell, Lincoln authorized the military governor to permit the Virginia legislators to reassemble to take the state's troops out of Lee's army. But even this met the disapproval of his Cabinet, and Lincoln withdrew the order. At his last Cabinet meeting he surveyed the problem of reconstruction, and in his last public speech he reviewed the situation and pleaded with the people to unite in doing the things necessary to bring the states back into their proper practical relations with the government. He promised then that he would have a new plan of reconstruction in a few days.

The new plan never came, and no hint of its nature was to be found among the President's papers. One can only guess at the thoughts that were in Lincoln's mind and speculate about the fresh difficulties that he might have had with the Radical element in Congress. But it is certain that the plan would have revealed Lincoln's practical approach to problems, his magnanimity, and his deep human understanding.

65

ABRAHAM LINCOLN AND THE ART
OF THE WORD

by Marianne Moore

"On principle I dislike an oath which requires a man to swear he *has* not done wrong. It rejects the Christian principle of forgiveness on terms of repentance. I think it is enough if the man does no wrong *hereafter*." It was Abraham Lincoln who said this—so ardent in temperament he exemplifies excellence both of the technician and of the poet.

Malcontents attack greatness by disparaging it—by libels on efficiency, by distortion, by ridicule, by interpreting needful silence as lack of initiative. "As a general rule," Lincoln said, "I abstain from reading the reports of attacks upon myself, wishing not to be provoked by that to which I can not properly offer an answer." Expert in rebuttal, however, as in strategy, he often won juries and disinterested observers alike, not always by argument but by anecdote or humorous implication that made evidence unnecessary. His use of words became a perfected instrument, acquired by an education that was largely self-attained—an education "picked up," he said, "under the pressure of necessity." That the books he read became part of him is apparent throughout his letters and addresses; in them one detects phrases influenced by the Bible, Shakespeare, *Pilgrim's Progress, Robinson Crusoe*, Burns, Blackstone's *Commentaries*, and, not least, the six books of Euclid, which he read and "nearly mastered," he said, after having been a member of Congress.

The largeness of the life entered into the writing, as with a passion Lincoln strove to persuade his hearers of what he believed. His adroit and ingenious mentality framed an art which, if it is not to be designated poetry, we may call a "grasp of eternal grace"—grace in both senses, figurative and literal. Nor was he unaware of having effected what mattered, as we realize by his determined effort to obtain a set of his debates with Douglas from the Chicago *Press and Tribune* "two copies of each number . . . in order to lay one away in the raw, and to put the other in a Scrapbook."

Of persuasive expedients those most constant with Lincoln are antithesis, reiteration, satire, metaphor, and, above all, *the meaning*, lucid and neat. Clearness and a determination "to express his ideas in simple terms became his ruling passion," as has been said—his every word being natural, cast in a mold made indigenous by ardor. In his address at the Wisconsin Agricultural Fair he said, regarding competitive awards about to be made, ". . . exultations and mortifications . . . are but temporary; . . . the victor shall soon be the vanquished, if he relax in his exertion; and . . . the vanquished this year, may be victor the next, in spite of all competition." At the Baltimore Sanitary Fair of 1864, in an address conspicuously combining antithesis and reiteration, he said, "The world has never had a good definition of the word liberty. . . . We all declare for liberty; but in using the same *word* we do not all mean the same *thing*. With some the word liberty may mean for each man to do as he pleases with himself, and the product of his labor; while with others the same word may mean for some men to do as they please with other men, and the product of other men's labor. Here are two, not only different, but incompatable things, called by the same name—liberty. . . . The shepherd drives the wolf from the sheep's throat, for which the sheep thanks the shepherd as a *liberator*, while the wolf denounces him for the same act as the destroyer of liberty, especially as the sheep was a black one." In 1859, declining an invitation to the Jefferson birthday dinner, he wrote, "The principles of Jefferson are the definitions and axioms of free society. . . . One dashingly calls them 'glittering generalities'; another bluntly calls them 'self evident lies'. . . ." And in combating repeal of the Missouri Compromise, which would extend slavery, he said, "Repeal the Missouri Compromise—repeal all compromises—repeal the declaration of independence—repeal all past history, you still can not repeal human nature."

Crystalline logic indeed was to be his passion. For example, on one occasion he wrote to General Schurz, "You think I could do better; therefore you blame me. . . . I think I could not do better; therefore I blame you for blaming me."

Unsurpassed in satire, Lincoln said that Judge Douglas, in his interpretation of the Declaration of Independence, offered "the arguments that kings have made for enslaving the people in all ages of the world . . . they always bestrode the necks of the people, not that they wanted to do it, but because the people were better off for being ridden." And of slavery as an institution he said, "Slavery is strikingly peculiar, in this, that it is the only good thing which no man ever seeks the good of, *for himself.*"

Metaphor is a force, indeed a magnet, among Lincoln's arts of the word. Urging that the new government of Louisiana be affirmed he says: "If we reject . . . them . . . We in effect say . . . 'You are worthless . . . we will neither help you, nor be helped by you.' To the blacks we say 'This cup of liberty which these, your old masters, hold to your lips, we will dash from you,' . . . discouraging and paralyzing both white and black. . . ." Passionate that the Union be saved, he uses a metaphor yet stronger than

380

the cup of liberty. He says, "By general law life *and* limb must be protected; yet often a limb must be amputated to save a life; but a life is never wisely given to save a limb. I could not feel that . . . to save slavery . . . I should permit the wreck of government, country, and Constitution all together."

Diligence underlay these verbal expedients—one can scarcely call them devices—so rapt was Lincoln in what he cared about. He had a genius for words, but through diligence became a master of them, affording hope to the most awkward of us. To Isham Reavis he wrote, "If you are resolutely determined to make a lawyer of yourself, the thing is more than half done already. It is but a small matter whether you read *with* any body or not. . . . It is of no consequence to be in a large town. . . . I read at New-Salem, which never had three hundred people living in it. The *books*, and your *capacity* for understanding them, are just the same in all places."

Diligence was basic. Upon hearing that George Latham, his son Robert's classmate at the Phillips Exeter Academy, had failed the Harvard entrance examinations Lincoln wrote, ". . . having made the attempt, you *must* succeed in it. '*Must*' is the word . . . you *can* not fail, if you resolutely determine, that you *will* not."

Lincoln was inflexible when sure he was right—as in his reply to Isaac M. Schermerhorn, who was dissatisfied with the management of the war. He said, "This is not a question of sentiment or taste, but one of physical force which may be measured and estimated as horse-power and Steam-power are measured and estimated. . . . Throw it away, and the Union goes with it."

There is much to learn from Lincoln's respect for words taken separately. He was determined "to be so clear" he said, "that no honest man can misunderstand me, and no dishonest one can successfully misrepresent me." Exasperated to have been misquoted, he protested a specious and fantastic arrangement of words by which a man can prove a horse chestnut to be a chestnut horse. He said of Stephen A. Douglas, "Cannot the Judge perceive the distinction between a purpose and an expectation. I have often expressed an expectation to die, but I have never expressed a *wish* to die." The Declaration of Independence he made stronger by saying, "I think the authors of that notable instrument intended to include *all* men, but they did not intend to declare all men were equal *in all respects*." And he said to quibblers after the surrender of the South, ". . . whether the seceded states, so-called, are in the Union or out of it, the question is bad . . . a pernicious abstraction!" "With malice toward none and charity for all," he said in his Second Inaugural Address, "let us strive on to finish the work we are in." *We are in*. Lincoln understood the art of emphasis—that one must be *natural*. Instead of placing the word "confidential" at the head of a private communication to A. H. Stephens, he wrote, and underlined *"For your eye only."* The result of this particularity and directness was such that in his so-called Lost Speech of 1856, which unified the Republican party, "Newspapermen forgot paper and pad . . . to sit enraptured," and instead of taking down his eulogy of Henry Clay, reporters "dropped their pens and sat as under enchantment from beginning, to quite the end."

Lincoln attained not force only but a natural cadence which indeed must be called poetry—a melodic creation as in the farewell address in Springfield. And consider the matchless stateliness of the three "can nots" in the Gettysburg Address: ". . . we can not dedicate—we can not consecrate—we can not hallow—this ground. The brave men, living and dead, who struggled here, have consecrated it, far above our poor power to add or detract. The world will little note, nor long remember what we say here, but it can never forget what they did here."

With consummate reverence for God, with insight that illumined his every procedure as a lawyer and as a President with civilian command of an army at bay, Lincoln was unique. He was notable in his manner of proffering consolation. He was instantaneous with praise. To General Grant, made commander of the Union Army some months after his brilliant flanking maneuver at Vicksburg, he said: "As the country herein trusts you, so, under

God, it will sustain you." To Grant "alone" he ascribed credit for terminating the war.

In 1849, during Zachary Taylor's Administration, Lincoln commented on the problem of presidential appointments and said that a President "must occasionally say, or seem to say . . . 'I take the responsibility.'" He referred back to the Jackson Administration and pointed out that "we dare not disregard the lessons of experience." He remembered, and put these lessons into practice when appointing Governor Chase to the position of Secretary of the Treasury. Pressed, almost persecuted, to appoint General Cameron instead, Lincoln stated: "It seems to me not only highly proper, but a *necessity*, that Gov. Chase shall take that place. His ability, firmness, and purity of character, produce the propriety." "Purity of character." The phrase is an epitome of Lincoln.

In faithfulness to a trust; in saving our constituted freedom and opportunity for all; declaring that "no grievance is a fit object of redress by mob violence"; made disconsolate by what he termed "a conspiracy" to "nationalize slavery," Lincoln—dogged by chronic fatigue—was a monumental contradiction of that conspiracy. An architect of justice, determined and destined to win his "case," he did not cease until he had demonstrated the mightiness of his "proposition." It is a Euclid of the heart.

Marianne Moore

66

LINCOLN'S HUMILITY

by Norman A. Graebner

Abraham Lincoln lacked no essential attribute of greatness, but that quality which gave distinction to his character and which has endeared him to successive generations of Americans was his forthright humility. Claims to humility are always subject to challenge. Humility is so universally regarded as an admirable trait that many have pretended to be humble who have seldom experienced emotions of inadequacy. Perhaps even Lincoln's reference to his "poor, lean, lank face" was an effort to turn his humility into a political asset. But Lincoln's entire being was so characterized by doubt that one can scarcely question his sincerity when he said that he was a humble man.

Throughout his life Lincoln never ceased to stress his humble beginnings. When he ran for his first political office in 1832 he told one audience: "I am young and unknown to many of you. I was born and have ever remained in the most humble walks of life. I have no wealthy or popular relations to recommend me." In New Haven, Connecticut, a year before he entered the White

House, he told an audience, "I am not ashamed to confess that twenty-five years ago I was a hired laborer, mauling rails, at work on a flatboat—just what might happen to any poor man's son!" Lincoln's progress to fame, if not fortune, during those intervening years merely deepened his conviction that America must remain a land of opportunity for all men, white and black alike.

Lincoln was too democratic to be arrogant; he spontaneously extended to others any right he claimed for himself. "As I would not be a slave," he said, "so I would not be a master." Lincoln's friendliness stemmed, in large measure, from the loneliness that came from his feeling of solitude. He would have accepted without question Walt Whitman's rhetorical question, "If you meet me and I meet you, why should we not speak to one another?"

Lincoln always made limited claims to wisdom. His doubts permitted him to retain an open mind and willingness to learn. "So soon as I discover my opinions to be erroneous," he said early in his political career, "I shall be ready to renounce them." His tolerance of people and views with which he disagreed reflected his acceptance of democracy as a pluralistic method of resolving issues. He believed that problems which emanated from differences of opinion could be settled only with the engineering of consent. "When the conduct of men is designed to be influenced," he said, "*persuasion*, kind, unassuming persuasion, should ever be adopted." To turn men adrift, to condemn them without remedy, so that good may abound, he added was "something so repugnant to humanity, so uncharitable, so cold-blooded and feelingless, that it never did, nor ever can enlist the enthusiasm of a popular cause. . . . The generous man could not adopt it. It could not mix with his blood." Lincoln would mitigate man's inhumanity not by claims to superior wisdom or morality but through tolerance and magnanimity.

Lincoln was never convinced that he had much to say or that he said it well. "I am not a professional lecturer," he wrote in 1860. "Have never got up but one lecture, and that I think rather a poor one." In addressing an audience at Springfield in December 1839 Lincoln voiced his apprehension that those who had come to hear him did so to spare him mortification rather than to hear his ideas. "This circumstance," he admitted, "casts a damp upon my spirits, which I am sure I shall be unable to overcome during the evening." He revealed this same humility toward his person at Rochester in February 1861, after he had been elected to the Presidency. "I am not vain enough," he said, "to believe that you are here from any wish to see me as an individual, but because I am, for the time being, the representative of the American people."

By the late 1850's Lincoln was being considered for the Republican nomination along with such leading politicians as William H. Seward and Salmon P. Chase. Again he expressed his doubts. To one friend he wrote, "I must, in candor, say I do not think myself fit for the Presidency." Even after his nomination in 1860, when many Republican editors wanted to know something of his early life, Lincoln insisted that there was nothing in his past worth noting. To one inquiring editor he said, "It is a great piece of folly to attempt to make anything out of me or my early life."

After his election Lincoln doubted his ability to handle the office of the Presidency. In Steubenville, Ohio, in February 1861, he warned an audience that he feared the great confidence placed in his ability was unfounded. When the great issue before the nation became the preservation of the Union Lincoln doubted that he could save it. "As to my wisdom in conducting affairs as to tend to the preservation of the Union, I fear too great confidence may have been placed in me." Lincoln's greatness as President stemmed at least partially from the humble view he took of his preparation and competence, for it caused him to respond thoughtfully and energetically to the intellectual and political challenges of his years in office.

Lincoln as President showed marked deference to those around him, although he was obviously superior to most of them in every respect. In his famous message to Congress in December 1862 he wrote, "I do not . . . forget that some of you are my seniors, nor that many of you have more experience than I, in the conduct of public affairs. Yet I trust that in view of the great responsibility resting upon me, you will perceive no want of respect to yourselves, in any undue earnestness I may seem to display."

He always assumed a posture of humility in his relations with his officers, although he revealed far more knowledge of strategy than most of them. When General George B. McClellan one day ignored the President's call Lincoln said, "I will hold McClellan's horse, if he will only bring us success." He told General Ulysses S. Grant at their first meeting in the spring of 1864 that he was no military man and did not know how campaigns should be conducted. He had issued his military orders, he said, only because of the procrastination of his commanders. He admitted that many of them were wrong. "All he wanted or had ever wanted," Grant recalled, "was some one who would take the responsibility and act. . . ."

Humility was an essential ingredient in Lincoln's wartime statesmanship. It was this that made him scrupulously honest. It set limits to his goals and caused him to expect no more of himself, of the nation, or of human nature than the tragic elements in American society would permit. Lincoln always distinguished between what his better nature desired and what the situation would allow. He understood that the confines of successful action were always far narrower than the visions of men. He rejected the will to perfection as the basis of policy because he knew that it was easily turned into fanaticism and would falter because it would expect too much. It was far more important to settle problems than to settle them perfectly. To pursue "pernicious abstractions" divided men unnecessarily and ruled out compromise.

Lincoln understood wisely and humbly that his responsibility ended at the limits of his power to create a better world. In keeping his sights low, but not too low, he did not misuse the power he wielded, or mislead and disappoint those for whom he spoke. He wielded the power to reforge the Union, but he never wielded the power to resolve the problems of human relations in the South. For that reason he made the Union, not the freedom of the slaves, the pervading object of the war. He would attempt only what he believed he could achieve.

Lincoln's true greatness as President lay in his willingness to assume the moral burden of leadership. In a moment of trial he was reported to have said, "Now I don't know what the soul is, but whatever it is, I know that it can humble itself." His great presidential addresses were expressions of that humility. The Presidency, for which Lincoln had sacrificed so much, was never a source of pride to him. He admitted that he was never at home in the White House, for there was no escape from the wearisome burdens of war. Once when a friend suggested a rest he replied: "I suppose it is good for the body. But the tired part of me is *inside* and out of reach."

Lincoln's humility prevented any callousness toward the awful slaughter and anguish of the war. Few men who have wielded power have been so chastened by it. To assure fairness in his decisions he made himself more available to callers at the White House than any other President in American history. Leaders who move about merely in official circles, he once remarked, tend to become officious and arbitrary and forget that they hold power only in a representative capacity. "So long as I have been here," he told a serenading throng on the White House lawn shortly after his re-election in 1864, "I have not willingly planted a thorn in any man's bosom." History illustrates that men often forgive their national enemies but seldom their personal antagonists. Lincoln, in his humility, refused to harbor resentment even against those who intentionally and maliciously sought to injure him.

Lincoln found solace in one phrase which he thought befitting to every situation. That phrase was *"And this, too, shall pass away."* "How chastening in the hour of pride!" he wrote in reference to it. "How consoling in the depths of affliction!" Perhaps for Lincoln the latter respite had the greater significance. If he seldom required chastening in a moment of pride he often required consolation in an hour of affliction.

Norman A. Graebner

67

LINCOLN AND THE FOURTEENTH AMENDMENT

by Sherrill Halbert

The events of Abraham Lincoln's Administration as President of the United States produced three amendments to the Federal Constitution. Of these the Fourteenth has had more written about it and is probably less understood than the other two. It was not the creation of Lincoln or of those who stood with him. It was conceived and pressed into enactment by those who opposed Lincoln in life and abused him in death. It was enacted in a way that was the antithesis of everything that Lincoln believed and stood for. It was born of malice, designed to punish, and pushed through in haste. The very amendment itself is Janus-faced. It opens in phrases exalted in character and purpose, but quickly casts off this mask. The later paragraphs show the true evil spirit that guided its sponsors.

A look at the Fourteenth Amendment reveals that it has four sections, exclusive of the enabling section by which Congress is authorized to enforce the amendment by appropriate legislation.

Section One is that which makes citizens of the United States citizens of the several states. It is more commonly known for its "due process of law" and "equal protection of the laws" provisions. If the wording of this section, apparently virtuous, could have been taken in full faith it probably would have pleased Abraham Lincoln.

But what of the remaining sections of the amendment? Those are the sinister portions. Nothing could be more deceitful than Section Two. It appears to give the freedman the right to vote. Actually it gave him nothing. It merely penalized a state for withholding the right to vote by reducing the state's representation in Congress. It was a double-talking provision and was intended to be so.

The third and fourth Sections were frankly designed to nullify the philosophy spoken by Abraham Lincoln in his Second Inaugural Address. No such exemplary thoughts were in the minds of the men responsible for these two sections. Their object was revenge against the South. The Fourteenth Amendment was the legal vehicle by which they intended to prosecute it.

While Lincoln was actually responsible for this amendment, in the sense that it was the outgrowth of the successful prosecution of the war, his every word and act indicate that he would have fought this particular amendment with all the vigor and ability at his command. It was he who said of his enemies: "Do I not destroy them when I make them my friends?"

It was Lincoln's view at all times that the Confederate states had never left the Union, for that was not legally possible. Therefore once the rebellion had been quelled nothing remained but to pardon the offenders wherever proper and return them to full citizenship. These views were openly and bitterly opposed by a group of men in Lincoln's own Republican party. One firebrand representative referred to the Southern states as "conquered provinces" and advocated that "the whole fabric of Southern society must be changed . . . though it drive her nobility into exile. If they go, all the better." At the same time, a powerful Senator was urging that Congress seize control of the handling of the Southern states from the President. To him the states that had attempted to secede had "committed suicide" and no longer existed.

These men placed social equality above all else, and magnified the issue so that to them all other problems became inconsequential. "If all whites vote," maintained this Senator, "then must all blacks. . . . Their votes are as necessary as our muskets. . . . Mr. Lincoln is slow in accepting truths."

To find the answer to this antipathy between President and Congress we must return to the constitutional problems which arose when the eleven Southern states sought to secede from the Union. Their acts of secession immediately created two serious problems. First, had the rebellious states succeeded in leaving the Union? Second, was the President or Congress responsible for the handling of reconstruction? Lincoln had consistently held, and publicly stated, that the purpose of the war between the states was "to preserve the Union." This conviction, coupled with his view that the Confederate states had never left the Union, brought him to the inescapable conclusion that reconstruction was to involve only the Union, and not the South as a territory. So he incurred the wrath of the Radicals in Congress.

In midwar, December 1863, Lincoln announced his plan of reconstruction. By sound reasoning and benevolence he sought to "bind up the nation's wounds." The opposition in Congress, ruled more by emotion than by logic, took a different view. They set about to make certain that the South was severely punished. When the President killed the Wade-Davis Bill the Radical Republicans were furious. In one breath they assailed him for being too lenient with the South, and in the next breath they accused him of unduly expanding the powers of his office.

Notwithstanding this conflict the Fourteenth Amendment might never have been enacted but for the unfortunate events of the year 1865. That the war ended when it did was, in Lincoln's view, providential, for Congress was not then in session. On April 14 Lincoln told his Cabinet that a wise and discreet course would get the Union re-established before Congress would again meet in the following December. This was his fond hope, but fate was to intervene that very evening. By the next morning Abraham Lincoln was dead, and the course of the nation was in the hands of an honest, conscientious, but inadequate President in the person of Andrew Johnson.

Abraham Lincoln had set a pattern for reconstruction which was merciful, just, and benign. What happened during the reconstruction was to leave a keloid scar on the nation which has not yet disappeared. That Lincoln's plan failed was the real tragedy. This was not the fault of his successor, Andrew Johnson. President Johnson did everything in his power to bring about a fair readjustment that would surely have been satisfactory to Lincoln. But he did not have the astuteness or the ability of his predecessor, and the cause was lost to a group of bitter legislators.

What Lincoln had feared actually came to pass when the lame-duck session of the Thirty-eighth Congress met in December 1865. The Congress refused to accept the policy recommended by President Johnson, even though it was evolved from the reconstruction program of Lincoln. Driven by Thaddeus Stevens, Representative from Pennsylvania, the purpose of Congress, thinly veiled, was to put the conqueror's heel on the throat of the South.

When the Thirty-ninth Congress met in 1865 its first step was the passage of the Civil Rights Act. This act conferred citizenship upon the former slaves and granted the same rights to all persons born in the United States. It was rushed through Congress and passed over the President's veto. Johnson held that the act was an unwarranted invasion of states' rights, and seventeen years later the Supreme Court of the United States was to sustain his view. Even at the time there were some calm thinkers who agreed with the President that the act was unconstitutional. As a result the Fourteenth Amendment was formulated and pushed through Congress. It was passed on June 13, 1866, and submitted to the states for ratification on June 16. By July 28, 1868, all hope of putting Lincoln's philosophy of the golden rule into the operation of reconstruction died. On that date the Secretary of State proclaimed that the Fourteenth Amendment had been ratified by thirty of the thirty-six states of the Union. Thereupon it became a part of the supreme law of the land.

Whether the Fourteenth Amendment would ever have been enacted if Abraham Lincoln had lived we shall never know. Of one thing we can be quite certain, however. That is that if his opponents had been as great and good as Abraham Lincoln there certainly would never have been any thought of its enactment at the time and in the manner that it was done.

And the course of history, and some of our distressing social problems would have been very different. Those of us who believe in Lincoln are sure that he would truly have healed the nation's wounds.

68

A PLAYWRIGHT LOOKS AT LINCOLN

by Mark Van Doren

A playwright wants to see his subject in the sharpest possible focus. His search is for the single moment that contains all time. There may in fact be no such moment in his particular story. Yet the playwright must feel that he has found it before he considers his first scene. If there is no such moment he must make it. He must settle upon some point in the present which explains the past and foreshadows the future. Past, present, and future are in any play. But since dialogue can take place only in the present, the other two dimensions have to be implied. The essence of drama is concentration. "Much in little" is its motto. A great deal has to happen in two hours or else the audience will feel that it is wasting its time. The best way to satisfy the audience is to reach back into the past of the subject at hand.

My experience in writing a play about Lincoln was not quite like this, for it was only at the last moment that I decided to write the play at all. When I did decide, however, the principle applied. It applied, for that matter, to the very process by which the decision was made. My original notion had been to write a long poem about Lincoln—about all of him, his whole life, from beginning to end. But then my interest in his life narrowed down to its concluding moments. The man seemed to be most clearly expressed in the way he behaved just before he died. His past was there—it was actually present—and all of it seemed visible in perspective. It was then that I knew I must write a play. For then I knew that I could dispense with the past and still save it. The end of Lincoln's life was not only its most interesting part. It was also the greatest part, for he was then the greatest man, with all of his depths revealed. So I settled upon *The Last Days of Lincoln* as my subject and title.

But what was the past I could dispense with even as I used it? It was the life of Lincoln as we know it. It was his childhood in Kentucky. It was his moving north to Indiana, and then to Illinois and Springfield, where he met his best friend and his wife. Where he practiced law, and where he got interested in politics. Where he found himself from the start a rival of the Little Giant, Stephen A. Douglas. Where he realized, in common with everybody else, the burning importance of the slavery question. Where he saw the awful possibility of a civil war that might be fought over this question. Where he experienced his first ambition to become a national figure. Where, in 1860, by his election to the Presidency of the United States, he became that figure. To restate his life in such terms is to leave out many details. For instance, his best friend was Joshua Speed, also from Kentucky, as was Mary Todd, whom he married in spite of an instinct that warned him against doing so. He always loved her, but she was high-strung and difficult, and the serenity of their union was something he had to achieve. He did so by being the man he always was—reasonable, charitable, and very intelligent, with a deep longing for peace. Even the details, I determined, must somehow be suggested in *The Last Days of Lincoln.*

The outstanding detail was Lincoln's love of peace, public as well as private. But that was where the irony came in. For any drama that interests us is full of irony—the impossible becomes the possible, and finally the actual. The crowning irony in Lincoln's career is that he presided over the greatest and most terrible war ever experienced by the American people. His fame has its foundation in this war, as his character was most completely expressed in it. But it was expressed against the grain. Lincoln proved himself a military genius, although there was nothing military in his nature. He became a master of men, although he hated the very idea of masters. He revealed in himself an iron will and an irresistible determination, although he was capable of as many doubts as Hamlet. And in doing all of these things he won the war. He triumphed over his enemies, although triumph was the last thing he loved.

The ordeal, as everybody knows, was agony for Lincoln. The war went on too long, it took too many lives, it generated too much hatred. On his own side it bred a fanaticism which he liked least of all. Another irony lies in this. The very fanaticism he disliked was necessary to the winning of the war. The President was forced to accept the help of men who could not have been his friends. Their incompatibility with him was indeed so great that as the war drew to a close, and he saw the task ahead of him of remaking peace between North and South, they could seem more hostile to him than the South itself. The South hated him —mistakenly, he thought. These men distrusted him, for the reason that he himself did not hate the South. The most difficult of all his times lay before him. How could he make a durable peace amid such bitterness? And here the final irony emerged. Just as he thought he had set the country on its course to a just and lasting peace he was assassinated. And by a Southerner who never knew how deeply his victim had desired that the South be free to live again.

My play *The Last Days of Lincoln* begins with the President on his deathbed in the house across the street from the theater where he was shot. But then it goes back three weeks in time, to gather up the events that preceded his death, which the final scene records. The heart of the play is in the scenes between.

Their tense is the present tense, but their reference is both forward and backward—chiefly backward, for the past is what plays are chiefly concerned with.

Joshua Speed has come to Washington, to visit his old friend, only to learn that Lincoln is planning to leave town for a few days. He is going down to City Point, Virginia, to Grant's headquarters on the James River near Richmond, to discuss with Grant the terms that shall be offered Lee when he surrenders. For the day of surrender is at hand, and the victorious army must be prepared. Lincoln desires that the terms shall be lenient. All he really wants is for the Southern fighters to lay down their arms and go home, there to resume their lives in the best circumstances possible, given the ruin around them. He does not know what is in Grant's mind, or in Sherman's either, and Sherman commands another great army, so he must be consulted, too. Lincoln makes his position clear to Speed, as well as his hopes. He says good-by to his friend for the time being.

In the next scene Lincoln is with Grant, feeling out that silent general's position on the terms of surrender. To Lincoln's delight Grant agrees with him. So the famous terms of Appomattox are sketched out. After Richmond falls Lincoln goes there and learns how much the Negroes love him and how little the white people do. Then he is back in Washington with Speed, who is with him till he dies.

Speed witnesses one of Mary Lincoln's hysterical scenes. He listens while Lincoln argues with Radical Senators who would repudiate the terms Grant had given Lee because their own view of peace is entirely punitive. He hears from Lincoln's lips what he intends to say in a speech from the balcony of the White House.

The speech, which was Lincoln's last, failed with the crowd because it was not vindictive. It merely asked how the seceded states could be restored to the Union, and suggested constitutional steps toward that end. Lincoln had destroyed the Southern army. He did not want to destroy the South. His aim was to treat it as if it had never seceded; to let it alone, now that it, too, was at peace. The failure of his policy was as much the result of his assassination as it was the victory of the vindictives. Decades of misery were to follow. There are those who say the country is still not united.

All of this is present somehow in the play, though much of it was past and some of it was future. And in the center of the play Lincoln himself, serious and humorous, energetic and tired, dominates those who are about him. He was a wonderful talker, and my attempt was to bring that talker back to life, if only for three weeks before he was doomed to say, as Hamlet did, "The rest is silence."

Mark Van Doren

69

MR. LINCOLN GOES TO THE THEATRE

by Randle B. Truett

All through his Presidency Abraham Lincoln was under constant pressure. For it was his policy to be accessible to anyone who sought him. Consequently office seekers descended upon him; mothers of soldiers arrived asking for special consideration; politicians called, hoping to obtain support for their particular legislation—there were few quiet moments.

He sought relief that could not be found within the Executive Mansion by living for a few weeks each year in the more relaxed atmosphere of the Anderson cottage, the summer White House. Also, he frequently escaped to the theater and the opera.

When the war prospects for the Union were darkest the New York *Herald* reported: "Mr. Lincoln, it is said, has become a devotee of the Italian opera. After attending one or two of the representations of Grau's troupe in Washington, he thinks like Oliver, he would take a little more. No wonder. From the troubles of the war it is natural that he should seek occasional relaxation. His happy faculty as a joker has doubtless done him a world of good but the wear and tear of the mind from the cares of the state demanded more substantial diversions. No wonder, therefore, that Honest Old Abe has become a lover of music and the opera."

Arrangements were worked out between the President and the managers of two theaters so that he could enter their establishments by the stage door and slip into a stage box without being seen by the audiences. Lincoln frequently moved about Washington without proper protection, and those responsible for his safety were constantly concerned. Carl Sandburg, in his great biography, relates one instance. "To Grover's one night came Mr. and Mrs. Lincoln with Speaker Colfax and no guard or other company. Grover met them at the curb, conducted them from their carriage through a private passage to their box." John Hay, one of the President's secretaries, recorded in his diary: "Spent the evening at the theatre with President, Mrs. L. . . . . J. Wilkes Booth was doing the *Marble Heart*. Rather tame than otherwise." Sandburg also states: "Alone often, yet again with varied companions . . . the President went to the drama, visiting Grover's Theater perhaps a hundred times since coming to Washington. When there was opera at Grover's, Mrs. Lincoln invariably attended with the President."

April 14, 1865, was the occasion for celebration and thanksgiving all over the North. After four years of war General Robert E. Lee, Commander of the Army of Northern Virginia, had surrendered to Grant at Appomattox, and the capitulation of Johnston to Sherman was a foregone conclusion.

This same day had been selected by Mrs. Lincoln for a theater party. The Lincolns had been invited by Grover to attend his theater, where he was going to stage a patriotic gala, including fireworks. Mrs. Lincoln decided against this, turning the tickets over to her son Tad. She chose to attend Ford's, where the popular Laura Keene was offering as her benefit and closing performance the comedy *Our American Cousin*.

General and Mrs. Grant had been invited to the party, but declined, saying they were leaving Washington to visit their children in New Jersey. Lincoln then asked several others to join them, but all declined. Late in the day Miss Clara Harris, daughter of Senator Ira T. Harris of New York, and her fiancé, Major Henry R. Rathbone, accepted the President's invitation.

Even though the President had attended Ford's Theater many times the news that he and his party would be present that evening threw the Tenth Street theater into a furor. Preparations would have to be made that would be adequate for the Chief Executive. The temporary partition between boxes 7 and 8 was removed, and the enlarged box made more comfortable by the addition of special furniture. A sofa and some easy chairs were brought from the property and reception rooms. Among them was a rocking chair, upholstered in red damask, which the President had occupied on his first visit to Ford's new theater. To carry out the patriotic theme American flags were placed on either side of the box and two others were placed on the front. The blue regimental flag of the U. S. Treasury Guards was suspended at the center pillar on a staff. An engraving of George Washington was hung on the front of the box directly below the Treasury Guard flag. When all these preparations had been completed the presidential box reflected the love and admiration in which the President was held by the theater management.

John Wilkes Booth, hearing that the President would attend Ford's Theater rather than Grover's, made a few frantic last-minute preparations.

The performance began promptly at 7:45 before a full house. The President and his party arrived at the theater at about 8:30. They entered the lobby, crossed over to the stairway at the north, and ascended to the dress circle. Passing behind the dress-circle seats, they proceeded down the aisle to the vestibule leading to the double box. When Lincoln entered the box the orchestra struck up "Hail to the Chief," and it was only then that the audience caught sight of him. They rose in a body, cheering again and again. The President smiled and bowed, and when his party was seated the play was resumed.

Booth entered the theater at about 10:10 leaving his horse in the alley back of the theater. Once in the lobby, he quickly crossed to the stairway, ascended to the dress circle, and passed behind the seats to the vestibule door which led to the President's box. He entered the vestibule, closed and secured the door. Since it had no lock he placed a pine bar against the door to prevent anyone in the dress circle from entering.

Observing the President through a small hole which had earlier been bored through the door of box 7, he entered the box silently and, directly behind Lincoln, fired one shot. Lincoln slumped forward in his chair.

Instantly Major Rathbone sprang upon the assassin. Booth dropped his derringer, broke from Rathbone's grasp, and lunged at him with a large knife. Rathbone avoided a direct stab but received a deep wound in his left arm.

All the time Booth was moving toward the front of the box. He placed one hand on the balustrade and vaulted over the railing. His right toe struck the framed engraving of Washington, and his spur caught in the fringe of the Treasury Guard flag. He lost his balance and fell awkwardly to the stage below. He landed in a kneeling position with a force that fractured the large bone of his left leg about two inches above the ankle. Nevertheless, with the agility of an athlete, he quickly regained his feet and dashed across the stage, shouting, *"Sic semper tyrannis!"* Seconds later he had gained the alley, mounted his horse, and swiftly disappeared into the night.

The audience was stunned for a moment by the sound of the pistol shot. Then Mrs. Lincoln's screams told them what they had just heard and seen. This drama was not part of the play but the assassination of the President.

Pandemonium broke out, the people confused and terrified. Finally the audience was quieted and the theater vacated—never to open again.

Three doctors from the audience made a preliminary examination of the wounded President. They ordered that he be moved to the nearest bed.

A ride over the rough cobblestone streets to the Executive Mansion would have caused a fatal brain hemorrhage. So the unconscious Lincoln was carried down the stairway and into the street.

On the other side of Tenth Street a man was seen silhouetted in the light of an open doorway. The surgeons ordered that Lincoln be taken to that house. He was carried up the curving steps and down a narrow hall to a small bedroom. The single bed was pulled out from the corner of the room and the wounded man tenderly laid diagonally across it, his extreme height not permitting any other position. By this simple emergency act the Petersen house was raised from obscurity to become a historic shrine in the nation's capital.

All through the night physicians, Cabinet members, and other distinguished men watched by Lincoln's bedside. Mrs. Lincoln spent the night in the front parlor, going back from time to time to kneel at her husband's bedside.

In the back parlor a hurriedly called meeting of the Cabinet was held, for from the moment the shot was fired the end was inevitable. Here also Secretary of War Stanton immediately began his investigation of the assassination, interviewing as many of the witnesses as possible.

At twenty-two minutes after seven the next morning Abraham Lincoln died, never having regained consciousness. The Reverend Phineas D. Gurley, pastor of the New York Avenue Presbyterian Church which Lincoln had often attended offered a prayer.

It was over. The war was won, the Union was saved, and the man who had done these things was destroyed. But if it had to be it is perhaps some solace to remember that Lincoln spent the last evening of his life free of the heavy trials and petty annoyances of his office, in quiet enjoyment of the relaxation he found most refreshing.

70

THE NATION MOURNS

by Arnold Gates

In a scene as wild and unreal as any staged melodrama the President of the United States had been shot in a theater, carried slowly through an excited throng to a house across the street, and stretched out on a bed to die. While doctors tried to think of some way in which they might save his life a great crowd milled restlessly in the street and waited. Through the long hours of anguish and grief men and women waited in the street and stopped in their talk whenever the door of the Petersen house opened. At about six in the bleak, dark morning Gideon Welles stepped out for a short walk. He recorded that people asked him if there was "no hope." When he replied that Lincoln could survive but a short time the expressions on the faces before him were of intense grief. It started to rain but the people remained and waited.

On the morning of Saturday, April 15, crisp, short messages flashed to the distant points of the country. The President was dead. The rain had stopped and the day promised to be sunny and bright with the tang of fresh-turned earth and new growth in the clean spring air.

So suddenly had all this occurred that many citizens of Washington knew nothing of the night's work until the newspapers or a friend told them the next morning. Noah Brooks, who was to have been Lincoln's private secretary during the second term, was so informed and hurried outdoors to find the streets crowded with bewildered and distressed people. Near the theater he met a procession of bareheaded Army officers leading a company of soldiers which carried the bier of the dead President. Every head was quickly bared and the silence was broken only by the sound of footsteps and sobs from the watching people.

Bells and artillery sounded throughout the day. Flags were at half-mast and buildings everywhere were shrouded in black. Across the land people would not believe what on first hearing sounded so much like a vicious rumor. And when they finally and reluctantly had to believe, the full realization affected them just as would the sudden loss of a father or dear relative. Father Abraham was no more.

Words were inadequate to express what it was the nation felt. Shops, stores, offices, and schools were closed, for people could no longer think of the tasks at hand. People wandered aimlessly through the streets of towns everywhere, could not eat their meals, sought the company of friends, and even tried to find some purpose in this mad act. In Boston's Common a large group of men marched in double column, saying nothing, going to no particular destination, working off the great emotion in the company of fellow mourners, and then drifting away to that solitude in grief that was so necessary in the face of so great a tragedy. While emotion cried for words only brooding silence seemed adequate. A great gloom descended upon everyone and brave soldiers and strong men cried.

General Sherman, meeting with Confederate General Joseph Johnston at a conference, said great beads of sweat appeared on Johnston's forehead as he read a telegram announcing Lincoln's assassination. "Mr. Lincoln," Johnston said, "was the best friend" the South had. General Lee at first would not listen to the story of the assassination but then did and said he regretted the death of Lincoln as much as any man in the North.

A funeral service was held in the White House's East Room just as it had appeared to Lincoln in one of his dreams. Six hundred generals, captains, and dignitaries crowded into the room and heard the Reverend Dr. Phineas D. Gurley read the funeral address. Mrs. Lincoln and Tad were too grief-stricken to attend, but Robert Lincoln braved the ordeal.

The coffin was then moved to the rotunda of the Capitol to be passed by pale soldiers from the Washington hospitals and an endless stream of people. During the night it stood alone while guards paced the vigil hours away.

On the sixth day after his death the body of Abraham Lincoln was placed aboard a special funeral train. While the engine bell tolled and the train moved slowly out of the railroad yard a great crowd of people stood uncovered and watched with infinite sadness Lincoln's final departure from Washington.

And now began a journey which has no equal in the annals of the American people. Only the grand tour of Henry Clay's casket compared with it. The funeral train of seven cars was to travel seventeen hundred miles and practically retrace Abraham Lincoln's journey to Washington four years before. It would stop at cities and villages along the way so that people could come and greet Honest Abe for the last time. In its sad journey it would slow down as it passed through hamlets so that the people might gather along the railroad track to remove their hats and throw flower bouquets.

Baltimore, Philadelphia, Newark, New York City, Albany. As great crowds passed Lincoln's coffin at the Albany capitol on April 26 John Wilkes Booth was killed by his pursuers near Bowling Green, Virginia, without pity or remorse.

Buffalo, Erie, Cleveland, Columbus, Indianapolis, Chicago, Springfield. At Springfield the funeral train had ended its seventeen-hundred-mile journey. More than seven million Americans had seen it as it made its slow way across the country. Farmers plowing in fields paused to remove their hats in humble tribute to its lifeless passenger. Men, women, and children came to stand for hours along the railroad track and say without words what a great loss they understood was theirs. At night no village failed to light fires along the train's way so that it could be seen. At lonely and isolated farmsteads families stood in the light of open doorways and raised hands in mute salute. In spite of rain and other discomforts the people waited everywhere until the train had arrived and passed. Then, having paid final respects to the memory of the man who had come to symbolize the Union, they returned to their wagons and drove home in silence.

Into the state capitol's hall of the lower house at Springfield old friends and neighbors carried the coffin. There, where he had been a member and where he had given his famous House Divided speech, a silent procession of fellow townspeople came to say farewell to Abraham Lincoln. When sadness and grief had weighed the spirits of people everywhere it was personal and doubly meaningful among his old neighbors. They could remember so many homely and commonplace things about his years among them. They could recall his farewell in 1861 and in particular his phrase "I now leave, not knowing when or whether ever I may return. . . ." How tinged with foreboding so many of his words seemed to be in retrospect.

On May 4, 1865, Abraham Lincoln was put to rest in a burial vault in Oak Ridge Cemetery. The man who had arrived in Illinois in 1830 as hardly more than a hewer of wood had returned as the sixteenth President of the United States. Throughout the nation, which he had guided during the grim and uncertain years of a Civil War, he had left his imprint. His words and deeds not only had gripped the imagination of thoughtful Americans but had also been warmly accepted by the peoples of other lands. Though he was dead the shadow of his influence continued to grow.

The great and the humble mourned the man's passing. From every pulpit in the land sermons on the man's life and work were read to the people. So many poems were written and submitted to newspaper editors that they had to point out that publishing them all would have crowded all news out of their pages.

The nation mourned as it never had before and never would afterward. Its writers and poets put their deepest feelings to prose and verse or into lectures given to great, silent audiences. Walt Whitman, newspaperman and Civil War nurse, visiting his mother on Long Island, sat down to meals he could not eat and reflected with deep intensity on what had come to pass. He remembered the courteous nods he had exchanged with President Lincoln as they passed each other on Washington's streets. Returning to the capital, Whitman paced its familiar streets, walked past the White House, and found a setting in keeping with his mood in the woodland outside the city. As deeply aware of the people as Lincoln had been, Walt Whitman knew its pulse beat. Out of the purple tinting of their great sadness he wrote his epic tribute to Abraham Lincoln:

> When lilacs last in the door-yard bloom'd,
> And the great star early droop'd in the western sky in the night,
> I mourn'd—and yet shall mourn with ever-returning spring.

As the great nation bound up its wounds and set to the unfinished tasks before it many men knew they, too, would mourn and yet mourn in many a returning spring.

71

THE FAITH OF ABRAHAM LINCOLN

by Richard Paul Graebel

Today Abraham Lincoln is portrayed as a man of trusting religious faith. This has not always been so. Some biographers took special delight in dwelling on his supposed spiritual poverty, immaturity, or nonconformity. But in the responsible writing of the past fifteen years there is accumulating a solid groundwork of proof that Lincoln was a man of faith. Moreover that he was a man whose faith had content—sturdy, religious content.

No one has ever questioned Lincoln's familiarity with the Judeo-Christian scriptures. He read his Bible regularly and knew it well. He astonished visitors on more than one occasion with his ready knowledge of where certain passages could be found. Biblical allusions in his published papers and recorded conversations number almost four score and are taken from twenty-two different books of the Old and New Testaments.

But even without the many recollected conversations we have today documentation for a lengthening portrait of a man who lived in the daily consciousness of God. We know that he became ever more dependent upon "that Divine Will" as the burdens of circumstance pressed upon him. And in very recent years we have come into possession of a document which proves the long-rumored story that Lincoln carried a pocket testament around with him and read it daily.

That testament is probably *The Believer's Daily Treasure*, published in 1852 by the Religious Tract Society of London. It is autographed by Lincoln—a thing he rarely did in his books.

Lincoln's religious faith took shape over a period of years, to reach its fullest development during the dark days of the war between brothers. His expression of that faith, both in word and deed is a part of the religious heritage of the American people.

Religious experience is not a static thing in the life of man, as Lincoln's life clearly illustrates. He undoubtedly had long thoughts when, still a child, he helped his father make a coffin for his mother's body and they laid it in the earth among the trees radiant with autumn colors. There was no preacher within thirty miles, and the family had its own funeral service for Nancy Hanks. They had done the same thing for her uncle and aunt only a few months before. They were people who knew the Book and the Gospel. It is said that youngsters grow up suddenly when they look into the face of death.

It is true that the young Abe Lincoln did not revel in the camp meetings of the time and shout "Hallelujah" with the saved.

Yet from the public utterances spoken in his mature years, under the conviction that "In times like the present, men should utter nothing for which they would not willingly be responsible through time and in eternity," we can safely say, This he believed:

He believed in God, the Father Almighty, Maker of heaven and earth.

He believed in praising God as beneficient; and that His truth and justice are eternal.

He believed that it is the duty of nations, as well as individuals, to own their dependence upon the overruling power of God. That it is their duty to invoke the influence of the Holy

Spirit. To confess their sins, and to be assured that genuine repentance will bring mercy and pardon.

He recognized that those nations only are blessed whose god is the Lord.

He realized in his own life that all human reliance is vain. "Without the assistance of that Divine Being," he told his friends in Springfield, "I cannot succeed; with that assistance, I cannot fail."

At another time he said, "I do not think I could myself be brought to support a man for office whom I knew to be an open enemy of, and scoffer at, religion."

Lincoln believed himself to be an instrument in the hands of God. He insisted that he had registered an oath in heaven to finish the work that he was in, fully cognizant of his responsibility to God.

The question might well be asked: "How did Lincoln come by such a faith?"

We cannot gauge the effect of the religion taught in the Pigeon Creek Baptist Church where Thomas and Sarah Bush Lincoln took their brood of five children. There were no Sunday schools in those days, and if there had been it is unlikely that the rigid Calvinism would have been teachable to youngsters except in terms of unlimited rewards and total punishments.

We know that Abe Lincoln came to Springfield feeling so uncouth that he didn't go to church for three months after his arrival. He wrote a friend that he wasn't sure he would know how to act in a city church. Whether this was a reason or an excuse is anybody's guess.

But we do know that when in February of 1850 his second son, Edward Baker, died Lincoln knew where to turn for help. He called upon Dr. James Smith, pastor of the First Presbyterian Church, to conduct the funeral service for the infant. The two became understanding friends thereafter.

While it is true that Lincoln rented pew number 20 in the First

by Richard Paul Graebel

Presbyterian Church in Springfield he never made a profession of faith in that church or any other during his life.

Perhaps it was this public display which deterred Lincoln. As his closest associates insisted, no one had a right to say he knew Lincoln intimately. There were areas of his life which he shared with no man.

By the time Lincoln rented his pew there were already three Presbyterian churches in Springfield. And although they dwelt "in unity of spirit and in the bonds of peace" they had their differences.

One of the trustees of First Church decided that what the church needed most was a pipe organ. The instrument was ordered and installed without consent of the congregation, which thereupon refused to pay for it. A suit was brought before the presbytery of Springfield, and the church trustees appointed Lincoln as one of three persons to assist the pastor, Dr. Smith, in defending the matter. Yet, interestingly enough, this was contrary to the Book of Discipline of the church, which stated:

"No professional counsel shall be permitted to plead in cases of process in any of our ecclesiastical courts."

One wonders whether Lincoln was passed off as a trustee of the church or if he appeared as a member of the congregation.

Certainly Lincoln gave the world the impression and set the example of a man with a profoundly religious sense of responsibility and faith. A New England Congressman, Henry C. Deming of Connecticut, said that Lincoln was once asked why, in light of his obvious piety, he did not join a church. And Lincoln reportedly replied: "When any church will inscribe over its altars, as its sole qualification for membership, the Saviour's . . . statement for the substance of both law and gospel, 'Thou shalt love the Lord thy God with all thy heart, and with all thy soul, and with all thy mind, and thy neighbor as thyself,' that church will I join with all my heart and soul."

A hundred years after his tragic, destined role upon the stage of world history we find new insights and strength in his example

413

for the trials of our difficult era. Even as in that time, many people today sense a certain new mystical quality. "Things came about not so much by preconceived method as by an impelling impulse," recollected one of Lincoln's contemporaries.

"The Almighty has His own purposes," said Lincoln, and wanted it known that he was on the side of God when he wrote, "I am conscious of no desire for my country's welfare that is not in consonance with His will, and of no plan upon which we may not ask His blessing."

The newest discoveries in the field of Lincoln lore give us cause to increase research into the religious attitudes of the man. For though the findings thus far take us no further toward placing Lincoln within any particular creed or denomination, they undoubtedly bear testimony to a truth we have know all along in our own hearts. Here was a man of profound and vital religious faith.

Lincoln belongs to the ages because he knew he belonged to the Eternal God.

Richard Paul Graebel

72

LINCOLN AND THE FAMILY OF MAN

by Ralph G. Newman

In discussing the personal philosophy from which Abraham Lincoln developed his political credo and which governed his every official act, we must remember a phrase he liked to use. He spoke of the "family of man." Not Northerners or Southerners, or Americans or British or Russians, but "the whole great family of man." His faith was not in parties or armies, but in men, mankind itself.

He was probably born with that faith, as surely all great men are. But he found it epitomized in words when as a boy in Indiana he read late into the night by the flickering light of a crude fireplace, studying and pondering over the Declaration of Independence, which maintained that all men were created equal. Only out of his complete assumption of that tenet could have come the determination and the staying power to educate himself and literally pull himself up by his own bootstraps. From it came both his humility and his authority, and his ability to grow into whatever task was set before him. It sustained him through the terrible trials of war. For he saw the Civil War as the final testing of that mighty principle.

One of the most striking affirmations of this democratic faith that Lincoln ever uttered was in a speech at Lewistown, Illinois, during his campaign against Stephen A. Douglas in 1858 for election to the United States Senate. He declared that the men who met in Independence Hall were speaking to the whole world of men when they enunciated their principles of human freedom and equality. Yes, even more than that, because "They grasped not only the whole race of man then living, but they reached forward and seized upon the farthest posterity. They erected a beacon to guide their children and their children's children, and the countless myriads who should inhabit the earth in other ages. Wise statesmen as they were . . . they established these great self-evident truths, that when in the distant future some man, some faction, some interest, should set up the doctrine that none but rich men, or none but white men, were entitled to life, liberty and the pursuit of happiness, their posterity might look up again to the Declaration of Independence and take courage to renew the battle which their fathers began—so that truth, and justice, and mercy, and all the humane and Christian virtues might not be extinguished from the land; so that no man would hereafter dare to limit and circumscribe the great principles on which the temple of liberty was being built."

In this speech Lincoln revealed his conception of the mission of America. He believed fervently that America does have a mission. He called Americans "God's almost chosen people," because to them it had been given not only to demonstrate democracy as a workable form of government but furthermore to cleanse it of the hypocrisies which, he said, "deprive it of its just example in the world."

Herein lies the most impelling reason for Lincoln's dislike of slavery. For while he hated human bondage as a monstrous injustice in itself ("I am naturally anti-slavery," he said. "If slavery is not wrong, nothing is wrong."), he hated it even more because "it . . . enables the enemies of free institutions, with plausibility, to taunt us as hypocrites. . . ."

Lincoln conceived of America as more than people, or homes, or wealth, or wheat, or corn, or steel, or factories. To him it embodied an idea. Common sacrifices for a new and better way of life were like "mystic chords of memory," he said, "stre[t]ching from every battle-field, and patriot grave, to every living heart and hearthstone, all over this broad land. . . ." America was a trustee for humanity. The Union of States was bound together by an idea. If the Union perished the idea would perish with it. Thus the issue of the Civil War to Lincoln was the preservation of democratic government, through the preservation of the American Union, in order that America might go on to fulfill its mission as the exemplar of democracy to the world.

No smaller conception of the struggle could forgive the awful cost. Lincoln knew that from the start. Very early in the war he explained his view to his young secretary John Hay, saying, "For my part, I consider the central idea pervading this struggle is the necessity that is upon us, of proving that popular government is not an absurdity. We must settle this question now, whether in a free government the minority have the right to break up the government whenever they choose. If we fail it will go far to prove the incapability of the people to govern themselves."

He explained this conception to Congress at his first opportunity—when it assembled on July 4, 1861, the war already three months old. He said: "This is essentially a People's contest. On the side of the Union, it is a struggle for maintaining in the world, that form, and substance of government, whose leading object is, to elevate the condition of men—to lift artificial weights from all shoulders—to clear the paths of laudable pursuit for all—to afford all, an unfettered start, and a fair chance, in the race of life."

Throughout the war, in letters, in addresses, in informal talks to soldiers, this was the theme that Lincoln stressed. In the Gettysburg Address, in which he pleaded for increased devotion to the ideals of our founding fathers so that government of the *people*, by the *people*, for the *people*, might not perish from the earth, he reached the loftiest expression of a concept that he had put forward many times before.

Lincoln's deep regard for the principles of human liberty and equality suggests a religious reverence. Even his political thinking was conditioned by belief in a supernatural force which lays down the laws of life. Though something of a doubter in his younger years he grew increasingly religious as his thought matured, and came finally to such complete acceptance of this belief in an overruling power that he looked upon himself as a mere instrument of what he called variously Divine Providence, the Almighty, and God.

Along with this concept of a higher power governing the affairs of man went the notion that man, given the proper environment, is capable of self-betterment to the point that human society, bringing its own laws and conduct into closer and closer accord with Divine Providence, may one day attain, or at least approach, perfection. In his mind the democratic form of government provided the most promising environment for such human improvement. "We propose to give *all* a chance," he said, "and we expect the weak to grow stronger, the ignorant to grow wiser; and all better and happier together."

But Lincoln knew that human nature cannot be changed by edicts and laws, that the struggle for human freedom and social justice will probably go on to the end of time, and that the only permanent advance mankind can hope for is such as can be made in the mind and conscience of mankind itself. He knew, too, that men's moral judgments differ, that moral standards change, and that good and evil are not easily separated by drawing a line between them. "The true rule, in determining to embrace, or reject any thing," he said, "is not whether it have *any* evil in it; but whether it have more of evil, than of good. There are few things *wholly* evil, or *wholly* good. Almost every thing, especially of governmental policy, is an inseparable compound of the two; so that our best judgment of the preponderance between them is continually demanded."

So, in the day-to-day conduct of the war, Lincoln was able to be practical, as practical a politician as any President we have ever had. Without in the least abandoning his ideals he learned to subordinate them to the considerations of the moment, and to limit his objectives to what was obtainable. Though detesting slavery, he saw no sense in destroying the whole edifice reared by the founding fathers because slavery constituted a defect in it. The reckless zeal of the abolitionists was wholly foreign to his nature.

The Emancipation Proclamation was only a half measure, a steppingstone. Lincoln knew that righteousness could not be established by presidential edict. It had to come, eventually, from the people themselves, in a constitutional amendment. The Proclamation was a temporary thing, a matter of war necessity. But it set the people to thinking in the right direction.

No one has been able to prove whether or not Lincoln really said that "you can fool all the people some of the time, and you can fool some of the people all of the time; but you can't fool all the people all of the time." Though he may never have said this in so many words it can be taken as a true expression of the way he felt. For a man can have no faith in democracy without deep faith in human nature. And Lincoln's faith in the integrity and mass judgment of plain people, the kind he had grown up with, was limitless and unwavering, provided only that the people were informed.

Therefore in his First Inaugural Address he asked, "Why should there not be a patient confidence in the ultimate justice of the people? Is there any better, or equal hope, in the world? In our present differences, is either party without faith of being in the right? If the Almighty Ruler of nations, with his eternal truth and justice, be on your side of the North, or on yours of the South, that truth, and that justice, will surely prevail, by the judgment of this great tribunal, the American people."

In identifying religion with democracy Lincoln made himself democracy's oracle. The spirit of democracy is moral. It emphasizes *right* as well as rights, and responsibility as well as freedom.

There are enduring lessons in Lincoln's philosophy. The nations of the earth will always need his faith in the people, in their judgment, in their ability to govern themselves. And America has, to the farthest generation, the obligation to maintain and fulfill the destiny prepared by the founding fathers for what Lincoln termed in affection and respect the "family of man."

APPENDIX

REFLECTIONS WHILE STANDING BEFORE
THE LINCOLN MEMORIAL

These two essays on the theme "Reflections While Standing before the Lincoln Memorial" were selected as prize-winning entries in a contest conducted by Broadcast Music, Inc., in co-operation with the American Association for State and Local History, and in association with *This Week Magazine*. The two winning authors, Helen M. Newell of Boise, Idaho, winner in the professional-writer category, and Nancy A. Potter of Voluntown, Connecticut, winner in the nonprofessional-writer category, received prizes of a thousand dollars each. Entries in the contest were received from every one of the United States.

I. by Helen M. Newell

What a quiet place it is. Not the quiet of the dead. Not a tranquil hush of peace. A meditative quietness.

Steadily up the broad steps people come, singly, in twos, in families, stopping to look back along the reflecting pool to Washington's monument—poised like a rocket on its launching pad—before they turn and come in through the columns. They pause below the chair of the great, gaunt, brooding man and study him, his absorbed face, his long arms resting on the arms of the chair, one hand clenched upon a problem. They move on to the allegorical paintings, the inscriptions—his dedication of the cemetery at the field of Gettysburg, the Second Inaugural Address. Then they come back and stand quiet again, meditating with the meditating figure. And then they walk slowly and thoughtfully down the steps.

How fitting the response! Above all else this man's distinction was the employment of his mind. He accepted that as the first responsibility of any citizen of a democracy, the condition for its survival. "My countrymen," he urged them, "think calmly and well . . ."

How came such mental quality from so unlikely a background? The son of unremarkable parents, a meager frontier boyhood, his energies almost to middle life swallowed up in making a living—what struck the spark? What combination of heritage produced the desire, the will, and the judgment to discipline his mind and develop a philosophy stout enough to lead a nation through the holocaust of civil war when the hand of history reached out and closed around him? It sets one pondering. Has anything half as triumphant come out of our laboratories? Off our drafting boards?

The sculptured face is not so worn and somber as his photographs show. Flesh takes pain more deeply than marble will. Fifty-six years? Was that really all? Could any face grow sadder in a century? Not one illusion left in it. No cynicism either—that's the wonder. The true realist. He took men as they were, finding something of value in most.

Finding it even behind the vicious tongues—tongues not only of Southern rebels, Northern copperheads, cotton-hungry Europeans, but of his own party, his officials, his military men, leading citizens and newspapers of the day. They sneered and hated. "Second-rate village lawyer," "poor-white trash," "despot," "gorilla," buffoon . . ." The droll parables he used to illuminate grave problems seemed to infuriate them most of all. They could not comprehend a man in whom humor worked with gravity. Already the cities were growing remote from the frontier; they had forgotten how lives of constant danger and hardship had to be bantered to be borne. Buffoon! This man whom depths of black despair twice drove to the edge of suicide, this man of so hard a discipline it could compel him to take up again what seemed to him his defeated life, what seemed to him his defeated country, and go on under the load.

Those vicious tongues! . . . Yet, now I think of it, are our tongues more responsible today? From the minute we elect our public servants, don't we bellow contempt of them, which, in a democracy, is contempt of ourselves, contempt of our system. And then we squawk our righteous wrath when the world, watching with interest, questions the supreme merits of democracy!

Lincoln ignored the name-calling; his mind was tough and he had no time for meanness. What harassed him was the advice. *Everybody* advised him. How did the man withstand the pressure of those violent, conflicting opinions? He respected his own abilities well enough, but no one had a clearer view of his deficiencies and inexperience. And he never came to believe final wisdom possible to anyone. Especially in war, there was no "right" way. All ways were wrong. The best you could do was try to judge which was least wrong. An agonizing responsibility. No doubt he prayed; but, though his nature was deeply religious, there was nothing orthodox about his beliefs. He held no conviction of being the chosen of God; he did not presume to interpret the purpose of God. In the South, he knew people were praying to the same God with sincere faith He was on *their* side.

Well, Lincoln was frontier-raised. He knew you didn't get anywhere scattering your shot over the whole landscape; you selected your target, and drew a bead on it. His whole political feeling, he said, was rooted in the Declaration of Independence: "all men are created equal . . . endowed by their Creator with certain unalienable Rights . . . to secure these rights, Governments are instituted among Men, deriving their just powers from the consent of the governed . . ." As he saw it, the one purpose for which the people had elected him President was to hold the Union together.

He aimed himself at that. He judged his every decision by it, with all the sagacity he had in him. Into that purpose he paid the rest of his life.

I like to read his sentences. He had such a feeling for words, "hefting" each one against the weight of his thought. There is something extraordinary in the way this unschooled man taught himself to get the pith out of a complex matter and express it in a few words. Nothing fuzzy, no padding. It sets one pondering again. How about the products of our vast educational system? Our Age of Communication?

". . . our fathers brought forth on this continent, a new nation, conceived in Liberty, and dedicated to the proposition that all men are created equal. Now we are engaged in a great civil war, testing whether that nation, or any nation so conceived and so dedicated, can long endure. . . ." November 1863. Almost a hundred years ago. . . . And now we are engaged in another great war. Not a civil war, thank God. And we call this one "cold," as if it were some new kind altogether—but there's nothing new in its purpose. Still testing whether a nation conceived in liberty and dedicated to the proposition that all men are created equal can endure. There are people who think it can't. There are people doing their best to see that it doesn't. Every day they prod, hunting out our weakness.

What about this weakness—where is it we're most vulnerable? Everywhere we're damned as materialistic; they say that's the beginning of the end for us as it was for the Romans. Is that true? Are we wholly engrossed in accumulation and prestige and comfort and entertainment? Is it true we run mentally in flocks and grow steadily more content with the second- and the third-rate? And is it true that fewer and fewer of us trouble ourselves to use our separate minds and abilities to work out principles and values honestly worth paying out our energies for, our talents, our time on this earth?

We don't hear much about principles any more. It hasn't become a dirty word, exactly; it just isn't fashionable. The fashion-

by Helen M. Newell

able word today is "Peace." All over the world people talk enthusiastically about Peace, as if Peace were the principle we could all agree to stand for. But Peace isn't a principle. Justice is the principle; Peace is only a result. Justice requires work and moral hardiness and stretching our minds till they hurt. Is that our trouble? Do we want the result without the effort?

Yet lately there's a hint in the air that the facts of democracy may be dawning on us. Bought by the minds and the lives of our forefathers, was it perhaps *not* an outright gift to us who came afterward? Was other men's blood, paid in civil war, not the end of it either? Could it be that democracy is not a gift at all, but a discipline? A proposition stated by the lives of its citizens? If the lives of any generation shirk that statement, can mere institutions guarantee that freedom, equality, self-government, will "long endure"?

I think of the sermon our pastor gave on the dangers besetting our nation. He named the threats of outside enemies, and suggested that a strong people united beyond self-interest in the good of our country could withstand outside enemies; we are a democracy, we choose our representatives, we vote. He was silent a long, thoughtful moment. "And how do we vote?" he inquired slowly. "How do the Republicans vote? How do the Democrats vote? How do the farmers vote? How does Labor vote? How do the businessmen vote? How do I vote? How do you vote? . . ."

There is nothing more to see here. I have read the inscriptions; I have looked at the paintings. I linger again beside the sculptured man whose absorbed face gazes out through the marble columns, along the reflecting pool, and beyond Washington's monument toward the buildings of our government. And then I go out with the other visitors and walk slowly down the steps.

Helen M. Newell

II. by Nancy A. Potter

Every day of the year Americans make pilgrimages here, alone and in groups—school children and retired businessmen, scientists and politicians, farmers and steelworkers, soldiers and sailors, housewives and diplomats. We come with separate purposes and thoughts, but finally all of us measure our time against yours, trying to learn what you would think of our century and our way of life.

Parts of our worlds coincide. Across the years we can share many things: the smell of white pine and freshly turned sod, of growing corn and harvested apples; the touch of rough bark, the thin pages of a loved book, and the hardness of work-worn hands; the taste of cold spring water and sun-drenched plums. Lilacs go on blooming in the same dooryards, and the thrush sings the same song. Spring awakens the country we love with the same freshets in the hills and blossoming trees in the valleys; we linger through slow rich summers and golden autumns, and we chill with the tightening of winter.

Our personal joys and sorrows are echoes of yours too. We love the weariness that follows honest labor, the release of holidays, the size and variety of our country, and the freedom to move about it and to come back home again. We like to recite the fables of the land, to boast of regional heroes, to champion one state over the others, but we are faithful to the entire nation. We share most of your fears and concerns. Like you, we have dreaded the sound of marching feet, the scars and pain of war, but, like you, we hated persecution and slavery more. Like you, we have loved the quiet years of peace, but, like you, we have despised intolerance enough to fight well when freedom and rights were lost. Like you, we have been unhappy with dissension and weary of tedious argument, but we realize that both are sometimes the necessary behavior of a democracy.

We come here to tell you of the changes in our patterns of life and to contrast our values with yours. There are new states and larger cities, greater harvests and bigger machines, more leisure and greater speed. We have harnessed the power of rivers, mastered the elements in the earth, and crossed the reaches of the sky. We pride ourselves on having mixed the best of the Old World together to gain a vigorous culture. We have assured ourselves longer and generally healthier lives, built ourselves larger houses and great universities, and guaranteed greater material security to our citizens. Our assurance is doubled by the abundance of resources and our belief in our way of life. The scenes from this daily life are those we wish we could share with you.

You would understand the spread of personalities across our continent and the vitality of a still-growing nation. You would delight in our mixing of backgrounds, our continual scrutiny of our government, our educational opportunities, our role in international politics. You would worry about some of the difficulties that still stand in the way of our being a perfect republic. You would hope that the sensitivity of our hearts might match our increased technical skills and our knowledge of the material world. You would hope that somehow we might have become better people as a result of our physical progress. You might believe that we would have been able to destroy all human fears in order that we might spend ourselves upon higher concerns, but instead we have often exchanged the old fears for new ones. We find ourselves constantly struggling to fulfill responsibilities thrust upon us by the progress it is impossible to deny.

Our speed and growth have diminished the forests and plains you knew into a tidy patchwork of alfalfa fields and towns and factories, all linked by concrete bands which we cross to visit the mountains, the coasts, and the ranch lands. News travels among us with the speed of wind, but answers to our problems sometimes come more slowly. We are aware of new situations, people, and places, but these are only variations of the ones that concerned you. Many of us are richer materially than you could have dreamed we would be. We have traveled more miles on what seems to be a smaller world, but it is doubtful that we can match your comprehension of the human heart. The years have magnified your abilities and clarified your singular importance to us.

That is the reason why we have come to this place. We need to measure our decisions against yours and in our short reflection here remember your life, work, and manner. Here random lines from your addresses ring through our minds, and vignettes from your life pass before our eyes, for yours is the most familiar of all American stories. In schoolbooks and legends and memory we trace your career from New Salem to the White House, from Bull Run to Gettysburg, through the fifty-six years from a winter day in a Kentucky clearing to a spring evening in Ford's Theatre. There are the tales of the honest storekeeper, the thorough surveyer, the gaunt young lawyer, the trusted congressman, the thoughtful husband, and the suffering President. The youngest school child knows the details of your biography, and the newest citizen has a strong impression of your personality. To every American for a century your name has summoned up a series of pictures which are the same no matter where we live or how old we are.

We see you patient in the general confusion, thoughtful of the smallest detail, and always sensitive to the destiny of a united nation you had to leave at the moment of its rebirth. We see you solicitous with the soldiers and the widows and kind to the weak and unfortunate, gentle with the stubborn and willful. Yet beneath this simple goodness and this homely charm lay a sturdy and lasting courage and a strength that helped the country torn apart come together again into a seamless whole. We have always drawn a double picture of you from the stories of the private man and the legends of the great American. We try to learn from the pattern of your life your virtues, your gentle self-reliance, and your dignified patience. We tell our children of your nobility and

430

bring them here to see a statue, but, more than that, to feel a presence.

When sometimes we worry that we are in danger of losing the directness, clarity, and honesty which you practiced, we seek your counsel here and hope for your sympathy. It is fitting that this quiet place should exist in the heart of our nation and that here we may thoughtfully pause to reflect upon the debt we owe to you and the virtues we may still learn from your life. We hope for more statesmen with your conscience and devotion to the whole country. Often we hope for the perspective of intelligent wit which you used to reduce the monumental fears of the minute to reasonable proportions. We wish for the quiet humility which still could vow that the possession of right would provide the means to establish it firmly.

You gave us the unsated need to establish justice and honesty where we can. Where we fail and your shadow stretches far beyond ours, our humility reaches toward it. One hundred and fifty years after Tom and Nancy Lincoln's son was born in Hardin County, we dedicate ourselves to his unfinished work.

Nancy A. Potter

LINCOLN IN THE ARCHIVES

by C. Percy Powell

Lincoln items may range from an entry in the daybook of a Springfield apothecary for a vial of ipecac to the official copy of the Emancipation Proclamation in the National Archives. The most important group of documents consists of the personal correspondence and manuscripts of Lincoln, beginning about 1825 and continuing until his death in 1865. A second group comprises the legal records of Lincoln's practice filed in the courthouses of the Illinois Eighth Judicial Circuit, the Illinois Supreme Court, the Federal courts at Springfield. A third and large group includes the records associated with Lincoln as President and now a part of the government archives. Still a fourth group consists of the correspondence of public figures of Lincoln's time.

The documents pertaining to the Lincoln story beyond his death usually originate with persons and institutions interested in collecting Lincoln materials or in perpetuating his memory. These collections may be, and often are, the beginning of a special library, the creation of a shrine, a monument, a painting, or a book. Such documents frequently contain information regarding the living Lincoln, and should be consulted.

The principal Lincoln collections are now in large libraries or universities. Where, then, should one go to find the personal correspondence of Abraham Lincoln? The letters written by Lincoln, so far as they are known, have been collected and printed from time to time. The latest publication is *The Collected Works of Abraham Lincoln*, edited by Roy P. Basler, Marion D. Pratt, and Lloyd A. Dunlap for the Abraham Lincoln Association of Springfield, Illinois, and published in 1953-55. Without such a publication one would have had to go to virtually every state in the Union to locate the estimated 5000 published manuscripts. The largest number of these is in the Library of Congress. There are, however, approximately 1100 in the Illinois State Historical Library, 800 in the Brown University Library, 300 in the Henry E. Huntington Library, and lots of fewer than 100 in the University of Chicago Library, the Lincoln National Life Foundation, and Lincoln Memorial University.

The other side of the correspondence—the letters received by Abraham Lincoln—is, with few exceptions, in the Library of Congress. These letters were deeded to the government in 1923 by Robert Todd Lincoln, oldest and only surviving son of the President, with the proviso that they be withheld from public examination for twenty-one years after the death of the donor. This time limit expired in 1947, and the letters have been available to the public since then. There are approximately 18000 of these documents, of which only a few hundred are in print.

The large collection of letters, documents, and other papers assembled by Lincoln's law partner, William H. Herndon, who devoted the remaining years of his life, after Lincoln's death, to collecting material relating to the life of his associate and friend, are in the Library of Congress. Together with the material assembled by Herndon's collaborator, Jesse W. Weik, this collection constitutes one of the great sources of Lincoln information and is invaluable to the biographer, student, and historian.

Occasionally a series of letters written by Lincoln to a personal friend becomes available for acquisition from some private source, such as his letters to Lyman Trumbull, now in the Huntington

Library, or the letters to Elihu B. Washburne and Joshua Speed, in the Illinois State Historical Library.

Lincoln's homemade arithmetic book, land surveys, poems, farewell address to the people of Springfield, autobiography, copies of the Gettysburg Address, scrapbooks, and the like are scattered among libraries and private citizens throughout the country. The arithmetic book, of which ten pages are known to exist, is divided among the University of Chicago, Brown University, the Chicago Historical Society, Columbia University, the Library of Congress, and several individuals. The Gettysburg Address, with five copies extant, is in the Illinois State Historical Library, Cornell University Library, the White House, and there are two drafts in the Library of Congress. The contract for the purchase of his house in Springfield, his marriage license, land surveys, and poll books kept by Lincoln are among the holdings of the Illinois State Historical Library. The original manuscript of the poem "My Childhood Home I see Again," two autobiographies, the farewell speech to the people of Springfield, the famous Cabinet agreement, and the Second Inaugural Address are in the Library of Congress.

Many of the legal manuscripts of Lincoln can be consulted in the respective county, state, and Federal archives. But many of these documents have found their way out of the archives and into libraries or the hands of collectors. For example there are 300 such legal items in the Illinois State Historical Library and 750 in the Library of Congress.

The official records of Lincoln as President and Commander-in-chief of the Armed Forces are in the National Archives. In addition there are Lincoln documents associated with the Black Hawk War of 1832, with Lincoln in Congress 1847-49, and with Lincoln the inventor. Official copies of his proclamations, treaties, executive orders, messages, and the like are there as part of the required routine government records. The departmental records were greatly enlarged during the Civil War, and standard procedures were not always followed in storing them. Consequently it is sometimes difficult to locate specific documents related to an action of Lincoln's. Anyone wishing to consult the Lincoln material in the National Archives should rely upon the expert guidance of the archivists there.

Perhaps the reason for the continuous research and writing on the Lincoln theme is the wealth of information about him in the correspondence of his contemporaries. Apart from his own letters to members of his Cabinet the Lincoln Administration is revealed in the papers of his Secretary of the Treasury, Salmon P. Chase; his Secretary of the Navy, Gideon Welles; and others. All these are in the Manuscript Division of the Library of Congress. The same is true for the correspondence of many publicized military figures and political appointees. The papers of Stephen A. Douglas, now in the University of Chicago Library, bear on the Lincoln story. The papers of Ward Hill Lamon, one-time Lincoln law partner and personal bodyguard, are revealing. They can be found in the Huntington Library. One should not overlook the papers of Cassius M. Clay, minister to Russia and self-appointed protector of Lincoln. These are owned by Lincoln Memorial University. The genealogical records of the Lincoln and Hanks families may be studied at the Lincoln National Life Foundation in Fort Wayne, Indiana.

The Lincoln story after 1865 seems to have developed certain aspects of a crusade. Individuals, organizations, institutions, and governments have been so zealous in their collecting and preserving that today we have a Lincoln legend. Consequently important collections of correspondence have been created in the search for and purchase of Lincoln materials. Letters to and from any major collector are part and parcel of the Lincoln story.

Organizations that have been created to serve the Lincoln theme are almost without number. Virtually every section of the country has an active local group today. A classic example of this type of organization is the Abraham Lincoln Association of Springfield, Illinois. The documentation in its files properly belongs to the Lincoln story. Organizations are often instrumental in promoting projects in the Lincoln tradition. There was, for instance, the restoration of the village of New Salem, Illinois, where Lincoln lived as a young man and served as postmaster. The correspondence resulting from such endeavors often reflects the living Lincoln.

Institutions, often receiving their incentive as well as their sustaining force from private collectors, are no doubt the principal source of the Lincoln legend. They may be a museum boasting only the carriage in which Lincoln rode to Ford's Theater on the night of his assassination, or the Lincoln Museum in Washington, D. C. In such archives can be found information on Lincoln in manuscripts and music, in statuary and pictures, stamps and bric-a-brac.

The Lincoln name has often been memorialized by both state and Federal governments. There is, for example, an Illinois state park at New Salem, and a national park at Hodgenville, Kentucky. It was to perpetuate the Lincoln tradition that the national Lincoln Highway was named. Perhaps the most popular means used by small governmental units is statuary. The contribution of the Federal Government to the lasting fame and memory of Lincoln is the Lincoln Memorial in Washington, D. C. The correspondence relating to all such projects tells the Lincoln story.

The two major sources, however, of keeping alive and fresh the memory of Lincoln and the Lincoln story are the American public education system and the National Republican Party. But who can examine archives of such magnitude!

In any event Lincoln nowadays seems to be in nearly everyone's archives.

C. Percy Powell

"THE FACTS . . . ARE MAINLY OLD AND FAMILIAR"

LINCOLN CHRONOLOGY

by Harry E. and Marion D. Pratt

The late Harry E. Pratt prepared a chronological compilation of the significant events in the life and story of Abraham Lincoln, which was first published in 1953. This chronology was revised and subsequently reprinted several times. Mrs. Pratt has revised and added to Dr. Pratt's original work to include the significant events and dates involved in the contributions which comprise the main portion of this book.

Pre-1809

1778, January 6. Abraham Lincoln's father, Thomas Lincoln, is born in Rockingham County, Virginia.

1782. Thomas Lincoln migrates with his parents to Kentucky.

1784, February 5. Abraham Lincoln's mother, Nancy Hanks, is born in western Virginia.

1806, June 12. Thomas Lincoln and Nancy Hanks are married in the cabin of Richard Berry, near Springfield, Kentucky, in Washington County. The Reverend Jesse T. Head performs the ceremony.

1807, February 10. Sarah, first child of Thomas and Nancy Lincoln, is born at Elizabethtown, Kentucky.

1808. Thomas Lincoln moves his family to a farm on the south fork of Nolin Creek in Larue County, Kentucky, after living on the George Bromfield farm earlier in the year.

1809

February 12. "I was born Feb. 12, 1809, in Hardin County, Kentucky." Thus wrote Abraham Lincoln in the autobiographical sketch he prepared for his friend Jesse W. Fell, on December 20, 1859. The birthplace cabin was located three miles south of present-day Hodgenville (now in Larue County).

1811

Spring. Thomas Lincoln moves his family to a better farm of 230 acres on Knob Creek, ten miles north and six miles east of Hodgenville.

1811. Thomas, third child of Thomas and Nancy Lincoln, is born and dies in infancy.

1815

Autumn. "Before leaving Kentucky he [Abraham] and his sister were sent for short periods, to A.B.C. schools." Later in Indiana he also "went to A.B.C. schools by littles. . . . The aggregate of all his schooling did not amount to one year." Thus Abraham Lincoln wrote in a third-person autobiography prepared in June 1860 for John L. Scripps.

1816

Autumn. "From this place [Knob Creek farm] he [Thomas Lincoln] removed to what is now Spencer county Indiana . . . A. then being in his eighth year."

1817

February. Abraham "took an early start as a hunter . . . a flock of wild turkeys approached the new log-cabin . . . and A. . . . shot through a crack, and killed one of them."

Autumn. Thomas and Elizabeth Sparrow (Nancy Lincoln's aunt and uncle) and their ward Dennis Hanks (nephew to Mrs. Sparrow) move to Indiana and settle in the half-face camp which the Thomas Lincoln family had occupied before moving into a new and more comfortable cabin.

1818

October 5. Abraham's mother, Nancy Hanks Lincoln, dies of milk sickness. She had nursed Thomas and Elizabeth Sparrow, who died of milk sickness in late September.

1819

December 2. Abraham's father Thomas Lincoln and Mrs. Sarah Bush Johnston are married in Elizabethtown, Kentucky. Thomas Lincoln returns to Indiana with Sarah and her three children.

1825

June 21. The names of Thomas and Sarah Lincoln appear on Pigeon Creek Baptist Church membership list. Thomas joined by letter, June 7, 1823.

1828

January 20. Lincoln's sister Sarah, who married Aaron Grigsby on August 2, 1826, dies in childbirth in her twenty-first year.

Autumn. "When he [Abraham] was nineteen, still residing in Indiana, he made his first trip upon a flat-boat to New Orleans."

1830

March 1. Thomas Lincoln's family, and the families of Mrs. Lincoln's two sons-in-law, a party of thirteen persons, start for Illinois. Abraham drives one of the ox wagons.

March 15. The Lincoln party arrives at Decatur, Illinois, and Abraham's father establishes a new home eight miles southwest of town on the Sangamon River. After the "deep snow" of the winter of 1830–31 Thomas Lincoln and family move to Coles County, Illinois. The last of their four homes in that county is now Lincoln Log Cabin State Park.

1831

March. Lincoln helps build a flatboat at Sangamo Town, seven miles northwest of Springfield.

April–July. Lincoln pilots the flatboat with produce of Denton Offutt to New Orleans and returns to New Salem, eighteen miles northwest of Springfield. "Here he rapidly made acquaintances and friends."

August 1. Lincoln casts his first vote and gains a reputation as a storyteller, and a month later becomes a store clerk.

1832

March 9. Lincoln announces his candidacy for the legislature in the Springfield *Sangamo Journal* to be published on March 15.

April 7. Lincoln is elected a captain in the Thirty-first Regiment, Illinois Militia.

April 21. Lincoln is elected captain of a volunteer company enlisted for thirty days to drive Black Hawk and his band west of the Mississippi River.

May 27. Lincoln is mustered out and re-enlists as a private in Captain Elijah Iles' company for twenty days.

June 16. Lincoln re-enlists for thirty days in Captain Jacob M. Early's Independent Spy Corps.

July 10. Lincoln writes the mustering-out roll for Captain Early. It is certified by Lieutenant Robert Anderson, who commanded at Fort Sumter in 1861.

August 6. Lincoln is defeated for the legislature in this day's election, "the only time I have been beaten by the people." He runs eighth in a field of thirteen candidates, but receives practically all votes cast in New Salem precinct.

1833

January 15. William F. Berry and Lincoln purchase the New Salem store formerly owned by Reuben Radford, but they go "deeper and deeper in debt. . . . The store winked out."

May 7. Lincoln is appointed postmaster of New Salem by President Jackson. He serves until the post office is moved to Petersburg on May 30, 1836.

1834

January 6. Lincoln's first survey, as a deputy surveyor of Sangamon County, is of 800 acres for Reason Shipley. He continues his surveying until late in 1836.

August 4. Lincoln is elected one of four Sangamon County members of the lower house of the Illinois General Assembly. He is re-elected in 1836, 1838, and 1840, serving until the end of the Twelfth General Assembly, March 1, 1841.

September 30. Lincoln makes his first town survey, New Boston on the Mississippi. In 1836 he surveys Petersburg, Huron, Albany, and Bath.

December 1. Lincoln takes his seat in the lower house of the Ninth General Assembly at Vandalia, which adjourns February 13, 1835.

1835

August 25. Lincoln's legendary sweetheart, Ann Rutledge, dies at the farm home seven miles northwest of New Salem.

December 7. Lincoln is in attendance at the second session of the Illinois General Assembly at Vandalia until January 18, 1836.

1836

Autmn. Lincoln begins a courtship of Mary Owens, who comes to New Salem from Kentucky to visit her sister Mrs. Bennett Abell. In an April Fool letter (1838) he burlesques the unsuccessful affair.

December 5. Lincoln takes his seat in the lower house of the Tenth General Assembly at Vandalia. The first session adjourns on March 6, 1837.

1837

January–February. Lincoln and the other members of the "Long Nine" from Sangamon County cast their votes for the Internal Improvements Bill, and Lincoln's skill gets agreement on moving the state capital from Vandalia to Springfield.

March 3. Lincoln and Dan Stone enter their protest in the *House Journal* against the anti-abolitionist resolutions adopted on January 20. Their real difference from the House view was moral—the injustice of slavery.

April 15. Lincoln, formally admitted to the bar March 1, moves to Springfield, rooms with Joshua F. Speed, and becomes the law partner of John T. Stuart in the firm of Stuart & Lincoln. In the autumn of 1836 Lincoln had obtained a license to practice law.

July 10–22. Lincoln is in attendance at the special session of the Tenth General Assembly at Vandalia.

1838

December 3. Lincoln is beaten in the election for speaker of the House at the opening of the Eleventh General Assembly at Vandalia, the first session adjourning March 4, 1839. (Lincoln is again beaten in the election for the speakership in the Twelfth General Assembly, 1840.) He serves as Whig floor leader.

1839

June 24. Lincoln begins a term as trustee of the town of Springfield. He serves until the new city charter goes into effect in April 1840.

July 4. By order of Governor Thomas Carlin, the state government is moved from Vandalia to Springfield.

September 23. Lincoln begins to practice on the newly organized Eighth Judicial Circuit. He continues to attend these courts until his nomination for the presidency.

October 8. Lincoln is chosen one of the presidential electors by the Whig convention. (He is likewise honored in 1844, 1852, and 1856.)

December 3. Lincoln is admitted to practice in the United States Circuit Court by Judge Nathaniel Pope.

December 9. Lincoln attends the second session of the Eleventh General Assembly, which meets in Springfield.

December 16. Lincoln is one of the "managers" of the Cotillion Party held at the American House. The guests include twenty-one-year-old Mary Todd of Lexington, Kentucky, who has come to reside with her sister, Mrs. Ninian W. Edwards.

1840

February 1. Lincoln is one of the editors of *The Old Soldier*, a Whig campaign newspaper, the first number of which appears on this date. Before the November election, seventeen issues will be published.

July 20. Lincoln "skins" Jesse B. Thomas, who had disparaged him in a campaign speech. Feeling remorseful the next day, Lincoln apologizes.

November 23–December 5. Lincoln attends the first session of the Twelfth General Assembly.

December 5. Lincoln and two other Whigs jump from the window of the Methodist Church in Springfield, where the House of Representatives is meeting (the Senate is in session in the new capital). They choose the easiest exit in the confusion following adjournment of the House sine die. This forces resumption of specie payments by the Illinois State Bank, a result which the Whigs do not want but which comes about because their presence completes a quorum.

December 7. Lincoln attends the second session of the Twelfth General Assembly, both the House and Senate convening in the new capital. The session adjourns March 1, 1841.

1841

January 1. Lincoln calls this "the fatal 1st of Jan'y. 1841," when an emotional crisis upsets his relations with Mary Todd, and causes him acute mental anguish.

April 14. The partnership of Stuart & Lincoln is dissolved and Lincoln becomes the junior partner of Stephen T. Logan.

August–September. Lincoln visits for three weeks with his intimate friend, Joshua Speed, at Farmington, Speed's home near Louisville, Kentucky. Revealing letters—especially concerning marriage and personal happiness—are to be exchanged between Lincoln and Speed.

1842

September 22. Lincoln's proposed duel with James Shields is averted when, without Shields' knowledge, his friends withdraw his note to Lincoln and read Lincoln's apology.

November 4. Lincoln and Mary Todd are married in the evening at the home of her brother-in-law, Ninian W. Edwards, by the Reverend Charles Dresser, minister of the Episcopal Church.

1843

August 1. Robert Todd Lincoln, first child of the Lincolns, is born at the Globe Tavern, where they are then residing.

1844

May 2. The Lincolns move from a cottage on South Fourth Street into the house at Eighth and Jackson streets, their home until February 1861. Lincoln had drawn up the contract for its purchase, signed by Lincoln and the Reverend Charles Dresser, the owner, on January 16.

October 30. Lincoln speaks at Rockport, Indiana, near his boy-hood home, at the close of his campaign tour of southern Illinois, Kentucky, and Indiana, for Henry Clay.

December 9. William H. Herndon is admitted to the bar. The firm of Lincoln & Herndon is organized soon afterward.

1846

March 10. Edward Baker Lincoln, second child of the Lincolns, is born and named for Edward Dickinson Baker, a friend and political associate.

May 1. Lincoln is nominated for Congress by the Whig District Convention in Petersburg.

July 31. Lincoln prepares a handbill replying to his oppoent's charges of infidelity. The handbill and a letter dated August 11 addressed to Editor Allen N. Ford appears in the August 15 issue of the *Illinois Gazette* of Lacon.

August 3. Lincoln is the only Whig among seven congressmen in Illinois elected on this day. His majority of 1511 votes over the Reverend Peter Cartwright is unprecedented.

1847

October 25. The Lincolns and their two boys start for Washington by way of Mary Todd Lincoln's girlhood home, Lexington, Kentucky.

December 6. Lincoln takes his seat in the Thirtieth Congress, the only congress of which he was a member.

December 22. Lincoln presents a series of resolutions requesting President Polk to inform the House whether the "spot" where American blood was first shed in the Mexican War was not within territory claimed by Mexico. Lincoln's stand is un-popular with his constituents.

1848

June 7–9. Lincoln attends his first national Whig convention, at Philadelphia, and is pleased with the nomination of General Zachary Taylor for President.

September 12–22. Lincoln concludes a summer of campaign labor in and around Washington with a ten-day speaking tour in New England.

1849

January 10. Lincoln reads in Congress a draft of a bill for compensated abolition of slavery in the District of Columbia. "Finding that I was abandoned by my former backers and having little personal influence," he never formally introduces the bill.

March 7–8. Lincoln is admitted to practice in the United States Supreme Court and makes his only appearance before the court, in Lewis *v.* Lewis. The opinion rendered by Chief Justice Roger B. Taney is unfavorable to Lincoln's contentions.

March 10. Lincoln applies for a patent on "a new and improved manner of combining adjustable buoyant chambers with steam boats or other vessels." The patent is granted on May 22.

June 21. Lincoln fails to get the appointment as commissioner of the General Land Office, for which he has made a special trip to Washington.

August 21. Lincoln declines appointment as secretary of Oregon Territory.

September 27. Lincoln declines appointment as governor of Oregon Territory.

1850

February 1. Edward Baker Lincoln dies after being "sick fifty-two days." Mortality schedule of 1850 federal census records "consumption" as the cause of death.

December 21. William Wallace Lincoln, third son of the Lincolns, is born.

1851

January 17. Lincoln's father, Thomas, dies in Coles County, Illinois.

1852

July 6. Lincoln delivers a eulogy on Henry Clay, his beau ideal of a statesman.

August 14. Lincoln opens his speaking campaign for Winfield Scott for president with an attack upon Stephen A. Douglas' speech at Richmond, Virginia.

1853

April 4. Thomas (Tad) Lincoln, fourth son of the Lincolns, is born.

1854

May 30. The Kansas–Nebraska Act is signed. Lincoln was to write in 1859: "From 1849 to 1854, both inclusive, practiced law more assiduously than ever before. . . . I was losing interest in politics, when the repeal of the Missouri Compromise aroused me again."

August 26. Lincoln delivers his first speech on the Kansas–Nebraska Act, at Winchester.

October 16. Lincoln delivers at Peoria one of his first great speeches—on "the repeal of the Missouri Compromise, and the propriety of its restoration." He had delivered substantially the same speech in Bloomington on September 12 and in Springfield on October 4.

November 7. Lincoln is elected to the Illinois legislature. He declines the office on November 27 in order to become a candidate for the United States Senate.

1855

February 8. Lincoln fails of election to the United States Senate. To forestall election by the General Assembly of Joel A. Matteson he throws his votes to Lyman Trumbull, to elect him on the tenth ballot.

1856

February 22. Lincoln attends a convention of anti-Nebraska editors at Decatur. He is instrumental in the adoption of a statement of principles on which all factions of anti-Nebraska men can agree.

Spring. The Lincoln home is enlarged from a story and a half to two full stories by Hannan & Ragsdale at a cost of thirteen hundred dollars.

May 29. Lincoln delivers his famous "Lost Speech" at the organization of the Republican Party at Bloomington, Illinois. A presidential elector for the fourth time, he "made over fifty speeches" during the campaign.

June 19. Lincoln receives 110 votes on the informal ballot for Vice President at the first Republican National Convention at Philadelphia.

August 27. Lincoln makes his only speech in Michigan, for Frémont to a crowd of ten thousand at Kalamazoo.

December 1. Lincoln presides over the Sangamon County Circuit Court in the absence of Judge David Davis. In five years he presides on seven occasions in four different counties.

1857

June 26. Lincoln delivers in Springfield his first major speech against the Dred Scott decision. He maintains that it was "erroneous," and urges that it not be accepted as a precedent.

August 12. Lincoln receives his largest legal fee, five thousand dollars, for winning Illinois Central Railroad *v.* County of McLean in the State Supreme Court.

1858

April 6. Lincoln delivers for the first time his lecture on "Discoveries and Inventions," in Centre Hall in Bloomington. He delivers a second address on the same subject at Jacksonville (February 11, 1859), Decatur (February 1859), Springfield (February 21, 1859, April 26, 1860), and Pontiac (January 27, 1860).

May 7. Lincoln clears "Duff" Armstrong, the son of his old New Salem friend Jack Armstrong, of the charge of murder, in the circuit court at Beardstown. He uses an almanac in discrediting the state's star witness.

June 16. "Abraham Lincoln is the first and only choice of the Republicans of Illinois for the United States Senate." Lincoln accepts the nomination and delivers the famous "House Divided" speech in the hall of the House of Representatives of the statehouse (present Sangamon County Courthouse).

August 21. The first Lincoln-Douglas debate is held at Ottawa. Subsequent debates are held at Freeport (August 27), Jonesboro (September 15), Charleston (September 18), Galesburg (October 7), Quincy (October 13), and Alton (October 15). Lincoln makes at least sixty-three speeches during his campaign which began in Chicago on July 10.

November 2. Lincoln gets a majority of the votes, but the gerrymandered legislative districts give Douglas his re-election to the United States Senate. Lincoln writes to a disheartened friend: "Quit that. You will soon feel better. Another 'blow-up' is coming; and we shall have fun again."

1859

September 16–17. Lincoln speaks twice in Columbus, Ohio, and in Dayton, Hamilton, and Cincinnati.

September 30. Lincoln addresses the Wisconsin State Fair at Milwaukee. He makes a political speech there in the evening, and in Beloit and Janesville the day following.

December 1–3. Lincoln speaks in Kansas, at Elwood, Troy, Doniphan, Atchison, and Leavenworth a few days before the territorial election.

December 20. Lincoln sends his autobiography to Jesse W. Fell. "If any thing be made out of it, I wish it to be modest."

1860

February 27. Lincoln delivers his famous Cooper Union Address in New York City, which is printed in full by the New York *Tribune*. Earlier in the day he visits Mathew B. Brady's studio and faces Brady's camera for the first time.

February 28. Lincoln begins a two-week speaking tour of New England. Included in the eleven speeches is one at Exeter, New Hampshire, where Robert Lincoln is attending Phillips Exeter Academy.

May 9–10. Lincoln attends the State Republican Convention at Decatur. The convention instructs the Illinois delegation for Lincoln the "Rail Splitter" for President.

May 18. Lincoln is nominated for President of the United States on the third ballot at the Republican National Convention in Chicago. Hannibal Hamlin of Maine is nominated for Vice President.

May 19. Lincoln is officially notified of his nomination by a committee headed by George Ashmun of Massachusetts, "President of the Republican National Convention," in the "large north parlor" of the Lincoln home. Lincoln's formal acceptance is dated May 23.

July. Robert Lincoln enrolls in Harvard University. After graduating in 1864, he becomes a captain on General Ulysses S. Grant's staff.

October 19. Lincoln replies to a letter from eleven-year-old Grace Bedell of Westfield, New York: "As to the whiskers, having never worn any, do you not think people would call it a piece of silly affection if I were to begin it now?" But he soon became the first bearded President.

November 6. Lincoln is the first Republican to be elected President of the United States, defeating Douglas (Northern Democrat), John C. Breckinridge (Southern Democrat), and John Bell (Constitutional Unionist).

December 20. South Carolina is the first state to secede.

January 31. Lincoln goes to Coles County to visit his aged step-mother.

February 4. Representatives of South Carolina, Georgia, Florida, Alabama, Mississippi, and Louisiana meet in Montgomery, Alabama, to form the Confederate States of America. Texas, which had also seceded, is not represented. Jefferson Davis is elected President and Alexander H. Stephens Vice President.

February 6. "The soiree at the private residence of the President-elect [Lincoln], is a brilliant affair."

February 11. Lincoln delivers his "Farewell Address" to the people of Springfield at the Great Western Railroad station.

February 23. Lincoln arrives secretly in Washington after a twelve-day trip and many public appearances and speeches.

March 4. Lincoln is inaugurated as the sixteenth President of the United States.

March 9. President Lincoln holds his first cabinet meeting. Lincoln's cabinet consisted of: Secretary of State William H. Seward; Secretary of the Treasury Salmon P. Chase, succeeded in 1864 by William P. Fessenden, and in 1865 by Hugh McCulloch; Attorney General Edward Bates, succeeded in 1864 by James Speed; Secretary of the Navy Gideon Welles; Secretary of War Simon Cameron, succeeded in 1862 by Edwin M. Stanton; Secretary of the Interior Caleb B. Smith, succeeded in 1863 by John P. Usher; and Postmaster General Montgomery Blair, succeeded in 1864 by William Dennison.

April 12–14. Fort Sumter is attacked, and after thirty-four hours of bombardment, surrenders to the Confederate forces and is evacuated. Relief of Fort Sumter had been ordered by Lincoln on March 29.

April 15. Lincoln convenes an extra session of Congress to meet on July 4, and calls for 75,000 volunteers. As a result Virginia, North Carolina, Tennessee, and Arkansas secede. The Confederate capital is soon moved to Richmond, Virginia.

April 19, 27. Lincoln proclaims a blockade of the Confederate states from Virginia to Texas.

May 3. By proclamation Lincoln calls for 42,034 three-year volunteers, 22,714 additional men for the regular Army, and 18,000 for the Navy.

May 24. Northern troops take over Alexandria and the Virginia heights, and begin the string of forts to protect Washington. Colonel E. E. Ellsworth, a former student in Lincoln's law office, is the first officer killed in the war.

June 3. Stephen A. Douglas dies in Chicago at the age of forty-eight. His stirring address in Springfield on April 25 had united Illinois and encouraged thousands to enter the Union Army.

July 2. Lincoln suspends the writ of habeas corpus from Philadelphia to New York. On May 10 he had done this for a portion of the Florida coast.

July 4. Lincoln delivers his first message to Congress in special session.

July 21. The President, Congress, and the North are shocked by the defeat of General Irvin McDowell's army at Bull Run.

July 22. Congress votes five hundred million dollars to support the war, and gives Lincoln war powers.

July 27. Lincoln brings General George B. McClellan to Washington to command all the forces there and the Army of the Potomac.

September 11. Lincoln revokes Frémont's emancipation proclamation, thus bringing a storm of abuse from the anti-slavery faction.

November 1. General Winfield Scott's resignation is accepted and McClellan is made General-in-Chief.

November 8. Mason and Slidell, Confederate commissioners to Great Britain and France, are seized on the British steamer *Trent*.

December 10. Congress resolves on the appointment of a joint committee to inquire into the conduct of the war. It is organized on December 20.

December 28. The surrender of Mason and Slidell to the British authorities is ordered by the government.

1862

January 13. Lincoln sends Simon Cameron as Minister to Russia, and replaces him with Edwin M. Stanton as Secretary of War. Another major appointment in January was that of Noah H. Swayne of Ohio as a justice of the United States Supreme Court; other appointments to the court in 1862 were Samuel F. Miller of Iowa and David Davis of Illinois, followed in 1863 by Stephen J. Field of California.

February 6, 16. Fort Henry on the Tennessee River and Fort Donelson on the Cumberland are taken by forces under General Grant, the first important victories of Northern armies.

February 20. William Wallace Lincoln, eleven-year-old son of the President, dies. His death and the illness of his younger brother, Tad, prostrate Mrs. Lincoln.

March 6. Lincoln recommends to Congress a plan for gradual, compensated emancipation.

March 8–9. The Confederate ironclad *Merrimac* destroys the Northern ships in Hampton Roads, but the Union ironclad *Monitor* forces it to retire.

April 2. McClellan arrives at Fortress Monroe to begin a four months' campaign on the Virginian Peninsula.

April 6–7. The Confederate attack at Pittsburg Landing or Shiloh, Tennessee, is repulsed with serious losses by both armies.

April 16. Lincoln signs act freeing the slaves in the District of Columbia.

April 25. New Orleans is captured by a Northern naval expedition under Admiral David G. Farragut.

May 15. Lincoln approves the act establishing the Department of Agriculture.

May 20. Lincoln signs the Homestead Law, which grants a quarter section of unoccupied land to homesteaders on payment of nominal fees after five years of actual residence.

June 20. Slavery is prohibited in the territories by an act of Congress.

July 1. Lincoln approves the Union Pacific Railroad Company charter.

July 2. The Morrill Agricultural College Land Grant Act becomes a law. The Seven Days battles culminate in the retreat of the Army of the Potomac.

July 11. Lincoln appoints Henry W. Halleck General-in-Chief.

July 17. Congress authorizes a draft of state militia, and empowers the President to accept Negroes for military and naval service.

July 22. Lincoln reads his first draft of an emancipation proclamation to his cabinet. The plan is deemed premature.

August 22. In reply to criticism of administration policy by Horace Greeley, Lincoln writes: "My paramount object in this struggle *is* to save the Union, and is *not* either to save or to destroy slavery."

August 30. Northern forces under General John Pope are defeated at Bull Run.

September 2. Lincoln removes Pope and again places McClellan in command of all troops around Washington.

September 17. McClellan stops General Robert E. Lee's Northern invasion in the Battle of Antietam or Sharpsburg, Maryland.

September 22. President Lincoln issues a preliminary proclamation of emancipation of slaves of rebels, to take effect January 1, 1863.

September 24. Lincoln suspends the writ of habeas corpus for all persons arrested by military authority.

October 1–4. Lincoln visits McClellan's army and the battlefield of Antietam.

December 13. The Army of the Potomac under command of General Ambrose E. Burnside is defeated at Fredericksburg, Virginia.

December 31. Lincoln reluctantly approves the bill admitting West Virginia to the Union.

1863

January 1. Lincoln issues the Emancipation Proclamation whereby slaves in areas held by Confederates are declared free.

February 25. Congress establishes a national currency; the National Bank Act is passed.

March 3. Lincoln approves the first draft law in the nation's history.

April 4–10. Lincoln, Mrs. Lincoln, and "Tad" visit the headquarters of the Army of the Potomac, commanded by General Joseph Hooker.

May 2–4. The Army under Hooker is defeated at Chancellorsville, Virginia.

May 5. Clement L. Vallandigham of Ohio, Copperhead leader and Democratic congressman, is arrested for violating General Burnside's "General Order No. 38" in a speech at Mount Vernon, Ohio, on May 1. On direction of the President, Vallandigham is ordered by Secretary of War Stanton to be banished beyond Union lines.

July 1–3. The Confederate invasion of Pennsylvania under Lee is defeated by General George G. Meade at Gettysburg.

July 4. The long siege of Vicksburg by Grant results in the surrender of the Confederates under General John C. Pemberton.

September 20. The Northern defeat at Chickamauga is offset on November 25 by victory at Chattanooga.

November 26. The first national observance of Thanksgiving is held, as proclaimed by the President on October 3.

December 8. Lincoln issues a proclamation of amnesty to Confederates who take the oath of allegiance.

1864

March 10. The President appoints Ulysses S. Grant, who had become a lieutenant general on March 2, Commander-in-Chief of the armies.

May 5–12. Grant and Lee are in constant battle in the Virginia Wilderness.

June 7–8. The National Union Convention at Baltimore renominates Lincoln for President; Andrew Johnson of Tennessee is nominated for Vice President.

June 20–24. Lincoln visits Grant's army in Virginia.

June 28. Congress repeals the Fugitive Slave Law.

July 4. Lincoln pocket vetoes the drastic congressional reconstruction bill, and on July 8 issues a Proclamation regarding reconstruction.

September 2. General William T. Sherman takes Atlanta, a Northern victory which, with that of Admiral Farragut at Mobile Bay on August 5, insures Lincoln's re-election. Invasion of eastern Tennessee, long sought by Lincoln, becomes a reality with the occupation of Knoxville.

November 8. Lincoln is re-elected President in an easy victory over McClellan, the Democratic candidate.

November 21. Lincoln writes a letter of sympathy to Mrs. Lydia Bixby, who he was incorrectly informed had lost five sons in battle.

December 6. Lincoln delivers his Fourth Annual Message to Congress. He nominates Salmon P. Chase as Chief Justice of the United States Supreme Court.

December 10. Sherman's march "from Atlanta to the sea" concludes at Savannah, Georgia, which surrenders on December 21.

1865

February 1. Lincoln approves the Thirteenth Amendment, abolishing slavery. Later in the day, Illinois is the first state to ratify the amendment, which became a part of the Constitution of the United States on December 18. The Fourteenth Amendment, adopted in 1868, was designed to grant citizenship and protect the civil liberties of the freedman. The Fifteenth Amendment, adopted in 1870, forbids a state to deprive a citizen of his right to vote because of race, color, or previous condition of servitude.

February 3. Lincoln confers with representatives of the Confederacy on board the *River Queen* in Hampton Roads, Virginia.

March 3. The Freedman's Bureau is established by Congress to aid the former slaves in adjusting themselves to a life of freedom.

March 4. Lincoln is re-inaugurated and delivers his Second Inaugural Address, "with malice toward none; with charity for all."

March 5. The first Negro entertained at the White House is Frederick Douglass.

March 23–April 8. Lincoln visits Grant's army at City Point, Virginia. His party includes Mrs. Lincoln and son "Tad." (Mrs. Lincoln left for Washington on April 1, and returned April 5.) Lincoln and "Tad" go to see the ruins of the evacuated city of Richmond, April 4–5. Lincoln and his party return to Washington from City Point, the evening of April 9.

April 9. Lee surrenders to Grant at Appomattox Court House, Virginia.

April 11. Lincoln delivers his last speech, from a window of the White House, in response to a serenade.

April 14. Lincoln is shot at Ford's Theater by the actor John Wilkes Booth.

April 15. Abraham Lincoln dies at 7:22 A.M. and the country goes into mourning.

April 19. Funeral services for President Lincoln are held in the White House.

April 21–May 3. The funeral train bears the remains of Lincoln on the journey to Springfield, Illinois.

May 4. Lincoln is buried in Oak Ridge Cemetery on the north edge of Springfield. He leaves a net estate of 110,296.80 dollars, exclusive of real estate, to his widow and two surviving children. Lincoln's body is moved from the public receiving vault on December 21, 1865, to the temporary vault, and on September 19, 1871, to a crypt in the partially completed monument.

(After 1865)

July 14, 1870. Congress Grants Mrs. Lincoln an annual pension of three thousand dollars. On January 16, 1882, it is increased to five thousand dollars, plus a gift of fifteen thousand dollars.

July 15, 1871. "Tad" Lincoln dies of dropsy of the chest, in Chicago. He is buried in the Lincoln Tomb in Springfield.

October 15, 1874. The National Lincoln Monument Association, organized May 11, 1865, dedicates the partially completed Lincoln Tomb designed by Larkin G. Mead, Jr. President Ulysses S. Grant speaks briefly; ex-Governor Richard J. Oglesby gives the principal address.

November 7, 1876. An attempt to steal Lincoln's body, to be held for ransom, is made by three men. Frightened away from the tomb by Secret Service men, they are apprehended in Chicago, tried in Springfield for burglary, and sentenced to the penitentiary for one year.

July 16, 1882. Mrs. Lincoln dies in the Springfield home of her sister, Mrs. Ninian W. Edwards, where Lincoln courted and married her. She is buried in the Lincoln Tomb with her husband and three of their four sons.

June 16, 1887. Robert Todd Lincoln and his wife Mary Harlan Lincoln present the Lincoln home in Springfield to the State of Illinois. The first floor has since been open to the public, visited by more than a third of a million people annually. The second floor was restored and opened to the public February 12, 1955.

by Harry E. and Marion D. Pratt

July 26, 1926. Robert Lincoln dies and is buried in Arlington National Cemetery. Five years earlier he had left 18,350 items of his father's papers on deposit in the Library of Congress, not to be open to the public for twenty-one years after his death (July 26, 1947).

June 17, 1931. The remodeled Lincoln Tomb is rededicated by President Herbert Hoover. It had been previously rebuilt in 1900–1.

Harry E. Pratt

Marion D. Pratt

459

BIOGRAPHICAL SKETCHES OF CONTRIBUTORS

PAUL MCCLELLAND ANGLE has been Director of the Chicago Historical Society since 1945. He was the Executive Secretary of the Abraham Lincoln Association from 1925 until 1932 and served as Illinois State Historian from 1932 to 1945. He is the author or editor of many distinguished works in the field of American history, including: *Mary Lincoln: Wife and Widow* (with Carl Sandburg), 1932; *Here I Have Lived,* 1935; *A Shelf of Lincoln Books,* 1946; *The Lincoln Reader,* 1947; *Bloody Williamson,* 1952; *By These Words,* 1954; *The Living Lincoln* (with Earl Schenck Miers), 1955; *Created Equal,* 1958; *and The Tragic Years* (with Earl Schenck Miers), 1960.

WILLIAM ELDON BARINGER is Professor of History and Social Sciences at the University of Florida. He was the executive secretary and editor of the *Abraham Lincoln Quarterly* from 1943 to 1947. He served as Executive Director of the national Lincoln Sesquicentennial Commission, 1957–60. He is the author or editor of *Lincoln's Rise to Power,* 1937; *A House Dividing,* 1947; *Lincoln's Vandalia,* 1949; *The Philosophy of Abraham Lincoln,* 1959; *Lincoln Day by Day,* 1960; and numerous historical articles. In 1959 Lincoln Memorial University awarded him the Lincoln Diploma of Honor.

Biographical Sketches of Contributors

ROY PRENTICE BASLER is the Director of the Reference Department of the Library of Congress. From 1947 until 1952 he was Executive Secretary of the Abraham Lincoln Association and editor of the *Abraham Lincoln Quarterly*. He is the author or editor of *The Lincoln Legend*, 1935; *Abraham Lincoln: His Speeches and Writings*, 1946; and *The Collected Works of Abraham Lincoln*, 1953–55 and numerous articles in many scholarly publications.

HOWARD KENNEDY BEALE was Professor of History at the University of Wisconsin from 1948 until his death in December 1959. Prior to that he was Professor of History at the University of North Carolina. He was the author or editor of *The Critical Year*, 1930; *The Diary of Edward Bates*, 1933; *Theodore Roosevelt and the Rise of America to World Power*, 1956; and *The Diary of Gideon Welles*, 1960.

KENNETH ANDERSON BERNARD is Professor of American History and Curator of Lincoln Collections at Boston University. He is President of the Lincoln Group of Boston, Honorary Member of the national Lincoln Sesquicentennial Commission, and a member of the Advisory Committee for the Massachusetts Civil War Centennial Commission. He is a contributor to the Lincoln Sesquicentennial Series of the United States Information Service and the author of many articles on Lincoln which have appeared in various publications. He is currently working on a book, *Lincoln and the Music of the Civil War*.

ROBERT VANCE BRUCE is Assistant Professor of History at Boston University. He is a member of the Lincoln Group of Boston, the Civil War Round Table, and the Society for the History of Technology. He is the author of *Lincoln and the Tools of*

War, 1956; and *1877: Year of Violence,* 1959. He was awarded a Guggenheim Fellowship, 1957–58.

OLIVE CARRUTHERS is a free-lance writer who has published more than 150 newspaper feature stories. She is a book reviewer for the Chicago *Tribune,* and has written publicity for Northwestern University and the American Library Association. She has specialized in research relating to the women in the Lincoln story. She is the author of *Lincoln's Other Mary* (with R. Gerald McMurtry), 1946; and *We'll Sing One Song,* 1947.

BRUCE CATTON is senior editor of *American Heritage* magazine. His writings on the Civil War have brought him many honors and awards, including the National Book Award, 1954, and the Pulitzer Prize, 1954. He is the author of *Mr. Lincoln's Army,* 1951; *Glory Road,* 1952; *A Stillness at Appomattox,* 1953; *U. S. Grant and the American Military Tradition,* 1954; *Banners at Shenandoah,* 1955; *This Hallowed Ground,* 1956; *America Goes to War,* 1958; and *Grant Moves South,* 1960. In addition to his articles in *American Heritage,* he has contributed many articles to *This Week, Holiday, Life,* and other leading national periodicals.

HENRY STEELE COMMAGER is Professor of History at Amherst College and Adjunct Professor of History at Columbia University. He is the author or editor of many distinguished works relating to American history, including *The Growth of the American Republic* (with Samuel Eliot Morison), 1931–42: *Theodore Parker,* 1936; *The Heritage of America* (with Allan Nevins), 1939; *The Blue and the Gray,* 1950; *America, Story of a Free Nation,* 1950; *The American Mind,* 1951; and *Living Ideas in America,* 1952.

NORMAN [LEWIS] CORWIN is an author, director, and producer. He is the recipient of many honors, including the Peabody Medal (twice) and the Bok Medal for his radio writings. He is the author of the screenplays of *Lust for Life, The Blue Veil,* and *The Story of Ruth.* His books include *Thirteen by Corwin,* 1942; *More by Corwin,* 1944; *On a Note of Triumph,* 1945; *Untitled and Other Plays,* 1947; *The Plot to Overthrow Christmas,* 1952; and *The Rivalry,* 1959. He wrote the radio adaptation of Carl Sandburg's *The People, Yes,* 1941, and produced the premier performance of *The Lonesome Train* in the same year. He is the adapter-director of the stage production *The World of Carl Sandburg,* 1959.

RICHARD NELSON CURRENT is Professor of History and Head of the Department of History and Political Science at The Woman's College of the University of North Carolina. He lectured at Deshisha University in Japan in 1958 and was State Department Lecturer (on Abraham Lincoln) in India in 1959 and Fulbright Lecturer at the University of Munich, Germany, in 1959. He is the author of *Old Thad Stevens,* 1952; *Secretary Stimson,* 1954; *Lincoln the President: The Last Full Measure* (with James G. Randall), 1955; *Daniel Webster and the Rise of National Conservatism,* 1955; and *The Lincoln Nobody Knows,* 1958.

IRVING DILLIARD is editorial writer for the St. Louis *Post-Dispatch.* He is a former President of the Illinois State Historical Society. He was the recipient of the American Bar Association Award for articles on the United States Supreme Court. He is the author or editor of *Mr. Justice Brandeis, Great American,* 1941; *I'm From Missouri,* 1951; and *The Spirit of Liberty,* 1952. He has contributed many articles to the Dictionary of American Biography, the Dictionary of American History, the Encyclopedia of the Social Sciences, and to many of the leading American magazines.

PAUL HOWARD DOUGLAS is the senior United States Senator from Illinois. He was Professor of Industrial Relations at The University of Chicago from 1925 until his election to the Senate. He was a Guggenheim Fellow in 1931. He is the author of many books, including *Wages and the Family,* 1925; *Real Wages in the United States,* 1930; *The Coming of a New Party,* 1932; *The Theory of Wages,* 1934; *Controlling Depressions,* 1935; *and Ethics in Government,* 1952. He has been a lifelong student of American history.

CLIFFORD [SHIRLEY] DOWDEY [JR.] is a professional writer and is currently a lecturer in creative writing at the University of Richmond. His novels and works of nonfiction relating to the Civil War have caused him to be recognized as one of the great influences in the revival of interest in the Civil War. His novel *Bugles Blow No More,* 1937, appears on all lists of the best Civil War novels. His other works include *Experiment in Rebellion,* 1946; *Weep for My Brother,* 1950; *The Land They Fought For,* 1955; *The Great Plantation,* 1957; and *Death of a Nation,* 1958.

LLOYD ALLEN DUNLAP is the Administrative Officer for the national Lincoln Sesquicentennial Commission. He is on loan from the Library of Congress, where he is Consultant in Lincoln Studies. He is the assistant editor of *The Collected Works of Abraham Lincoln,* 1953–55 and the editor of *Lincoln 1809– 1959,* the catalogue of the sesquicentennial exhibit of Lincolniana at the Library of Congress. He is the author of numerous periodical articles on the Lincoln theme, as well as many book reviews.

JOSEPH THOMAS DURKIN, S.J. Father Durkin is Professor of United States History at Georgetown University. He is a member of the board of directors of the Civil War Centennial Association and has devoted many years to a study of the American War of 1861–65, with particular emphasis on the Confederacy. He is the editor or author of *John Dooley: Confederate Soldier,* 1945; *Stephen R. Mallory: Confederate Navy Chief,* 1954; and *General Sherman's Son,* 1959.

OTTO EISENSCHIML is Chairman of the Board, Scientific Oil Compounding Co., Inc., and is one of the country's leading industrial chemists. He is the recipient of many honors in the fields of history and chemistry, including an honorary degree from Lincoln Memorial University and the Honor Scroll of the American Institute of Chemists. He is the author or editor of *Why Was Lincoln Murdered?* 1937; *In the Shadow of Lincoln's Death,* 1940; *Without Fame,* 1942; *The American Iliad* (with Ralph Newman), 1947; *As Luck Would Have It* (with E. B. Long), 1948; *The Celebrated Case of Fitz John Porter,* 1950; *The Civil War* (with Ralph Newman and E. B. Long), 1956; *Why the Civil War?* 1958; and *Vermont General,* 1960.

AVARD [TENNYSON] FAIRBANKS is Professor of Sculpture and Dean of the College of Fine Arts at the University of Utah. A distinguished sculptor, he has created many great works, including "The Pony Express," for the Utah Centennial; "Marcus Whitman" (representing the State of Washington), in Statuary Hall, Washington, D. C.; "Abraham Lincoln From New Salem," for New Salem State Park; "The Chicago Lincoln"; "Lycurgus," in Sparta, Greece; and "Lincoln, The Friendly Neighbor," in Berwyn, Illinois.

JOHNSON EDDY FAIRCHILD is the Director of Adult Education and Assistant to the President of The Cooper Union for the Advancement of Science and Art. He is Chairman of The Cooper Union Forum. He is the geography editor of the Crowell-Collier Encyclopedia and is the editor of *The European Possessions in the Caribbean Area,* 1941; *Women, Society and Sex* (with Margaret Mead and others), 1952; *Personal Problems and Psychological Frontiers,* 1957; and *Basic Beliefs,* 1959. He has written articles for many learned societies and journals.

MARGARET ALICE FLINT is the Assistant State Historian of Illinois. She was formerly Reference Librarian, Illinois State Historical Library. She is the author of *Chronology of Illinois, 1673–1954* and *Chronological History of Chicago* for the *Illinois Blue Books,* 1941–54. Her familiarity with the manuscript resources of the Illinois State Historical Library and her knowledge of the Lincoln–Civil War story have made her an invaluable friend to all researchers and writers concerned with this period of our history.

SHELBY FOOTE is a free-lance writer. He is the author of five novels: *Tournament,* 1949; *Follow Me Down,* 1950; *Love in a Dry Season,* 1951; *Shiloh,* 1952; and *Jordan Country,* 1954. In 1955–56 and 1959 he was awarded a Guggenheim Fellowship. He has been interested in the Civil War since childhood and is currently at work on a multivolume history, *The Civil War,* the first volume of which was published in 1958. He lives in Memphis, Tennessee.

JOHN HOPE FRANKLIN is Professor and Chairman, Department of History, Brooklyn College. He has been the recipient of a President's Fellowship, Brown University, a Guggenheim

Fellowship, and a Rosenwald Fellowship. He is the winner of the Bancroft Prize awarded by the *Journal of Negro History*. He is the author or editor of *From Slavery to Freedom*, 1947; *Free Negro in North Carolina, 1790–1860*, 1943; *The Civil War Diary of James T. Ayers*, 1947; and *The Militant South, 1800–1861*, 1956.

ARNOLD GATES is in the Estimating Department, Lehigh Structural Steel Company. He has been a Lincoln student for the past twenty-seven years. He has been the literary editor of the *Lincoln Herald* since 1956 and is the editor of *The Round Table*, the publication of the Civil War Round Table of New York. He has written book reviews for many publications, including *Civil War History* and the New York *Times Book Review*. He is the author of a series of Lincoln pamphlets and is a contributor to *Abraham Lincoln: A New Portrait*, 1959 (edited by Henry B. Kranz).

RICHARD PAUL GRAEBEL is the pastor of the First Presbyterian Church of Springfield, Illinois. Mrs. Abraham Lincoln was a member of this church. He is a devoted student of the Lincoln story and has delivered many lectures and sermons on the Lincoln theme. He is a member of the Illinois State Historical Society and was a member of the Abraham Lincoln Association. He is a director of the Vachel Lindsay Association. He is the author of many articles that have appeared in religious, musical, and social-action journals.

NORMAN ARTHUR GRAEBNER is Professor of History, University of Illinois. He previously taught at Iowa State College and Stanford University. He is a contributing editor of *Current History* and associate editor of *World Affairs Quarterly*. He is the author or editor of *Empire on the Pacific,* 1955; *The New Isolationism,* 1956; *The Enduring Lincoln,* 1959; and *The Troubled Union,* 1960. In January–February, 1959, he delivered the Commonwealth Fund Lectures at the University of London. He is the author of many articles that have appeared in well-known historical journals of the United States.

ULYSSES SIMPSON GRANT, III, Major General Grant, United States Army, Retired, is Chairman of the national Civil War Centennial Commission. He is President of the Columbia Historical Society and of the American Peace Society. He is a trustee of the National Trust for Historic Preservation. He is the recipient of the Gold Medal from the Civil War Round Table of the District of Columbia, the John McAneny Medal for Historic Preservation, and many other honors. He is the author of many historical reports, brochures, and professional reports. He is the grandson of the eighteenth President of the United States.

WOOD GRAY is Professor of American History, The George Washington University. He is the contributing editor of the section on the United States in the *American Historical Review.* He is the author or editor of *The Marcus W. Jernegan Essays in American Historiography* (with William T. Hutchinson), 1937; *The Hidden Civil War,* 1942; and (with others) *Historian's Handbook: A Key to the Study and Writing of History,* 1959.

SHERRILL HALBERT is the United States District Judge for the Northern District of California. A distinguished lawyer and jurist, he has been a Lincoln student for many years. He is a member of the Board of Trustees of the California Historical Society and the President of the Sacramento Book Collector's Club. He is a member of the Board of Directors of the American Society for Legal History and is the author of "The Suspension of the Writ of Habeas Corpus by President Lincoln," which was first published in the April, 1958, issue of *The American Journal of Legal History*.

ROBERT S[TORY] HARPER is the Public Information Officer for the Ohio Historical Society. For twenty-seven years he has been a newspaper writer and editor. He was the recipient of the Grand Medal of the Ohioana Library Association in 1951. He is the author of *Trumpet in the Wilderness*, 1940; *The Road to Baltimore*, 1942; *Lincoln and the Press*, 1951; and of many booklets, including "The Ohio Lincoln Calendar," "A Lincoln Reading List," and "Lincoln's Other Scrapbook." He has written many articles and short stories for magazines.

RICHARD BARKSDALE HARWELL is the Associate Executive Director, American Library Association, and Executive Secretary, Association of College and Research Libraries. From 1956 to 1957 he was Director of Publications, Virginia State Library. He is the author or editor of *Confederate Belles-Lettres*, 1941; *Confederate Music*, 1950; *Songs of the Confederacy*, 1954; *Cornerstones of Confederate Collecting*, 1953; *Stonewall Jackson and the Old Stonewall Brigade*, 1954; *Destruction and Reconstruction*, 1955; *The Confederate Reader*, 1957; *More Confederate Imprints*, 1957; *Cities and Camps of the Confederate States*, 1958; *The Union Reader*, 1958; *Kate: The Journal of a Confederate Nurse*, 1959.

CARL HAVERLIN is President, Broadcast Music, Inc. He has been a student and collector of Lincolniana for more than forty years. He is President of the Civil War Centennial Association and is a member of the Board of Trustees, Lincoln Memorial University. He has been responsible for the creation and development of *The American Story* and *The Abraham Lincoln Story* radio and television series, and other projects designed to give American history a wider acceptance and better literary appeal. He has written articles for various historical journals. He is an honorary member of the national Lincoln Sesquicentennial Commission.

WILLIAM BEST HESSELTINE is Professor of History, University of Wisconsin. In 1958 he was given the Award of Merit by the American Association for State and Local History. He is the author of 130 articles, 260 encyclopedia articles, and 330 book reviews. His books include *Civil War Prisons*, 1930; *Ulysses S. Grant, Politician*, 1935; *Lincoln and the War Governors*, 1958; *The Rise and Fall of Third Parties*, 1948; *Confederate Leaders in the New South*, 1950; *Pioneer's Mission*, 1954; *The South in American History*, 1957; *Lincoln's Plan of Reconstruction*, 1960.

ROBERT LEE KINCAID was President Emeritus of Lincoln Memorial University and President of the Citizens News Company, Middlesboro, Kentucky. For more than twenty years as Executive Vice-President and President of L.M.U., he devoted himself to the Lincoln story. As editor of The *Lincoln Herald* he was responsible for many articles in that publication. He was the author of *Jinny and Jim*, 1941; *Joshua Fry Speed*, 1943; and *The Wilderness Road*, 1947. He was President of the Cumberland Gap National Historical Park Association and a member of the Tennessee Historical Commission until his death in May 1960.

WILLARD LEROY KING is an attorney at law, member of the firm of King, Robin, Gale and Pillinger. He is a trustee of the Chicago Historical Society. He was the recipient of honorary degrees from Bowdoin College in 1951 and Knox College in 1954. He is the author of *Law of Opinion Evidence in Illinois* (with Douglas Pillinger), 1942; *Melville Weston Fuller*, 1950; and *Lincoln's Manager, David Davis*, 1960. He has written many articles for legal publications.

LEO ALFRED LERNER is the editor and publisher of a chain of Chicago newspapers. He was a member of the Illinois Lincoln Sesquicentennial Commission and Chairman of the Abraham Lincoln Memorial Commission of the State of Illinois. In 1951 he was the winner of the Herrick Award given by the National Editorial Association. He is a member of the Civil War Round Table. He has written two books, *Continental Journey*, 1947; and *The Itch of Opinion*, 1956.

MORT REIS LEWIS is a television writer, producer, and program creator. He is past president of the Civil War Round Table of Southern California and Vice-President of the Lincoln Sesquicentenial Association of California. He has been the creator, producer, and writer of many historical television and radio programs, including the NBC series "Stroke of Fate." He has written several articles on the Lincoln story for various publications. He is regarded as one of the foremost authorities on Lincoln's humor. He resides in Los Angeles, California.

E[VERETTE] B[EACH] LONG is chief of research for Bruce Catton and the *Centennial History of the Civil War*, to be published beginning in 1961. He is former president of the Civil War

Round Table of Chicago. For many years he was an editor for the Associated Press and was later associate editor of the *American People's Encyclopedia*. He is the author or editor of *As Luck Would Have It* (with Otto Eisenschiml), 1948; *The Personal Memoirs of U. S. Grant*, 1952; *The Civil War* (with Ralph Newman and Otto Eisenschiml), 1956; and, in addition to his research assignment, is currently working on *The Civil War Almanac*.

R[OBERT] GERALD MCMURTRY is Director of the Lincoln National Life Foundation in Fort Wayne, Indiana. From 1936 until 1956 he was Director of the Department of Lincolniana, Lincoln Memorial University. He was editor of the *Lincoln Herald* from 1947 to 1956. He has written more than 50 magazine articles about Abraham Lincoln. Among his books are *The Kentucky Lincolns on Mill Creek*, 1939; *Let's Talk of Lincoln*, 1939; *Ben Hardin Helm*, 1943; *Lincoln's Other Mary* (with Olive Carruthers), 1946; and *Lincoln's Favorite Poets* (with David J. Harkness), 1959. He is a member of the national Lincoln Sesquicentennial Commission.

ROBERT DOUTHAT MEADE is Chairman, Department of History, Randolph-Macon Woman's College. He is a former member of the history faculties of the University of Illinois, Vanderbilt University, and the University of North Carolina. In 1943 he received the Southern Authors Award for the best book of the year by a Southern author. He has written some two dozen biographical sketches for the Dictionary of American Biography, and a great many book reviews and articles. He is the author of *Judah P. Benjamin, Confederate Statesman*, 1943; and *Patrick Henry, Patriot in the Making*, 1957.

DAVID CHAMBERS MEARNS is Assistant Librarian for American Collections; Chief, Manuscript Division; incumbent of the Chair of American History, Library of Congress. He is a member of the national Civil War Centennial Commission, National Historical Publications Commission, and Board of Directors of the Civil War Centennial Association. He has written many articles for Lincoln, historical, and professional journals. He is the author or editor of *The Story Up to Now*, 1947; *The Lincoln Papers*, 1948; *The Declaration of Independence: The Story of a Parchment*, 1950; *Three Presidents and Their Books* (co-author), 1955; and *Herbert Putnam: Librarian of the United States*, 1955.

ROY MEREDITH is a consultant for the Westinghouse Broadcasting Company and is currently engaged in writing a motion-picture-television series for that firm. He has been both a writer and director in films and television. He is regarded as one of the foremost authorities on Civil War photography. His books include *Mr. Lincoln's Cameraman*, 1946; *The Face of Robert E. Lee*, 1947; *Mr. Lincoln's Contemporaries*, 1951; *The American Wars*, 1955; *Storm Over Sumter*, 1957; *This Was Andersonville*, 1957; *Mr. Lincoln's General*, 1959.

EARL SCHENCK MIERS is one of the most brilliant and versatile writers of our time. He is also a gifted editor, and prior to devoting full time to his writing was Director of the Rutgers University Press and editor for Alfred A. Knopf. He has been responsible for some of the great books (written by others) of our time in the American-history field and is himself the author or editor of a long list of distinguished titles, including *Gettysburg* (with R. A. Brown), 1946; *General Who Marched to Hell*, 1951; *The Web of Victory*, 1955; *The Living Lincoln* (with Paul M. Angle), 1955; *The American Story*, 1956; *Rob-*

ert E. Lee, 1956; *The Great Rebellion*, 1958; *Johnny Reb and Billy Yank*, 1959; and *The Tragic Years* (with Paul M. Angle), 1960. He is editor-in-chief of the national Lincoln Sesquicentennial Commission publication, *Lincoln Day by Day*, 1960.

[ROBERT] JUSTIN MILLER is consultant for Broadcast Music, Inc., and the National Association of Broadcasters. A lawyer, he was Associate Justice of the United States Court of Appeals from 1937 to 1945. He served as President of the National Association of Broadcasters, 1945–51, and was Chairman of the Board and General Counsel for the National Association of Radio and TV Broadcasters, 1951–54. He has written many articles that have appeared in legal and other magazines. He was Dean of the Law School, University of Southern California, 1927–30 and Dean of the Law School, Duke University, 1930–35.

HERBERT MITGANG is a member of the editorial staff of the Sunday New York *Times*. His interest in Lincoln and the Civil War dates back to his childhood. He is the author or editor of *Lincoln As They Saw Him*, 1956; *Washington in Lincoln's Time*, 1958; *The Return*, 1959; and *Civilians Under Arms: The American Soldier from the Civil War to Korea*, 1959.

[JAMES] JAY MONAGHAN is Consultant, Wyles Collection of Lincolniana, University of California, Santa Barbara. He was formerly Illinois State Historian. He was the recipient of the Diploma of Honor from Lincoln Memorial University in 1944. He is the author of *Lincoln Bibliography*, 1839–1939; *Diplomat in Carpet Slippers*, 1945; *The Overland Trail*, 1947; *Civil War on the Western Border*, 1955; *The Man Who Elected Lincoln*, 1956; *Custer, The Life of George Armstrong Custer*, 1959; and other titles.

Biographical Sketches of Contributors

MARIANNE CRAIG MOORE is one of the great poets of our time. She has been the recipient of many awards, including the Dial Award, 1924; Helen Haire Levinson Prize, 1933; Shelley Memorial Award, 1940; Harriet Monroe Poetry Award, 1944; Guggenheim Memorial Fellowship, 1945; National Book Award, 1951; Pulitzer Prize, 1951; and National Institute Art and Letters Gold Medal, 1953. Her books include *Poems*, 1921; *Observations*, 1924; *Selected Poems*, 1935; *The Pangolin and Other Verse*, 1936; *What Are Years*, 1941; *Nevertheless*, 1944; *Collected Poems*, 1951; *The Fables of La Fontaine* (translator), 1954; *Predilections*, 1955; *Like a Bulwark*, 1956; and *O To Be a Dragon*, 1959. She has written many reviews and essays, and her poetry has been published in many magazines.

ALLAN NEVINS is Senior Research Associate, Henry E. Huntington Library and Art Gallery. He was Professor of American History at Columbia University from 1931 until 1959. He is President of the Society of American Historians and in 1959 was President of the American Historical Association. He has been the recipient of almost every honor that can come to an historian: Pulitzer Prize for biography, 1933 and 1937; Scribner Centenary Prize, 1947; Bancroft Prize, 1948; and Gold Medal for history and biography of the American Academy of Arts and Letters. Among his many books are included *The Ordeal of the Union*, 1947; *The Emergence of Lincoln*, 1950; *Statesmanship of the Civil War*, 1953; and *The War for The Union*, 1959. He has written hundreds of articles and book reviews for almost every major magazine in the English-speaking world.

HELEN MARIE NEWELL is a free-lance writer. During the teacher shortage after World War II she taught English in Balmorhea High School in Texas. She is the author of *The Hardhats*, a novel published in 1956 and issued in London under the title *The Dam*. Her essay "Reflections While Standing before the Lincoln Memorial" was the winner in the professional-writer group in competition with several thousand entrants from every one of the United States. She is a resident of Boise, Idaho.

RALPH GEOFFREY NEWMAN is the proprietor of the Abraham Lincoln Book Shop in Chicago. He is also a free-lance writer and consultant in public service and history to many American business organizations. He was the founder of the Civil War Round Table in Chicago, a movement that has spread to some one hundred American cities and to England. He is currently the President of the Illinois State Historical Society. In 1952 he was the recipient of the Lincoln Diploma of Honor from Lincoln Memorial University. He has written articles for many magazines and is the author or editor of *The Diary of a Public Man*, 1945; *The American Iliad* (with Otto Eisenschiml), 1947; *The Railsplitter*, 1950; and *The Civil War* (with Otto Eisenschiml and E. B. Long), 1956.

ROY FRANKLIN NICHOLS is Vice-President and Dean of the Graduate School of the University of Pennsylvania. He is also Professor of History at the same institution. He was the winner of the Pulitzer Prize in History in 1949. He is the author of many distinguished works, including *Growth of American Democracy* (with Jeannette P. Nichols), 1939; *The Republic of the United States: A History* (with Jeannette P. Nichols), 1942; *Franklin Pierce*, 1931; *Disruption of American Democracy*, 1947; and *Advance Agents of American Destiny*, 1956.

STERLING NORTH is the general editor of North Star Books (Houghton Mifflin Company) and is also a free-lance writer. For thirty years, until 1958, he was literary critic for metropolitan newspapers in Chicago, New York, and elsewhere. He has been the winner of three prizes for his poetry: the Witter Bynner Prize, *Poetry* magazine's Young Poet's Prize, and a special prize by the Friends of American Writers. His articles, poetry, and fiction have appeared in many of our leading magazines. He is the author of more than twenty books, including *So Dear to My Heart*, 1947; *Abe Lincoln, Log Cabin to White House*, 1956; *George Washington, Frontier Colonel*, 1956; *Young Thomas Edison*, 1958; and *Thoreau of Walden Pond*, 1959.

DAVID M[ORRIS] POTTER is William R. Coe Professor of American History, Yale University. In 1947–48 he was Harmsworth Professor of American History and Fellow of Queen's College, Oxford. He was editor of the *Yale Review*, 1949–51. He is the author of the chapter on the "Background of Civil War" in a forthcoming volume of the new edition of the *Cambridge Modern History*. He is the author or editor of *Lincoln and His Party in the Secession Crisis*, 1942; *Trail to California: The Overland Diary of Vincent Geiger and Wakeman Bryarly*, 1945; *A Union Officer in the Reconstruction* (with J. H. Croushore), 1948; and *People of Plenty: Economic Abundance in the American Character*, 1954.

NANCY ANGELINE POTTER is Associate Professor of English at the University of Rhode Island. She received her B.A. and M.A. degrees from Tufts College and her Ph.D. from Boston University. She was an entrant in the nonprofessional category in the competition for the best essay on the theme "Reflections While Standing before the Lincoln Memorial." The distinguished board of judges, which included three Pulitzer Prize winners, selected Miss Potter's essay as the best in her category. Her home is in Voluntown, Connecticut.

C[HARLES] PERCY POWELL is in the Manuscript Division of the Library of Congress. He is head of Public Reader Service. He was Research Director for the national Lincoln Sesquicentennial Commission, 1958–60. He was among the select group who catalogued the Robert Todd Lincoln Papers prior to the opening of this collection to the public in 1947. In 1948 Lincoln Memorial University awarded him the Lincoln Diploma of Honor. He was the recipient of the Philadelphia Civil War–Lincoln Association Plaque for Meritorious Service, 1958. He is co-editor of the *Alumni History,* University of North Carolina, and the author of the *Handbook of the Lincoln Sesquicentennial Commission.*

HARRY EDWARD PRATT was Illinois State Historian from 1950 until his death in 1956. From 1936 to 1943 he was the Executive Secretary of the Abraham Lincoln Association. He was perhaps the greatest "fact" man the Lincoln field has ever known. Many of the leading Lincoln historians of our time were indebted to Dr. Pratt for his counsel and for his help in checking on details, dates, and minute facts in the Lincoln story. He received the Lincoln Diploma of Honor from Lincoln Memorial University. He edited *The Life of Abraham Lincoln* by W. D. Howells, 1938. He was the author of *Lincoln, 1840–46,* 1939; *Lincoln, 1809–1839,* 1941; *The Personal Finances of Abraham Lincoln,* 1943; *Concerning Mr. Lincoln,* 1944; and many articles for numerous historical publications.

MARION DOLORES PRATT is Archival Assistant, Illinois State Archives. She was Acting Illinois State Historian from February to September, 1956, succeeding her late husband, Dr. Harry E. Pratt. From 1945 to 1952 she was Assistant Executive Secretary of the Abraham Lincoln Association and assisted in editing the *Abraham Lincoln Quarterly.* In 1953 she received the Lincoln Diploma of Honor from Lincoln Memorial University. She is the Assistant Editor of *The Collected Works of Abraham Lincoln* (with Roy P. Basler and Lloyd A. Dunlap), 1953–55. She has written articles for many historical magazines. She is an honorary member of the national Lincoln Sesquicentennial Association.

RUTH PAINTER RANDALL is the wife of the late Professor James G. Randall, one of the greatest Lincoln scholars of all time. She is herself a distinguished Lincoln student and worked with her late husband on his great work, *Lincoln, the President*. She has written many articles for some of our leading newspapers and magazines. She is the author of the following books: *Mary Lincoln: Biography of a Marriage*, 1953; *Lincoln's Sons*, 1956; *The Courtship of Mr. Lincoln*, 1957; and *Lincoln's Animal Friends*, 1958. Mrs. Randall lives in Urbana, Illinois.

DONALD WAYNE RIDDLE is Professor of History, Head of the Division of Social Sciences, University of Illinois, Chicago Undergraduate Division. He has been interested in the Lincoln story for many years and has specialized in researches into Lincoln's career in Congress. He is the author of *Lincoln Runs for Congress*, 1948; and *Congressman Abraham Lincoln*, 1957. Dr. Riddle is a resident of Naperville, Illinois.

CARL SANDBURG has become in his own lifetime one of the great literary figures in American history. Poet, collector of folk songs, novelist, biographer, historian, storyteller for children, and essayist, his versatility and genius have made him a living legend. He has been the recipient of many awards and honorary degrees, including Phi Beta Kappa Poet, Harvard, 1928; Pulitzer Prize for Poetry, 1950; Gold Medal for History, American Academy of Arts and Letters, 1952; Gold Medal for Poetry, Poetry Society of America; and Gold Medal, Lincoln Sesquicentennial Commission, 1960. He has written for almost every distinguished publication in this country, and his articles and books have been reprinted in almost every language. His books include *Rootabaga Stories,* 1922; *Abraham Lincoln: The Prairie Years,* 1926; *The American Songbag,* 1927; *Steichen the Photographer,* 1929; *The People, Yes,* 1936; *Abraham Lincoln: The War Years,* 1939; *Home Front Memo,* 1943; *Remembrance Rock,* 1948; *Lincoln Collector,* 1949; *Complete Poems,* 1950; *Always the Young Strangers,* 1953; and *The Sandburg Range,* 1957. His memorable address before the Joint Session of the United States Congress on February 12, 1959, is one of the great literary moments in our history.

DORE SCHARY is a well-known theatrical and motion-picture director and producer. He has been a contributor to most of the major American magazines. He was the winner of an Academy Award for his original screenplay, *Boys' Town,* 1938, and received the Tony Award for his play, *Sunrise at Campobello,* 1958. He is a member of the Civil War Round Table of Southern California and an honorary member of the Civil War Centennial Commission. His books include *Case History of a Movie,* 1950; *Sunrise at Campobello,* 1957; and *The Highest Tree,* 1959.

FRED[ERIC DELBERT] SCHWENGEL is the Representative in the United States Congress from the First Congressional District of Iowa. He is the President of the Lincoln Group of the District of Columbia and a member of the national Civil War Centennial Commission. He was the Chairman of the Joint Session of Congress commemorating the one hundred and fiftieth anniversary of the birth of Abraham Lincoln. He has written many articles dealing with masonic orders, fraternal and historical activities. He is an honorary member of the national Lincoln Sesquicentennial Commission and a collector of books relating to Abraham Lincoln and the Civil War.

LOUIS M[ORRIS] STARR is the Director, Oral History Research Office, and Associate Professor of Journalism, Columbia University, where his chief occupation is serving as Director of the International Division of the Graduate School of Journalism. He has written articles for *American Heritage* and the Dictionary of American Biography. In 1958–59 he was a lecturer on "Civil War and Reconstruction" at the Hunter College graduate school. He is the author of *Bohemian Brigade: Civil War Newsmen in Action,* 1954.

PHILIP VAN DOREN STERN is a free-lance writer and consultant to NEA newspaper service on Civil War history. During World War II he was General Manager, Editions for the Armed Services. He has been a contributor to *American Heritage, Holiday,* and other national magazines. In 1959 he was awarded a Guggenheim Fellowship for work on the history of the navy in the Civil War. He has written or edited many books, including *The Man Who Killed Lincoln,* 1939; *The Life and Writings of Abraham Lincoln,* 1940; *An End to Valor: The Last Days of the Civil War,* 1958; *and They Were There: The Civil War in Action Pictures as Seen by Its Combat Artists,* 1959.

ADLAI EWING STEVENSON is a partner in the law firm of Stevenson, Rifkind and Wirtz, Chicago. He was Governor of Illinois, 1949–53 and Democratic candidate for President of the

United States in 1952 and 1956. His interest in history and particularly in Abraham Lincoln comes naturally—he is the great-grandson of Jesse W. Fell, who was one of the prime backers of his friend, Abraham Lincoln, for the Republican nomination for President in 1860. Governor Stevenson has been the recipient of numerous awards and honorary degrees from organizations and institutions of learning all over the world. He has written many newspaper and magazine articles, and the following books: *The Stark Reality of Responsibility,* 1952; *Major Campaign Speeches of Adlai E. Stevenson,* 1952; *Call to Greatness,* 1955; *What I Think,* 1956; *The New America,* 1957; *Friends and Enemies,* 1959; and *Putting First Things First,* 1960.

WILLIAM GRANT STRATTON is the thirty-second Governor of the State of Illinois and, prior to his election to the highest office in his state, served in the United States Congress and as Treasurer of the State of Illinois. He is the son of the late Secretary of the State of Illinois, William J. Stratton. He has always been interested in history and is particularly fascinated with the Lincoln–Civil War period. He is a member of the Illinois State Historical Society and the Civil War Round Table. He served as President of the Council of State Governments in 1958 and is a member of the national Lincoln Sesquicentennial Commission.

WILLIAM ANDREW SWANBERG devotes his entire time to writing. He is a member of the Society of American Historians, the Civil War Round Table of New York, and the New York Historical Society. He is the author of *Sickles the Incredible,* 1956; *First Blood: The Story of Fort Sumter,* 1957; and *Jim Fisk,* 1959. *First Blood* was the winner of both the Christopher Award and the Minnesota Centennial Award.

Biographical Sketches of Contributors

WAYNE CALHOUN TEMPLE is Director of the Department of Lincolniana, editor-in-chief of the *Lincoln Herald,* and Professor of History at Lincoln Memorial University. From 1954 until 1958 he was Historian for the Illinois State Museum. He is Secretary-Treasurer of the national Lincoln–Civil War Council and an honorary member of the national Lincoln Sesquicentennial Commission. He has written numerous articles dealing with historical subjects and on the Lincoln story. He is the author of *Indian Villages of the Illinois Country,* 1958, and is the editor of the forthcoming new edition of Horace Porter's *Campaigning with Grant.*

WALTER TROHAN is Chief of the Washington Bureau of the Chicago *Tribune.* He has been an active newspaperman for thirty-eight years and has traveled to Asia, Europe, and South America on special assignments. He has been a radio news commentator since 1951. He was President of the White House Correspondents Association, 1937–38 and is a member of the Civil War Round Table and the Chicago and Illinois State Historical Societies. He serves as a member of the editorial advisory board, *Civil War History* quarterly, and is the author of many articles for various magazines and historical journals.

RANDLE BOND TRUETT is the Chief Park Historian, National Capital Parks, National Park Service. In this position he has in his jurisdiction Ford's Theater, where President Lincoln was shot, and the Peterson house, where he died. Previous to his work with the National Park Service he was President, Lincoln Institute of Kentucky, and Instructor, History and Political Science, University of Louisville. He has been the recipient of many awards, including the Grand Cross of the Floy Alfaro International Foundation and an Honor Award from the Freedoms Foundation, Valley Forge. He is an honorary member of the national Lincoln Sesquicentennial Commission. He has written many books, booklets, and articles, including *History of Civilization, Medieval and Modern* (a syllabus), 1932; *The Lee Mansion,* 1943; *Lincoln, The Story of the Assassination,* 1949; and *The White House: Home of the Presidents,* 1949.

FRANK E[VERSON] VANDIVER is Professor of History, Rice Institute. He was a Rockefeller Fellow, 1946–48 and a Guggenheim Fellow, 1955. In 1958 he received the Carr P. Collins Award, Texas Institute of Letters. He has written numerous articles and reviews in the field of Civil War history. He is the author or editor of *The Diary of Josiah Gorgas,* 1947; *Ploughshares into Swords: Josiah Gorgas and Confederate Ordnance,* 1952; *Rebel Brass,* 1957; and *Mighty Stonewall,* 1957. He is currently engaged in work on a biography of General John J. Pershing.

MARK VAN DOREN is Professor Emeritus of English, Columbia University. He was the recipient of the Pulitzer Prize for poetry in 1940. He is the editor of various compilations including *Anthology of World Poetry,* originally issued in 1928 and revised and reissued in many editions, and is the author of *Collected Poems,* 1939; *Shakespeare,* 1939; *Nathaniel Hawthorne,* 1949; *Introduction to Poetry,* 1951; *Nobody Say a Word and Other Stories,* 1953; *Selected Poems,* 1954; *The Autobiography of Mark Van Doren,* 1958; *The Last Days of Lincoln: A Play,* 1959; and many other works.

CLYDE CAMERON WALTON is Illinois State Historian and Secretary-Treasurer of the Illinois State Historical Society. He is the founder and was the editor of *Civil War History* and is the editor of the *Journal of the Illinois State Historical Society.* He is a member of the Illinois Civil War Centennial Commission and an honorary member of the national Lincoln Sesquicentennial Commission. He has written articles for many historical journals and is art editor of *Lewis Henry Morgan: The Indian Journals 1859–62,* 1959.

LOUIS AUSTIN WARREN is the Director Emeritus of the Lincoln National Life Foundation. He was Director of this institution for twenty-eight years until his retirement in 1956. He edited *Lincoln Lore,* 1929–56, the weekly publication, invaluable to all Lincoln students and the *Lincoln Kinsman,* 1938–42, a monthly publication devoted to Lincoln genealogy. For his distinguished services he was awarded the Transylvania University Citation in History. He is the author of almost 200 Lincoln articles, booklets, and brochures. He has written two books, *Lincoln's Parentage and Childhood,* 1926; and *Lincoln's Youth: Indiana Years,* 1959.

T[HOMAS] HARRY WILLIAMS is Boyd Professor of History, Louisiana State University. He was President of the Southern Historical Association, 1958–59 and a member of the Historical Advisory Committee, Department of the Army, 1955–59. He was an American History Research Center Fellow, 1956–57 and a Guggenheim Fellow, 1957. In 1956 he received the Lincoln Memorial University Lincoln Diploma of Honor. He has written articles for numerous historical journals and is the author or editor of many books, including *Lincoln and the Radicals,* 1941; *Lincoln and His Generals,* 1952; *P.G.T. Beauregard: Napoleon in Gray,* 1955; *With Beauregard in Mexico,* 1956; *Selected Writings and Speeches of Abraham Lincoln,* 1957; and *A History of the United States,* 1959.

ALBERT ALEXANDER WOLDMAN is Judge of the Juvenile Court of Cuyahoga County (Cleveland), Ohio. He is the President of Abraham Lincoln Association of Ohio and the Vice Chairman, Ohio Abraham Lincoln Sesquicentennial Committee. In commemoration of the Lincoln sesquicentennial, the United States Information Agency broadcast excerpts from his books via Voice of America into Russia, Poland, and other Iron Curtain countries. He has written numerous magazine articles on Lincoln and is the author of *Lawyer Lincoln,* 1936; *Lincoln and the Russians,* 1952; and *The Governors of Ohio,* 1954 (co-author).

RALPH WEBSTER YARBOROUGH is United States Senator from the State of Texas. A brilliant lawyer, he has been a student of American history and of the life and times of Abraham Lincoln since his schooldays. He has spoken to the Civil War Round Table and other similar groups on various topics related to Lincoln and the Civil War. He is a member of the national Lincoln Sesquicentennial Commission and the Southern Historical Association. He has written many articles on Texas land law.

"I DO BUT QUOTE FROM ONE OF THOSE SPEECHES"

REFERENCE SOURCES FOR QUOTATIONS
USED AS TITLES

All chapter and section titles in this volume are taken from Abraham Lincoln's writings and speeches, with the exception of two instances where other sources are indicated. With these two exceptions, all references are taken from *The Collected Works of Abraham Lincoln,* 9 volumes, Rutgers University Press, 1953–55.

FOREWORD "Take hold with an honest heart and a strong hand" —Letter to Frederick Steele, January 27, 1864, *Collected Works,* Volume VII, page 155.

INTRODUCTION "Let us proceed in the great task which events have devolved upon us"—Annual Message to Congress, December 3, 1861, *Collected Works,* Volume V, page 53.

ACKNOWLEDGMENTS "The better part of one's life consists of his friendships"—Letter to Joseph Gillespie, *Collected Works,* Volume II, page 57.

1. "*We* cannot escape history"—Annual Message to Congress, December 1, 1862, *Collected Works,* Volume V, page 537.

2. "The present subject"—Autobiography written for John Locke Scripps (ca. June, 1860), *Collected Works,* Volume IV, page 61.

3. "I know so little of our family history"—Letter to Solomon Lincoln, March 6, 1848, *Collected Works,* Volume I, page 456.

4. "My parents were both born in Virginia"—Autobiography written for Jesse W. Fell, December 20, 1959, *Collected Works*, Volume III, page 511.

5. "Abraham though very young, was large of his age"—Autobiography written for John Locke Scripps, (ca. June, 1860), *Collected Works*, Volume IV, page 62.

6. "There I grew up"—Autobiography written for Jesse W. Fell, December 20, 1859, *Collected Works*, Volume III, page 511.

7. "I am young and unknown to many of you"—Communication to the people of Sangamon County, March 9, 1832, *Collected Works*, Volume I, page 8.

8. "Whatever woman may cast her lot with mine"—Letter to Mary S. Owens, May 7, 1837, *Collected Works*, Volume I, page 78.

9. "Every man is said to have his peculiar ambition"—Communication to the people of Sangamon County, March 9, 1832, *Collected Works*, Volume I, page 8.

10. "I shall be governed by their will"—Letter to the editor of the Sangamo *Journal*, June 13, 1836, *Collected Works*, Volume I, page 48.

11. "Love is eternal"—Inscription on the gold wedding band Abraham Lincoln placed on the finger of Mary Todd, November 4, 1842.

12. "Let reverence for the laws . . . become the political religion"—Address before the Young Men's Lyceum of Springfield, Illinois, January 27, 1838, *Collected Works*, Volume I, page 112.

13. "Never *plead* what you *need* not"—Letter to Usher F. Linder, February 20, 1848, *Collected Works*, Volume I, page 453.

14. "I wish to do justice to all"—Speech in United States House of Representatives on the presidential question, July 27, 1848, *Collected Works*, Volume I, page 515.

15. "Billy, I can trust you, if you can trust me"—Conversation with William H. Herndon (ca. December, 1844), *Herndon's*

Lincoln, by Wiliam H. Herndon and Jesse W. Weik, Volume II, page 266; *Lincoln's Herndon,* by David Donald, pages 18–19.

16. "These principles can not stand together—Speech at Peoria, Illinois, October 16, 1854, *Collected Works,* Volume II, page 275.

17. "Here I have lived"—Farewell Address at Springfield, Illinois, February 11, 1861, *Collected Works,* Volume IV, page 190.

18. "I want to see you, and our dear—*dear* boys very much"—Letter to Mary Todd Lincoln, June 12, 1848, *Collected Works,* Volume I, page 478.

19. "The Union is a house divided against itself"—First debate with Stephen A. Douglas, at Ottawa, Illinois, August 21, 1858, *Collected Works,* Volume III, page 18.

20. "It reminds me of the story"—Second debate with Stephen A. Douglas at Freeport, Illinois, August 27, 1858, *Collected Works,* Volume III, page 74.

21. "Let us have faith that right makes might"—Address at Cooper Institute, New York City, February 27, 1860, *Collected Works,* Volume III, page 550.

22. "I accept the nomination tendered me by the Convention"—Letter to George Ashmun, May 23, 1860, *Collected Works,* Volume IV, page 52.

23. "I do not think myself fit for the Presidency"—Letter to Thomas J. Pickett, April 16, 1859, *Collected Works,* Volume III, page 377.

24. "I am not a master of language"—Speech at Chicago, Illinois, July 10, 1858, *Collected Works,* Volume II, page 491.

25. "I bid you an affectionate farewell"—Farewell Address at Springfield, Illinois, February 11, 1861, *Collected Works,* Volume IV, page 190.

26. "If any personal description of me is thought desirable"—Autobiography written for Jesse W. Fell, December 20, 1859, *Collected Works,* Volume III, page 512.

27. "I have been selected to fill an important office"—Remarks at Lawrenceburg, Indiana, February 12, 1861, *Collected Works*, Volume IV, page 197.

28. "I shall unselfishly try to deal fairly with all men"—Letter to William Cullen Bryant, December 29, 1860, *Collected Works*, Volume IV, page 163.

29. "We are not enemies, but friends"—First Inaugural Address, March 4, 1861, *Collected Works*, Volume IV, page 271.

30. "In *your* hands, my dissatisfied fellow countrymen"—First Inaugural Address, March 4, 1861, *Collected Works*, Volume IV, page 271.

31. "What I deal with is too vast for malicious dealing"—Letter to Cuthbert Bullitt, July 28, 1862, *Collected Works*, Volume V, page 346.

32. "In the midst of unprecedented political troubles"—Annual Message to Congress, December 3, 1861, *Collected Works*, Volume V, page 35.

33. "The success of your army and the cause of the country are the same"—Letter to George B. McClellan, May 9, 1862, *Collected Works*, Volume V, page 209.

34. "I have no prejudice against the Southern people"—Speech at Peoria, Illinois, October 16, 1854, *Collected Works*, Volume II, page 255.

35. "I happen temporarily to occupy this big White House"—Speech to One Hundred Sixty-sixth Ohio Regiment, August 22, 1864, *Collected Works*, Volume VII, page 512.

36. "Public opinion in this country is everything"—Speech at Columbus, Ohio, September 16, 1859, *Collected Works*, Volume III, page 424.

37. "Peace has been preserved with all nations"—Proclamation of Thanksgiving, October 3, 1863, *Collected Works*, Volume VI, page 496.

38. "This is essentially a People's contest"—Message to Congress in Special Session, July 4, 1861, *Collected Works*, Volume IV, page 438.

39. "Shall be then, thenceforward, and forever free"—Emancipation Proclamation, January 1, 1863, *Collected Works*, Volume VI, page 29.

40. "Let every one play the part he can play best"—Letter to William H. Herndon, June 22, 1848, *Collected Works*, Volume I, page 491.

41. "What news from the front?"—Letter to George B. McClellan, August 27, 1862, *Collected Works*, Volume V, page 396.

42. "We are met on a great battle-field"—Address delivered at the dedication of the cemetery at Gettysburg, November 19, 1863, *Collected Works*, Volume VII, page 17.

43. "We must think anew, and act anew"—Annual Message to Congress, December 1, 1862, *Collected Works*, Volume V, page 537.

44. "The gallant Navy stood ready"—Last public address, April 11, 1865, *Collected Works*, Volume VIII, page 400.

45. "Work, work, work, is the main thing"—Letter to John M. Brockman, September 25, 1860, *Collected Works*, Volume IV, page 121.

46. "I begin to see it. You will succeed"—Telegram to Ulysses S. Grant, June 15, 1864, *Collected Works*, Volume VII, page 393.

47. "These measures, whether strictly legal or not"—Message to Congress in Special Session, July 4, 1861, *Collected Works*, Volume IV, page 421.

48. "We must disenthrall ourselves"—Annual Message to Congress, December 1, 1862, *Collected Works*, Volume V, page 537.

49. "The Presidency . . . is no bed of roses"—Eulogy on Zachary Taylor, July 25, 1850, *Collected Works*, Volume II, page 89.

50. "Every foul bird comes aboard"—Letter to Charles D. Drake and others, October 5, 1863, *Collected Works*, Volume VI, page 500.

51. "The Union of these States is perpetual"—First Inaugural

Address, March 4, 1861, *Collected Works*, Volume IV, page 252.

52. "Let the Supreme Court be of convenient number"—Annual Message to Congress, December 3, 1861, *Collected Works*, Volume V, page 42.

53. "I abstain from reading the reports of attacks upon myself"—Last public address, April 11, 1865, *Collected Works*, Volume VIII, page 401.

54. "We can not have free government without elections"—Response to a serenade, November 10, 1864, *Collected Works*, Volume VIII, page 101.

55. "I suppose they got my shaddow"—Letter to Harvey G. Eastman, April 7, 1860, *Collected Works*, Volume IV, page 39.

56. "I too, am a Kentuckian"—Fragment of speech intended for Kentuckians (ca. February 12, 1861), *Collected Works*, Volume IV, page 200.

57. "Such alone can meet and cover all cavils"—Reply to committee notifying Lincoln of his renomination, June 9, 1864, *Collected Works*, Volume VII, page 380.

58. "I have always thought 'Dixie' one of the best tunes"—Response to serenade, April 10, 1865, *Collected Works*, Volume VIII, page 393.

59. "Not in sorrow, but in gladness of heart"—Last public address, April 11, 1865, *Collected Works*, Volume VIII, page 399.

60. "I have seen very little of the drama"—Letter to James H. Hackett, August 17, 1863, *Collected Works*, Volume VI, page 392.

61. "I will take care of myself"—Letter to Edwin M. Stanton, April 3, 1865, *Collected Works*, Volume VIII, page 385.

62. "For man's vast future,—thanks to all"—Letter to James C. Conkling, August 26, 1863, *Collected Works*, Volume VI, page 410.

63. "Writing . . . is the great invention of the world"—Second

lecture on discoveries and inventions, (February 11, 1859), *Collected Works*, Volume III, page 360.

64. "A merely pernicious abstraction"—Last public address, April 11, 1865, *Collected Works*, Volume VIII, page 403.

65. "In using the same *word* we do not all mean the same *thing*" —Address at Sanitary Fair, Baltimore, Maryland, April 18, 1864, *Collected Works*, Volume VII, page 301.

66. "In this view, humble as I am"—Speech in United States House of Representatives on internal improvements, June 20, 1848, *Collected Works*, Volume I, page 481.

67. "Do nothing merely for revenge"—Letter to William S. Rosecrans, November 19, 1864, *Collected Works*, Volume VIII, page 116.

68. "I think nothing equals Macbeth"—Letter to James H. Hackett, August 17, 1863, *Collected Works*, Volume VI, page 392.

69. "The last full measure of devotion"—Address delivered at the dedication of the cemetery at Gettysburg, November 19, 1863, *Collected Works*, Volume VII, page 18.

70. "The grief of a loss so overwhelming"—Letter to Mrs. Lydia Bixby, November 21, 1864, *Collected Works*, Volume VIII, page 117.

71. "I have never denied the truth of the Scriptures"—Handbill replying to charges of infidelity, July 31, 1846, *Collected Works*, Volume I, page 382.

72. "An unfettered start, and a fair chance, in the race of life"— Message to Congress in Special Session, July 4, 1861, *Collected Works*, Volume IV, page 438.

APPENDIX

REFLECTIONS . . . "Let him have the marble monument"—Letter to John H. Bryant, May 30, 1864, *Collected Works*, Volume VII, page 366.

LINCOLN IN THE ARCHIVES "It is a little curious . . . to look over those old letters"—Letter to Henry Asbury, November 19, 1860, *Collected Works*, Volume IV, page 140.

A BASIC LINCOLN LIBRARY

It has been said that more books have been written about Abraham Lincoln than about any other historical figure with the possible exception of Napoleon; and in recent years the number of titles referring to him has probably passed the total referring to the Little Corsican. Jay Monaghan's *Lincoln Bibliography,* published in 1943–45, lists 3958 separate titles which appeared in the one-hundred-year span between 1839 and 1939. It has been estimated that over 6000 separate titles, books and pamphlets, have been issued about or by Abraham Lincoln since the appearance early in 1839 of the Illinois Legislature House of Representatives Eleventh Assembly document in which "Mr. Lincoln, from the Committee on Finance," made a report on Public Lands in Illinois. This modest three-page folder began a flood of printed material which has averaged a title every week in the intervening one hundred and twenty-one years.

The specialist in the Lincoln field is constantly requested to furnish a list of the "best" books about Abraham Lincoln, or a list of the "essential" titles necessary for a good basic collection. In 1935, Dr. Louis A. Warren selected "Fifty Important Lincoln Books" in "Lincoln Lore No. 316," the weekly publication of the Lincoln National Life Foundation. In 1936, Paul M. Angle in two articles which appeared in "Bulletins" Nos. 43 and 44 of the Abraham Lincoln Association under the title "Basic Lincolniana," recorded what he considered to be the most worth-while Lincoln books. A few years later the late Harry J. Lytle of Davenport, Iowa, supplied a list of "100 Best Lincoln Books" which appeared as a supplement to "The Education of Abraham Lincoln," a pamphlet by M. L. Houser. In 1946 Paul M. Angle's *A Shelf of Lincoln Books* was published, and the eighty-one titles specified in this volume immediately became accepted as the ownership goal of every Lincoln enthusiast and collector. In 1951 the editor of this work prepared a list of "One Hundred Books About Abraham Lincoln," being in the main a modification of Angle's *Shelf,* adding some new books published during the intervening five years and eliminating a few titles rendered obsolete by new publications.

495

The use of the word "best" in connection with a selective listing of this type is unfortunate. Perhaps a more appropriate term would be "useful." While accuracy and detail in research, good writing, and depth of information made available to the reader, have been important factors governing the selection of the titles, perhaps the main consideration has been the assembling of the most compact group of books which, in the estimation of the compiler, will present the most knowledge concerning the life and times of our sixteenth President. This has necessitated the elimination of many superbly written volumes because they duplicate, in part, other excellent titles included in the selection. It has also resulted in some titles' being chosen, not for excellence of style, but because they offer special information not available elsewhere.

Ten years have passed since the last list appeared, but the flood of new titles has continued. During this period some of the greatest contributions to Lincolniana have made their appearance, including the definitive edition of *The Collected Works of Abraham Lincoln*, Benjamin P. Thomas's *Abraham Lincoln*, James G. Randall's *Lincoln the President*, Ruth Painter Randall's *Mary Lincoln*, Kenneth P. Williams' *Lincoln Finds a General*, and the first five volumes of Allan Nevins' magnificent *The Ordeal of the Union*. To limit a list to an exact figure, whether it be fifty or one hundred, is too arbitrary, and I am rather embarrassed when I recall that I, too, was guilty of doing so. It is much more important to attempt to determine (at least to the satisfaction of a few people) just what the most useful books about Abraham Lincoln are than it is to limit or stretch a list to fit a preconceived number.

This restriction is certainly not intended to discourage those who are building, or hope to build, all-inclusive Lincoln collections. Realizing the limitations that confront most collectors and readers, who, if they do not lack the necessary funds, are short of shelf space, I submit this foundation group as a contribution toward solving the Lincoln student's book-housing problem. In preparing this section of this book, the editor consulted many of the leading writers, libraries, collectors, and students prominently identified with the Lincoln story. Many suggestions were received and gratefully incorporated into the final list. It must be emphasized, however, that final responsibility for the selection, nevertheless, rests wholly on his shoulders.

No attempt has been made to include every edition of every work. The first edition and the latest revised edition are here recorded, and occasionally some special edition worthy of notice. Many excellent books have been omitted because of space limitations and because the goal here is necessarily narrow. Your forgiveness is asked if any of your favorite books have been overlooked. This is, primarily, one-man's opinion. No two students or collectors could or would compile identical lists—which is as it should be, and explains in part why there always will be new Lincoln books. We each seek our own Lincoln and some of us, for better or for worse, go so far as to presume to write or edit *another* book on the subject.

ANGLE, PAUL MCCLELLAND. *"Here I Have Lived." A History of Lincoln's Springfield, 1821–1865.* Springfield: The Abraham Lincoln Association, 1935. New edition, New Brunswick: Rutgers University Press, 1950.

ANGLE, PAUL MCCLELLAND. *A Shelf of Lincoln Books: A Critical Selective Bibliography.* New Brunswick: Rutgers University Press, 1946.

ANGLE, PAUL MCCLELLAND, editor. *The Lincoln Reader.* New Brunswick: Rutgers University Press, 1947. New edition, New York: Pocket Books, Inc., 1954.

ANGLE, PAUL MCCLELLAND, editor. *Created Equal? The Complete Lincoln-Douglas Debates of 1858.* Chicago: The University of Chicago Press, 1958.

ANGLE, PAUL MCCLELLAND, and EARL SCHENCK MIERS, editors. *The Living Lincoln: His Mind, His Times, and the War He Fought. Reconstructed from His Own Writings.* New Brunswick: Rutgers University Press, 1955.

ARNOLD, ISAAC NEWTON. *The Life of Abraham Lincoln.* Chicago: Jansen, McClurg & Company, 1885.

BALLARD, COLIN ROBERT. *The Military Genius of Abraham Lincoln.* New York: Oxford University Press, London: Humphrey Milford, 1926. New edition, with a Preface by Fletcher Pratt and photographs from the Meserve Collection. Cleveland and New York: The World Publishing Company, 1952.

BARINGER, WILLIAM ELDON. *Lincoln's Rise to Power.* Boston: Little, Brown and Company, 1937.

BARINGER, WILLIAM ELDON. *A House Dividing: Lincoln as President Elect.* Springfield: The Abraham Lincoln Association, 1945.

BARINGER, WILLIAM ELDON. *Lincoln's Vandalia: A Pioneer Portrait.* New Brunswick: Rutgers University Press, 1949.

BARTON, WILLIAM ELEAZAR. *The Paternity of Abraham Lincoln: Was He the Son of Thomas Lincoln? An Essay on the Chastity of Nancy Hanks.* New York: George H. Doran Company, 1920.

BARTON, WILLIAM ELEAZAR. *The Soul of Abraham Lincoln.* New York: George H. Doran Company, 1920.

BARTON, WILLIAM ELEAZAR. *The Lineage of Lincoln.* Indianapolis: The Bobbs-Merrill Company, 1929.

BARTON, WILLIAM ELEAZAR. *Lincoln at Gettysburg: What He Intended to Say; What He Was Reported to Have Said; What He Wished He Had Said.* Indianapolis: The Bobbs-Merrill Company, 1930.

BASLER, ROY PRENTICE. *The Lincoln Legend: A Study in Changing Conceptions.* Boston and New York: Houghton Mifflin Company, 1935.

BASLER, ROY PRENTICE, editor. *Abraham Lincoln: His Speeches and Writings.* Preface by Carl Sandburg. Cleveland and New York: The World Publishing Company, 1946.

BEVERIDGE, ALBERT JEREMIAH. *Abraham Lincoln, 1809–1858.* 2 volumes. Boston and New York: Houghton Mifflin Company, 1928. Library edition, Boston and New York: Houghton Mifflin Company, 1928. 4 volumes.

BLEGEN, THEODORE CHRISTIAN. *Lincoln's Imagery: A Study in Word Power.* La Crosse: Emerson C. Wulling, Sumac Press, 1954.

BROOKS, NOAH. *Washington In Lincoln's Time.* New York: The Century Company, 1895. New edition, edited, with an Introduction by Herbert Mitgang, New York: Rinehart & Company, Inc., 1958.

BROWNE, FRANCIS FISHER, editor. *The Every-day Life of Abraham Lincoln.* New York and St. Louis: N. D. Thompson Publishing Co., 1886. Revised edition, Chicago: Browne & Howell Company, 1913.

BRUCE, ROBERT VANCE. *Lincoln and the Tools of War.* Foreword by Benjamin P. Thomas. Indianapolis, New York: The Bobbs-Merrill Company, Inc., 1956.

BRYAN, GEORGE SANDS. *The Great American Myth.* New York: Carrick & Evans, Inc., 1940.

BULLARD, FREDERICK LAURISTON. *Abraham Lincoln & The Widow Bixby.* New Brunswick: Rutgers University Press, 1946.

BULLARD, FREDERICK LAURISTON. *Lincoln in Marble and Bronze.* New Brunswick: Rutgers University Press, 1952.

CARMAN, HARRY JAMES and REINHARD HENRY LUTHIN. *Lincoln and the Patronage.* New York: Columbia University Press, 1943.

CARPENTER, FRANCIS BICKNELL. *Six Months in the White House with Abraham Lincoln: The Story of a Picture.* New York: Hurd and Houghton, 1866.

CHARNWOOD, GODFREY RATHBONE BENSON, LORD. *Abraham Lincoln.* London: Constable & Company, Ltd., 1916. New edition, New York: Pocket Books, Inc., 1951.

CURRENT, RICHARD NELSON. *The Lincoln Nobody Knows.* New York, Toronto, London: McGraw-Hill Book Company, Inc., 1958.

CUTHBERT, NORMA BARRETT. *Lincoln and the Baltimore Plot: From Pinkerton Records and Related Papers.* San Marino, California: The Huntington Library, 1949.

DENNETT, TYLER, editor. *Lincoln and the Civil War in the Diaries and Letters of John Hay.* New York: Dodd, Mead & Company, 1939.

DEWITT, DAVID MILLER. *The Assassination of Abraham Lincoln and Its Expiation.* New York: The Macmillan Company, 1909.

DODGE, DANIEL KILHAM. *Abraham Lincoln: Master of Words.* New York: D. Appleton and Company, 1924.

DONALD, DAVID. *Lincoln's Herndon.* Introduction by Carl Sandburg. New York: Alfred A. Knopf, 1948.

DONALD, DAVID, editor. *Inside Lincoln's Cabinet: The Civil War Diaries of Salmon P. Chase.* New York: Longmans, Green and Co., 1954.

DORRIS, JONATHAN TRUMAN. *Pardon and Amnesty Under Lincoln and Johnson.* Chapel Hill: The University of North Carolina Press, 1953.

DUFF, JOHN JOSEPH. A. *Lincoln, Prairie Lawyer.* New York, Toronto: Rinehart & Company, Inc., 1960.

EISENSCHIML, OTTO. *Why Was Lincoln Murdered?* Boston: Little, Brown and Company, 1937. New edition, New York: Grosset & Dunlap, Inc., 1957.

EVANS, WILLIAM AUGUSTUS. *Mrs. Abraham Lincoln: A Study of Her Personality and Her Influence on Lincoln.* New York: Alfred A. Knopf, 1932.

HARNSBERGER, CAROLINE [THOMAS], editor. *A Lincoln Treasury.* Chicago: Wilcox & Follett Co., 1950.

HARPER, ROBERT S[TORY]. *Lincoln and the Press.* New York: McGraw-Hill Book Company, Inc., 1951.

HENDRICK, BURTON JESSE. *Lincoln's War Cabinet.* Boston: Little, Brown and Company, 1946.

HERNDON, WILLIAM HENRY, and JESSE WILLIAM WEIK. *Herndon's Lincoln: The True Story of a Great Life.* 3 volumes. Chicago, New York, and San Francisco: Belford, Clarke & Company, 1889. New edition, with an Introduction and Notes by Paul M. Angle. Illustrated with photographs from the Meserve Collection, Cleveland and New York: The World Publishing Company, 1949.

HERTZ, EMANUEL, editor. *The Hidden Lincoln: From the Letters and Papers of William H. Herndon.* New York: The Viking Press, 1938.

HERTZ, EMANUEL, editor. *Lincoln Talks: A Biography in Anecdote.* New York: The Viking Press, 1939.

HESSELTINE, WILLIAM BEST. *Lincoln and the War Governors.* New York: Alfred A. Knopf, 1948.

HOLLAND, JOSIAH GILBERT. *The Life of Abraham Lincoln.* Springfield, Massachusetts; Gurdon Bill, 1866.

HOWELLS, WILLIAM DEAN. *Lives and Speeches of Abraham Lincoln and Hannibal Hamlin.* Columbus: Follett, Foster & Co., 1860. New edition, *Life of Abraham Lincoln by W. D. Howells. This campaign biography corrected by the hand of Abraham Lincoln . . .* edited by Harry E. Pratt; Introduction by Clyde C. Walton, Bloomington: Indiana University Press, 1960.

JONES, EDGAR DEWITT. *Lincoln and the Preachers.* Introduction by William H. Townsend. New York: Harper & Brothers, 1948.

JUDSON, CLARA INGRAM. *Abraham Lincoln: Friend of the People,* Pen Drawings by Robert Frankenberg. Chicago: Wilcox and Follett Company, 1950.

KECKLEY, ELIZABETH. *Behind the Scenes . . . or, Thirty Years a Slave, and Four Years in the White House.* New York: G. W. Carleton & Co., 1868. New edition, with one-page Foreword by James H. Stansil, Buffalo: Stansil and Lee, 1931.

LAMON, WARD HILL. *The Life of Abraham Lincoln: From His Birth to Inauguration as President.* Boston: James R. Osgood and Company, 1872.

LEARNED, MARION DEXTER. *Abraham Lincoln: An American Migration.* Philadelphia: William J. Campbell, 1909.

LEWIS, LLOYD [DOWNS]. *Myths After Lincoln.* New York: Harcourt, Brace and Company, 1929. New edition, with an Introduction by Carl Sandburg, New York: Harcourt, Brace and Company, 1940.

LINCOLN, ABRAHAM. *The Collected Works of Abraham Lincoln.* Roy P. Basler, editor; Marion Dolores Pratt and Lloyd A. Dunlap, assistant editors. 9 volumes. New Brunswick: Rutgers University Press, 1953–55.

LINCOLN, WALDO. *History of the Lincoln Family: An Account of the Descendants of Samuel Lincoln of Hingham, Massachusetts, 1637–1920.* Worcester: Commonwealth Press, 1923.

LORANT, STEFAN. *Lincoln: His Life in Photographs.* New York: Duell, Sloan and Pearce, 1941. Revised and enlarged edition, *Lincoln: A Picture Story of His Life,* New York: Harper & Brothers, 1957.

LUTHIN, REINHARD HENRY. *The First Lincoln Campaign.* Cambridge: Harvard University Press, 1944.

MCCARTHY, CHARLES HALLAN. *Lincoln's Plan of Reconstruction.* New York: McClure, Phillips & Co., 1901.

MCCLURE, ALEXANDER KELLY. *Abraham Lincoln and Men of War Times: Some Personal Recollections of War and Politics during the Lincoln Administration.* Introduction by Dr. A. C. Lambdin. Philadelphia: The Times Publishing Company, 1892.

MEARNS, DAVID CHAMBERS, editor. *The Lincoln Papers.* 2 volumes. Introduction by Carl Sandburg. Garden City: Doubleday & Company, 1948.

MESERVE, FREDERICK HILL and CARL SANDBURG. *The Photographs of Abraham Lincoln.* New York: Harcourt, Brace and Company, 1947.

MIERS, EARL SCHENCK, editor-in-chief. *Lincoln Day by Day: A Chronology, 1809–1865. Volume I: 1809–1848: Volume II: 1849–1860: Volume III: 1861–1865.* Compiled by William E. Baringer and based on the work of Paul M. Angle, Lloyd A. Dunlap, C. Percy Powell, Harry E. Pratt, and Benjamin P. Thomas. Washington, D. C.: Lincoln Sesquicentennial Commission, 1960.

MITGANG, HERBERT, editor. *Lincoln: As They Saw Him.* New York, Toronto: Rinehart & Company, Inc., 1956.

MONAGHAN, [JAMES] JAY. *Lincoln Bibliography, 1839–1939.* 2 volumes. Foreword by James G. Randall. Springfield: Illinois State Historical Library, 1943–45.

MONAGHAN, [JAMES] JAY. *Diplomat in Carpet Slippers: Abraham Lincoln Deals with Foreign Affairs.* Indianapolis, New York: The Bobbs-Merrill Company, 1945.

NEVINS, ALLAN. *The Ordeal of the Union.* 2 volumes. *Volume I: Fruits of Manifest Destiny, 1847–1852. Volume II: A House Dividing, 1852–*

1857. The Emergence of Lincoln. 2 volumes. *Volume I: Douglas, Buchanan, and Party Chaos, 1857–1859. Volume II: Prologue to Civil War, 1859–1861. The War for the Union. Volume I: The Improvised War, 1861–1862.* New York: Charles Scribner's Sons, 1947–59.

NICOLAY, HELEN. *Lincoln's Secretary: A Biography of John G. Nicolay.* New York: Longmans, Green and Co., 1949.

NICOLAY, JOHN GEORGE and JOHN HAY. *Abraham Lincoln: A History.* 10 volumes. New York: The Century Co., 1890, 1914.

NORTH, STERLING. *Abe Lincoln: Log Cabin to White House.* Illustrated by Lee Ames. New York: Random House, 1956.

PETERSEN, WILLIAM FERDINAND. *Lincoln-Douglas: The Weather as Destiny.* Springfield: Charles C. Thomas, 1943.

PHILLIPS, ISAAC NEWTON, editor. *Abraham Lincoln by Some Men Who Knew Him.* Bloomington: Pantagraph Printing & Stationery Co., 1910. New edition, re-edited with Notes and Foreword by Paul M. Angle, Chicago: Americana House, 1950.

POTTER, DAVID M[ORRIS]. *Lincoln and His Party in the Secession Crisis.* New Haven: Yale University Press, 1942.

PRATT, HARRY EDWARD. *The Personal Finances of Abraham Lincoln.* Springfield: The Abraham Lincoln Association, 1943.

PRATT, HARRY EDWARD, editor. *Concerning Mr. Lincoln: In which Abraham Lincoln is Pictured as He Appeared to Letter Writers of His Time.* Springfield: The Abraham Lincoln Association, 1944.

RANDALL, JAMES GARFIELD. *Constitutional Problems Under Lincoln.* New York: D. Appleton and Company, 1926. Revised edition, Urbana: The University of Illinois Press, 1951.

RANDALL, JAMES GARFIELD. *Lincoln the President.* 4 volumes (volume IV edited and completed by Richard N. Current after Dr. Randall's death). New York: Dodd, Mead & Company, 1945–55. One-volume edition, *Mr. Lincoln,* edited by Richard N. Current, New York: Dodd, Mead & Company, 1957.

RANDALL, JAMES GARFIELD. *Lincoln: The Liberal Statesman.* New York: Dodd, Mead & Company, 1947.

RANDALL, RUTH PAINTER. *Mary Lincoln: Biography of a Marriage.* Boston: Little, Brown and Company, 1953.

RANDALL, RUTH PAINTER. *Lincoln's Sons.* Boston: Little, Brown and Company, 1955.

REEP, THOMAS PHILIP. *Lincoln at New Salem.* Petersburg: The Old Salem Lincoln League, 1927.

RICE, ALLEN THORNDIKE, editor. *Abraham Lincoln by Distinguished Men of His Time.* New York: North American Publishing Company, 1886. Revised edition, New York: Harper & Brothers, 1909.

RIDDLE, DONALD WAYNE. *Lincoln Runs for Congress.* New Brunswick: Rutgers University Press, 1948.

RIDDLE, DONALD WAYNE. *Congressman Abraham Lincoln.* Urbana: The University of Illinois Press, 1957.

ROSCOE, THEODORE. *The Web of Conspiracy: The Complete Story of the Men Who Murdered Abraham Lincoln.* Englewood Cliffs, New Jersey: Prentice-Hall, Inc., 1959.

SANDBURG, CARL. *Abraham Lincoln: The Prairie Years, The War Years.* 6 volumes. New York: Harcourt, Brace & Company, 1926–39. One-volume edition, New York: Harcourt, Brace & Company, 1954; paperbound edition, Laurel Edition, 3 volumes, New York: Dell Publishing Co., 1959.

SANDBURG, CARL. *Lincoln Collector: The Story of Oliver R. Barrett's Great Private Collection.* New York: Harcourt, Brace & Company, 1950.

SANDBURG, CARL, and PAUL MCCLELLAND ANGLE. *Mary Lincoln: Wife and Widow.* New York: Harcourt, Brace & Company, 1932. New edition, New York: Harcourt, Brace & Company, 1940.

SHAW, ARCHER, editor. *The Lincoln Encyclopedia: The Spoken and Written Words of A. Lincoln Arranged for Ready Reference.* New York: The Macmillan Company, 1950.

SILVER, DAVID MAYER. *Lincoln's Supreme Court.* Urbana: The University of Illinois Press, 1956.

STEPHENSON, NATHANIEL WRIGHT. *Lincoln: An Account of His Personal Life, Especially of Its Springs of Action as Revealed and Deepened by the Ordeal of War.* Indianapolis: The Bobbs-Merrill Company, 1922.

STERN, PHILIP VAN DOREN, editor. *The Life and Writings of Abraham Lincoln.* Introduction by Allan Nevins. New York: Random House, 1940. Revised edition, New York: The Modern Library, 1942.

TARBELL, IDA MINERVA. *The Life of Abraham Lincoln.* 2 volumes. New York: The Doubleday & McClure Co., 1900. Revised edition, New York: The Macmillan Company, 1928, 2 volumes.

TARBELL, IDA MINERVA. *In the Footsteps of the Lincolns.* New York: Harper & Brothers, 1924.

THOMAS, BENJAMIN PLATT. *Lincoln's New Salem.* Drawings by Romaine Proctor. Springfield: The Abraham Lincoln Association, 1934. New and revised edition, New York: Alfred A. Knopf, 1954.

THOMAS, BENJAMIN PLATT. *Portrait for Posterity: Lincoln and His Biographers.* Illustrations by Romaine Proctor. New Brunswick: Rutgers University Press, 1947.

THOMAS, BENJAMIN PLATT. *Abraham Lincoln: A Biography.* New York: Alfred A. Knopf, 1952.

TOWNSEND, WILLIAM HENRY. *Lincoln and His Wife's Home Town.* Indianapolis: The Bobbs-Merrill Company, 1929. Revised and enlarged edition, *Lincoln and the Bluegrass: Slavery and Civil War in Kentucky.* Lexington: University of Kentucky Press, 1955.

TOWNSEND, WILLIAM HENRY. *Lincoln and Liquor.* New York: The Press of the Pioneers, 1934.

WARREN, LOUIS AUSTIN. *Lincoln's Parentage & Childhood: A History of the Kentucky Lincolns Supported by Documentary Evidence.* New York: The Century Co., 1926.

WARREN, LOUIS AUSTIN. *Lincoln's Youth: Indiana Years. Seven to Twenty-One: 1816–1830.* New York: Appleton-Century-Crofts, Inc., 1959.

WEIK, JESSE WILLIAM. *The Real Lincoln.* Boston and New York: Houghton Mifflin Company, 1922.

WELLES, GIDEON. *Diary of Gideon Welles: Secretary of the Navy Under Lincoln and Johnson.* With an Introduction by John T. Morse, Jr. 3 volumes. Boston and New York: Houghton Mifflin Company, 1911. New edition, with Foreword and notes by Howard K. Beale, (3 volumes), New York: W. W. Norton & Company, 1960.

WHITNEY, HENRY CLAY. *Life on the Circuit with Lincoln. With Sketches of Generals Grant, Sherman and McClellan, Judge Davis, Leonard Swett and other contemporaries.* Boston: Estes and Lauriat, 1892. New edition, Introduction and Notes by Paul M. Angle, Caldwell, Idaho: The Caxton Printers, 1940.

WILLIAMS, KENNETH POWERS. *Lincoln Finds A General: A Military Study of the Civil War.* 5 volumes. New York: The Macmillan Company, 1949–59.

WILLIAMS, T[HOMAS] HARRY. *Lincoln and the Radicals.* Madison: The University of Wisconsin Press, 1941.

WILLIAMS, T[HOMAS] HARRY. *Lincoln and His Generals.* New York: Alfred A. Knopf, 1952.

WILSON, RUFUS ROCKWELL, editor. *Lincoln Among His Friends: A Sheaf of Lincoln Memories.* Caldwell, Idaho: The Caxton Printers, 1942.

WILSON, RUFUS ROCKWELL, editor. *Intimate Memories of Abraham Lincoln.* Elmira: Primavera Press, 1945.

WILSON, RUFUS ROCKWELL, editor. *Lincoln in Caricature. 165 Poster Cartoons and Drawings from the Press.* Elmira: The Primavera Press, 1945. New edition, Introduction by R. Gerald McMurtry, New York: Horizon Press, 1953.

WOLDMAN, ALBERT ALEXANDER. *Lawyer Lincoln.* Boston & New York: Houghton Mifflin Company, 1936.

WOLF, WILLIAM JOHN. *The Almost Chosen People: A Study of the Religion of Abraham Lincoln.* Garden City: Doubleday & Company, Inc., 1959.

ZORNOW, WILLIAM FRANK. *Lincoln and the Party Divided.* Norman: University of Oklahoma Press, 1954.

INDEX

Index

Bowles, Samuel, 109
Bowne, Captain John, 41
Bowne, Richard and Sarah, 40
Bowne, William, 39, 40
Boyd, Andrew, 23
Brady, Mathew B., 137, 139, 320–21, 323
Bragg, General Braxton, 246, 298
Brandt, Willy, 25
Brayman, Mason, 138
Breckinridge, John C., 128, 147, 149
Briggs, James A., 136
Bright, John, 220–21
Brooks, Noah, 188, 189, 190, 218, 338, 347, 406
Brown, John, 142
Browne, Judge, 81
Browning, Orville H., 276
Bruce, Robert V., 252–57, 461
Brumfield, Nancy Lincoln, 37, 151
Brumfield, William, 37
Bryant, William Cullen, 109, 137, 138
Buchanan, James, 127, 149, 183, 333, 365
Buell, Don Carlos, 374–75
Bullard, F. Lauriston, 23
Bull Run, battles of, 198, 200, 227, 245, 285
Butler, General Benjamin F., 375
Butler, William, 80

Cabinet, Lincoln's, 172–75, 184
Caccia, Sir Harold, 25
Calhoun, John C., 286
Cameron, John M., 58
Cameron, Simon, 143, 148, 174, 175, 185, 227, 383
Campbell, Justice John Archibald, 295, 298, 302, 360
Carpenter, Francis Bickness, 19
Carrie Martin, steamship, 188
Carruthers, Olive, 63–68, 462
Cartter, David K., 140
Cass, Lewis, 98
Catron, Justice John, 304, 305
Catton, Bruce, 197–202, 462
Chambrun, Marquis Adolphe de, 349
Champaign, Ill., 92
Chancellorsville, battle of, 229
Chandler, Zachariah, 239, 315
Charleston, S.C., 176, 180
Charnwood, Lord, 368
Chase, Salmon P., 142, 143, 147, 173, 174, 189, 216, 240, 306, 314, 315,

317, 383, 386, 435
Chattanooga, battle of, 246, 268, 270
Chicago Press and Tribune, 141, 142
Chicago Times, 250
Chicago Tribune, 250
Choate, Joseph R., 138
Chronology, Lincoln, 437–59
Cincinnati Gazette, 250
City Point, Va., 344, 356, 398
Civil Rights Act, 393
Civil War, 185, 191–96, 197–202, 221, 226–30, 268–72, 273–78, 368, 373, 417
Clausewitz, General, 199
Clay, Cassius M., 435
Clay, Henry, 82, 108, 407
Clifford, Justice Nathan, 304, 305
Cobden, Richard, 220–21
Cogedale, Isaac, 158
Cold Harbor, 269
Coles County, Ill., 159
Colfax, Speaker, 401
Collected Works of Abraham Lincoln, The, 433
Commager, Henry S., 362–66, 462
Committee on the Conduct of the War, 191–96, 227
Compromise of 1850, 108, 146
Confederate States of America, 176, 220, 221, 240, 366
Conkling, James, 364
Conscription, 229
Cooke, John Esten, 205
Cooper, Gary, 353
Cooper, Peter, 136
Cooper Union Address, 135–39, 142
Copperheads, 238, 240, 289–94
Corwin, Norman, 248–51, 463
Crimean War, 224
Crittenden Compromise, 156
Crook, Colonel, 355, 358, 359, 360, 361
Crume, Mary Lincoln, 37
Crume, Ralph, 37
Current, Richard N., 171–75, 463

Dahlgren, Captain John A., 255, 256, 261
Dalton, Test, 351
Daniel, Justice Peter Vivian, 302
Davis, Judge David, 90, 91, 92, 93–94, 141, 143, 265, 305, 306
Davis, Henry Winter, 315, 316, 375, 376

505

Index

507

Index